ENSLAVING SPIRITS

THE ATLANTIC WORLD

Europe, Africa and the Americas, 1500-1830

EDITORS

Wim Klooster (Clark University)
Benjamin Schmidt (University of Southern Maine)

VOLUME II

ENSLAVING SPIRITS

*The Portuguese-Brazilian Alcohol Trade at Luanda
and its Hinterland, c. 1550-1830*

BY

JOSÉ C. CURTO

BRILL
LEIDEN · BOSTON
2004

This book is printed on acid-free paper.

Library of Congress Cataloging-in-Publication Data

Curto, José C.
  Enslaving spirits : the Portuguese-Brazilian alcohol trade at Luanda and its hinterland, c.
1550-1830 / by José C. Curto.
    p. cm. — (The Atlantic world, ISSN 1570-0542 ; v. 2)
  Includes bibliographical references and index.
  ISBN 90-04-13175-2
    1. Liquor industry—Angola—History. 2. Slave trade—Angola—History. I. Title. II.
Atlantic world (Leiden, Netherlands) ; v. 2.

HD9390.A52C87 2003
382'.456635'0096730903—dc22

2003059602

ISSN   1570–0542
ISBN   90 04 13175 2

PRINTED IN THE NETHERLANDS

In memory of my father, Francisco da Cruz Curto, otherwise
known as "Chico Padeiro."

CONTENTS

ACKNOWLEDGEMENTS

This book is a refurbished version of my doctoral dissertation submitted in 1996 at the University of California, Los Angeles, and recently published in its integrity by Editora Vulgata, Lisbon, in Portuguese translation. Although the dissertation attempted to cover much of West Central Africa from the late fifteenth century to 1830, from the Kingdom of Kongo in the north to Benguela and the central Angolan plateau further south, my concern here is almost exclusively with Luanda and its hinterland from about 1550 until the end of legal slaving in the South Atlantic in 1830. Such a focus results from the fact that this was the area in West Central Africa where the exchange of imported alcoholic beverages for exportable slaves was most intense. Moreover, while the dissertation was heavily based upon documentation from archives in Portugal, this refurbished version is further underpinned by subsequent research in a number of archives both in Angola and in Brazil. The documentation subsequently located in Angolan and Brazilian archives has not led to major modifications in my original arguments. It has, however, reinforced them further still.

This book, "in progress" for such a long time, owes a great deal to teachers, financial institutions, archival personnel, colleagues, and family spread across the Atlantic world. Professors Frank Chalk and Michael Mason were the first to spark my interest in the history of Africa at Concordia University, Montreal. Later at the University of California, Los Angeles, Professors Edward A. Alpers, Boniface Obichere, Christopher Ehret, and Robert Griffeth were responsible for my professional training in the African past. Professors Temma Kaplan, Geoffrey Symcox, E. Bradford Burns, and James Lockhart, also of the University of California, Los Angeles, directed my training in Early Modern European and Latin American history. I am extremely grateful to all for the knowledge which they passed on to me and the patience with which they oversaw the development of my analytical and writing skills. Professor Alpers, in particular, proved a constant source of intellectual stimulation and constructive criticism as chair of my doctoral committee. His faith in my being able to complete the dissertation never waivered and the amount of time he put into it went far beyond the call of duty. *Muito obrigado*, Ned.

A number of other scholars also deserve to be mentioned for their collegiality. Over the years, I have gained much from discussions and exchanges of information on Angola with Professors Susan Herlin of the University of Louisville, Linda Heywood of Howard University, Joseph Miller of the University of Virginia, John Thornton of Millersville University, Manolo G. Florentino of the Universidade Federal do Rio de Janeiro, Rosa da Cruz e Silva of the Arquivo Histórico Nacional de Angola, Alberto da Costa e Silva, President of the Academia Brasileira de Letras, Isabel Castro Henriques of the Universidade de Lisboa, Joana Pereira Leite of the Universidade Técnica de Lisboa, and Alfredo Margarido of the Universidade Lusófona. I have also learned a great deal about things African and beyond from Paul E. Lovejoy, with whom I have worked closely over the last six years at York University. My thanks to all.

I am further indebted to the directors and personnel of the archives and specialized libraries in Angola, Brazil, Portugal, and the United States where I have conducted research over the years. Whether at the Biblioteca da Sociedade de Geografia de Lisboa, the Biblioteca Nacional de Lisboa, the Instituto Nacional de Estatística, the Arquivo Histórico do Ministério das Obras Públicas, the Arquivo Histórico Ultramarino, and the Biblioteca Pública de Évora, all in Portugal, the Arquivo Histórico da Biblioteca Municipal de Luanda and the Arquivo Histórico Nacional in Angola, the Biblioteca Nacional do Rio de Janeiro, the Arquivo do Instituto Histórico e Geográfico Brasileiro, and the Arquivo Nacional do Rio de Janeiro in Brazil, or the Library of Congress and the Lilly Library (Indiana University) in the United States, these individuals kindly introduced me to the organizational aspects of the Angolana holdings of their respective institutions and always promptly answered my requests for information. Their assistance has been invaluable. I am also grateful to Mr. Eugene Onutan, webmaster of the Harriet Tubman Resource Centre on the African Diaspora at York University, for is work on the maps and illustrations found in this volume.

If to begin, continue in, and complete a program of graduate study is an expensive affair, carrying out a sustained research program in no less than four continents is even more so. As a graduate student, I was fortunate to have received financial assistance from the Fonds FCAC (Québec), the Luso-American Foundation (Oakland), the Social Sciences and Humanities Research Council of Canada, the University of California, Los Angeles, and the Fundação Calouste Gulbenkian (Lisbon) to pursue graduate studies at UCLA and to begin my archival research. Since then I have benefited from the financial assistance of institutions such as the Fundação Calouste Gulbenkian (once again) and the Instituto Camões in Lisbon, as well as Trent University where I spent the 1996–1997 academic year as a Visiting Assistant Professor, to carry on with my research agenda. And, last but not least, further financial assistance from the Department of History, the Faculty of Arts, and the Harriet Tubman Resource Centre on the African Diaspora at York University has enabled me to conclude the research underpinning the pages that follow. Without their support, this book would not have materialized.

My final words of thanks go to three very special people. Talia, my spouse, has stuck with this project through thick and thin. She provided not only much needed moral support, but also sustained the family alone during periods when I was unemployed. Deanna Kathryn, our daughter, came into the world at a time when the future of my venture was uncertain. Roberto Francisco, our son, arrived at a moment when the venture was still far from secure. Each has had to give up a lot to see this project, finally, completed.

LIST OF ABBREVIATIONS

AHBML	Arquivo Histórico da Biblioteca Municipal de Luanda
AHMOP	Arquivo Histórico do Ministério das Obras Publicas, Lisbon
AHNA	Arquivo Histórico Nacional de Angola, Luanda
AHU	Arquivo Histórico Ultramarino, Lisbon
AIHGB	Arquivo do Instituto Histórico e Geográfico Brasileiro, Rio de Janeiro
ANRJ	Arquivo Nacional do Rio de Janeiro
BNL	Biblioteca Nacional de Lisboa
BNRJ	Biblioteca Nacional do Rio de Janeiro
BPE	Biblioteca Pública de Évora
BSGL	Biblioteca da Sociedade de Geografia de Lisboa
Cód.	*Códice* (codex)
Cx.	*Caixa* (box)
Doc.	*Documento* (document)
ft.	footnote
INE	Instituto Nacional de Estatística, Lisbon
LC	Library of Congress, Washington, D.C.
No.	*Número* (number)

MAPS AND ILLUSTRATIONS

The maps and illustrations can be found between the pages 88 and 89

INTRODUCTION

ALCOHOL AS HISTORY IN AFRICA

Consumer goods not only have a past of their own, but are also part and parcel of historical processes. In Africa, for example, cloves, kola, maize, tobacco, and salt all played significant economic, political, and social roles both in the more distant and the not too distant past.[1] These items, however, were not the only consumer goods of significance in the African past. Not a few others were of equal, possibly even greater, significance in the history of Africa. One of these was intoxicating beverages.

Indeed, the history of alcohol in Africa is more than a trivial element in the economic, political, and social development of the continent. The beginning of this past, which stretches very deep in time,

---

[1] See, for example, Babatunde A. Agiri, "Kola in Western Nigeria, 1850–1950: A History of the Cultivation of Colanitida in Egba-Owode, Ijebu-Remo, Iwo and Oto Arewa," Unpublished Ph.D. dissertation, University of Wisconsin, 1972; George E. Brooks, "Kola Trade and State Building: Upper Guinea Coast and Senegambia, 15th–17th Centuries," *Working Paper no. 38*, African Studies Center, Boston University, 1980; Paul E. Lovejoy, *Caravans of Kola: The Hausa Kola Trade, 1700–1900*. Ibadan, 1980; idem, *Salt of the Desert Sun: A History of Salt Production and Trade in the Central Sudan*. Cambridge, 1986; Elizabeth A. McDougall, "The Ijil Salt Industry: Its Role in the Pre-Colonial Economy of the Western Sudan," Unpublished Ph.D. dissertation, University of Birmingham, 1980; Marvin P. Miracle, *Maize in Tropical Africa*. Madison, 1966; Joan C. Power, "The History of Keana's Salt Industry c. 1780–1900: The Mechanics of Gender in a Precolonial Economy," Unpublished M.A. thesis, Dalhousie University, 1985; J. W. Purseglove, "The Origins and Migrations of Crops in Tropical Africa," in J. R. Harlan, Jan de Wet, and A. B. L. Stemler, eds. *Origins of African Plant Domestication*. The Hague, 1976, pp. 291–310; Dominique Jhue-Beaulaton, "La diffusion du maïs sur les Côtes de l'Or et des Esclaves aux XVIIᵉ et XVIIIᵉ siècles," *Revue française d'histoire d'outre-mer*. Vol. 77, 1990, pp. 177–198; Mahmoud A. R. El Sheikh, "State, Cloves, and Planters: A Reappraisal of British Imperialism in Zanzibar, 1890–1938," Unpublished Ph.D. dissertation, University of California at Los Angeles, 1986; Abdul Sheriff, *Slaves, Spices and Ivory in Zanzibar: Integration of an East African Commercial Empire into the World Economy, 1770–1873*. London, 1987; Joaquim Lino da Silva, "O *Zea mays* e os milhos africanos na costa oriental da África: Discussão em torno de documentos Antigos," *Garcia de Orta, Série Geográfica*. Vol. 14, 1993, pp. 15–40; Pierre Verger, "Rôle joué par le tabac de Bahia dans la traite des esclaves au Golfe de Bénin," *Cahiers d'études africaines*. Vol. 4, 1964, pp. 349–369; and Jan Vansina, "Histoire du manioc en Afrique centrale avant 1850," *Paideuma*. Vol. 43, 1997, pp. 255–279.

can not be precisely dated.[2] Nevertheless, the production and consumption of intoxicating drinks may well have begun when Africans
started to shift their subsistence from hunting and gathering to agriculture. Following this transition, which took place at different times
in different regions of the continent, five main groups of intoxicants
were already being produced: beverages fermented from cereals,
honey water, fruits and juices, and sap from various species of palm
trees, as well as drinks made from milk.[3] Because these alcoholic
beverages were made from items that were part and parcel of the
food supply, this must have placed limits on both their production
and consumption. Thus, while it is unlikely that production was carried out on a large scale, whatever amounts of alcoholic beverages
existed were primarily consumed during more or less strictly defined
social and religious occasions.[4] By and large, these early characteristics of intoxicants in Africa seem to have remained stable for mil-
lennia. But, with the arrival of Europeans in the continent, alcohol
consumption patterns began to undergo significant changes.

As Europeans slowly reconnoitred the western coast of Africa during the 1400s, captives became an important part of the emerging
Euro-African trade to supply the labour demands of the sugar plantations being established in the islands off West Africa and, later, in
the Americas. One of the favoured goods which European traders
used to acquire captives from African political authorities and other
slave producing individuals near the coast was alcoholic beverages:
grape wine and a variety of distilled intoxicants such as sugar cane
rum, gin, and brandy.[5] Initially, most of the foreign alcoholic bev-

---

[2] See Jan Vansina, "Finding Food and the History of Precolonial Africa: A Plea,"
African Economic History. Vol. 7, 1979, p. 11, for the specific case of palm wine in
Equatorial Africa. On beer, see: Jeremy R. Geller, "Predynastic Beer Production
at Hierakonpolis, Upper Egypt: Archaeological Evidence and Anthropological
Implications," Unpublished Ph.D. dissertation, Washington University, 1992; and
D. N. Edwards, "Sorghum, Beer, and Cushite Society," *Norwegian Archaeological Review*.
Vol. 29, 1996, pp. 65–77.

[3] B. S. Platt, "Some Traditional Alcoholic Beverages and their Importance in
Indigenous African Communities," *Proceedings of the Nutrition Society*. Vol. 14, 1955,
p. 115.

[4] Lacking contemporaneous evidence for earlier periods, this assumption is based
on a reconstruction of existing alcohol consumption patterns during the initial contact of West Central African societies with Europeans. See Chapter One below and
the supporting documentation therein.

[5] See, for example: I. A. Akinjogbin, *Dahomey and its Neighbours 1708–1818*. London,
1967, pp. 75, 104, 135, and 144; Stanley B. Alpern, "What Africans Got for Their

erages, all of which possessed a higher alcoholic continent than any of the intoxicants produced within Africa, were consumed by the socio-economic groups engaged in the Euro-African commerce, not only during traditionally accepted occasions but, increasingly, outside of them, as well. But as Atlantic demand for captives increased significantly following the mid-1600s, so did the volume of European alcohol to acquire them. By the 1780s, according to a recent estimate, western Africa was already importing some 2.9 million litres

Slaves: A Master List of European Trade Goods," *History in Africa*. Vol. 22, 1995, pp. 24–25; Jay Coughtry, *The Notorious Triangle: Rhode Island and the African Slave Trade 1700–1807*. Philadelphia, 1981, pp. 16, 81–86, 107–120, and 170–174; Philip D. Curtin, *Economic Change in Precolonial Africa: Senegambia in the Era of the Slave Trade*. Madison, 1975, pp. 242 243, 252, 258–259, 262, 313, 316–318, 321, and 326 327; Kwame Y. Daaku, *Trade and Politics on the Gold Coast, 1600–1720: A Study of the African Reaction to European Trade*. Oxford, 1970, pp. 59, 64 65, 87, 98–99, 104, and 116; K. G. Davies, *The Royal African Company*. New York, 1970, pp. 45, 115–116, 173, 190, 234, 238, and 271; K. Onwuka Dike, *Trade and Politics in the Niger Delta, 1830–1885: An Introduction to the Economic and Political History of Nigeria*. London, 1956, pp. 105–106; David Eltis and Lawrence C. Jennings, "Trade between Western Africa and the Atlantic World in the Precolonial Era," *American Historical Review*, Vol. 93, 1988, pp. 951–952 and 955; Adam Jones, ed., *Brandenburg Sources for West African History 1680–1700*. Stuttgart, 1985, pp. 24–26, 31, 39, 50, 61–69, 76–80, 86, 95–106, 119, 126, 130–138, 147, 151, 168, 177, 182, and 196–199, Robin Law, *The Oyo Empire c. 1600–1836: A West African Imperialism in the Era of the Atlantic Slave Trade*. Oxford, 1977, p. 225; idem, *The Slave Coast of West Africa, 1550 1750: The Impact of the Atlantic Slave Trade on an African Society*. Oxford, 1991, p. 202; John J. McCusker, *Rum and the American Revolution: The Rum Trade and the Balance of Payments of the Thirteen Colonies*. New York, 1989, Vol. 1, pp. 20, 480–483, and 492–497; George Metcalfe, "A Microcosm of Why Africans Sold Slaves: Akan Consumption Patterns In the 1770s," *Journal of African History*. Vol. 20, 1987, pp. 379 380, 382–383, 385–386, 388–390, and 392–394; Colin W. Newbury, *The Western Slave Coast and its Rulers: European Trade and Administration among the Yoruba and Adja-speaking Peoples of South-Western Nigeria, Southern Dahomey and Togo*. London, 1961, pp. 28–29; Karl Polanyi (in collaboration with Abraham Rotstein), *Dahomey and the Slave Trade: An Analysis of an Archaic Economy*. Seattle, 1966, pp. 35, 155, 162, and 165; Johannes M. Postma, *The Dutch in the Atlantic Slave Trade, 1600–1815*. Cambridge, 1990, pp. 104–105; James A. Rawley, *The Transatlantic Slave Trade: A History*. New York, 1981, pp. 154, 208, 311, 343–345, 355, and 361; David Richardson, "West African Consumption Patterns and Their Influence on the Eighteenth-Century English Slave Trade," in Henry A. Gemery and Jan S. Hogendorn, eds. *The Uncommon Market: Essays in the Economic History of the Atlantic Slave Trade*. New York, 1979, pp. 308–315 and 324–326; Walter Rodney, *A History of the Upper Guinea Coast, 1545 to 1800*. New York, 1980, pp. 135, 178–180, 187–189, and 242; Allen F. C. Ryder, *Benin and the Europeans, 1485–1897*. New York, 1969, pp. 86, 160, 167, 207–209, 335–336; James F. Searing, *West African Slavery and Atlantic Commerce: The Senegal River Valley, 1700–1860*. Cambridge, 1994, pp. 33, 51, 66–68, and 71–74; and Pierre Verger, *Trade Relations Between the Bight of Benin and Bahia from the 17th to the 19th Century*. Ibadan, 1976, pp. 12, 28–33, 48, 88, 110, 122, 132, 156, 222–225, 232, 259, and 595.

of foreign alcohol per year.[6] This allowed individuals along the littoral, regardless of socio-economic class, to gain access to ever larger amounts of the foreign intoxicants.

The succeeding era of bulk commodity commerce in the 1800s saw the acquisition and consumption of imported alcohol by Africans further accentuated. Along the western coast of Africa alone, alcohol imports are estimated to have jumped from an annual average of 3.8 million litres in the 1820s to slightly over 23 million litres in the 1860s.[7] Throughout this century, European merchants used greater and greater quantities of inexpensively produced intoxicants such as gin, spirited wine, and brandy, as items of exchange to acquire African rubber, wax, palm oil, and ivory for the expanding industries of Europe and North America.[8] As long-distance trade caravans penetrated deeper into the interior of the continent in search of these primary resources, the volume of imported liquor available to the population settled along the commercial routes rose significantly. This led directly to a proportionate increase in the amount of alcoholic beverages consumed throughout the interior both within and outside of traditionally accepted occasions.

In the late 1800s, following the rise of prohibitionist movements throughout Europe and North America, various international conventions attempted the curb the flow of alcohol to Africa. Instead of decreasing, however, the amount of foreign alcohol available increased further still. Many of the signatory powers at these conventions were also engaged in carving out colonies to establish protected markets and secure sources of raw materials for their then stagnating industries. Coinciding with this trend was the fact that one of

---

[6] Eltis and Jennings, "Trade between Western Africa and the Atlantic World," p. 955.

[7] Ibid.

[8] Lynn Pan, *Alcohol in Africa*. Helsinki, 1975, pp. 8–27. Emmanuel A. Ayandele, *The Missionary Impact on Modern Nigeria, 1872–1914*. London, 1966, especially Chapter 10—"The Triumph of Gin", pp. 307–327; Raymond E. Dumett, "The Social Impact of the European Liquor Trade on the Akan of Ghana (Gold Coast and Asante), 1875–1910," *Journal of Interdisciplinary History*. Vol. 1, 1974, pp. 69–101; A. Olorunfemi, "The Liquor Traffic Dilemma in British West Africa: The Southern Nigerian Example, 1895–1918," *International Journal of African Historical Studies*. Vol. 17, 1984, pp. 229–241; and Gregory R. Pirio, "Commerce, Industry and Empire: The Making of Modern Portuguese Colonialism in Angola and Mozambique," Unpublished Ph.D. dissertation, University of California at Los Angeles, 1982, especially Chapter 7—"The Political Economy of Alcohol in the Portuguese Empire," pp. 234–302.

the European industries most in need of protected colonial markets was that of alcohol. As a result, even larger quantities of European alcohol eventually found their way into Africa, where they were invariably used as a trade import exchanged for local agricultural produce and primary resources, a luxury item to lure individuals into labour contracts, a form of payment in exchange of labour, a tool to recuperate wages in industrial compounds and company towns, a stimulant (in the short run) for labourers to withstand long working hours and difficult working conditions, and a mechanism to control labour forces.[9] In the Gold Coast (Gold Coast Colony, Ashanti, Northern Territories, and Togoland), for example, potable spirit imports increased from 4.4 million litres in 1890 to 4.7 million in 1900 and then to 7.2 million in 1910.[10] In the case of Angola, on the other hand, alcohol imports jumped from 2.9 million litres in 1870 to some 5.1 million in 1890 and then to 8.8 million litres in late 1920s.[11] Not surprisingly, the ever rising amounts of European alcohol exported to Africa soon became the object of widespread consumption. Moreover, the colonial period also saw the development of cottage and small-scale industrial brewing and distilling based on a large number of crops and fruits to cater to the continuously growing African demand for cheap alcoholic beverages.[12] Following

---

[9] Analysis of this development has been particularly concentrated on Southern Africa. See Charles van Onselen, "Randlords and Rotgut, 1886–1903," *History Workshop*. Vol. 2, 1976, pp. 32–89; and the pertinent chapters in the important collection by Charles H. Ambler and Jonathan Crush, eds. *Liquor and Labor in Southern Africa*. Athens, OH, 1992. For Lusophone Africa, see José Capela, *O Vinho para o Preto: Notas e Textos Sobre a Exportação do Vinho para a África*. Lisbon, 1973.

[10] Pan, *Alcohol in Africa*, p. 68.

[11] *Boletim Official do Governo Geral de Angola*. No. 11, 18–03–1871, pp. 124–128, No. 51, 23–12–1871, pp. 643–645, and No. 52, 30–12–1871, pp. 658–660 for 1870; idem, No. 10, Appendix 3, 07–03–1891, pp. 7–15, No. 19, Appendix 5, 09–05–1891, pp. 1–6, No. 27, Appendix 7, 04–07–1891, pp. 1–9, and No. 32, Appendix 10, 08–08–1891, pp. 1–8 for 1890; and A. Brandão de Mello, *Angola: Monographie Historique, Géographique et Économique de la Colonie Destinée à l'Exposition Coloniale Internationale de Paris de 1931*. Luanda, 1931, pp. 67–68, for the late 1920s.

[12] The case of beer cottage brewing is the best documented. See the following essays in Ambler and Crush, *Liquor and Labor in Southern Africa*: Helen Bradford, "'We Women Will Show Them': Beer Protests in the Natal Countryside, 1929," pp. 208–234; Sean Redding, "Beer Brewing in Umtata: Women, Migrant Labor, and Social Control in a Rural Town," pp. 325–251; and Steven Haggblade, "The Shebeen Queen and the Evolution of Botswana's Sorghum Beer Industry," pp. 395–413. See also: M. Hedlund and M. Lundahl, "The Economic Role of Beer in Rural Zambia," *Human Organization*. Vol. 43, 1984, pp. 61–65; Patrick A. McAllister, "Indigenous Beer in Southern Africa: Functions and Fluctuations," *African Studies*.

the "Winds of Change" which swept European colonial powers to withdraw from the continent between the late 1950s and the early 1970s, many of the newly established African states inherited alcoholism as a serious socio-economic and health problem.

The outline presented above is but a rough sketch of major trends. From this cursory presentation it is clear that alcohol, too, is part and parcel of some of the more important historical processes that have shaped the African continent. However, the long history of alcohol in Africa, unlike that of kola, maize, or salt, has yet to attract the attention that it deserves.

The study of alcohol in Africa began in the late nineteenth century, primarily as a result of a Victorian perception of the "dark continent" as an insatiable guzzler of booze. Since then, alcoholism has been considered a major social, economic, and health problem of increasing proportion throughout much of the continent. Whether the perception is right or wrong, an ever-growing corpus of literature has nevertheless appeared with the aim of explaining this phenomenon.[13] The overwhelming majority of this literature can be divided into three distinct categories: work produced by missionaries, philanthropists, colonial and postcolonial government officials, by biological and health scientists, and by social scientists. The work generated by missionaries, philanthropists, and colonial and postcolonial government officials is mainly devoted to depicting the socio-economic effects occasioned by heavy drinking, usually in a prohibitionist mould. The studies carried out by biological and health scientists, on the other hand, have largely concentrated on property analysis of indigenous alcoholic beverages and on the effects of alcohol consumption upon the digestive and nervous systems. Social scientists, in turn, have focused their work primarily on the description, social and economic functions, and the attitudinal and behavioral patterns of problem

Vol. 52, 1993, pp. 71–88; and the pertinent essays in Deborah Fahy Bryceson, ed., *Alcohol in Africa: Mixing Business, Pleasure, and Politics*. Portsmouth, NH, 2002.

[13] Much of this literature is listed in the following bibliographies: Simon Heap, "Alcohol in Africa: A Supplementary List of Post-1875 Literature," *Current Bibliography on African Affairs*. Vol. 26, 1994–95, pp. 1–14; Kebede Gessesse and Louis Molamu, *Alcohol and Alcoholism in Africa: A Bibliography*. National Institute of Development Research and Documentation, University of Botswana, 1988, Working Bibliography no. 15; and José C. Curto, "Alcohol in Africa: A Preliminary Bibliography of the Post-1875 Literature". *A Current Bibliography on African Affairs*. Vol. 21, 1989, pp. 3–31.

drinkers in various ethnic and social groups.[14] From these studies, a
better understanding can be obtained of the types and functions of
intoxicating drinks consumed throughout much of the continent, the
psychological and physiological problems of certain ethnic and socio-
economic groups prone to heavy drinking, and the social and economic effects occasioned by widespread alcohol consumption in the
twentieth century. But, if the problems raised by alcohol in Africa
during the 1900s have been the object of numerous studies, rarely
have these works been the product of historians.

Historians have not been particularly interested in the question of
alcohol in Africa. Some two decades ago, Raymond Dumett, the
author of one of the first historical studies on the impact of the
European alcohol trade in Africa, pleaded for an end to this indifference
in the following manner:

> [Although] pioneering case studies of drinking patterns in traditional
> and transitional societies in Africa are beginning to be undertaken by
> social anthropologists who have already advanced a number of impor-
> tant hypothesis and conceptual models based on ethnographic data
> and cross-cultural analysis, [. . .] Africanist historians have rarely ven-
> tured into this field. Yet historians need not leave this important aspect
> of African social history entirely to behavioral scientists. By combin-
> ing their own investigative techniques with insights gained from other
> disciplines, historians can place African drinking practices in cultural
> context and time perspective; they can attempt to identify the major
> causes and patterns of change; and they can expose the errors and
> imprecise knowledge [. . .] which has impeded understanding of African
> customs and culture to the present day. The latter task provides a con-
> tinuing background theme for much of the present day inquiry.[15]

The appeal made by Dumett, however, was largely ignored. The
subsequent contribution by historians to the literature on this issue
remained comparatively small. As a result, only a few have ventured
to investigate any of the topics surrounding the question of alcohol
in Africa. And, of those who have, most have limited their research
primarily to the post-1875 era: that is, the period beginning with the
advent of formal European colonialism.[16] Moreover, the investigations

---

[14] See the survey of this literature in Curto, "Alcohol in Africa: A Preliminary
Bibliography," pp. 3–31.
[15] Dumett, "Social Impact of the European Liquor Trade on the Akan," pp.
70–71.
[16] See the studies listed in ft. 8 and 9. Other notable exceptions include Charles

carried out by historians have been further restricted to three major
topics: the European alcohol trade with Africa after the mid-nineteenth
century;[17] the utilization of alcoholic beverages in the acquisition and
control of African labour;[18] and more recently the social history of
alcohol.[19] Historical research on alcohol in Africa thus remains not

---

H. Ambler, *Alcohol and Disorder in Precolonial Africa.* African Studies Center, Boston
University, Working Papers # 126, 1987; Thomas J. Herlehy, "Ties that Bind: Palm
Wine and Blood Brotherhoods at the Kenya Coast during the 19th Century,"
International Journal of African Historical Studies. Vol. 17, 1984, pp. 285–308; Wallace
G. Mills, "Cape Smoke: Alcohol Issues in the Cape Colony in the Nineteenth
Century," *Contemporary Drug Problems.* Vol. 12, 1985, pp. 1–12; idem, "The Roots
of African Nationalism in the Cape Colony: Temperance, 1865–1898," *International
Journal of African Historical Studies.* Vol. 13, 1980, pp. 197–213; Mary I. Rayner,
"Wine and Slaves: The Failure of an Export Economy and the Ending of Slavery
in the Cape Colony, 1806–1835," Unpublished Ph.D. dissertation, Duke University,
1986; and Emmanuel K. Akyeampong, *Drink, Power, and Cultural Change: A Social
History of Alcohol in Ghana, c. 1800 to Recent Times.* Portsmouth: Heinemann, 1996,
especially Chapter 2—"Alcohol, Ritual, and Power among the Akan, Ga-Adangme,
and Ewe in Precolonial Southern Gold Coast," pp. 21–46; and David Gordon,
"From Rituals of Rapture to Dependence: The Political Economy of Khoikhoi
Narcotic Consumption, c. 1487–1870," *South African Historical Journal.* Vol. 35, 1996,
pp. 62–88.

[17] Aside from the studies listed in ft. 8 above, see: Raymond Dumett, *Merchants
versus moralists: the impact of the liquor trade in the Gold Coast and Asante in the late nineteenth century.* Waltham, Mass.: African Studies Association, 1970; Simon Heap,
"Before 'Star': The Import Substitution of Western Style Alcohol in Nigeria, 1870–
1970," *African Economic History.* Vol. 24, 1996, pp. 69–89; and Susan Diduk, "European
Alcohol, History, and the State in Cameroon," *African Studies Review.* Vol. 36, 1993,
pp. 1–42.

[18] See the work of van Onselen cited in ft. 9 above, as well as: the essays by
Ambler and Crush, Ambler, Crush, Edgecombe, and Scully in Ambler and Crush,
Liquor and Labor in Southern Africa; Charles H. Ambler, "Drunks, Brewers and Chiefs:
Alcohol Regulation in Colonial Kenya, 1900–1939," in Susanna Barrows and Robin
Room, eds. *Drinking: Behavior and Belief in Modern History.* Berkeley, 1991, pp. 165–183;
and Patrick A. McAllister, *Bulding the Homestead: Agriculture, Labour and Beer in South
Africa's Transkei.* Aldershot, 2001.

[19] Emmanuel K. Akyeampong and Pashington Obeng, "Spirituality, Gender and
Power in Asante History," *International Journal of African Historical Studies.* Vol. 28,
1995, pp. 481–508; Emmanuel K. Akyeampong, "What's in a Drink? Class Struggle,
Popular Culture and the Politics of *Akpeteshie* (Local Gin) in Ghana, 1930–1967,"
Journal of African History. Vol. 37, 1996, pp. 215–236; idem, *Drink, Power, and Cultural
Change*; Charles H. Ambler, "Alcohol, Racial Segragation and Popular Politics in
Northern Rhodesia," *Journal of African History.* Vol. 31, 1990, pp. 295–313; Ayodeji
Olukoju, "Prohibition and Paternalism: The State and the Clandestine Liquor Traffic
in Northern Nigeria, c. 1889–1918," *International Journal of African Historical Studies.*
Vol. 24, 1991, 349–368; idem, "Race and Access To Liquor: Prohibition as Colonial
Policy in Northern Nigeria, 1919–45," *Journal of Imperial and Commonwealth History.*
Vol. 24, 1996, pp. 218–243; Simon Heap, "'We Think Prohibition is a Farce':
Drinking in the Alcohol-Prohibited Zone of Colonial Northern Nigeria," *International
Journal of African Historical Studies.* Vol. 31, 1998, pp. 23–52; Helen Bradford, "'We

only sparse, but what does exist is more often than not limited to the post-1875 era. In short, the discourse on alcohol in Africa during the twentieth century continues to be pursued in ignorance of the more distance past.

The present work is designed to redress, in part, this situation. Historians have generally recognized that the opening of the Atlantic slave trade introduced new, more alcoholized intoxicants in Africa, particularly for the acquisition of captives.[20] Few, however, have investigated the relationship between European alcohol and the acquisition of slaves throughout the continent in any thorough or systematic way.[21] And, equally significant, none have researched the impact

---

Are Now Men': Beer Protests in the Natal Countryside, 1929," in Belinda Bozzoli, ed. *Class, Community and Conflict: South African Perspectives*. Johannesburg, 1987, pp. 292–323; Elizabeth Colson and Thayer Scudder, *For Prayer and Profit: The Ritual, Economic and Social Importance of Beer in the Gwembe District, Zambia, 1950–1982*. Stanford, 1988; Paul La Hausse, *Alcohol, the Ematsheni and Popular Struggle in Durban. The Origins of the Beer Hall in South Africa, 1902–09*. Cape Town, 1983; idem, *The Struggle for the City: Alcohol, the Ematsheni and Popular Culture in Durban, 1902–1936*. Durban, 1984; idem, *Brewers, Beerhalls and Boycotts: A History of Liquor in South Africa*. Johannesburg, 1988; Alan G. Cobley, "Liquor and Leadership: Temperance, Drunkenness and the African Petty Bourgeoisie in South Africa," *South African Historical Journal*. Vol. 31, 1994, pp. 128–148; Justin Willis, "*Enkurma sikitoi*: drink, commoditization and power in Maasai society," *International Journal of African Historical Studies*. Vol. 32, 1999, pp. 339–358; and idem, *Potent Brews: A Social History of Alcohol in East Africa, 1850–1999*. Athens, OH, 2002.

[20] Akinjogbin, *Dahomey and its Neighbours 1708–1818*, pp. 75, 104, 135, and 144; Coughtry, *Notorious Triangle: Rhode Island and the African Slave Trade*, pp. 16, 81–86, 107–118, 120, and 170–174; Curtin, *Economic Change in Precolonial Africa*, pp. 242–243, 252, 258–259, 262, 313, 316–318, 321, 326, and 327; Daaku, *Trade and Politics on the Gold Coast, 1600–1720*, pp. 50, 61–65, 87, 98–99, 104, and 116; Davies, *Royal African Company*, pp. 45, 115–116, 173, 190, 234, 238, and 271; Dike, *Trade and Politics in the Niger Delta*, pp. 105–106; Eltis and Jennings, "Trade between Western Africa and the Atlantic World," pp. 951–952 and 955; Jones, *Brandenburg Sources for West African History*, pp. 24–26, 31, 39, 50, 61–69, 76–80, 86, 95–106, 119, 126, 130–138, 147, 151, 168, 177, 182, and 196–199; Law, *Oyo Empire c. 1600–1836*, p. 225; idem, *Slave Coast of West Africa*, p. 202; McCusker, *Rum and the American Revolution*, Vol. 1, pp. 20, 480–483, and 492–497; Metcalfe, "Microcosm of Why Africans Sold Slaves," pp. 379–380, 382–383, 385–386, 388–390, and 392–394; Newbury, *Western Slave Coast and its Rulers*, pp. 28–29; Polanyi, *Dahomey and the Slave Trade*, pp. 35, 155, 162, and 165; Postma, *Dutch in the Atlantic Slave Trade*, pp. 104–105; Rawley, *Transatlantic Slave Trade*, pp. 154, 208, 311, 343, 345, 355, and 361; Richardson, "West African Consumption Patterns," pp. 308–315 and 324–326; Rodney, *History of the Upper Guinea Coast*, pp. 135, 178–180, 187–189, and 242; Ryder, *Benin and the Europeans*, pp. 86, 160, 167, 207–209, 335–336; Searing, *West African Slavery and Atlantic Commerce*, pp. 33, 51, 66–68, and 71–74; and Verger, *Trade Relations Between the Bight of Benin and Bahia*, pp. 12, 28–33, 48, 88, 110, 122, 132, 156, 222–225, 232, 259, and 595.

[21] See, for example: José C. Curto, *Álcool e Escravos: O comércio luso-brasileiro do*

which foreign alcohol had upon African societies during this era.[22] Yet, given the importance attained by foreign alcohol between the fifteenth and the nineteenth centuries, these questions require an answer if a fuller understanding of Africa during this epoch of fundamental economic, political, and social changes is to be achieved. This is the aim of the present work.

Our investigation will concentrate on the Portuguese-Brazilian alcohol trade in Luanda and its hinterland during the era of the legal Atlantic slave trade. A number of factors make this area a particularly fertile ground for analysis. First, from its foundation in 1575 to the end of legal Atlantic slave trading in 1830, Luanda was the single most important slave-export town along the western coast of Africa. Of the roughly twelve million victims removed from this part of the continent via the insidious Atlantic slave trade, some 1.2 million were supplied through Luanda between 1710 and 1830 alone.[23]

Álcool em Upinda, Luanda e Benguela durante o tráfico Atlântico de escravos (c. 1480–1830) e o seu impacto nas sociedades da África Central Occidental. Lisbon, 2002; idem, "Luso-Brazilian Alcohol and the Legal Slave Trade at Benguela and its Hinterland, c. 1617–1830," in Hubert Bonin and Michel Cahen, eds. *Négoce Blanc en Afrique Noire: L'évolution du commerce à longue distance en Afrique noire du 18ᵉ au 20ᵉ siècles.* Paris, 2001, pp. 351 369; and idem, "Vinho verso Cachaça: A Luta Luso-Brasileira pelo Comércio do Álcoól e de Escravos em Luanda, 1648–1703," in Selma Pantoja and José F. S. Saraiva, eds. *Angola e Brasil nas Rotas do Atlântico Sul.* Rio de Janeiro, 1999, pp. 69–97. There is also, of course: Coughtry, *Notorious Triangle: Rhode Island and the African Slave Trade*; and McCusker, *Rum and the American Revolution.* But neither are Africanists: they are Americanist historians.

[22] The only studies presently available on the impact of the European alcohol trade are limited to the later nineteenth and early twentieth centuries. See Ayandele, *Missionary Impact on Modern Nigeria, 1872–1914*, pp. 307–327; Dumett, *Merchants versus moralists*; idem, "Social Impact of the European Liquor Trade on the Akan, pp. 69–101; and Olorunfemi, "Liquor Traffic Dilemma in British West Africa," pp. 229–241.

[23] José C. Curto, "A Quantitative Re-assessment of the Legal Portuguese Slave Trade from Luanda, Angola, 1710–1830," *African Economic History.* Vol. 20, 1992, pp. 1–25. The recent contention by David Eltis and David Richardson, "West Africa and the Transatlantic Slave Trade: New Evidence and Long-Run Trends," *Slavery and Abolition.* Vol. 18, 1997, p. 22, that Ouidah, with "probably well over one million slaves exported from the 1670s to the 1860s, was "perhaps the single most important oceanic outlet for slaves in sub-Saharan Africa," does not hold. Luanda, aside from the known 1710–1830 export figures, also shipped considerable numbers of captives prior to 1710 and following 1830. See: Joseph C. Miller, "The Slave Trade in Congo and Angola," in Martin L. Kilson and Robert I. Rotberg, eds. *The African Diaspora: Interpretive Essays.* Cambridge, 1976, pp. 75–113, for the period before 1710; and, for the post–1830 era, Roquinaldo A. Ferreira, "Dos Sertões ao Atlântico: Trafico Ilegal de Escravos e Comercio Licito em Angola, 1830–1860," Unpublished M.A. thesis, Universidade Federal do Rio de Janeiro, 1996.

However, studies of this slaving port and its relation to the Atlantic slave trade remain few and far in between, particularly when compared to slaving ports in West Africa, the other major region involved in the traffic.[24] Moreover, Luanda and its hinterland during the Atlantic slave trade also happens to be an area where foreign alcohol was especially important in the acquisition of captives through the activities of Portuguese and Brazilian slave traders established there. And last, but not least, as a result of the Luso-Brazilian presence centered

---

[24] The only scholar to have researched systematically this connection is Joseph C. Miller. See his "Legal Portuguese Slaving from Angola: Some Preliminary Indications of Volume and Direction, 1760–1830," *Revue française d'histoire d'outre-mer.* Vol. LXII, 1975, pp. 135–176; "Slave Trade in Congo and Angola"; "Some Aspects of the Commercial Organization of Slaving at Luanda, Angola, 1760–1830," in Henry A. Gemery and Jan S. Hogendorn, eds. *The Uncommon Market: Essays in the Economic History of the Atlantic Slave Trade.* New York, 1979, pp. 77–106; "Capitalism and Slaving: The Financial and Commercial Organization of the Angolan Slave Trade, According to the Accounts of Antonio Coelho Guerreiro (1684–1692)," *International Journal of African Historical Studies.* Vol. 17, 1984, pp. 1–57; "Slave Prices in the Portuguese Southern Atlantic, 1600–1830," in Paul E. Lovejoy, ed. *Africans in Bondage: Studies in Slavery and the Slave Trade.* Madison, 1986, pp. 43–77; *Way of Death: Merchant Capitalism and the Angolan Slave Trade, 1730–1830.* Madison, 1988; and "The Numbers, Origins, and Destinations of Slaves, in the Eighteenth Century Angolan Slave Trade" in Joseph. E. Inikori and Stanley L. Engerman, eds. *The Atlantic Slave Trade; Effects on Economies, Societies, and Peoples in Africa, the Americas, and Europe.* Durham, 1992, pp. 77–115. Complementing Miller's important work there is also Frédéric Mauro, "L'Atlantique Portugais et les Esclaves (1570–1670)," *Revista da Faculdade de Letras da Universidade de Coimbra.* Vol. 22, 1966, pp. 5–55; Manuel dos Anjos da Silva Rebelo, *Relações entre Angola e Brasil (1808–1830).* Lisbon, 1970; Herbert S. Klein, "The Portuguese Slave Trade from Angola in the 18th Century," *Journal of Economic History.* Vol. XXXII, 1972, pp. 849–918; idem, "O Tráfico de Escravos Africanos para o Porto do Rio de Janeiro, 1825–1830," *Anais de História.* No. 5, 1973, pp. 85–101; Corcino M. dos Santos, "Relações de Angola com o Rio de Janeiro (1736–1808)," *Estudos Históricos.* No. 12, 1973, pp. 7–68; Anne W. Pardo, "A Comparative Study of the Portuguese Colonies of Angola and Brazil and their Interdependence from 1648–1825," Unpublished Ph.D. Dissertation, Boston University, 1977; Luiz-Felipe de Alencastro, "La Traite Négrière et les Avatars de la Colonisation Portugaise au Brésil et en Angola (1550–1825)" *Cahiers du Centre de Recherches Ibériques et Ibéro-américaines de L'Université de Rouen.* Vol. 1, 1981, pp. 9–76; idem, *O Trato dos Viventes: Formação do Brasil no Atlântico Sul.* São Paulo, 2000; Manolo Florentino, *Em Costas Negras: Uma História do Tráfico de Escravos entre a África e o Rio de Janeiro.* São Paulo, 2002, 2nd edition; Jerker Carlsson, "Brazilian Trade with West Africa and Angola within the Portuguese Colonial Empire, 1500–1850: The Dialectics of South-South Exchange," in Jerker Carlsson and Timothy M. Shaw, eds. *Newly Industrialized Countries and the Political Economy of South-South Relations.* London, 1988, pp. 151–183; Curto, "A Quantitative Re-assessment of the Legal Portuguese Slave Trade from Luanda"; idem, "Vinho verso Cachaça"; and José C. Curto and Raymond R. Gervais, "The Population History of Luanda During the Late Atlantic Slave Trade, 1781–1844," *African Economic History.* Vol. 29, 2001, pp. 1–59.

in this colonial port, effectively and nominally controlling a hinterland that stretched for hundreds of kilometres inland, the Atlantic slave trade era here is endowed with an extremely large corpus of written sources dating back to the very beginnings of this commerce.[25] The relation between European alcohol, the acquisition of slaves, and the impact of foreign intoxicants in Luanda and its hinterland can thus be examined in great detail.

The primary documents which bear witness to the Luso-Brazilian alcohol commerce at Luanda and its interior during the Atlantic slave trade fall into five major categories. They are export and import statistics, missionary travelogues, traders' accounts, official governmental reports, and narratives of commercial enterprises. Exception may be taken that these sources, most of which were written by Europeans, present an exclusively Eurocentric point view on the alcohol commerce and its impact upon indigenous societies inland from Luanda. It might be argued, for example, that African evidence, particularly oral data, provide a more appropriate body of documentation to fully understand this trade and its effects. Such reasoning, however, would be mistaken. Oral sources, traditions excepted, rarely provide information that goes back beyond three generations.[26] Any historical data which such materials could provide would fall outside the chronological limit of our study, 1830. Oral traditions, on the other hand, do stretch far deeper in time. But their use for our purposes is similarly marginal. Of the many published oral traditions from West Central Africa, none provide substantive information on changing consumer patterns in the distant past. And the specific case of alcohol, whether of local or of trans-Atlantic origin, is no exception. A few examples will suffice to prove the limits here of these otherwise

---

[25] José C. Curto, "The Angolan Manuscript Collection of the Arquivo Historico Ultramarino, Lisbon: Toward a Working Guide," *History in Africa*. Vol. 15, 1988, pp. 163–189.

[26] Jan Vansina, *Oral Tradition: A Study in Historical Methodology*. Chicago, 1965, (trans. by H. M. Wright) p. 155; Daniel F. McFall, *Africa in Time-Perspective: A Discussion of Historical Reconstruction from Unwritten Sources*. New York, 1970, (originally published in 1964) p. 59; Joseph C. Miller, "Listening for the African Past," in Joseph C. Miller, ed. *The African Past Speaks: Essays on Oral Tradition and History*. Folkestone, 1980, p. 10; and David Henige, *Oral Historiography*. New York, 1982, pp. 106–112. For this reason, oral data has been primarily used for the colonial period, especially when other sources are either not available or biased. See Jan Vansina, "Memory and Oral Tradition," in Miller, *The African Past Speaks*, pp. 262–279.

more chronologically comprehensive documents. In the extensive work of Jan Vansina, a tireless proponent, collector, and interpreter since the late 1950s of precolonial Central African oral traditions, only a few passing references on intoxicants are to be found.[27] The same occurs in the *magnum opus* of Mesquitela Lima, where oral traditions describing the genesis of the Ovimbundu are thoroughly analyzed.[28] The early 1900's oral data used by John Janzen to reconstruct the Lemba, a therapeutic cult of adepts on the north side of the lower Zaire River perceived to be afflicted with a social disease caused by the goods and wealth obtained through the Atlantic economic, do contain significantly more references to alcoholic beverages, especially palm wine, used in various rituals.[29] Yet, one can only guess to what degree the passages on intoxicants in Lemba rituals can be retrojected beyond the late 1800s, since Janzen does not investigate but merely documents the presence of the cult in earlier periods. The particular case of Luba-Lunda oral traditions, as analyzed by Luc de Heusch, is even more illuminating. Although a relative large number of references to palm wine may be found in these primary documents, connecting anti-social drinking behaviour to the rise of states, they are essentially symbolic.[30] Moreover, even though export and import statistics, missionary travelogues, traders' accounts, official governmental reports, and narratives of commercial enterprises were mainly the product of Europeans, these written sources do not necessarily represent a Eurocentric view. As Robin Law, one of the more prolific and astute students of West Africa during the era of the Atlantic slave trade, has recently indicated:

---

[27] Jan Vansina, *Kingdoms of the Savanna: A History of Central African States Until European Occupation.* Madison, 1966, p. 23; idem, *The Tio Kingdom of the Middle Congo, 1880–1892.* London, 1973, p. 148; idem, *The Children of Woot: A History of the Kuba Peoples.* Madison, 1978, pp. 52, 173, 178, and 183; and idem, "Equatorial Africa and Angola: Migrations and the Emergence of the First States," in D. T. Niane, ed. *General History of Africa—IV: Africa from the Twelfth to the Sixteenth Century.* Paris, 1984, pp. 558 and 574.

[28] Mesquitela Lima, *Os Kyaka de Angola.* Lisbon, 1988, 3 Vols. In this otherwise extensive work, only two, very short references to beer made from millet or sorghum are found: Vol. 1, pp. 158 and 210.

[29] John M. Janzen, *Lemba, 1650–1930: A Drum of Affliction in Africa and the New World.* New York, 1982, pp. 105–272.

[30] Luc de Heusch, *Le Roi Ivre ou l'origine de l'État.* Paris, 1972, p. 112, 115, 117–118, 130–132, 140, 142–144, 150, 168, 178–180, 180–186, 204, 206, and 217–221.

The 'eternality' of the European documentation can be exaggerated, since for the most part Europeans reported what they had been told by African informants. European accounts of African societies thus represent a sort of second-hand internal rather than a truly external testimony.[31]

This is exactly the same conclusion that another student of West Africa during the Atlantic slave trade era, Adam Jones, has more recently reached with respect to European quantitative sources on commerce with Africans. He, too, has perceptively pointed out that:

Until recently, such information was regarded merely as a narrow branch of European economic history. Yet increasingly it is becoming clear that trade statistics reflect consumption patterns, which provide indispensable clues towards an 'internal' perspective on precolonial West African societies.[32]

Last but not least, as intimated above, the extant written documentation for the pre-1830 history of Luanda and its hinterland was not penned exclusively by Europeans. Brazilians and, more importantly Africans and Euro-Africans, especially political and religious authorities, not to mention traders, also contributed to this body of evidence.[33] Consequently, rejecting the value of written documents in European languages for understanding the African past is as myopic as denying the use of oral sources and traditions for the history of the continent.

---

[31] Law, *Slave Coast of West Africa*, p. 8.

[32] Jones, ed. and trans., *West Africa in the Mid-Seventeenth Century: An Anonymous Dutch Manuscript*. Atlanta, 1995, p. 11.

[33] See the many letters of the early Christian Kings of Kongo published in Visconde Paiva Manso, ed., *História do Congo (Documentos) 1492–1772*. Lisbon, 1877; and António Brásio, ed., *Monumenta Missionaria Africana: Africa Occidental*. Lisbon, 1952–1985, 1st series, Vols. I and II. Extracts of a few of these letters have been published in English in Basil Davidson, *The African Slave Trade: Precolonial History, 1450–1850*. Boston, 1961, pp. 146–148. On the *problématique* of this corpus of documents, see John K. Thornton, "The Correspondence of the Kongo Kings, 1614–35: Problems of Internal Written Evidence on a Central African Kingdom," *Paideuma*. Vol. 33, 1987, pp. 407–421. For other sources from the region written by Africans, see: António de Almeida, "Relações com os Dembos: Cartas do Dembado de Kakulu-Kahenda," in *1° Congresso da História da Expansão Portuguesa no Mundo: 4ª Secção—Africa*. Lisbon, 1938, Vol. III, pp. 3–98 and 151–179; and Ilídio do Amaral and Ana Amaral, "A Viagem dos pombeiros angolanos Pedro Baptista e Amaro José entre Mucari (Angola) e Tete (Moçambique), em princípios do século XIX, ou a história da primeira travessia da Africa central," *Garcia de Orta, Série Geográfica*. Vol. 9, 1984, pp. 17–58. See also the pertinent studies in Ana P. Tavares and Catarina M. Santos, eds., *Africae Monumenta—A Apropriação da Escrita pelos Africanos*. Lisbon, 2002.

Four objectives are central to this study. The first is to estimate the quantitative dimensions of the Luso-Brazilian alcohol commerce at Luanda. An analysis of its role in the slave trade of this port and its hinterland constitutes the second goal. The third objective is to demonstrate how Luso-Brazilian alcohol came to be insinuated into the economic, social, and cultural fabric not only of Luanda, but especially also African formations inland. And the fourth goal is to assess the impact of this history on the area under investigation. To achieve these objectives, not only is a thorough, critical reading of the available primary sources required, but so is an equally meticulous, analytical re-examination of all previous readings of such primary evidence. The development of a critical methodology towards both primary and secondary sources is still too often lacking in reconstructions of African history. In the case of Luanda and its hinterland during the Atlantic slave trade, as will be seen below, this is crucial.

Our reconstruction of the Luso-Brazilian alcohol trade in and its impact upon Luanda and its interior during the Atlantic slave trade is as follows. Chapter One sets the stage by examining the types and functions of indigenous alcoholic beverages in the societies of West Central Africa during their early contact with Europeans. The introduction of European alcohol throughout the region is the subject of Chapter Two. Here two fundamental questions, in particular, are tackled: Why did the Portuguese introduce their intoxicants and why did Africans accept them? Thereafter follows a series of five chapters dealing exclusively with the Luso-Brazilian alcohol trade in Luanda and its hinterland, a sub-region of West Central Africa that was the most important recipient of foreign alcohol. Chapter Three investigates the flux of the Portuguese wine trade at Luanda to the mid-1600s, Chapter Four continues the analysis by concentrating on the struggle between Portuguese merchant capitalists and Brazilian colonial traders for the alcohol trade that took place in this slaving port during the second half of the seventeenth century, and Chapter Five concludes the chronological investigation by examining the substantial Brazilian alcohol commerce at Luanda from the about 1700 to 1830, the year in which legal slave trading in the South Atlantic was banned. The profitability of Luso-Brazilian alcohol in slave trading at Luanda and its hinterland throughout the period under consideration is the object of Chapter Six. Chapter Seven, on the other hand, focuses on the non-commercial uses of Luso-Brazilian alcohol in Luanda and its hinterland throughout the whole period of the legal Atlantic slave trade, especially the mechanisms which Luso-Brazilians used to make their alcoholic drinks widely accepted in the area. Finally, our investigation concludes with an assessment of the impact of Luso-Brazilian alcohol upon the societies of West Central African throughout the period under consideration.

Such a scheme is conditioned both by the historical specificity of the Luso-Brazilian alcohol commerce at Luanda and its interior during the Atlantic slave trade and by the extant documentation which informs this past. Quantification, here, is very much in evidence. But the end product is not quantitative history *per se*. Indeed, quantification by itself is meaningless. Series of statistical data, whatever their comprehensiveness, are only valuable insofar as they throw light on various aspects of historical processes. Consequently, although extensive series of numerical data are provided in the pages that follow, these are primarily used to inform the socio-economic aspects of its topic.

In short, we seek to reconstruct the important roles of Luso-Brazilian alcohol in the slave trade at Luanda and its hinterland, as well as much of the history of alcohol in a specific sub-region of the continent before the middle of the nineteenth century. Nevertheless, the import of this study goes beyond the purely regional level. With much of the west African coast, the Cape colony, and even parts of eastern African experiencing similar developments during the era of slaving, it challenges other Africanists to historicize the problematic of alcohol past the "threshold" represented by the era of legitimate commerce. At the same time, this case-study also offers striking comparative insights on the use and abuse of distilled beverages in a number of other geographical contexts during the early modern era: the similarly ubiquitous alcohol trade carried out with Amerindian societies in British, French and Hispanic America;[34] the crucial role

---

[34] See, for example: Peter C. Mancall, *Deadly Medicine: Indians and Alcohol in Early America*. Ithaca, NY, 1995; Bruce M. White, "'Give Us a Little Milk': The Social and Cultural Significance of Gift Giving on the Lake Superior Fur Trade," *Minnesota History*. Vol 48, 1982, pp. 66–71; idem, "A Skilled Game of Exchange: Ojibway Fur Trade Protocal," *Minnesota History*. Vol 50, 1987, pp. 232–236; André Vachon, "L'Eau-de-vie dans la société indienne," *Report of the Canadian Historical Association*. 1960, pp. 22–32; G. F. Stanley, "The Indians and the Brandy Trade during the Ancien Régime," *Revue d'Histoire de l'Amérique Française*. Vol. 6, 1953, pp. 489–505; Thomas F. Schilz, "Brandy and Beaver Pelts: Assiniboine-European Trading Patterns, 1695–1805," *Saskatchewan History*. Vol. 37, 1984, pp. 95–102; Edmund S. Carpenter, "Alcohol in the Iriquois Dream Quest," *American Journal of Psychiatry*. Vol. 116, 1959, pp. 148–151; R. C. Dailey, "The Role of Alcohol among North American Indian

played by drink in settler societies of the Atlantic world (and beyond);[35] and the centrality of alcohol in pre-industrial European societies.[36]

Tribes as Reported in the *Jesuit Relations*," *Anthropologica*. Vol. 10, 1968, pp. 45–59; F. W. Howay, "The Introduction of Intoxicating Liquors Amongst the Indians of the Northwest Coast," *British Columbia Historical Quarterly*. Vol. 6, 1942, pp. 157–169; William B. Munro, "The Brandy Parliament of 1678," *Canadian Historical Review*. Vol. 2, 1921, pp. 172–189; William B. Taylor, *Drinking, Homicide, and Rebellion in Colonial Mexican Villages*. Stanford, 1979; Michael C. Scardaville, "Alcohol Abuse and Tavern Reform in Late Colonial Mexico City," *Hispanic American Historical Review*. Vol. 60, 1980, pp. 643–671; M. Moreno, "Aguardientes y alcoholismo en el Mexico colonial," *Cuadernos hispanoamericanos*. Vol. 52, 1985, pp. 81–96; M. Rice, "Wine and Brandy Production in Colonial Peru," *Journal of Interdisciplinary History*. Vol. 27, 1998, pp. 455–479; G. Mora de Tovar, *Aguardiente y Conflictos Sociales en la Nueva Grenada durante el Siglo XVIII*. Bogotá, 1988; and G. Mezza Cuadra, "Le pisco, eau de vie du Pérou," *Premier Symposium International sur les eaux-de-vie traditionnelles d'origine viticole*. Paris, 1991, pp 28–31. See also, for the case of Australia, Marcia Langton, "Rum, Seduction, and Death: 'Aboriginality' and Alcohol," *Oceania*. Vol. 63, 1993, pp. 195–206.
[35] The case of British North America is particularly well studied. The most important works are: William Rorabaugh, *The Alcohol Republic: An American Tradition*. New York, 1979; Paton Yoder, "Tavern Regulation in Virginia: Rationale and Reality," *Virginia Magazine of History and Biography*. Vol. 87, 1979, pp. 259–278; Mark E. Lender and James K. Martin, *Drinking in America: A History*. New York, 1982; Richard P. Gildrie, "Taverns and Popular Culture in Essex County Massachusetts, 1678–1686," *Essex Institute Historical Collections*. Vol. 124, 1988, pp. 158–185; Peter Thompson, "'The Friendly Glass'· Drink and Gentility in Colonial Philadelphia," *Pennsylvania Magazine of History and Biography*. Vol. 133, 1989, pp. 549–573; David W. Conroy, "Puritans in Taverns: Law and Popular Culture in Colonial Massachusetts, 1630–1720," in Susanna Barrows and Robin Room, eds. *Drinking: Behavior and Belief in Modern Times*. Berkeley, 1991, pp. 29–60; Robert D. Arner, "Politics and Temperance in Boston and Philadelphia: Benjamin Franlin's Journalistic Writings on Drinking and Drunkenness," in J. A. Leo Lemay, ed. *Reappraising Benjamin Franklin: A Bicentennial Perspective*. Newark, Del., 1993, pp. 52–77; Allan M. Winkler, "Drinking on the American Frontier," *Quarterly Journal of Studies on Alcohol*. Vol. 29, 1968, pp. 413–445; Harry G. Levine, "The Discovery of Addiction: Changing Conceptions of Habitual Drinkenness in America," *Journal of Studies on Alcohol*. Vol. 39, 1978, pp. 143–174; Harry G. Levine, "The Vocabulary of Drunkenness," *Journal of Studies on Alcohol*. Vol. 42, 1981, pp. 1038–1051; Rebecca H. Warner and Henry Rosett, "The Effects of Drinking on Offspring: An Historical Survey of American and British Literature," *Journal of Studies on Alcohol*. Vol. 36, 1975, pp. 1395–1420; Joel Bernard, "The Transit of 'Small, Merry' Anglo-American Culture: Sir John Barley-Corne and Sir Richard Dum (Captain Whiskey)," *Proceedings of the American Antiquarian Society*. Vol. 100, 1990, pp. 81–136; A. Pinson, "The New England Rum Era: Drinking Styles and Social Change in Newport, R. I., 1720–1770," *Alcoholism* (Zagreb). Vol. 16, 1980, pp. 26–42; and Peter Thompson. *Rum Punch and Revolution: Taverngoing and Public Life in Eighteenth-Century Philadelphia*. Philadelphia, 1999. See also the works listed in the preceding ft. for francophone and hispanophone regions of the Americas, as well as Luis da Camâra Cascudo, *Prelúdio da Cachaça: etnografia, história e sociologia da aguardente no Brasil*. Rio de Janeiro, 1968, for Brazil.
[36] See, in particular, A. Lynn Martin. *Alcohol, Sex, and Gender in Late Medieval and*

The phenomenon was not specific to Africa. Rather, it was part and parcel of world-wide historical developments.[37]

Early Modern Europe. New York, 2001; Judith M. Bennett, *Ale, Beer, and Brewsters in England: Women's Work in a Changing World, 1300–1600*. New York, 1996; John M. Bowers, "'Dronkennesse is Ful of Stryvyng': Alcoholism and Ritual Violence in Chaucer's *Pardoner's Tale*," *English Literary History*. Vol. 57, 1990, pp. 757–784; Keith Wrightson, "Alehouses, Order and Reformation in Rural England, 1590–1660," in Eileen Yeo and Stephen Yeo, eds. *Popular Culture and Class Conflict, 1590–1914: Explorations in the History of Labour and Leisure*. Brighton, 1981, pp. 2–11; Harris G. Hudson, *A Study of Social Regulations in England under James I and Charles I: Drink and Tobacco*. Chicago, 1933; Peter Clark, *The Alehouse: A Social History, 1200–1830*. London, 1983; Peter Clark, "The 'Mother Gin' Controversy in the Early Eighteenth Century," *Transactions of the Royal Historical Society*. 5th Series, Vol. 38, 1988, pp. 63–84; George Rude, "'Mother Gin' and the London Riots of 1736," *Guildhall Miscellany*. Vol. 10, 1959, pp. 53–63; T. G. Coffey, "Beer Street, Gin Lane: Some Views of Eighteenth-Century Drinking," *Quarterly Journal of Studies on Alcohol*. Vol. 27, 1966, pp. 669–692; Hans Medick, "Plebeian Culture in the Transition to Capitalism," in Raphael Samuel and Gareth S. Jones, eds. *Culture, Ideology and Politics: Essays for Eric Hobsbawn*. London, 1982, pp. 84–113; Thomas B. Gilmore, "James Boswell's Drinking," *Eighteenth-Century Studies*. Vol. 24, 1991, pp. 337–357; Lee Davison, "Experiments in the Social Regulation of Industry: Gin Legislation, 1729–1751," Lee Davidson, *et. al.*, *Stilling the Grumbling Hive: Responses to Social and Economic Problems in England, c. 1869–1750*. London, 1992, pp. 25–48; Sidney Webb and Beatrice Webb, *The History of Liquor Licensing, Principally from 1700 to 1800*. Hamden, Conn., 1963 (but originally published in 1903); David Christian, *'Living Water': Vodka and Russian Society on the Eve of Emancipation*. Oxford, 1990; and Thomas Brennan, *Public Drinking and Popular Culture in Eighteenth Century Paris*. Princeton, 1988.

[37] See, for example, Wolfgang Schivelbusch, *Tastes of Paradise: A Social History of Spices, Stimulants, and Intoxicants*. New York, 1992 (trans. by David Jacobson); and Jordan Goodman, Paul E. Lovejoy, and Andrew Sherrat, eds., *Consuming Habits: Drugs in History and Anthropology*. New York, 1995.

CHAPTER ONE

ALCOHOL IN EARLY MODERN
WEST CENTRAL AFRICA

In his account of the mid-fifteenth century Portuguese "discoveries" along the coast of West Africa, the chronicler Gomes Eanes de Zurara stated with some astonishment that the inhabitants of this region did not know of *vinho* or wine extracted from grapes.[1] Although unaware of it, Zurara could have extended the geographical breath of this comment to cover nearly all of the continent.[2] The reason is that the vine, so dear to Europeans throughout the ages for the alcoholized juice produced by its grapes, was just not found in most of Africa.[3] This is not to suggest that Africans did not produce and consume their own indigenous alcoholic beverages. Quite the con-

---

[1] Gomes Eanes da Zurara, *Crónica da Guiné*. Barcelos, 1937, p. 126.

[2] The one exception is northern Africa, from ancient Egypt to Morocco. See T. D. Crothers, "Inebriety in Ancient Egypt and Chaldea," *Quarterly Journal of Inebriety*. Vol. 25, 1903, pp. 142–150; W. I. Adams, *Nubia: Corridor to Africa*. London, 1984, pp. 363–364; Robert E. Popham, "The Social History of the Tavern," in Y. Israel, F. B. Glaser, H. Kalant, R. E. Popham, W. Schmidt, and R. G. Smart, eds. *Research Advances in Alcohol and Drug Problems: Vol. 4.* New York, 1978, pp. 231 and 236–238; L. H. Lesko, *King Tut's Wine Cellar.* Berkeley, 1977; Hildebert Isnard, *La Vigne en Algérie.* Gap, 1951–1954, 2 Vols., and Hugh Johnson, *The Story of Wine.* London, 1988, pp. 24–34.

[3] Northern Africa aside, the timing of the introduction of the vine in the rest of the continent is uncertain. According to W. G. L. Randles, *L'Ancien royaume du Congo des origines à la fin du XIXe siècle.* Paris, 1968, p. 188, it was introduced in the kingdom of Kongo by the Portuguese during the middle of the 1600s. Although possibly representing the first occurrence of this phenomenon, the vines planted in Kongo did not take root for long. See Curto, *Álcool e Escravos*, Chapter 3 "O Comércio Do Álcool Luso-brasileiro no Reino do Kongo Durante o Tráfico Atlântico de Escravos, c. 1480–1830." The only two areas in the continent, again with the exception of ancient Egypt, where the introduction of grape vines was significantly more lasting and wine production became important industries were: South Africa, following the arrival of the Dutch in the mid-1600s; and Algeria, after the beginning of French colonization in the early 1800s. For South Africa see Charles J. G. Niehaus, "The Birth of our Wine Industry on the 2nd of February 1659," *Wine and Spirit.* Vol. 15, 1946, pp. 11–15; C. Louis Leipoldt, *300 Years of Cape Wine.* Cape Town, 1974; and Mary I. Rayner, "Wine and Slaves: The Failure of an Export Economy and the Ending of Slavery in the Cape Colony, 1806–1835," Unpublished Ph.D. dissertation, Duke University, 1986. For Algeria see Isnard, *La Vigne en Algérie*.

trary. Like most other non-European cultures before their contact with Europeans, the peoples of Africa had long acquired the knowledge to produce their own alcoholic drinks and developed the desire to consume them.[4]

As noted above in the "Introduction," the precolonial history of alcohol in the African continent, whether it be its economic, social, or cultural dimensions, remains to be written. One of the major stumbling blocks impeding the reconstruction of this past has been the question of documentation. Written and oral sources containing information on alcohol in African societies before the later 1800s do exist. But the further one goes back in time, fewer and fewer of these records become available.

One region where such a reconstruction is less problematic is West Central Africa. Indeed, for this part of the continent, there exists a comparatively larger corpus of sources chronicling the economic, social, and cultural facets of alcohol from the late 1400s onwards. Primarily generated by the first European missionaries, traders, and government officials, these documents allow us to draw a picture of alcohol and its roles at an extremely important time in the past of this region: its encounter with Europeans. Such a reconstruction is not without methodological difficulties. The sources available are not from the era of initial contact, but come mainly from the 1500s and the 1600s. By this time, alcohol consumption patterns in West Central African were already beginning to change due to the importation of European and American booze.[5] Nevertheless, in spite of these changes, the consumption of traditional alcohol was to remain fairly

---

[4] For some early references to western African alcoholic beverages, aside from those listed below specifically for the West Central region, see Diogo Gomes, "A Relação dos Descobrimentos da Guiné e das Ilhas," in Vitorino de Magalhães Godinho, ed., *Documentos sôbre a Expansão Portuguesa*. Lisbon, 1943–1956, Vol. I, p. 86; Th. Monod, A. Teixeira da Mota, and Raymond Mauny, *Description de la Côte Occidentale d'Afrique (Sénégal au Cap de Monte, Archipels, par Valentim Fernandes, 1505–1510)*. Bissau, 1951, pp. 68–70; Richard Jobson, *The Golden Trade: Or, a Discovery of the River Gambra, and the Golden Trade of the Aethiopians*. London, 1968 (but originally published in 1623), pp. 157–159; and Olifert Dapper, *Description de l'Afrique contenant les noms, la situation & les confins de toutes les parties, leurs rivieres, leurs villes & leur habitations, leurs plantes & leurs animaux; les mouers, les coûtumes, la langue, les richesses, la religion & le gouvernement de ses peuples*. Amsterdam, 1686, p. 255.

[5] The crucial testing ground in this region was the Kingdom of Kongo. See Curto, *Álcool e Escravos*, Chapter 3 "O Comércio Do Álcool Luso-brasileiro no Reino do Kongo Durante o Tráfico Atlântico de Escravos, c. 1480–1830."

constant throughout the region for centuries to come. Palm wine and beer, as we will see below, are a case in point. Many of the roles which these alcoholic beverages played in the 1500s and the 1600s were, as elsewhere in the continent, still current in the twentieth century.[6] As a result, the picture which can be drawn for the sixteenth and seventeenth centuries may be viewed tentatively as a reflection of West Central African alcohol consumption patterns not only during, but also before, the initial era of contact with Europeans.

In the 1500s and the 1600s, there were already a number of local alcoholic beverages from which West Central Africans could choose to drink.[7] Of these, two seem to have been widely consumed: one, known as *malafu* or *malavu*, was wine extracted primarily from the raphia variety of palm tree;[8] and the other, known as *ovallo* or *walo*,

---

[6] According to Théophile Obenga, "Histoire du Monde Bantu," in Théophile Obenga and Simão Souindoula, eds. *Racines Bantu/Bantu Roots*. Libreville, 1991, p. 126, palm wine and beer have long been essential to social life in Central, Eastern, and Southern Africa. For the specific case of Angola, see Isabel C. Henriques, *Percursos da Modernidade em Angola: Dinâmicas comerciais e transformações sociais no século XIX*. Lisbon, 1997, pp. 292-298.

[7] Aside from those discussed below, there was *quilunda*, a drink first described by Giovanni António Cavazzi de Montecúccolo, *Descrição Histórica dos Três Reinos do Congo, Matamba e Angola*. Lisbon, 1965, (translated and edited by Graziano Maria da Legguzzano) Vol. I, p. 188, as simply being made with an infusion of precious aromas by the Jagas in the interior of Luanda during the mid-1600s. (On the Jagas see ft. 22 below.) Another alcoholic drink was a blend of bee honey and *walo*, which António de Oliveira de Cadornega, *História Geral das Guerras Angolanas*. Lisbon, 1972, (edited by José Matias Delgado and Manuel Alves da Cunha) Vol. III, p. 97, first reported as consumed in Kisama, south of Luanda, around 1650. *Ochasa* (also *quiaça*) was a similar concoction which, according to Jean-Luc Vellut, "Diversification de l'économie de cuillette: miel et cire dans les sociétés de la forêt claire d'Afrique centrale (c. 1750-1950)," *African Economic History*. Vol. 7, 1979, p. 96, was to become a favoured drink of the emerging Ovimbundu in the central Benguela plateau. Yet another intoxicant found in the central Benguela plateau was mead, considered by Vellut (*ibid.*) as the oldest alcoholic beverage known to humanity. The first report on this intoxicant, known as *mingundo* (also *migundi, ekundi, ingundi*) amongst the Ovimbundu, comes from Paulo Martins Pinheiro de Lacerda, "Noticia da Cidade de S. Filippe de Benguella, e dos Costumes dos Gentios Habitantes daquelle Sertão, 1797," *Annaes Marítimos e Coloniaes* (Parte Não Official). Sér. 5, 1845, p. 490. Early references with more ample information on these alcoholic drinks are not available to adequately reconstruct their use. A useful discussion, however, is found in Henriques, *Percursos da Modernidade em Angola*, pp. 292-298.

[8] For the kingdom of Kongo see Père Jésuite Jácome Dias, 01-08-1548, in Willy Bal, ed., *Le Royaume du Congo aux XVe et XVIe Siècles: Documents d'histoire*. Léopoldville, 1963, p. 41; Filippo Pigafetta and Duarte Lopes, *Description du Royaume de Congo et des Contrées Environantes (1591)*. Louvain, 1965, 2nd edition (translated and annotated by Willy Bal), pp. 76-77 and 123; "De la situation du royaume du Congo," 25-11-1595, in Jean Cuvelier and Louis Jadin, eds., *L'Ancien Congo d'après les Archives*

was beer produced from a variety of local grains, especially millet and sorghum.[9] Each of these two drinks probably then had an alcoholic content similar to that found four and a half centuries later.

Romaines, 1518–1640. Brussels, 1954, p. 197; the early 1600s anonymous report in Luciano Cordeiro, ed., *Viagens, Explorações e Conquistas dos Portugueses: Collecção de Documentos—Estabelecimentos e Resgates Portugueses na Costa Occidental da Africa, 1607*. Lisbon, 1881, pp. 20–21; António Brásio, ed., *História do Reino do Congo*. Lisbon, 1969, pp. 39–40 and 60; the report of canon André Cordeiro, 24–01–1622, in Louis Jadin, "Relations sur le Congo et l'Angola tirées des archives de la Compagnie de Jésus, 1621–1631," *Bulletin de l'Institut Historique Belge de Rome*. Vol. XXXIX, 1968, p. 367; Cavazzi de Montecúccolo, *Descrição Histórica dos Três Reinos*, Vol. I, pp. 39–47 and 281, and Vol. II, p. 147; Bonaventure d'Alessano to Mgr. Ingoli, 04–06–1645, Gianuario de Nole to P. Gio-Battista da Napoli, 06–06–1645, and P. José de Pernambuco to Provincial de Castille, 25–03–1648, in Louis Jadin, ed., *L'Ancien Congo et l'Angola, 1639–1655, d'après les Archives Romaines, Portugaises, Neerlandaises, et Espagnoles*. Rome, 1975. Vol. II, pp. 664, 684, and 972, respectively; Jean-François de Rome, *La Fondation de la Mission des Capucins au Royaume de Congo (1648)*. Louvain, 1964, (Edited by François Bontinck), pp. 91, 93, and 122; P. Hildebrand, *Le Martyr Georges de Geel el les Débuts de la Mission du Congo (1645–1652)*. Anvers, 1940, pp. 187–188; Giuseppe Simonetti, "P. Giacinto Brugiotti da Vetralla e la sua Missione al Congo (1651–1657)," *Bolletino della Società Geografica Italiana*. Vol. 8, 1907, p. 317; Carlo Toso, ed. *L'Anarchia Congolese nel sec. XVII. La relazione inedita di Marcellino d'Atri*. Genoa, 1984, pp. 149–150; and Girolamo Merolla da Sorrento, "A Voyage to Congo and Several Other Countries Chiefly in Southern Africa," in John Churchill, ed., *A Collection of Voyages and Travels*. London, 1732, Vol. I, p. 564.

For the hinterland of Luanda see Irmão Antonio Mendes to Padre Leão Henriques, 29–10–1562, in Gastão Sousa Dias, ed., *Relações de Angola (Primordios da Ocupação Portuguesa) Pertencentes ao Cartorio do Colégio dos Padres da Companhia de Luanda, e Transcritas do Codice Existente na Biblioteca Nacional de Paris*. Coimbra, 1934, p. 34; idem to Padre Geral, 09–05–1563, in Brásio, *Monumenta Missionaria Africana*, 1st series, Vol. III, pp. 500–501; Garcia Simões to Provincial de São Paulo de Loanda, 20–10–1575, and Padre Diogo [da Costa] to Provincial de Portugal, 31–05–1586, both in "Descoberta de Angola e Congo: Relações de Angola, Tiradas do Cartorio do Collegio dos Padres da Companhia," *Boletim da Sociedade de Geografia de Lisboa*. Vol. 4, 1883, pp. 343 and 383, respectively; Lino d'Assumpção, "Exploração á Africa nos Ineditos da Bibliotheca de Evora," *Boletim da Sociedade de Geografia de Lisboa*. Vol. 6, 1885, p. 356; E. G. Ravenstein, ed., *The Strange Adventures of Andrew Battell of Leigh in Angola and the Adjoining Regions*. London, 1901, pp. 15, 25, and 30; the 1621 report of Garcia Mendes Castello Branco, in Luciano Cordeiro, ed., *Viagens, Explorações e Conquistas dos Portugueses: Collecção de Documentos—Da Mina ao Cabo Negro, 1574–1620*. Lisbon, 1881, p. 21; the 1622 report of Bento Banha Cardoso, in idem, ed., *Viagens, Explorações e Conquistas dos Portugueses: Collecção de Documentos—Producções, Commercio e Governo do Congo e de Angola, 1620–1629*. Lisbon, 1881, p. 19; Louis Jadin, "Pero Tavares, missionaire jésuite, ses travaux apostoliques au Congo et en Angola, 1629–1635," *Bulletin de l'Institut Historique Belge de Rome*. Vol. XXXIX, 1967, p. 359; Cadornega, *História Geral das Guerras*, Vol. III, pp. 358–363; and Cavazzi de Montecúccolo, *Descrição Histórica dos Três Reinos*, Vol. II, p. 147.

[9] For the kingdom of Kongo see "Un religieux au Provincial du Portugal," 15–12–1587, in Bal, *Royaume du Congo*, p. 42; Rome, *Fondation de la Mission des Capucins*, pp. 91–93; and François Bontinck, ed., *Diaire Congolaise de Fra Luca da Caltanisetta (1690–1701)*. Louvain, 1970, pp. 145–146.

According to a mid-1950s study of alcohol production and consumption in Katanga, the alcoholic content of traditional beer made
from cereals was no more than two percent, while that of palm wine
reached five percent.[10] Circumstantial evidence from some of the first
sources on indigenous alcohol in Kongo and Angola also point to
the low alcoholic contents of local beer and *malavu*. In the case of
the latter, for example, the mid-1580s informants of Filippo Pigafetta,
who compiled one of the first detailed accounts of the region, indicated that only when drunk too freely would it cause intoxication.[11]
Similarly, Giovanni António Cavazzi de Montecúccolo, a particularly well-travelled Italian missionary of the mid-1600s, suggested,
probably from first hand experience, that it took a jar of this beverage to "completely alter the senses and to inebriate."[12] Otherwise,
palm wine was believed even to possess medicinal qualities.

Some of the earliest documented consumers of this beverage actually thought it was quite healthful, especially for the stomach.[13] Thus,

---

For Luanda and its hinterland see Padre Garcia Simões to Provincial [de São
Paulo de Loanda], 20-10-1575, in Brásio, *Monumenta Missionaria Africana*, 1st series,
Vol. III, p. 137; the letter of Father Baltasar Afonso, dated 25-08-1578, in Sousa
Dias, *Relações de Angola*, p. 92; and Cadornega, *História Geral das Guerras*, Vol. III,
p. 97.
For the hinterland of Benguela, where beer made from millet and sorghum was
known as *ocimbombo* (also *kimbombo*), see the oral traditions on Ovimbundu genesis
in Lima, *Os Kyaka de Angola*, Vol. 1, pp. 158 and 210; and Pinheiro de Lacerda,
"Noticia ... de Benguella ... e dos Costumes dos ... Habitantes daquelle Sertão,
1797," p. 490. These are the only early sources documenting the use of *ocimbombo*.
Nineteenth century references are found in Henriques, *Percursos da Modernidade em
Angola*, pp. 292–298. For modern references, see Gladwyn M. Childs, *Umbundu
Kinship & Character*. London, 1949, p. 33; A. C. Edwards, *The Ovimbundu under Two
Sovereignties: A Study of Social Control and Social Change among a People of Angola*. London,
1962, p. 121; Wilfrid W. Hambly, *The Ovimbundu of Angola*. Chicago, 1934, p. 149;
Alfred Hauenstein, "L'Ombala de Caluquembe," *Anthropos*. Vol. 58, 1963, pp. 63,
73, 77, and 113; and Linda M. Heywood, "Production, Trade and Power: The
Political Economy of Central Angola, 1850–1930," Unpublished Ph.D. dissertation,
Columbia University, 1984, pp. 40 and 65.
   [10] See G. Bernier and A. Lambrechts, "Étude sur les Boissons Fermentées
Indigènes du Katanga," *Problèmes Sociaux Congolais*. No. 48, 1960, p. 32. A decade
earlier, E. L. Adriaens, "Contribution à l'étude des vins de palme au Kwango,"
Bulletin des Sceances de l'Institut Royale Colonial Belge. Vol. 22, 1951, p. 339, found the
alcoholic content of palm wine amongst the Pende to be a maximum of six percent.
   [11] Pigafetta and Lopes, *Description du Royaume de Congo*, pp. 76–77. Impressionistic
references to the low alcoholic content of palm wine and beers of West Central
Africa are found in Miller, *Way of Death*, pp. 83 and 465.
   [12] Cavazzi de Montecúccolo, *Descrição Histórica dos Três Reinos*, Vol. I, p. 45. I
have been unable to determine the volume of such a jar.
   [13] See, for example, Padre Garcia Gomes to Provincial, 20-10-1575, in Brásio,

in the opinion of Pigafetta's informants, this alcoholic beverage was so "diuretic" when drunk fresh "that no one in this country suffers from gravel or stones in the bladder."[14] A parallel link was suggested some forty years later by the author of another early description of Kongo: as a result of drinking *malavu*, he wrote, "there is no one who suffers from stones or the kidneys."[15] And such opinions were not just the result of a view, then dominant in Europe, of alcohol as medicine.[16] As recently as the mid-1900s, at least one modern physician was still exalting the medicinal qualities of palm wine.[17]

The low alcoholic content of beer made from local grains and palm wine, as well as the "medicinal" qualities of the latter, could lead us to think that the consumption of both beverages was relatively widespread amongst the peoples of West Central Africa at the time of contact with Europeans. Let us see what can be pieced together from the available contemporaneous documentation: first from the more numerous sources relating to *malavu* and then the scanty records dealing with beer made from local grains.

I. *Palm Wine: Production, Consumption, and Uses*

The production of palm wine in West Central Africa involved either of two processes. According to Pigafetta's informants, *malavu*, a liquor resembling milk, was "obtained by perforating the top of the [palm] tree."[18] This required that individuals, males in each and every case, possess the skills to safely climb up the tree, make the necessary inci-

---

Monumenta Missionaria Africana, 1st series, Vol. III, p. 137; and Padre Diogo da Costa to Provincial de Portugal, 31–05–1586, in Sousa Dias, *Relações de Angola*, p. 179.

[14] Pigafetta and Lopes, *Description du Royaume de Congo*, p. 77.

[15] "Description du Congo," extracts of which are found in Cuvelier and Jadin, *L'Ancien Congo d'après les Archives Romaines*, p. 108.

[16] On this point, see Fernand Braudel, *The Structures of Everyday Life: The Limits of the Possible. Civilization & Capitalism 15th–18th Century, Vol. 1.* (trans. and rev. Siân Reynolds) New York, 1982, pp. 241–243.

[17] B. Bergeret, "Note préliminaire à l'étude du vin de palme au Cameroun," *Médecine Tropicale.* Vol. 6, 1957, pp. 901–904.

[18] Pigafetta and Lopes, *Description du Royaume de Congo*, p. 77. Similar details are also found in Ravenstein, *Adventures of Andrew Battell*, p. 30; "Description du Congo," in Cuvelier and Jadin, *L'Ancien Congo d'après les Archives Romaines*, p. 108; Rome, *Fondation de la Mission des Capucins*, p. 91; Simonetti, "Giacinto Brugiotti da Vetralla," p. 317; and Sorrento, "Voyage to Congo and Several Other Countries," Vol. I, p. 564.

sion, and collect the liquid.[19] Once these palm wine tappers made
the initial incision, the sap was collected on a daily basis, usually
both in the morning and in the evening, with no other work required
except the occasional cutting of a few branches.[20] Not a few of these
individuals, especially along the Zaire River, were in fact specialists
who made part of their living by tapping the raphia palms and selling their alcoholized milky juice.[21] A second, most likely less utilized,
method involved cutting down raphia palms by the root and, after
a ten day waiting period, making a hole in the top and heart of the
trees so that their sap could be easily collected every morning and
night for as long as forty days until they dried up.[22] Although requiring

---

[19] The first two recorded detailed descriptions of this process date from the second and third quarters of the 1600s, respectively: Rome, *Fondation de la Mission des
Capucins*, pp. 91–93; and Cadornega, *História Geral das Guerras*, Vol. III, p. 358. In
the hinterland of Luanda, these tappers were known as *engemas*. See Adriano Parreira,
Dicionário Glossográfico e Toponímico da Documentação sobre Angola, Séculos XV–XVII. Lisbon,
1990, pp. 12–13. A comparison with their mid-twentieth century counterparts in
Sénégal, as found in A. Adandé, "Le Vin de Palme chez les Diola de la Casamance,"
Notes Africaines. No. 61, 1954, pp. 1–6, reveals many similarities.

[20] Ravenstein, *Adventures of Andrew Battell*, p. 30; Rome, *Fondation de la Mission des
Capucins*, p. 91; and Girolamo Merolla as quoted in John K. Thornton, *The Kingdom
of Kongo: Civil War and Transition, 1641–1718*. Madison, 1983, p. 29.

[21] Dapper, *Description de l'Afrique*, p. 348. Amongst the Kongo, professional palm
wine tappers have continued to exist until the present century. See Gilles Sautter,
De l'Atlantique au Fleuve Congo: une géographie de sous-peuplement. Paris, 1966, Vol. 1,
p. 524.

[22] The first description of this method was provided by Andrew Battell in reference to the "Jagas", believed to have been expatriated Lunda title holders who
developed the military cult known as Imbangala that overrun much of West Central
Africa in the second half of the 1500s and the early 1600s. See Ravenstein, *Adventures
of Andrew Battell*, p. 30. A second description, relating to the territory in the interior of Luanda restructured in the mid-1600s by the wandering "Jagas", is found
in Cadornega, *História Geral das Guerras*, Vol. III, p. 361. On the changing percep-
tions of the "Jaga" by modern historians, see Jan Vansina, "The Foundation of the
Kingdom of Kasanje," *Journal of African History*. Vol. IV, 1963, pp. 355–374; David
Birmingham, "The Date and Significance of the Imbangala Invasion of Angola,"
Ibid., Vol. VI, 1965, pp. 143–152; Jan Vansina, "More on the Invasions of Kongo
and Angola by the Jaga and the Lunda," *Ibid.*, Vol. VII, 1966, pp. 421–429; Joseph
C. Miller, "The Imbangala and the Chronology of Early Central African History,"
Ibid., Vol. XIII, 1972, pp. 549–574; idem, "Requiem for the 'Jaga'", *Cahiers d'études
africaines*. Vol. XIII, 1973, pp. 121–149; idem, *Kings and Kinsmen: Early Mbundu States
in Angola*. Oxford, 1976, especially Chapter VII—"The Imbangala and the Portuguese";
John K. Thornton, "A Resurrection for the Jaga," *Cahiers d'études africaines*. Vol. 18,
1978, pp. 223–228; Joseph C. Miller, "Thanatopsis," *Ibid.*, 18, pp. 229–231; François
Bontick, "Un mausolée pour les Jaga," *Cahiers d'Études Africaines*. Vol. 20, 1979, pp.
387–389; and Anne Hilton, "Reconsidering the Jaga," *Journal of African History*. Vol.
22, 1981, pp. 191–202.

less investment in labour, this easier method of obtaining *malavu* reduced the lifespan of the sap-giving raphia palms and was environmentally unsustainable over the long run in any given area.[23] It appears to have been practised predominantly, though not exclusively, in the hinterland of Luanda.[24]

Whether collected from standing or felled raphia palms, the palm wine quickly turned sour. Indeed, this alcoholic beverage was best only when consumed on the same day that it was collected. By the second day, it started to become acidic and was thereafter used as vinegar.[25] As a result of its rapidly turning sour, *malavu* could thus neither be stored for future consumption nor transported to markets over long distances. It had to be consumed daily within a relatively short distance from where it was collected. For example, when Jean

---

[23] Vansina, *Children of Woot*, p. 178. A totally different interpretation of felling palms is found in Joseph C. Miller, "The Significance of Drought, Disease and Famine in the Agriculturally Marginal Zones of West-Central Africa," *Journal of African History*. Vol. XXIII, 1982, p. 26. Here, drawing upon the Imbangala example as reported by Battell, Miller argues that "during times of dearth in sixteenth-century Angola . . ., the edible pith of these . . . trees served as a last recourse for starving populations. (p. 26) Moreover, he adds, "[f]elling palms to obtain the edible pulp turns up repeatedly as [a] desperation tactic to avoid starvation." (p. 40) The time period during which Battell lived amongst the Imbangala, however, was one characterized by relatively good rainfall. Contemporaneous conditions of significant drought in West Central Africa, as Miller himself documents, existed only during the 1570s–1580s and then again during the later 1610s (pp. 21 and 35–42). Equally important, if the connection between drought-induced desperation and felling palms for food "turns up repeatedly", one can only wonder why Miller provides but one primary source: Battell, which he has re-interpreted to fit into this scheme. Consequently, the argument that cutting down palms in West Central Africa was a desperation tactic to obtain food during times of drought is both tenuous and devoid of historicity.

[24] Ravenstein, *Adventures of Andrew Battell*, p. 30; and Cadornega, *História Geral das Guerras*, Vol. III, p. 361. During the late 1800s, the Tio also used this method along the middle Zaire River. See Vansina, *Tio Kingdom of the Middle Congo*, p. 148. The collection of palm wine from felled trees may thus have been practised before then in areas other than Luanda's hinterland.

[25] Padre Diogo da Costa to Provincial de Portugal, 31–05–1586, in Brásio, *Monumenta Missionaria Africana*, 1st series, Vol. III, p. 338; Pigafetta and Lopes, *Description du Royaume de Congo*, p. 77; Rome, *Fondation de la Mission des Capucins*, pp. 91–92; and Jean Cuvelier, ed., *Relations sur le Congo du Père Laurent de Lucques, 1700–1717*. Brussels, 1953, pp. 77–78. This problem is still found wherever traditional palm wine is available. See, for example, David J. Parkin, *Palms, Wine, and Witnesses: Public Spirit and Private Gain in an African Farming Community*. San Francisco, 1972, p. 10, for Kenya; Ifekandu Umunna, "The Drinking Culture of a Nigerian Community: Onitsha," *Quarterly Journal of Studies on Alcohol*. Vol. 28, 1967, p. 530 for Nigeria; and Sautter, *De l'Atlantique au Fleuve Congo*, Vol. 1, pp. 523–524, for areas bordering the Zaire River.

Barbot visited the Nsoyo coast in 1700, he found that its inhabitants could provide "no refreshments besides some few pots of palm-wine, which they fetch[e]d from a good distance inland."[26] This probably meant a radius of between thirty-five and fifty kilometres over land.[27]

If palm wine had to be consumed locally on a daily basis, not all West Central African societies had access to this alcoholic beverage. Indeed, more than a few habitats in the region did not sustain palm trees. According to Jan Vansina, the raphia palm was only introduced east of the Lulua and the Lubudi rivers during the late nineteenth century.[28] Luc de Heusch has similarly maintained, based on an anthropological investigation of oral traditions, that this tree first appeared east of the Kasai River during the initial period of Luba-Lunda state formation.[29] In the case of the central African savanna, both Vansina and Heusch thus place the origin of the raphia palm and its milk-like alcoholized juice in the western part of the region, from where a slow, eastward expansion took place. But even in the western part of West Central Africa there were geographical niches where raphia palms were either entirely absent or where their number was relatively small. For example, when the English sailor Andrew Battell met up with the Imbangala south of the Kuvo River in 1601 he observed that this area lacked palm trees of any variety.[30] Further inland, in the central Benguela plateau, palms were also lacking. This would later lead the emerging Ovimbundu to pillage the lower river valleys of the highlands in search of these trees,[31] presumably for their sap.

The kingdom of Kongo constitutes an excellent microcosm of the irregular distribution of the raphia palm throughout the region. During the middle of the seventeenth century, in the opinion of the

---

[26] Jean Barbot, "Voyage to the Congo River or the Zaire in the Year 1700," in Churchill, *Collection of Voyages and Travels*, Vol. V, p. 503.

[27] According to Thornton, *Kingdom of Kongo*, p. 20, this was a critical distance for the overland transportation of foodstuffs. The Kongo, unlike the Bobangi and the Mpama up the Zaire River who used waterways to market palm wine, did not have navigable rivers to transport this alcoholic beverage over long distances. For the Bobangi and the Mpama see Robert W. Harms, *River of Wealth, River of Sorrow: The Central Zaire Basin in the Era of the Slave and Ivory Trade, 1500–1891*. New Haven, 1981, pp. 56–57.

[28] Vansina, *Kingdoms of the Savanna*, p. 23.

[29] Heusch, *Le Roi Ivre*, p. 221.

[30] Ravenstein, *Adventures of Andrew Battell*, p. 22.

[31] Joseph C. Miller, "Angola central e sul por volta de 1840," *Estudos Afro-Asiáticos*. Vol. 32, 1997, pp. 19 and 36.

particularly well informed Cavazzi de Montecúccolo, Kongo possessed every variety of palm tree, more so than any other area in
West Central Africa.[32] Yet, in Mbamba, its southern coastal province
neighbouring the kingdom of Ndongo, there were none.[33] In Kongo's
northern coastal province of Nsoyo, on the other hand, two other
mid-seventeenth century European missionaries found that the amount
of *malavu* available to the local ruling class was quite small, suggesting that raphia palms there were not in abundance.[34] Consequently,
the consumption of palm wine was limited to environments which
were endowed with an abundance of the raphia palms from which
the sap was collected: the inland rainforest-savanna areas lying south
of the dense forest and north of the drier savanna.[35]

Although the areas where West Central Africans had access to
malavu can be easily delineated, establishing the broad historical drinking patterns prevalent there is far more complex. Aside from the
number of *engema* involved in collecting the sap, the consumption of
palm wine had to be conditioned by at least two other factors: the
volume of the milk-like liquid given by each tree and the amount
of trees tapped in any one area.[36] At beginning of the 1600s, Battell
found that each of the raphia palms felled by the Imbangala north
of the Kuvo River provided an average of two quarts, or just over
one litre, per day of wine.[37] In the case of the palm trees left standing, similar data on output are not available. It may well be that
the daily output of each standing raphia palm in West Central Africa
was similar to that obtained in Senegambia during the early 1500s:
a maximum of .75 litres.[38] But the value of such quantitative infor-

[32] Cavazzi de Montecúccolo, *Descrição Histórica dos Três Reinos*, Vol. I, p. 39.

[33] See F. Capelle to Count de Nassau, 1642, in Louis Jadin, "Rivalités luso-néer-
landaise au Soyo, Congo, 1600–1675," *Bulletin de l'Institut Historique Belge de Rome*.
Vol. XXXVII, 1966, p. 227; Rome, *Fondation de la Mission des Capucins*, p. 93; and
Cuvelier, *Relations sur le Congo du Père Laurent de Lucques*, pp. 168–169.

[34] See Gianuario da Nola to P. Gio-Battista da Napoli, 06–06–1645, and P. José
de Pernambuco to P. Provincial de Castille, 25–03–1648, in Jadin, *L'Ancien Congo
et l'Angola, 1639–1655*, Vol. II, pp. 684 and 972, respectively.

[35] Vansina, *Children of Woot*, pp. 173 and 178.

[36] The consumption of *malavu* was most probably conditioned by another factor.
According to Sautter, *De l'Atlantique au Fleuve Congo*, Vol. 1, p. 524, production
reached its maximum during the dry season, coinciding with Kongo feasts, and
thereafter waned. Exactly the same point is made by Adandé, "Vin de Palme chez
les Diola," p. 4, for the Diola of Casamance, Sénégal.

[37] Ravenstein, *Adventures of Andrew Battell*, p. 30.

[38] See Monod, Teixeira da Mota, and Mauny, *Description de la Côte Occidentale*

mation is limited in light of the fact that data on the number of trees tapped do not exist. In order to develop more worthwhile insights, we must return to the qualitative evidence at hand.

With respect to the kingdom of Kongo in the 1580s, Pigafetta's informants indicated that its inhabitants did not take much palm wine.[39] Such an evaluation most certainly represents an oversimplified generalization, given the irregular distribution of the raphia palm throughout the realm. As we have already seen above, *malavu* was a relatively scarce consumer item in the dry coastal provinces of Nsoyo and Mbamba. But in the wetter, more elevated, inland areas of the kingdom, the situation was totally different. Thus, not a few observers were impressed by the amount of local wine available in the capital of the realm, *Mbanza* Kongo, and in its northeastern provinces, all of which possessed extensive groves of palm trees.[40] Similar details also caught the attention of eyewitnesses in the more southeasterly kingdom of Ndongo and its immediate surroundings, habitats in which palm trees also flourished.[41] Not surprisingly, these are the areas referred to by the extant scattered sources which specifically point to large amounts of *malavu* being consumed.[42] In other words, whether the volume drunk by West Central Africans was moderate or excessive depended on the local availability of the raphia palm.

---

d'Afrique, pp. 68–70. In the mid-1900s, a not too dissimilar amount of half a litre per tree was obtained daily in Casamance, Sénégal. See Adandé, "Vin de Palme chez les Diola," pp. 5–6.

[39] Pigafetta and Lopes, *Description du Royaume de Congo*, p. 123.

[40] See, for example, the report of canon André Cordeiro, 24 01–1622, in Jadin, "Relations sur le Congo et l'Angola," p. 367; Dapper, *Description de l'Afrique*, pp. 345 and 348; and Bontinck, *Diaire Congolaise de Fra Luca da Caltanisetta*, pp. 194–195.

[41] Irmão Antonio Mendes to Padre Leão Henriques, 29 10 1562, in Sousa Dias, *Relações de Angola*, p. 34; idem to Padre Geral, 09–05–1563, in Brásio, *Monumenta Missionaria Africana*, 1st series, Vol. III, pp. 500–501; Padre Francisco de Gouveia to Padre Diogo Mirão, 1564, in Sousa Dias, *Relações de Angola*, p. 43; the letters of Padre Diogo [da Costa], dated 04–06–1585 and 20–07–1585, in *ibid.*, pp. 154 and 161, respectively; idem to Provincial de Portugal, 31–05–1586, in "Descoberta de Angola e Congo: Relações de Angola," p. 383; Ravenstein, *Adventures of Andrew Battell*, pp. 20 and 22; Jadin, "Pero Tavares, missionaire jésuite," p. 359; and Cadornega, *História Geral das Guerras*, Vol. III, pp. 359–363.

[42] See the letters of Padre Diogo [da Costa], dated 04–06–1585, 20–07–1585, and 31–05–1586, in Sousa Dias, *Relações de Angola*, pp. 154, 161, and 179, respectively, for Ndongo in the mid-1580s; Ravenstein, *Adventures of Andrew Battell*, pp. 20 and 25, for the area immediately north of the Kuvo River at the beginning of the seventeenth century; and Cadornega, *História Geral das Guerras*, Vol. III, pp. 359–363, for the hinterland of Luanda in the third quarter of the 1600s. See also the other sources listed in the notes supporting the following paragraph.

However, regardless of the varying amounts of palm wine actually consumed throughout Kongo and Angola, one fact is inescapable. Wherever the raphia palm proliferated, a single group of individuals drank disproportionate quantities of its fermented sap: the ruling elites.[43] When Antonio Mendes, one of the first Portuguese missionaries to sojourn in the kingdom of Ndongo, visited the court of the *Ngola* or King in 1562, he found him constantly guzzling *malavu*, because "all of the nobles have to drink."[44] A year later, the same Mendes wrote that both his host and the latter's nobles imbibed palm wine all day long, a custom which they viewed as very honourable, more so than eating.[45] Similarly, when in 1601 Battell met up with the expatriated Lunda title holders near the present port town of Benguela, he noticed these to be particularly avid consumers of the milk-like alcoholized beverage.[46] The evidence on this type of consumption pattern amongst the nobility in the kingdom of Kongo is no less evocative. Even in the province of Nsoyo, which was not particularly well endowed with raphia trees, the most refined beverage of the wealthy lords during the mid-1600s was the smaller amounts of palm wine that were locally available.[47] Moreover, when the Italian missionary Luca da Caltanisetta travelled through Kongo's eastern province of Nkusu in 1694 and in 1699, he found the nobles there also to be heavy drinkers of *malavu*. Here, too, "inebriety [was not considered] shameful but an honour."[48] In the hinterland of Luanda,

---

[43] A symbolic, but nevertheless telling, view of the palm wine drinking patterns of early Luba-Lunda elites is found in Heusch, *Le Roi Ivre*, pp. 112–118, 130–132, 142–144, 150, 168, 178–186, 204–206, and 217–221. A more tangible example on the propensity of West Central African ruling elites towards heavy palm wine consumption comes from the modern Pende. Around 1950, according to Adriaens, "Contribution à l'étude des vins de palme au Kwango," p. 338, Pende chiefs ingested anywhere from four to six litres of palm wine per day, while their subjects drunk between one and one and a half litres.

[44] Irmão Antonio Mendes to Padre Leão Henriques, 29–10–1562, in Sousa Dias, *Relações de Angola*, p. 35.

[45] Irmão Antonio Mendes to Padre Geral, 09–050–1563, in Brásio, *Monumenta Missionaria Africana*, 1st series, Vol. II, pp. 500–501.

[46] Ravenstein, *Adventures of Andrew Battell*, pp. 20, 22, and 30.

[47] See Gianuario de Nole to P. Gio-Battista da Napoli, 06–06–1645, in Jadin, *L'Ancien Congo et l'Angola, 1639–1655*, Vol. II, p. 684.

[48] Bontinck, *Diaire Congolaise de Fra Luca da Caltanisetta*, pp. 28–29 and 156. Further evidence on heavy drinking by the Kongo ruling elite is provided by Marcellino d'Atri, a companion of Caltanisetta. See Toso, *L'Anarchia Congolese nel sec. XVII*, pp. 149–150.

there was even one type of palm wine, *kimdimbu*, the consumption of which was the exclusive reserve of kings, nobles, and chiefs.[49]

The strong inclination on the part of region's elites for drinking palm wine must have required a steady and relatively voluminous supply of this alcoholic beverage. How was such a supply obtained? Joseph C. Miller has argued that "wealthy lords in the wetter regions maintained groves of palms from which they drew sap that fermented rapidly into wine."[50] The early evidence which he cites, relating exclusively to the kingdom of Ndongo, does not however point to ownership or control of palm groves by nobles.[51] There are, to be sure, a few documents which could be read in this light. An Ndongo lord in the mid-1580s, after rebelling against the Portuguese, is reported to "have been destroyed, his land burnt and his palm trees cut down" in retaliation.[52] Another example comes from the Kimbangu mountainous area east of the Kongo's capital where, again according to Caltanisetta, nobles in the late 1690s "were taking their wine" from its abundant palms.[53] Although groves of raphia palms may have been controlled or owned by nobles, to imply from these meagre and vague sources that this was in fact the case is stretching the point. It is just as likely, if not more probable, that lords in West Central Africa secured *malavu* through the tribute paid by their subjects. According to one source from the early 1600s, the wealth of the King of Kongo derived from tribute, of which palm wine was an integral part, paid by his nobles.[54] This same point was picked up about a half century later by the "armchair" geographer Olifert Dapper: "there are vassals," he wrote, "that, aside from the regular

---

[49] Cadornega, *História Geral das Guerras*, Vol. III, p. 363.

[50] Miller, *Way of Death*, p. 83.

[51] This includes the following letters: Garcia Simões to Provincial de São Paulo de Luanda, 20–10–1575; Padre da Costa, 04–06–1585; and Padre Diogo da Costa to Provincial de Portugal, 31–05–1586. All of these are found in Sousa Dias, *Relações de Angola*, pp. 58–59, 154, and 179, respectively. In the first case, Miller confuses political control of the land with control over its resources. In the second, all that is said is that palm trees are abundant throughout the realm. Finally, the only thing mentioned in the third source is that many palm trees exist in the three provinces of the kingdom and from these is extracted a great quantity of wine.

[52] Padre Baltasar Afonso, 19–01–1585, in Sousa Dias, *Relações de Angola*, p. 149.

[53] Bontinck, *Diaire Congolaise de Fra Luca da Caltanisetta*, pp. 194–195.

[54] Anonymous report of 1607 in Cordeiro, *Viagens, Explorações e Conquistas dos Portugueses: Collecção de Documentos—Estabelecimentos e Resgates Portugueses na Costa Occidental da África, 1607*, pp. 20–21. See also Vansina, "Equatorial Africa and Angola," p. 574.

tribute, pay homage to this Prince with palm wine . . ."[55] As it happens, the tribute which the Kongo nobility paid their suzerain was
previously acquired from their subjects.[56] And this was by no means
a process merely limited to the kingdom of Kongo.[57] The larger
amounts of *malavu* consumed by the ruling elites of West Central
Africa could thus have been just as easily acquired through tribute
as from groves of raphia palm which they may have controlled or
owned. Whatever the case, and here the possibility of both meth-
ods being used can not be discarded, another important fact is indis-
putable: nobles did not themselves draw the sap from raphia palms.
Historically, the ruling elites in West Central Africa did not engage
in menial tasks. The more voluminous amounts of *malavu* which they
drank were collected by peasants, perhaps even slaves, whose social
condition and skills in climbing trees made the tapping of the raphia
palms their preserve.

Even though it was the elites of West Central Africa who drank
disproportionate amounts of *malavu* wherever the raphia palm proliferated, palm wine was central to the entire socio-cultural and economic fabric of many of the region's societies. As far as can be
determined, much of the *malavu* consumed appears to have been
drank by West Central Africans, whether of noble, peasant, or slave
status, to wash down the starchy foodstuffs which they ingested on
a daily basis.[58] Nevertheless, this was not the only occasion when

---

[55] Dapper, *Description de l'Afrique*, p. 350.

[56] On this point see, in particular, John K. Thornton "The Kingdom of Kongo,
ca. 1390–1678: The Development of an African Social Formation," *Cahiers d'études
africaines*. Vol. 23, 1982, pp. 325–342; idem, *Kingdom of Kongo*, especially pp. 15–55;
and David Birmingham, *Central Africa to 1870: Zambezia, Zaire, and the South Atlantic*.
Cambridge, 1981, p. 27.

[57] Thomas Reefe, *The Rainbow and the Kings: A History of the Luba Empire to 1891*.
Berkeley, 1981, p. 156, for example, reports that part of the tribute received by
the royal Luba court in the eighteenth century from nearby client villages was also
in the form of palm wine. Another early case of palm wine used in tribute payments to local lords relates to the Kanyok. See John C. Yoder, *The Kanyok of Zaire:
An Institutional and Ideological History to 1895*. Cambridge, 1992, p. 39.

[58] See, for example, [Irmão Antonio Mendes] au Père Général, 09–05–1563, in
Bal, *Royaume du Congo*, pp. 106–107; Pigafetta and Lopes, *Description du Royaume de
Congo*, p. 123; "De la situation du royaume du Congo," 25–11–1595, in Cuvelier
and Jadin, *L'Ancien Congo d'après les Archives Romaines*, p. 197; Rome, *Fondation de la
Mission des Capucins*, pp. 91 and 93; Serafino da Cortona to Prefect of Tuscany,
20–03–1648, in Brásio, *Monumenta Missionaria Africana*, 1st series, Vol. X, p. 98;
Dapper, *Description de l'Afrique*, p. 352; Giralamo Merolla as quoted in Thornton,
Kingdom of Kongo, p. 29; and Cuvelier, *Relations sur le Congo du Père Laurent de Lucques*,
pp. 77–78.

individuals, whatever their socio-economic group, sipped the milk-like alcoholic beverage. In one of the first major, modern studies of the "old" kingdom of Kongo, the French anthropologist Georges Balandier stressed that between the sixteenth and eighteenth centuries palm wine was present in every aspect of the daily lives of individuals, be it social gatherings, commercial transactions, feasts, marriages, rituals, or ancestor worship. In his view, "palm wine [was] the blood which animated the body of Kongo society and civilization."[59] Balandier has been taken to task for generally pushing his sources too far into the distant past.[60] But, on this specific point, he can hardly be criticized.[61]

Wherever available, palm wine was nearly always offered by hosts to visitors. When Rui de Sousa headed the first official Portuguese embassy to the kingdom of Kongo in 1491, he was promptly provided along the way to its capital with *malavu* by emissaries of the King.[62] During the early 1560s, the first group of Portuguese missionaries to sojourn in the kingdom of Ndongo was also kept well supplied with palm wine by the *Ngola* and his lords.[63] While travelling throughout the northeastern provinces of Kongo more than one century later, Caltanisetta was presented on at least two occasions with offerings of this alcoholic beverage by local lords.[64] Nor was this practice engaged in solely by the ruling elites. In the mid-1600s, for example, Cavazzi de Montecúccolo found that in certain places even ordinary Kongo routinely offered one *cabuça* or calabash of *malavu* to visiting missionaries.[65] Clearly, both in Kongo and in

---

[59] Georges Balandier, *La vie quotidienne au Royaume de Kongo du XVIe au XVIIIe Siècle*. Paris, 1965, pp. 155–156.

[60] See, especially, Jan Vansina, "Anthropologists and the Third Dimension," *Africa*. Vol. XXXIX, 1969, pp. 62–68.

[61] It is worth noting here that a geographer and another anthropologist have both come to the same conclusion regarding the place of palm wine amongst mid-twentieth century Kongo. See Sautter, *De l'Atlantique au Fleuve Congo*, Vol. 1, p. 524; and Wyatt MacGaffey, *Custom and Government in the Lower Congo*. Berkeley, 1970, pp. 103–109.

[62] "Chegada da Embaixada Portuguesa à Corte do Congo," 29–04–1491, in Brásio, *Monumenta Missionaria Africana*, 1st series, Vol. I, pp. 113 and 117.

[63] Irmão Antonio Mendes to Padre Geral, 09–05–1563, in *ibid.*, 1st series, Vol. II, pp. 500–501.

[64] Bontinck, *Diaire Congolaise de Fra Luca da Caltanisetta*, pp. 119 and 127–129. Marcellino d'Atri, Caltanisetta's contemporary and sometimes companion, received *malavu* from Kongo rulers on no less than four occasions. See Toso, *L'Anarchia Congolese nel sec. XVII*, pp. 72, 93, 149–150, and 188.

[65] Cavazzi de Montecúccolo, *Descrição Histórica dos Três Reinos*, Vol. I, p. 39.

Ndongo, customarily offering palm wine to visitors was a symbol of hospitality that was intended to facilitate new social and political relations.[66]

Malavu also played an important role in rituals.[67] In Kongo, according to Jean-François de Rome, it was used during the mid-seventeenth century to evoke the tears of mourners immediately following burials.[68] Two decades earlier, the Portuguese missionary Pedro Tavares noted palm wine being left at ancestor's shrines further south in the kingdom of Ndongo.[69] An identical practice was described some fifty years later by Dapper in relation to the various obligations which people in the interior of Luanda, where Ndongo was situated, had towards their deceased.[70] Even the notorious Imbangala, Miller informs us: "made extensive and prodigious use of palm wine in their rituals, . . . pouring [it] over the graves of their ancestors and using it in attempts to contact the dead through intoxication, trances, and spirit possession."[71] The "thirst" of the dead had to be appeased in the form of libations to the ancestors.[72]

---

[66] This long-standing custom is still current among the Kongo and, indeed, other African societies with access to palm wine. For the Kongo, see MacGaffey, *Custom and Government in the Lower Congo*, pp. 110–111. See also: Ndolamb Ngokwey, "Varieties of Palm Wine among the Lele of the Kasai," in Mary Douglas, ed., *Constructive Drinking: Perspectives on Drink from Anthropology*. Cambridge, 1987, p. 115, for the Lele; Umunna, "Drinking Culture of a Nigerian Community," pp. 531–533, for the Onitsha; and Parkin, *Palms, Wine, and Witnesses*, p. 42, for the Giriama.

[67] One of these may well have been the opening of the cultivation season and the search for good harvests by Kongo rulers, a ceremony which was attended by the whole population and where palm wine was plentiful. See Cuvelier, *Relations sur le Congo du Père Laurent de Lucques*, pp. 110–112 and 118–119. This ritual, and the place of *malavu* in it, is not however described in the earlier extant documentation.

[68] Rome, *Fondation de la Mission des Capucins*, p. 122. While describing the same ritual in Kongo during the 1650s, Barthélemy de Massiac noted that a great deal of wine was then consumed if the deceased was a noble or a wealthy person. See P. Salmon, "Mémoires de la relation de voyage de M. de Massiac a l'Angola et a Buenos-Aires," *Bulletin des Sceances de l'Académie Royal des Sciences d'Outre-Mer*. Vol. 6, 1960, pp. 586–604. In this latter case, however, it is not possible to specify whether the drink referred to was palm or grape wine.

[69] d'Assumpção, "Exploração á Africa nos Ineditos da Bibliotheca de Evora," p. 356.

[70] Dapper, *Description de l'Afrique*, p. 367. The same custom may have been further practised in the kingdom of Kongo. One of the more recent historians of this kingdom indicates that the Kongo, during the late 1500s, left wine and food at the graves of their relatives on a daily basis. See Anne Hilton, *The Kingdom of Kongo*. Oxford, 1985, p. 12. But it is not clear if this wine was *malavu*.

[71] Miller, *Kings and Kinsmen*, p. 177, ft. 6.

[72] In the kingdom of Ngoyo, according to Carlos M. H. Serrano, *Os Senhores da Terra e os Homens do Mar: Antropologia de um reino africano*. São Paulo, 1983, p. 105,

Yet another instance where palm wine was nearly always present was during matrimonial transactions. During the early 1680s, another Italian missionary, Girolamo Merolla da Sorrento, noted *malavu* being used in Kongo's coastal province of Nsoyo during discussions for marriage contracts.[73] One of his subsequent replacements, Lorenzo da Lucca, while referring to the same area at the beginning of the 1700s, was even more explicit: this alcoholic beverage was essential to successfully conclude any matrimonial transaction.[74] Similarly, Andrea da Pavia, who proselytized throughout Kongo during the last decade and a half of the eighteenth century, found that marriage contracts in this realm could only be concluded with *malavu*.[75] And here Kongo, again, was no exception. As pointed out by Heusch, palm wine frequently featured in the marriage contracts negotiated throughout much of the Central African savanna.[76]

Malavu further was prominent in at least a few other occasions. In spite of the fact that it was not particularly abundant in the coastal province of Nsoyo, Kongo princes in the late 1600s nevertheless secured relatively large volumes of this alcoholic drink to supply the annual banquets organized there in honour of Saint James.[77] And in the kingdom of Ndongo, at least up to the early 1620s, palm wine also appears both as a toll collected by the Ngola from slave dealers travelling through his realm or visiting his slave-mart and a form of compensation paid to individuals for restituting fugitive slaves.[78] Moreover, malavu seems to have been required, at least in Kongo's

---

a variant of *malavu* was also used in similar rituals. Furthermore, the utilization of this alcoholic drink in ancestor worship and funerals has, once again, persisted amongst African societies with access to palm wine. See Adandé, "Vin de Palme chez les Diola," p. 6; Parkin, *Palms, Wine, and Witnesses*, p. 11; Umunna, "Drinking Culture of a Nigerian Community," p. 534; Janzen, *Lemba, 1650–1930*, p. 196; and MacGaffey, *Custom and Government in the Lower Congo*, pp. 157, 159, 168, and 171.

[73] Sorrento, "Voyage to Congo and Several Other Countries," Vol. I, p. 564.

[74] Cuvelier, *Relations sur le Congo du Père Laurent de Lucques*, pp. 136–138.

[75] Louis Jadin, "Andrea da Pavia au Congo, à Lisbonne, à Madère: Journal d'un missionaire capucin, 1685–1702" *Bulletin de l'Institut Historique Belge de Rome.* Vol. XLI, 1970, p. 435.

[76] Heusch, *Le Roi Ivre*, p. 220. The geographical extent of this practice can be further expanded to other parts of Africa where palm wine remains available. See, for example, Serrano, *Os Senhores da Terra*, p. 111; Umunna, "Drinking Culture of a Nigerian Community," pp. 533–534; and Parkin, *Palms, Wine, and Witnesses*, p. 11; and Adandé, "Vin de Palme chez les Diola," p. 6.

[77] Jadin, "Andrea da Pavia au Congo, à Lisbonne," p. 450.

[78] Beatrix Heintze, ed., *Fontes para a História de Angola do Século XVII: Memórias, Relações, e outros Manuscriptos da Colectânea Documental de Fernão de Sousa, 1622–1635.*

province of Nsoyo, during the various stages of commercial transactions.[79]

Palm wine, then, was central to the socio-cultural and economic
fabric of West Central African societies that happened to live where
the raphia palm proliferated. Here, the raphia palm and its sap were
valued as much as the vine and the alcoholized juice it produced
were by Europeans. That is why, whenever military campaigns were
engaged in, one of the worst atrocities which belligerents could com-
mit was cutting down the raphia trees of their opponents. This was
a favoured tactic used by the Kongo against the kingdom of Ndongo
before the mid-1500s, when the latter were attempting to secure
their political independence from the former.[80] It was also adopted
by the Luanda-based Portuguese in their numerous late sixteenth
and early seventeenth century campaigns against the Ngola of Ndongo
and his lords.[81] Yet another group known to have utilized this strat-
egy were the early seventeenth century Imbangala during their incursions against Mbundu polities north of the Kuvo River.[82] In the
wake of these military operations, whole groves of raphia palms were
destroyed and not a few West Central Africans were denied their
malavu.

II. *Beer: Production, Consumption, and Uses*

Compared to the large number of early sources on palm wine, those
documenting the production, consumption, and uses of local beer in
West Central Africa at the time of its early contact with Europe are
relatively scarce. Nevertheless, if *malavu* was restricted to areas where
the raphia palm proliferated, *walo* made from local grains was much
more democratic in terms of its geographic availability. Wherever
raphia trees were lacking, particularly in the drier coastal areas and
plains of the savanna, palm wine was replaced by beer made from

---

Stuttgart, 1985, Vol. I, p. 121. Thereafter, transit tolls and payment for the recapture of slaves came to be received in the form of other merchandise.

[79] Barbot, "Voyage to the Congo River," pp. 504 and 506.
[80] Brásio, *História do Reino do Congo*, p. 40.
[81] See Padre Baltasar Afonso, 19–01–1585, in Sousa Dias, *Relações de Angola*,
p. 149; and Governor Fernão de Sousa to King, 26–06–1631, in Heintze, *Fontes
para a História de Angola*, Vol. I, p. 378.
[82] See Ravenstein, *Adventures of Andrew Battell*, p. 30.

grains such as millet and sorghum.[83] But even in the *malavu* rich areas of the rainforest-savanna, *walo* was present. This was so both in the inland areas of Kongo and in the hinterland of Luanda.[84]

No contemporaneous detailed account of the production of local beer seems to have been left by the numerous European missionaries, traders and government officials who were stationed in Kongo and Angola during the 1500s and the 1600s.[85] But, as in the case of palm wine, the production of *walo* during this period probably approximated that of traditional beer in Katanga in the mid-1900s. The base materials for *walo* were local grains, millets and sorghums, which had to be previously grown and harvested. Once collected, the grains were winnowed and, thereafter, immersed in water. Following this operation, which lasted for a few days, the millet and sorghum grains were then dried under the sun. As soon as this was done, the grains were pounded into flour. Immediately thereafter, the flour was added to water over a fire, with the paste being constantly mixed. When the first bubbles appeared, the blend was removed from the heat. After being infused with roots to liquify the paste, it was then poured into containers. Following a two to four day fermentation period, the *walo* was finally ready for consumption.[86]

The production of beer, even if one excludes the work involved in cultivating and harvesting the base grain crops, clearly involved a great deal of labour. Moreover, the preparation of *walo* fell exclusively upon the shoulders of women.[87] As a result, the production of beer throughout West Central Africa was significantly different from

---

[83] Miller, *Way of Death*, p. 83;

[84] See "Un religieux au Provincial du Portugal," 15–12–1587, in Bal, *Royaume du Congo*, p. 42; Rome, *Fondation de la Mission des Capucins*, pp. 91–93; and Bontinck, *Diaire Congolaise de Fra Luca da Caltanisetta*, pp. 145–146, for the kingdom of Kongo. For the hinterland of Luanda see Padre Garcia Simões to Provincial [de São Paulo de Loanda], 20–10–1575, in Brásio, *Monumenta Missionaria Africana*, 1st series, Vol. III, p. 137; the letter of Father Baltasar Afonso, dated 25–08–1578, in Sousa Dias, *Relações de Angola*, p. 92; and Cadornega, *História Geral das Guerras*, Vol. III, p. 97. According to Vansina, *Tio Kingdom of the Middle Congo*, p. 148, even in the middle Zaire River, were palm wine was abundant, beer was produced from maize (a grain imported from the Americas) by the Tio during the late 1800s.

[85] In the case of the Kongo, there is one short reference from the mid-1600s indicating that people made a beverage with flour cooked in water. See Rome, *Fondation de la Mission des Capucins*, p. 93.

[86] The method here summarized is described in Bernier and Lambrechts, "Étude sur les Boissons Fermentées Indigènes du Katanga," pp. 17–21.

[87] Vansina, *Tio Kingdom of the Middle Congo*, p. 148.

that of *malavu*, which was the sphere of males and required relatively little labour. The only area where *walo* was similar to palm wine was in its durability. It too did not last long and had to be consumed close to where it was produced.

Aside from the labour involved in production and those who performed the work, there was another important difference between *walo* and *malavu*. This was the socio-economic composition of those who consumed beer made from local grains. Of the few extant contemporaneous references to this drink, nearly all point to consumption by individuals who belonged to the commoner classes. For example, while describing the inhabitants of Luanda Island in the late 1570s, Father Baltasar Afonso noted that "this poor people sustain themselves only by eating fish and drinking wine made from grain flour."[88] A decade later, another European missionary indicated that the common beverages of the Kongo were water and sometimes *walo*.[89] During the mid-1600s, the Capuchin Rome found that the *peuplades* or poor folk in this realm who did not have palm wine consumed beer made from grains.[90] The chronicler of the late sixteenth and seventeenth century Angolan wars, António de Oliveira de Cadornega, similarly reported that beer made from local grains was the beverage which the *gentio* or the common people of Kisama ordinarily drank.[91] And last, but not least, in the late 1690s the Italian missionary Luca da Caltanisetta angrily recounted that in Kongo "this poor, misled people worship[ed] more a dirty cooking pot and a fetid calabash of *walo* than things consecrated to the divine cult."[92] Given the palm wine drinking patterns elucidated above, these sources evidence an important class difference in the consumption of alcohol: the ruling classes drinking primarily *malavu* and the lower classes consuming predominantly *walo*. This fundamental distinction is further borne out by the fact that none of the early references on local alcohol mention local beer being consumed by the ruling elites. Consequently, even though its preparation required

---

[88] See the letter of Father Baltasar Afonso, 25–08–1578, in Sousa Dias, *Relações de Angola*, p. 92.
[89] "Un religieux au Provincial du Portugal," 15–12–1587, in Bal, *Royaume du Congo*, p. 42.
[90] Rome, *Fondation de la Mission des Capucins*, p. 93.
[91] Cadornega, *História Geral das Guerras*, Vol. III, p. 97.
[92] Bontinck, *Diaire Congolaise de Fra Luca da Caltanisetta*, pp. 145–146.

significantly more labour, *walo* was comparatively more democratic not only in its geographic distribution, but also in terms of its consumers. As was the case in Europe, particularly during periods of economic hardship,[93] brews from local grains were the drink of the poorer folk throughout West Central Africa.

Precisely because *walo* was the alcoholic beverage of commoners, no documentation has survived on the roles which this drink may have played on occasions other than the washing down of daily meals. The relatively numerous European traders, missionaries, and government officials who wandered throughout West Central Africa during the 1500s and 1600s and wrote about their travels were generally far more concerned with the ruling elites they encountered than their subjects. There are, however, two recent references to other roles played by local beer in West Central Africa during the period that concerns us here. David Birmingham has maintained that during the 1500s a provincial governor who faithfully paid his taxes to the *Mani* Kongo could expect to be rewarded with beer.[94] And Vansina has affirmed that kings, chiefs, and councillors throughout Equatorial Africa and Angola before 1500 acquired followers in part by distributing palm wine and beer.[95] In both cases, the evidence to support these claims is not supplied. Nevertheless, there is no reason to believe that *walo* did not also then play a variety of roles similar to those of traditional beer amongst lower class Africans in the twentieth century, whether these be in social gatherings, commercial transactions, feasts, marriages, rituals, ancestor worship, or other occasions.[96]

---

[93] See Braudel, *Structures of Everyday Life: The Limits of the Possible*, pp. 238–240.

[94] See Birmingham, *Central Africa to 1870*, p. 27.

[95] Vansina, "Equatorial Africa and Angola," p. 558.

[96] The literature on the social values of traditional beer-drinking throughout Africa in the 1900s is too vast to list here. For a representative sample see: Thomas Beidelman, "Beer Drinking and Cattle Theft in Ukaguru: Intertribal Relations in a Tanganyika Chiefdom," *American Anthropologist*. Vol. 63, 1961, pp. 534–549; P. K. Eguchi, "Beer Drinking and Festivals amongst the Hide," *Kyoto University African Studies*. Vol. 9, 1975, pp. 69–90; Ellen Hellman, "The Importance of Beer-Brewing in an Urban Native Yard," *Bantu Studies*. Vol. 8, 1934, pp. 39–60; Ivan Karp, "Beer Drinking and Social Experience in an African Society: An Essay in Formal Sociology," in Ivan Karp and C. S. Bird., eds. *Explorations in African Systems of Thought*. Bloomington, 1980, pp. 83–119; Jensen E. Krige, "The Social Significance of Beer among the Balobedu," *Ibid.*, Vol. 4, 1932, pp. 343–357; Robert McC. Netting, "Beer as a Locus of Value among the West African Kofyar," *American Anthropologist*. Vol. 66, 1964, pp. 375–384; Platt, "Traditional Alcoholic Beverages and their Importance,"

Conclusion

During their early encounter with Europeans, West Central Africans thus possessed two alcoholic beverages that were widely consumed: palm wine and beer made from local grains. Each of these was predominantly consumed by a different socio-economic group of individuals, especially to wash down daily meals. Both *malavu* and *walo* were also consumed during other occasions, social gatherings, commercial transactions, feasts, marriages, rituals, ancestor worship, and possibly even the display of the rulers' power, all of which were central to the societies of the region. This suggests that the amounts of local alcoholic beverages consumed, wherever and whenever they were available, must have been relatively large.

It is unlikely, however, that inebriety was rampant throughout West Central Africa during the 1500s and 1600s. First of all, as we have seen above, *malavu* and *walo* were beverages with relatively low alcoholic contents. Second, as Heusch points out for the early Luba-Lunda, drinking was something done mainly in the company of others since solitary drinking was regarded as extravagant, disorderly, and anti-social behaviour.[97] This explains why many of the early references to heavy drinking in West Central Africa are specifically made to group, not solitary, drinking.[98] Moreover, the consumption of local alcoholic beverages was not engaged in solely for the sake of inebriation. Whatever the circumstances, *malavu* and *walo* were also ingested for the nutritional supplements which they provided to the diets of West Central Africans. *Walo*, as we have seen above, was reported during the late 1570s as constituting a major item of nourishment for the inhabitants of Luanda Island. Similarly, palm

---

pp. 115–124; Walter H. Sangree, "The Social Functions of Beer Drinking in Bantu Tiriki," in D. J. Pittman and C. S. Snyder, eds. *Society, Culture, and Drinking Patterns.* New York, 1962, pp. 6–21; and Mahir Saul, "Beer, Sorghum and Women: Production for the Market in Rural Upper Volta," *Africa* (London). Vol. 51, 1981, pp. 746–764.

[97] Heusch, *Le Roi Ivre*, p. 219.

[98] See, in particular, Irmão Antonio Mendes to Padre Leão Henriques, 29–10–1562, in Sousa Dias, *Relações de Angola*, p. 34; idem to Padre Geral, 09–05–1563, in Brásio, *Monumenta Missionaria Africana*, 1st series, Vol. III, pp. 500–501; Rome, *Fondation de la Mission des Capucins*, p. 122; Cavazzi de Montecúccolo, *Descrição Histórica dos Três Reinos*, Vol. I, p. 188 and Vol. II, p. 147; Salmon, "Relation de voyage de M. de Massiac a l'Angola," p. 597; Jadin, "Andrea da Pavia au Congo, à Lisbonne," p. 450; Bontinck, *Diaire Congolaise de Fra Luca da Caltanisetta*, pp. 127–129; and Cuvelier, *Relations sur le Congo du Père Laurent de Lucques*, pp. 81, 110–112, and 118–119.

wine was found by a Jesuit priest from the late 1540s to be one of the edible items with which the Kongo sustained themselves.[99] *Malavu* was also considered "very nutritious" by the 1580s informants of Pigafetta.[100] And, in the early 1620s, another observer further detected that palm wine and palm oil were the major foodstuffs of people in the interior of Luanda.[101] In short, just like alcoholic beverages in Europe and in coastal British North America roughly at the same time,[102] *malavu* and *walo* were consumed in sixteenth and seventeenth century West Central Africa as much for their nutritional values as for their powers to inebriate.

---

[99] See the letter of Jácome Dias, 01–08–1548, in Bal, *Royaume du Congo*, p. 41.
[100] Pigafetta and Lopes, *Description du Royaume de Congo*, p. 77.
[101] See the 1622 report of Bento Banha Cardoso, in Cordeiro, *Viagens, Explorações e Conquistas dos Portugueses: Collecção de Documentos—Producções, Commercio e Governo do Congo e de Angola*, p. 19.
[102] On this point see, especially: Braudel, *Structures of Everyday Life: The Limits of the Possible*, p. 237; and McCusker, *Rum and the American Revolution*, Vol. 1, pp. 478–479.

CHAPTER TWO

THE INTRODUCTION OF BACCHUS INTO WEST CENTRAL AFRICA

The surprise of Zurara with respect to the lack of *vinho* along the coast of West Africa is quite understandable. By the fifteenth century, the material life of any Portuguese individual was unthinkable without the pleasures enjoyed from drinking this alcoholic beverage.[1] Grape wine, along with olive oil and bread, formed a trilogy of basic consumption items that radically differentiated the material world of the Lusophone population, as well as of other Mediterranean Europeans, from that of peoples who inhabited other continents.[2] However, as the Portuguese pushed their caravels deep into the southern Atlantic and Indian oceans in search of new lands and, especially, commercial partners, this differentiation slowly but surely withered away. With the establishment of trade entrepôts along the coasts of Africa, India, and Latin America, *vinho* was introduced everywhere the Portuguese set up shop.

I. *The Arrival of Bacchus*

Precisely how grape wine was first introduced by the Portuguese in West Central Africa and in the kingdoms located in the hinterlands of Mpinda, Luanda, and Benguela is a difficult process to analyze due to the limited number of contemporaneous documents that refer to this alcoholic drink. The extant manuscripts that inform us about Portuguese overseas expansion in the fifteenth and sixteenth centuries, for example, rarely describe the type of European goods carried aboard the caravels, let alone their quantities. Similarly, the first

---

[1] On the importance of this alcoholic drink during the medieval period see A. H. de Oliveira Marques, *Daily Life in Portugal in the Late Middle Ages*. Madison, 1961, pp. 16 and 25–29.

[2] See Vitorino de Magalhães Godinho, *Os Descobrimentos e a Economia Mundial*. Lisbon, 1982, Vol. III, p. 217 and Vol. IV, pp. 7–9.

Portuguese accounts relating to Mpinda, Luanda, and Benguela and their respective interiors seldom mention *vinho* at all. As a result, the historical reconstruction of the introduction of this European alcoholic drink in West Central Africa must necessarily remain tentative.

In spite of this limitation, it is an established fact that the Portuguese caravels involved in the explorations of this period transported significant volumes of *vinho*. The fleet with which Vasco da Gama set out to find the sea route to India in 1497, for example, carried large quantities of it. According to the chronicler Duarte Pacheco Pereira, the volume of *vinho* transported in the bowels of Gama's ships was "in excess of what was needed for such a voyage."[3] Significant amounts of grape wine were similarly present in the naval expedition led by Pedro Alvares Cabral to India in 1500 via the land of Vera Cruz, as Brazil was initially known. It has been estimated that some 763,112 litres of this alcoholic drink were carried for the 1,200 men engaged in this venture.[4] Furthermore, the fleet which sailed for Kongo in 1512 under the command of Manuel A. Simão da Silva must also have transported a large amount of *vinho* since, prior to departure, he was ordered by the King to provide enough of this beverage to last the duration of the voyage.[5]

Why was so much grape wine transported by the Portuguese caravels during their missions of discovery? One of the more important reasons was of a technical nature. This bulky and heavy alcoholic beverage furnished excellent ballast for these vessels.[6] Moreover, unlike hewn stones, ingots of iron and other heavy metals, *vinho* could also serve as a consumable that kept well for relatively long periods of time. Given the length of the voyages of discovery, which lasted for months on end, this was not a negligible factor. Indeed, along with biscuits, dried meats, and fresh water, grape wine constituted one of the key provisions with which the caravels sailed from Lisbon.[7] Last,

---

[3] Duarte Pacheco Pereira, *Esmeraldo de Situ Orbis*. London, 1937, p. 166.

[4] William Brooks Greenlee, *The Voyage of Pedro Alvares Cabral to Brazil and India from Contemporary Documents and Narratives*. London, 1938, p. 194.

[5] See the "Regimento de D. Manuel A. Simão da Silva (1512)" in Brásio, *Monumenta Missionaria Africana*, 1st series, Vol. I, p. 228.

[6] Charles R. Boxer, *The Portuguese Seaborne Empire, 1415–1825*. London, 1969, p. 215.

[7] Magalhães Godinho, *Os Descobrimentos*, Vol. IV, p. 10; Frédéric Mauro, *Le Portugal, le Brésil et l'Atlantique au XVII*e *Siècle, 1570–1670*. Paris, 1983, pp. 84–89; and Boxer, *Portuguese Seaborne Empire*, p. 215.

but not least, this alcoholic drink provided Portuguese sailors with a stimulant to temporarily overcome their fear of sailing through unknown waters and with a distraction to break the monotony of everyday life on the high seas.

The alcohol consumption rate aboard the early caravels was consequently relatively high. Quantitative data from a Portuguese ship engaged in the Indian Ocean trade during the first years of the sixteenth century place the daily *vinho* consumption rate aboard at 3 *quartilhos* or about 1.2 litres per person.[8] This may well have represented a maximum, since high levels of grape wine consumption could not be sustained aboard every Portuguese vessel.[9] Nevertheless, some one hundred years later, equally significant amounts of this alcoholic beverage continued to be imbibed. For a three month voyage in the Atlantic, a fleet transporting 980 men required 220 *pipas* (wooden casks with a capacity of about 500 litres) or almost 110,000 litres of this alcoholic beverage to satisfy its crew and passengers, which works out to an average daily intake of 1.25 litres per individual.[10] Considering the various roles played by grape wine aboard the early Portuguese caravels, such consumption rates should not be surprising.

But there were additional factors that contributed to the inclusion of large quantities of *vinho* aboard the early caravels. By the 1400s, this alcoholic beverage was already of crucial importance to the economy of Portugal.[11] During the later Middle Ages, production had

---

[8] Greenlee, *Voyage of Pedro Cabral*, p. 194.

[9] Indeed, consumption patterns varied greatly from one ship to another. Thus data found in José R. do Amaral Lapa, *A Bahia e a Carreira da India*. São Paulo, 1968, p. 165, place the wine consumption rate aboard another early sixteenth century Portuguese vessel engaged in the Indian Ocean commerce at slightly over half a litre per day, per person. Similarly, data provided for an outbound Portuguese Indiamen c. 1600 by Charles R. Boxer, ed., *The Tragic History of the Sea: 1589–1622: Narratives of the Shipwrecks of the Portuguese East Indiamen* São Thome *(1589)*, Santo Alberto *(1593)*, São João Baptista *(1622)*, *and the Journeys of the Survivors in South East Africa*. Cambridge, 1959, p. 276, work out to an average wine consumption rate of .75 litres per day, per person.

[10] Frédéric Mauro, *L'Expansion Européenne (1600–1870)*. Paris, 1967, p. 116. Once again, however, other figures indicate lower daily wine consumption rates per person. From data provided by Charles R. Boxer, *From Lisbon to Goa, 1500–1750: Studies in Portuguese Maritime Enterprise*. London, 1984, I, p. 72, on a Portuguese Indiaman outfitted in 1636, the average intake translates to .8 litres. On the volume of the *pipa*, see the concluding chapter below.

[11] In spite of the importance of wine to the economy and culture of Portugal over the centuries, its history remains a neglected field of study. A few exceptions

surpassed the volume required by the small Portuguese population.[12] As a result, surplus grape wine emerged as a valuable export item in Portugal's growing overseas commerce with northern Europe, where the vine could not grow, primarily to acquire grain and manufactured goods not produced within its own borders. In the process, this intoxicant became one of the few items produced nationally on a very large scale which the Portuguese could offer to sustain their expanding maritime trade of the later medieval era.[13] Given the fact that trade with new commercial partners was a major objective of the fifteenth century voyages of discovery, some of the *vinho* aboard the Portuguese vessels was also destined for the potentates of newly discovered lands, most likely in the hope developing new markets.[14] If the whole cargo of grape wine was imbibed while these vessels were at sea, its value as ballast would have been squandered.

In the case of the kingdoms near the West Central African coast, it is not evident that gifts in the form of *vinho* were in fact presented to their rulers. Extant documentary sources do not always list the types of presents offered to these African potentates by the first Portuguese expeditions sent to establish diplomatic and commercial

---

are Herlander Alves Machado, *O Vinho na Economia Portuguesa: Alguns Aspectos*. Lisbon, 1987; the essays in Joaquim V. Serrão, ed. *O Vinho na História Portuguesa, Séculos XIII–XIX*. Porto, 1983; Alberto Vieira, ed. *História do Vinho da Madeira. Textos e Documentos*. Funchal, 1993; Susan Schneider, *O Marquês de Pombal e o Vinho do Porto: Dependência e Subdesenvolvimento em Portugal no Século XVIII*. Lisbon, 1980; Maria de Lurdes de Freitas Ferraz, "O vinho da Madeira no século XVIII: produção e mercados internacionais," in *Actas do I Colóquio Internacional de História da Madeira 1986* Funchal, 1990. Vol. 2, pp. 935–965; Norman R. Bennett, "The Golden Age of the Port Wine System, 1781–1807," *International History Review*, Vol. 12, 1990, pp. 221–248; idem, "The Vignerons of the Douro and the Peninsular War," *Journal of European Economic History*, Vol. 21, 1992, pp. 7–29; idem, "The Wine Growers of the Upper Douro, 1780–1800," *Portuguese Studies Review*, Vol. 2, 1992–1993, pp. 28–45; idem, "The Port Wine System in the 1890s," *International History Review*, Vol. 16, 1994, pp. 251–266; and idem, "Port Wine Merchants: Sandeman in Porto, 1813–1831," *Journal of European Economic History*, Vol. 24, 1995, pp. 239–269.

[12] By the 1500s, roughly 120,000 to 150,000 *pipas* of *vinho* were being produced per annum. See Mauro, *Le Portugal, le Brésil et l'Atlantique*, p. 407; and A. H. de Oliveira Marques, *História de Portugal*. Lisbon, 1978, Vol. I, p. 241.

[13] On Portugal's rising trade with northern Europe, and the place of wine in this commerce, see A. H. de Oliveira Marques, *Ensaios de História Medieval*. Lisbon, 1965.

[14] Diogo Gomes, "A Relação dos Descobrimentos da Guiné e das Ilhas, in Vitorino de Magalhães Godinho, *Documentos Sôbre a Expansão Portuguesa*. Lisbon, 1943, Vol. 3, p. 86 for the Senegambia in the mid-fifteenth century; and "Carta de Pedro Vaz da Caminha a el-Rei, 1–05–1500," in João M. da Silva Marques, ed. *Descobrimentos Portugueses: Documentos para a Sua História*. Lisbon, 1971, Vol. 3, pp. 597 and 604 for Brazil immediately upon its "discovery" by Cabral.

relations. This is the case of the missions led by Diogo Cão in 1482, 1484, and 1487, and by João Soares in 1493 to the *Mani* or King of Kongo,[15] as well as those under the command of Manuel Pacheco and Balthasar de Castro in 1520 and Paulo Dias de Novais in 1575 to the *Ngola* or King of Ndongo, inland from what later became Luanda.[16] Similarly, none of the accounts of the first expeditions sent to the Ovimbundu kingdoms in the interior of Benguela refer to *vinho* amongst the gifts presented on these occasions.[17] Furthermore, even when contemporaneous documents differentiate the presents offered by the first Portuguese diplomatic and commercial missions to the potentates of West Central African kingdoms, this alcoholic beverage is not listed. Nowhere is *vinho* found amongst the gifts presented by Rui de Sousa in 1491 or by Simão da Silva in 1512 to the *Mani*-Kongo and by Novais to the King of Ndongo in 1560.[18]

The lack of documentation, however, should not lead us to conclude hastily that presents in the form of grape wine were not given to the rulers of these West Central African kingdoms. Part of the

---

[15] See the chronicles by Rui de Pina, Garcia de Resende, and João de Barros on the "discovery" of Kongo in Brásio, *Monumenta Missionaria Africana*, 1st series, Vol. I, pp. 32–43; and the *Regimento* (royal instructions that defined the responsibilities of an office or the competence of an institution within the Portuguese imperial administration) of Manuel Pacheco and Balthasar de Castro in José Ramos-Coelho, ed. *Alguns Documentos do Archivo Nacional da Torre do Tombo acerca das Navegações e Conquistas Portuguesas*. Lisbon, 1892, pp. 436–441. Later documentation, while more comprehensive in many respects, presents exactly the same problem. A case in point is Pigafetta's account of the kingdom of Kongo which is primarily based on information collected from Duarte Lopes. In 1578, Lopes left Lisbon for Kongo in a vessel which stopped at Madeira to take on provisions of wine. But nowhere is it mentioned in Pigafetta's report that any of this alcoholic beverage was later offered to Kongo political authorities. See Pigafetta and Lopes, *Description du Royaume de Congo*.

[16] *Regimento* of Manuel Pacheco and Balthasar de Castro in José Ramos-Coelho, ed. *Alguns Documentos do Archivo Nacional da Torre do Tombo acerca das Navegações e Conquistas Portuguesas*. Lisbon, 1892, pp. 436–441; and the account of Novais' administration of Angola by Garcia Mendes Castelo Branco in Sousa Dias, *Relações de Angola*, pp. 239–245.

[17] Ralph Delgado, *Ao Sul do Cuanza: Ocupação e Aproveitamento do Antigo Reino de Benguela, 1483–1942*. Lisbon, 1944, Vol. I; and the account of the expedition to Benguela and its hinterland led by Governor Furtado de Mendonça in the last years of the sixteenth century in Ravenstein, *Strange Adventures of Andrew Battel*, p. 16.

[18] See the descriptions of these expeditions by Rui de Pina and Garcia de Resende, as well as the *Regimento* of Simão da Silva, in Brásio, *Monumenta Missionaria Africana*, 1st series, Vol. I, pp. 61–62, 72, and 247–253, respectively; and the instructions given by King Sebastião to Novais upon his mission to Ndongo in 1559 in Sousa Dias, *Relações de Angola*, pp. 25–30.

vinho aboard the early Portuguese caravels was usually destined for the potentates of newly "discovered" lands. Ultimately, grape wine presents were to become an important component of the diplomatic and commercial relations established by the Portuguese with the potentates of Kongo, Ndongo, and the Ovimbundu kingdoms. It is quite possible, therefore, that this practice was instituted early on in Lusophone contact with these realms. Yet, if this is what actually took place, the quantity of *vinho* thus introduced must have been rather small, since the number of Portuguese diplomatic and commercial expeditions sent to these West Central African realms were few and far between.

Far greater amounts of grape wine must have been intended to quench the insatiable thirst of Portuguese individuals who arrived in Kongo after the early 1490s, in Ndongo following the mid-sixteenth century, and in Benguela after the late 1610s. How could it have been otherwise, when these individuals were accustomed to consume large quantities of this alcoholic beverage in their home-land and while at sea? To be sure, none of the early available sources confirm this to have been the case. After all, the sight of Portuguese drinking *vinho* was too much of a commonplace occurrence to have caught the attention of the chroniclers who first reported on West Central Africa, since they were much more concerned with the exotic. Nevertheless, the general pattern seems clear. Once the Portuguese established themselves in West Africa during the second half of the fifteenth century, they had to be regularly supplied with *vinho* from mainland Portugal, Madeira, the Azores, and the Canary islands.[19] The same occurred in India, which became a significant importer of wine from Lisbon to supply the relatively large Portuguese communities that set up shop along the coast of this sub-continent following the late 1490s.[20] Brazil, too, was no exception, as the even greater number of Portuguese individuals who emigrated there after the mid-sixteenth century soon turned this colony into the major

---

[19] John W. Blake, ed., *European Beginnings in West Africa*. London, 1942, pp. 102 and 105; Magalhães Godinho, *Os Descobrimentos*, Vol. IV, pp. 46–48; John Vogt, *Portuguese Rule on the Gold Coast 1469–1682*. Athens, 1979, pp. 67–73; Ivana Elbl, "The Portuguese Trade with West Africa, 1440–1521," unpublished Ph.D. dissertation, University of Toronto, 1986, p. 414; and Alberto Vieira, *Os Escravos no Arquipélago da Madeira: Séculos XV a XVII*. Funchal, 1991, pp. 24–31.

[20] Magalhães Godinho, *Os Descobrimentos*, Vol. III, p. 71.

importer of *vinho* from the metropole.[21] Old habits, whether at sea or on foreign soil, clearly died hard.

Compared with the tens of thousands of Portuguese who established themselves in India and Brazil during the 1500s, however, those who set up shop at Mpinda, Luanda, and Benguela were just a handful.[22] When Portugal's influence in Kongo was at its height during 1491–1575, the number of Portuguese residents there does not seem to have surpassed one or two hundred at any given time.[23] Relatively few Portuguese also settled in Ndongo during the mid-sixteenth century and in Luanda after 1575.[24] Even fewer installed themselves in Benguela and in the Ovimbundu kingdoms following the late 1610s.[25] Consequently, the early *vinho* trade of Portugal with West Central Africa could not have been as substantial, or as profitable, as that with India or Brazil.

This was fully appreciated by Mamede de Góis, a government official stationed in São Jorge da Mina, another Portuguese foothold along the western coast of Africa with a very small European population. Writing to King Manuel in 1510, Gois explained that little gain ensued from the sale of metropolitan *vinho* to Portuguese residents. A much higher return was obtained, on the other hand, by exchanging this imported alcoholic beverage to the substantially larger African population for local commodities.[26] If Portugal's *vinho* trade

---

[21] Mauro, *Le Portugal, le Brésil et l'Atlantique*, pp. 415–418. Salvador was importing an annual average of over 1,250,000 litres of this alcoholic drink by the mid-1650s, while Rio de Janeiro imported an average of 1,603,000 litres per annum during the 1780s. See, respectively, Thales de Azevedo, *Povoamento da Cidade do Salvador*. São Paulo, 1955, p. 404 and Corcino M. dos Santos, *Relações do Rio de Janeiro com Lisboa (1763–1808)*. Rio de Janeiro, 1980, p. 191.

[22] On the comparatively small demographic presence of the Portuguese in Angola see A. J. R. Russell-Wood, *A World on the Move: The Portuguese in Africa, Asia, and America, 1415–1808*. Manchester, 1992, pp. 60–62 and 109–110.

[23] Birmingham, *Central Africa to 1870*, p. 55; and John K. Thornton, "Early Kongo-Portuguese Relations: A New Interpretation," *History in Africa*. Vol. 8, 1981, pp. 196–197.

[24] See Chapter Three below. A more detailed analysis of the early population history of Luanda is found in José C. Curto and Raymond R. Gervais, "The Population History of Luanda During the Late Atlantic Slave Trade, 1781–1844," *African Economic History*. Vol. 29, 2001, pp. 1–59. See also José C. Curto, "The Anatomy of a Demographic Explosion: Luanda, 1844–1850," *International Journal of African Historical Studies*. Vol. 32, 1999, pp. 381–405.

[25] Delgado, *Ao Sul do Cuanza*, Vol. I.

[26] A. A. de C. Almada, "Tratado Breve dos Rios da Guiné do Cabo Verde, 1594," in Brásio, *Monumenta Missionaria Africana*, 1st series, Vol. 3, 1964, p. 276; Blake, *European Beginnings*, p. 105; Vogt, *Portuguese Rule*, pp. 34 and 71; Elbl, "Portuguese

with West Central Africa were to develop into a profitable enterprise, the indigenous populations of this region also had to be turned into consumers of this foreign alcoholic drink. This is exactly what took place, as grape wine (and, later, other non-African alcoholic beverages) introduced by the Portuguese quickly became a crucial item of exchange in the emerging slave trade from this region.

II. *The Acceptance of Bacchus and Other Spirits*

If the Portuguese had reason to introduce *vinho* in West Central Africa, why should consumers there necessarily have accepted this new alcoholic drink? It is possible that the region was then experiencing a decrease in the production of alcoholic beverages. As we have seen in Chapter One, the two centuries following 1480 witnessed the periodic destruction of wine palm groves through military and other means. The introduction of *vinho* may thus have occurred precisely at a time when the production of *malavu* was falling. If this were the case, however, it is difficult to see how a decrease in *malavu* production could have played a decisive, as opposed to a contributing, role in this process. Although some palm wine groves were periodically destroyed, this could have hardly forced *malavu* production to completely dry up. The decisive factor that led to the acceptance of *vinho*, not to mention other subsequently introduced foreign alcoholic drinks, lies elsewhere.

In a most controversial, but nevertheless extremely sophisticated, book written on western Africa and the Atlantic world, John K. Thornton, a preeminent student of the "old" kingdom of Kongo, has recently argued that "one of the most interesting facts of the early Atlantic trade was that Europe offered nothing to Africa that Africa did not already produce—a fact often overlooked in the analyses of trade."[27] With respect to alcoholic beverages, which he views as nonutilitarian items, this was certainly true. At the time of contact with Europeans, as we have seen in Chapter One, West Central Africans possessed at least two alcoholic beverages, palm wine and

Trade," p. 414; and J. Bato'ora Ballong-wen-Mewuda, *São Jorge da Mina, 1482–1637: La vie d'un comptoir portugais en Afrique occidentale*. Lisbon, 1993, Vol. I, pp. 315–317.

[27] John K. Thornton, *Africa and Africans in the Making of the Atlantic World, 1400–1800*. Cambridge, 1998, 2nd edition, p. 44.

beer made from local grains, that were widely consumed. Consequently, Thornton concludes:

> It was . . . not to meet African needs that the trade developed . . . Rather, Africa's trade with Europe was largely moved by prestige, fancy, changing taste, and a desire for variety . . .[28]

But was the integration of *vinho* and, later, other foreign alcoholic beverages into West Central African consumption patterns really just a question of prestige, fancy, and changing tastes and desires? Aside from these issues, was there nothing else different between locally produced alcoholic beverages and those imported from Europe and, later, elsewhere?

In his *magnum opus* on the Angolan slave trade, Miller had earlier arrived at a conclusion that is not too far removed from that of Thornton. Imported alcohol, in his view:

> allowed prodigiously increased consumption of the psychoactive substances that intensified communication with the spiritual component of power in Africa. Intoxicants also carried strong connotations of status in the political economy of goods and people, confirming the mundane prestige of those able to distribute them liberally among dependents and guests.[29]

But Miller did not fail also to add that the newly imported beverages contained a much higher alcoholic content than the locally fermented alternatives and that their sharp taste was taken by African drinkers as a symbol of strength and quality. This last point, although weakened by a lack of evidence to support it,[30] is crucial for an understanding of why foreign alcoholic beverages attracted West Central Africans.

It was argued in Chapter One that the alcohol content detected by mid-twentieth century researchers in the palm wine and beer made traditionally in Katanga was most probably comparable to that of the same beverages made throughout West Central Africa during its early contact with Europeans: in the case of traditional beer made from cereals it was roughly two percent and in that of palm wine about five percent. Data on the alcohol levels of sixteenth century Portuguese wine are similarly wanting. But the alcohol content of

---

[28] *Ibid.*, p. 45.
[29] Miller, *Way of Death*, p. 83.
[30] *Ibid.*

Portuguese wine available in Angola during the early 1960s also provide a point of reference: regular metropolitan red wine ranged from nearly nine to just over eleven percent, while fortified Madeira wine reached seventeen percent.[31] As it happens, regular *vinho* seems to have been the least and Madeira the most alcoholized of the various types of wine introduced by the Portuguese in West Central Africa during the late fifteenth and sixteenth centuries.[32] Compared to *malavu* and *walo*, the alcohol content of regular *vinho* would thus have been two and four times greater, respectively, while that of Madeira wine jumped to three and almost nine times higher.[33]

In short, the wine introduced by the Portuguese was more potent than any of the major alcoholic beverages then available in West Central Africa. Whether, as Miller suggests, this new psychoactive substance also "intensified communication with the spiritual component of power" and "carried strong connotations of status in the political economy of goods and people" is, given the paucity of evidence he presents on this point, open to debate. What is clearer is that *vinho* probably provided African drinkers throughout the region with a much greater buzz than the *malavu* and *walo* their own societies produced. This was the fundamental difference, whatever the circumstances, traditional or new, under which consumption took place, that led West Central Africans to accept *vinho* and, later, even more potent foreign alcoholic drinks.

---

[31] See Antero J. Pena, "O Alcool na Ração Alimentar," *Boletim do Instituto de Angola*. No. 21, 1965, pp. 92–94.

[32] See Curto, *Alcoól e Escravos*, Chapter 3 "O Comércio Do Álcool Luso-brasileiro no Reino do Kongo Durante o Tráfico Atlântico de Escravos, c. 1480–1830."

[33] Around 1650, two other, far more potent, foreign alcoholic beverages came into use in West Central Africa: *aguardente*, a Portuguese brandy distilled from the must of grapes; and, especially, *gerebita*, a cheap Brazilian brandy distilled from sugar cane. According to Cascudo, *Prelúdio da Cachaça*, p. 12, *aguardente* possessed an alcohol content of around twenty-five degrees Cartier, or about sixty-seven percent. For the percentage equivalency of degrees Cartier see Yves Renouil, *Dictionnaire du Vin*. Bordeaux, 1962, p. 495. The alcohol content of *gerebita*, on the other hand, was roughly forty-five to sixty percent. See Cascudo, *Prelúdio da Cachaça*, p. 12, with original values expressed in degrees Cartier. The alcoholic content of both distillates was nine to thirteen times that of *malavu* and twenty-two to thirty-three times that of *walo*.

Conclusion

During the 1400s, Portugal was already a large producer of wine. Production not only sufficed to meet the needs of its population but also to sustain its overseas commerce with northern Europe. As the Portuguese set out to reconnoitre the western coast of Africa, relatively large amounts of this alcoholic beverage were found aboard their caravels of "discovery." Much of this *vinho* was destined for consumption by the crews of these ships. But when the Portuguese realized that it was not part of the alcoholic beverages consumed in these "newly discovered" lands, they began to systematically introduce their most prized intoxicant, which also happened to be one of their few exportable items produced nationally on a large-scale, to the populations which they encountered. This appears to have been done first by including *vinho* amongst the presents which they made to the potentates of the coastal areas where they landed. For these African rulers, the foreign alcohol constituted an intoxicant that was probably more potent than any of the locally available alcoholic drinks. Thereafter, as the remainder of this work shows, the Portuguese started to expand their newly created consumer market by turning the far more numerous subjects of these potentates into avid drinkers of *vinho*, soon to be followed by more alcoholized imported beverages, through the Atlantic slave trade.

CHAPTER THREE

THE REIGN OF BACCHUS: PORTUGUESE ALCOHOL AT
LUANDA AND ITS HINTERLAND DURING THE EARLY
SLAVE TRADE, c. 1550–1649

During the mid-1500s, the growing southern Atlantic pressure for
enslaved labour led Portuguese merchants previously operating in
Kongo to expand their search for more abundant sources of slaves
south to Ndongo. These slave traders established themselves around
the court of the *Ngola* or King of Ndongo, then about 150 or so
kilometres inland from Luanda Bay.[1] Here they operated on their
own account or as agents of slave dealers in the island São Tomé,
who provided them with assortments of European and Asian goods
appropriate for this commerce. Obtained directly through commercial
transactions from Ndongo political officials, the early export slaves
were initially drawn from a semi-independent group of individuals
made up of criminals, indebted persons, foreigners captured in war,
and people without the protection of kin,[2] By the late 1570s, such
initiatory transactions had developed to such an extent that some
10,000 appear to have been shipped yearly from Luanda Bay to São
Tomé, while the trade goods stockpiled around the *Ngola*'s court represented the cargoes of ten to twelve ships valued, in Portuguese
currency, at 8,000$000 *réis*.[3] Whether these early dealings were carried
out along the same lines as those struck throughout the kingdom of
Kongo, where generous portions of *vinho* were commonplace from

---

[1] The *Ngola*'s court, and consequently the capital of the kingdom, traditionally
referred to as Kabasa, was not fixed in any one specific territorial point. See Ilídio
do Amaral, *O Reino do Congo. Os Mbundu (ou Ambundos), o Reino dos 'Ngola' (ou de
Angola) e a Presença Portuguesa, de Finais do Século XV a Meados do Século XVI.* Lisbon,
1996, pp. 173–212; and, especially, Virgílio Coelho, "Em Busca de Kábàsà: Uma
Tentativa de Explicação da Estrutura Político-Administrativa do "Reino de Ndongo",
in *Actas do Seminário Encontro de Povos e Culturas em Angola: Luanda, 3 a 6 de Abril de
1995.* Lisbon, 1997, pp. 443–77.
[2] Miller, "Slave Trade in Congo and Angola," p. 85.
[3] David Birmingham, *Trade and Conflict in Angola: The Mbundu and Their Neighbours
Under the Influence of the Portuguese, 1483–1790.* Oxford, 1966, pp. 50–51.

the late fifteenth century onwards,[4] can not be determined from the evidence at hand. Nevertheless, the role played by grape wine in Kongo was soon replicated in Ndongo and elsewhere throughout the interior of Luanda Bay.

I. *Vinho and the Rise of Luanda's Slave Trade*

The success of the Portuguese slave traders operating in Kabasa led Paulo de Novais in 1571 to ask for and to obtain from the King of Portugal a donation charter to found and govern a colony at Luanda Bay. One of the provisos included in this charter stipulated that no one in the metropole could forward *vinho* to the new colony except to Novais himself, lest a penalty of 4$000 *réis* per 500 litre wooden cask was paid to the Crown, which committed itself to send the export duties collected on this alcoholic drink to the future Governor or his heirs and successors.[5] Steep by contemporary standards,[6] this export tax effectively limited the number of individuals in Luanda to whom *vinho* could be dispatched. This provided Novais with a virtual monopoly over the importation and wholesale distribution of this European alcoholic drink in the future colonial capital of Angola.

What influenced Novais to seek and obtain from the Portuguese Crown the inclusion of this proviso is a matter of conjecture. Perhaps he merely wished to control a consumer item that had already developed into a relatively important trade good for the acquisition of slaves in Ndongo. The fact that the São Tomé slave dealers who supplied Portuguese merchants in Kongo with *vinho*, as well as other European and Asian trade goods, were the same individuals who

---

[4] See Curto, *Álcool e Escravos*, Chapter 3 "O Comércio Do Álcool Luso-brasileiro no Reino do Kongo Durante o Tráfico Atlântico de Escravos, c. 1480–1830."

[5] "Minuta inédita da confirmação da doação da Capitania de Angola tal como Paulo Dias a desejava," *Arquivos de Angola*, 2nd series, Vol. I, No. I, 1943, p. 29. This proviso was reconfirmed in 1589 by King Philip I. See "Doação de D. Filipe I a Paulo Dias de Novais (1589)," in *Ibid.*, 2nd series, Vol. XVII, Nos. 67–70, 1960, p. 167.

[6] In the latter 1500s, for example, a *pipa* of Madeira wine was valued at an average price of 3$000 *réis*. This was 25% less than the penalty imposed upon wine exports from the metropole to anyone in Luanda aside from Governor Novais. Moreover, in the case of Madeira wine, the export duty then in effect was only 1% per *pipa*. See Frédéric Mauro, "Économie et Budget à Madère (1591–1641)," *Annales économiques, sociales et culturelles*. Vol. VII, 1952, pp. 504–505.

expedited consumer and luxury items to those established around the *Ngola*'s court strongly suggests such a possibility. But what is more certain is that Novais must have been fully aware that both on the Gold Coast and in Kongo *vinho* had become a major item of trade to obtain slaves. Named Governor for life of an area where the volume of the slave trade had steadily increased since the mid-1500s, his intention could not have been but to monopolize a consumer item that, under analogous circumstances, was destined to turn into one of the principal European trade goods with which slaves were acquired throughout the hinterland of Luanda.

Novais arrived early in 1575 off the Bay of Luanda to implement his donation charter. Yet, the projected rise in volume of *vinho* as an important item of exchange in the slave trade conducted throughout Ndongo did not materialize as expected. Diplomatic overtures failed to obtain from the political authorities of this kingdom the right to tax the local African population, control over the salt and precious metal production believed to take place throughout the area, recognition of Luanda as the only commercial entrepôt through which slaves from the interior could be legally shipped upon payment of a colonial export duty, and relocation of the Portuguese merchants around the *Ngola*'s court in the colonial capital of Angola. Burdened by the need to recoup the large outlay incurred with the colonization scheme, Novais began in 1579 a series of military ventures to acquire through force what he could not accomplish by peaceful means.[7] The unanticipated strong military resistance offered by Ndongo and the Portuguese merchants established there effectively blocked his attempt to gain command over these potentially significant sources of colonial revenue. In spite of repeated defeats on the battlefield, his efforts were not totally in vain. The relatively large number of Africans made prisoner during these conflicts provided Novais with a valuable export commodity which found a readily available outlet in the ever expanding southern Atlantic, especially Brazilian, demand for slaves.[8]

Yet, the military ventures undertaken against Ndongo considerably reduced the number of slaves exported both illegally by Portuguese

---

[7] For a discussion of Novais' administration see Birmingham, *Trade and Conflict*, pp. 46–55.

[8] Miller, "Slave Trade in Congo and Angola," pp. 86–87; and Birmingham, *Trade and Conflict*, pp. 46–51.

merchants based around the *Ngola*'s court and legally by Novais. While 10,000 slaves were exported from Luanda in the 1570s, the following decade saw the number decrease to 6,000.[9] Under these circumstances, it is doubtful that many were acquired other than through warfare. Of the slaves obtained through commercial transactions, few could have been acquired in exchange for *vinho*. The larger amounts of this European alcoholic drink arriving under Novais's name were consumed by the Portuguese settlers, soldiers, and missionaries in and around this emerging West Central African port.[10] The steep export duty imposed as part of his charter, on the other hand, surely limited the volume of *vinho* imported by other Portuguese individuals for trade with Africans.[11] Consequently, the near monopoly granted to Novais could not have yielded the anticipated returns. Although some 2,340 Portuguese individuals arrived in the colonial capital of Angola between 1575 and 1592, sickness and warfare significantly reduced their number to about 300 by 1594.[12] This small European population base was hardly sufficient to turn Novais' monopoly of the *vinho* trade into a large and profitable venture.

After the early 1590s, the incipient metropolitan wine trade at Luanda underwent a radical transformation. The death of Novais in 1589 enabled the Portuguese Crown, now under the dual monarchy headed by Philip II of Hapsburg, to regain direct control over the colony by revoking all of the monopolies and privileges granted to his heirs and successors. As a result, the restrictions imposed by Novais' donation charter on wine exports to this West Central African port were lifted. *Vinho* could henceforth be forwarded to any indi-

---

[9] See Graph 1.

[10] João M. dos Santos, "Angola na Governação dos Filipes: Uma Perspectiva de História Económica e Social," *Revista de História Económica e Social*. No. 3, 1979, pp. 60–61; and the 1600 report of Jerónimo Castãno in Claudio Miralles de Imperial y Gomes, *Angola en Tiempos de Felipe II y de Felipe III*. Madrid, 1951, p. 60.

[11] This is clearly suggested by the fact that in 1578 Novais asked his father in Lisbon to have 150 *pipas* (75,000 litres) of Madeira wine forwarded to him for commerce in the backlands of Luanda: i.e., the Kingdom of Ndongo. See Adriano A. T. Parreira, *The Kingdom of Angola and Iberian Interference: 1483–1643*. Uppsala, 1985, p. 57; and idem, "Primórdios da presença militar portuguesa em Angola: O tráfico de escravos: 1483–1643" in *Portugal no Mundo*. Lisbon, 1989, pp. 228.

[12] These population estimates are taken from the "História da Residência dos Padres da Companhia de Jesus em Angola, e Cousas Tocantes ao Reino, e Conquista," 1-05-1594, in Brásio, *Monumenta Missionaria Africana*, 1st series, Vol. IV, pp. 564–565.

vidual in Angola upon payment of a small export duty to *assientistas*, or persons who rented from the Crown the right to collect royal taxes for a determined period of time.[13] Furthermore, to make these contracts more attractive to *assientistas*, the Crown committed itself not to issue special licenses for the export of this alcoholic drink to the colonial capital of Angola.

As a result of this new policy, the alcohol trade at Luanda soon grew out of its depressed state. Portuguese merchant capitalists began to export increasing quantities of *vinho* to the colonial capital of Angola. Moreover, because the 1580 unification of Portugal and Spain allowed them access to the Spanish home and overseas economies, they also started to send equally low-cost and fortified wine from Seville, Cadiz, and the Canary Islands to this West Central African seaport.[14] According to an unsigned and undated report, most probably dating from the late 1610s or early 1620s, an annual average of about 20,000 *pipas* or some 10,000,000 litres were being loaded by Portuguese merchant capitalists in the Canary Islands alone for Brazil and Angola.[15] Much of this wine evidently found its way to the land of Vera Cruz, by far the most important colonial

---

[13] Alfredo de A. Felner, *Angola: Apontamentos Sobre a Ocupação e Início do Estabelecimento dos Portugueses no Congo, Angola, e Benguela*, Coimbra, 1933, p. 267. More often than not, these were the same individuals that rented the contract on slave export taxes. See, for example, article XI of the "Contracto de Angola, Congo e Loango, 1628–1636" obtained by Andre R. de Estremoz in Padre Ruela Pombo, ed., *Anais de Angola (1630–1635), Época de Decadencia no Governo de D. Manuel Pereira Coutinho: Fontes Documentais e Narrativas com Indicações, Comentários e Notas*. Lisbon, 1944, p. 72. A good discussion of the *assientos* and *assientistas* of the Angolan slave export contract is found in Mauro, "L'Atlantique Portugais et les Esclaves," pp. 22–34.

[14] See Francisco Demax to João de Argomedo, 23–06–1609, in Felner, *Angola*, pp. 504–519;" Memórias de Pedro Sardinha," in Brasio, *Monumenta Missionaria Africana*, 1st series, Vol. VI, pp. 105–106; "Relação de António Dinis," in *ibid.*, 1st series, Vol. VII, p. 67; and Bento Banha Cardoso to the King, 1622, in Cordeiro, ed., *Viagens, Explorações e Conquistas dos Portugueses: Colecção de Documentos—Producções, Commercio e Governo do Congo e de Angola, 1620–1629*. Lisbon, 1881, p. 11. The unification of Portugal and Spain also provided Spanish merchant capitalists access to the Portuguese home and overseas economies. Following the early 1590s, they too began to forward vessels laden with wine and other trade goods from Cadiz, Seville, and the Canary Islands to the colonial capital of Angola to acquire slaves destined for New Spain. See Carlos S. Assadourian, *El Trafico de Esclavos en Córdoba de Angola a Potosí siglos XVI–XVII*. Córdoba, 1966, pp. 3–28. According to data collected by Pièrre and Huguette Chaunu, *Seville et l'Atlantique, 1504–1650*. Paris, 1955–1960. Vol. 6, pp. 402–403, while only one Spanish vessel left Luanda between 1586 and 1590 with 330 slaves, the 1591–1615 total rose to 19 ships with 6,230 slaves aboard.

[15] See document #56 in Felner, *Angola*, pp. 488–489.

consumer of this alcoholic drink. But even if a mere 1% or 100,000 litres reached Luanda each year, a conservative estimate by any standards, it would nonetheless represent a relatively important figure for this port.

At the same time that the liberalization and expansion of the wine trade at Luanda was taking place, an even more profound change was occurring amongst the settler population of this seaport. Although subsequent governors of the colony did not fail to continue the conflict against Ndongo and even to expand military operations over neighbouring societies so as to obtain captives which they could then export to increase their meagre salaries, the acquisition of slaves in the hinterland of Angola's colonial capital nevertheless began to develop slowly into more of a commercial operation. The first Portuguese colons had originally established themselves in and around this emerging port to found a colony based on plantation agriculture. But by the late 1500s, these had become disillusioned with the unsuitability of the soil near the coast for such an endeavour. Spurred on by the ever rising demand for enslaved labourers resulting from the rapidly expanding Brazilian sugar plantation economy and the high mortality in the precious metal mines of New Spain, many thereafter set themselves up as slave traders working on their own account or as agents of merchant capitalists in Lisbon.[16] From their newly established commercial houses, these colons-turned-settlers soon began to forward caravans laden with cloths, ceramics, textiles, metal and glass wares, silk, and, after 1600 or so, guns and gunpowder imported from the metropole, as well as raphia cloth, copper, red dyewood, and elephant tail hair acquired from Kongo and Loango, and local salt and cowrie-shells to acquire slaves from groups of semi-independent individuals in the kingdoms of Ndongo and neighbouring areas.[17] Moreover, with greater amounts of *vinho* becoming available, they also started to include larger amounts of this alcoholic beverage amongst the items of trade transported by their slave searching

---

[16] Even Jesuits did not escape this process. By mid-1593, they complained from Luanda that "when merchants arrive here to sell biscuit, *vinho* and other things, they want no payment from us except in the currency of the country, that is slaves . . . which are anually shipped to Brazil and the Indies. See "Fundação de um Colégio em Angola dos Padres da Companhia (15–06–1593)," in Brásio, *Monumenta Missionaria Africana*, 1st series, Vol. XV, p, 333.

[17] Birmingham, *Trade and Conflict*, pp. 78–79; and Miller, "Slave Trade in Congo and Angola," pp. 87–91.

caravans.[18] Because of its lower cost compared to many of the other exchange goods imported from the metropole and its elastic capacity through dilution, *vinho* was an item of trade that, from the point of view of Portuguese merchants, was tailor made for the acquisition of slaves.

By the second decade of the seventeenth century slave exports from the colonial capital of Angola equalled the volume of the 1570s. An increasing number were now procured through commercial means and in exchange for *vinho*.[19] This fact did not escape the attention of Pedro Sardinha. In a report written *circa* 1612 for the Crown, he listed this alcoholic drink as one of the prominent trade goods with which slaves were obtained in the hinterland of Luanda. The exchange of *vinho* for slaves, he informed Phillip III, did not take place in regular markets. Instead, with commercial relations in the interior still in their infancy, these transactions were conducted wherever exportable slaves were available.[20] Throughout these backlands, as one of the first modern historians of Angola aptly put it, "even the most reluctant chiefs could be persuaded to sell slaves . . . [i]n return for good wine."[21]

But as Portuguese military forces painstakingly brought African social formations under colonial domination and influence during the first half of the seventeenth century, a network of permanent slave markets was established to the east, especially in the capitals of Ndongo and the newly founded kingdom of Kasanje, that reached as far as the Kwango River valley and the southern edges of the middle Kwanza River.[22] These *feiras* offered considerable numbers of slaves, which were no longer merely drawn from semi-independent groups of individuals but were increasingly procured through raids on neighbouring villages, chiefdoms, and kingdoms, for trade

---

[18] "História da Residência dos Padres da Companhia de Jesus em Angola," 1-05-1594, in Brásio, *Monumenta Missionaria Africana*, 1st series, Vol. IV, p. 561.

[19] Santos, "Angola na Governação dos Filipes," p. 67. This may well have been due to the significantly increased presence of Spanish slavers and, presumably, wine from Cadiz, Seville, and the Canary Islands at Luanda following 1615. Between 1616 and 1640, a total of 376 Spanish vessels left this seaport with 54,610 slaves for New Spain. See Chaunu, *Seville et l'Atlantique, 1504–1650*, Vol. 6, pp. 402–403.

[20] "Memórias de Pedro Sardinha ao Conselho de Estado," c. 1612, in Brásio, *Monumenta Missionaria Africana*, 1st series, Vol. IV, pp. 105–106.

[21] Birmingham, *Trade and Conflict*, p. 114.

[22] Miller, "Slave Trade in Congo and Angola," p. 89; and Birmingham, *Trade and Conflict*, pp. 72–103.

in one locality. Within a very short period of time, they quickly became the favourite destination of the slave searching caravans from the littoral. Here, as the documentation presented below suggests, the *vinho* transported by them in *peroleiras* was utilized as a stimulant to increase the already powerful lure that trade goods exercised upon local slave suppliers, an intoxicant to render the bargaining capabilities of the latter less effective, and as a cheap, expandable consumer item directly exchanged for slaves: all with the objective of enhancing the profits derived from the slave trade.

The commercial transactions conducted in the hinterland of this West Central African port, however, were based on mutual mistrust, as Lusophone and African trading parties sought to outdo each other in deviousness. The leaders of the caravans, mainly trusted slaves or retainers of Portuguese merchants in Luanda, attempted to intoxicate local African slave suppliers to such an extent as to slip without detection low quality trade goods into the deals agreed upon. The latter, on the other hand, sought to swap old and unhealthy captives for slaves in their prime so as to turn the terms of trade in their favour.[23] Fuelled by more than generous amounts of *vinho*, these trade negotiations often resulted in violent disputes. This situation reached such proportions by the 1620s that Governor Fernão de Sousa felt compelled to intervene. Almost immediately after his arrival in Angola, he made it illegal for Portuguese merchants to dispatch *vinho* to the interior slave markets.[24] As in the case of numerous other colonial laws, this ban proved ineffective.

The role of alcohol in the slave trade carried out in the interior had, by then, become too fundamental for Portuguese traders to refrain from utilizing it in the acquisition of slaves. In 1627 Governor Sousa still found it necessary to instruct the *Ngola* to ban the sale of wine in his *feira*.[25] This indicates that it most probably continued to be transported into the interior for the purpose of acquiring slaves.

---

[23] General discussions of these practices are found in Jean Cuvelier, *L'Ancien Royaume de Congo*. Brussels, 1954, pp. 228–229 and ff.; and Ralph Delgado, *História de Angola*. Benguela and Lobito, 1948–1955, Vol. II, p. 95.

[24] See the instructions penned by this Portuguese official for the *feira* of Ambaca on 3–10–1624 in Felner, *Angola*, p. 519; and his undated report to the Crown in Heintze, *Fontes para a História de Angola*, Vol. I, p. 222.

[25] Governor Sousa to Ngola Are, 26–03–1627, in Heintze, *Fontes para a História de Angola*, Vol. I, p. 283.

At least one merchant, António de Oliveira, is known to have persisted in forwarding *vinho* to *feiras* east of Luanda in spite of the ban.[26] And, in the case of slaves acquired from the Imbangala, the outlawed alcoholic drink remained the principal mode of payment.[27] Thus, even though it was prohibited, many nevertheless continued to dispatch *vinho* to inland markets for the purpose of obtaining slaves.

If, or when, this ban was revoked is not known. Given the growing importance of *vinho* in the interior *feiras*, it is quite possible that it was annulled by Manuel Pereira Coutinho, who governed the colony from 1630 to 1635. One of Governor Sousa's preoccupations after he implemented the restriction was that, once his successor arrived in Luanda, Portuguese merchants would exert enough pressure to have the forwarding of this intoxicant to the inland slave markets declared legal again.[28] Legal or not, however, much of the wine unloaded in Angola's colonial capital during the 1630s continued to find its way into the hinterland for the purpose of acquiring slaves. This was surely the case of the relatively significant amounts of wine, as well as other trade staples, that arrived from Cadiz, the Canary Islands, and Seville despite a 1629 ban on this commerce[29] and the large cargo of *vinho* brought in by Diogo F. da Silva around 1638 through a special license obtained from the Crown.[30] With the number of Lusophone consumers at Luanda still rather small, most of this alcohol had only one venue: the *feiras* in the interior to be exchanged for slaves.

The Dutch captured Luanda late in August, 1641, as part of their global onslaught against Lusitanian colonies, forcing many of its

[26] Undated report written by Governor Sousa for the King of Portugal in Heintze, *Fontes para a História de Angola*, Vol. I, pp. 291–292.

[27] Beatrix Heintze, "Traite de 'Pieces' en Angola: Ce Qui N'est Pas Dit Dans Nos Sources" in Serge Daget, ed. *De la Traite à l'Esclavage, du XVIᵉ au XVIIIᵉ Siècle: Actes du Colleque International sur la Traite des Noirs, Nantes, 1985.* Paris, 1988, Vol. I, p. 164.

[28] Undated report by Governor Sousa for the Portuguese Crown in Heintze, *Fontes para a História de Angola*, Vol. I, p. 292.

[29] The ban failed to be put into effect by no other than Governor Sousa because, in his view, Luanda would find itself short of consumer goods without the wine and other foodstuffs transported by Spanish vessels. See his letter to the government in the metropole, 9–01–1630, in Beatrix Heintze, ed. *Fontes para a História de Angola do Século XVII: Cartas e Documentos Oficiais da Colectânia de Fernão de Sousa (1624–1635).* Stuttgart, 1988, Vol. II, pp. 251–252.

[30] Magalhães Godinho, *Os Descobrimentos*, Vol. III, p. 244.

Portuguese inhabitants to flee to Massangano, a town some 140 kilometres inland from the coast. Amongst the loot apprehended by the invaders were some 140 *pipas* or about 70,000 litres of *vinho*,[31] most of which probably originated from Portugal.[32] With Angola's colonial capital in enemy hands, the flow of *vinho* required by Portuguese slave merchants in the interior to conduct their business was suddenly and effectively blocked off. Fleets transporting troops, provisions, and trade goods were periodically sent from Brazil and Portugal to supply the loyal settlers, but were seldom able to get through the Dutch.[33] In spite of the shortage of European and Asian trade goods, Portuguese loyalists in the interior continued their slave trading operations on an illegal basis. However, because most African slave suppliers preferred to trade with the Dutch, who offered better quality goods at lower prices than their Lusitanian competitors, loyal Portuguese traders in the hinterland acquired smaller numbers of slaves illegally than they did legally prior to 1641.[34]

It is very doubtful that any of the modest numbers of slaves illegally procured in the interior of Luanda during the 1640s were obtained in transactions involving *vinho*. The decision taken in 1645 to provision the Portuguese relief fleets with large quantities of this alcoholic beverage indicates that its availability in Massangano was most probably scarce.[35] Indeed, whatever small amounts of grape wine that were available in Massangano were obtained from the Dutch in Luanda, who had but little of it themselves, at exorbitant prices in exchange for slaves. According to one source, a single *peroleira* of this wine was then valued at no less than the cost of two prime slaves, or 36$000 *réis*.[36] But if grape wine was a rarity, *aguardente*

---

[31] See Dapper, *Description de l'Afrique*, p. 371 and, especially, the report of P. Moortamer and C. Nieulaut, August 25–September 17, 1641, in Jadin, *L'Ancien Congo d'après les Archives Romaines*, Vol. I, p. 102.

[32] Following 1640, when Portugal regained its independence, Spanish wine could no longer legally circulate in the Portuguese home and overseas economies. Political separation of also led to a significant decrease in direct slave trading between Luanda and Spanish America. See Enriqueta Vila Vilar, "La Sublevacion de Portugal y la Trata de Negros," *Ibero-Amerikanisches Archiv.* Vol. 2, 1976, pp. 171–192.

[33] This episode of Angolan history is best analyzed in Charles R. Boxer, *Salvador de Sá and the Struggle for Brazil and Angola, 1602–1686.* London, 1952. But see also Maria L. Esteves, "Os Holandeses em Angola: Decadência do comércio externo e soluções locais adoptadas," *Studia.* No. 52, 1994, pp. 49–82.

[34] Esteves, "Os Holandeses em Angola," pp. 62–64.

[35] Mauro, *Le Portugal, le Brésil et l'Atlantique*, p. 417.

[36] Cadornega, *História Geral das Guerras*, Vol. I, p. 429.

certainly was not. Indeed, once in Massangano, Portuguese loyalists "invented their *aguardente*" from sugar cane, corn, fruits, honey, and nuts to replace the unavailable *vinho*.[37] Contemporaneous sources do not inform us if these locally produced distilled brandies were used to obtain slaves. Yet, given the importance which *vinho* had acquired in the slave trade prior to the Dutch invasion, it is more than likely that local *aguardentes* substituted, albeit on a reduced scale, this alcoholic drink as a stimulant and intoxicant during commercial transactions and as a cheap consumer good directly exchanged for slaves.

The colonial capital of Angola was recaptured from the Dutch in 1648 by an expeditionary forced dispatched from Brazil. This allowed most of the Portuguese settlers established in and around Massangano to flock back to their former dwellings. Here they resumed their legal slave trading operations with European and Asian consumer and luxury goods obtained mainly, now once again, from Portugal, as well as with regional and local items of exchange. The renewed availability of large quantities of *vinho* from the metropole,[38] in particular, enabled them to abandon the utilization of local brandies for the acquisition of slaves throughout the interior.[39] As António de Oliveira de Cadornega, the most authoritative contemporaneous source for the history of the colony during the second half of the seventeenth century, makes plain, much of the metropolitan alcoholic drinks that arrived in Luanda after 1648, especially the less expensive *vinho*, found their way to the *feiras* located in the capitals of Kasanje and the kingdom of Matamba, where the majority of the slaves exported through this coastal town were henceforth procured.[40]

What proportion of the slave trade at Luanda can be accounted for by *vinho*? Data are not available to allow a meaningful estimate of the proportionate contribution of imported alcohol to the slowly growing dimensions of slave trading in the colonial capital of Angola

[37] *Ibid.*, Vol. I, pp. 488–489.

[38] A mid-seventeenth century source reports that one Genoese merchant, alone, held 4,000 *peroleiras* of wine (roughly 68,000 litres) for the purpose of trading in slaves. See Simonetti, "P. Giacinto Brugiotti da Vetralla," p. 316.

[39] As it happens, this was a timely development. The firewood required for the distillation of *aguardente* was always in short supply, which rendered the cost of this intoxicant considerably higher than that of *vinho*. See Delgado, *História de Angola*, Vol. III, p. 315.

[40] Cadornega, *História Geral das Guerras*, Vol. II, pp. 79–80.

during the period under consideration.[41] It is nevertheless clear from the preceding discussion that, by the mid-1600s, *vinho* had developed into one of the major trade goods with which the growing number of slaves procured in the hinterland through commercial relations were obtained.

Indeed, shortly after the Dutch captured this commercial entrepôt from the Portuguese, they realized how central grape wine was for the acquisition of slaves in the interior. Within five months, the 140 *pipas* of *vinho* which they had seized were nearly all empty. The Dutch Council in Recife had made plans in November of 1641 to supply Luanda with some 100 *pipas* of Spanish wine and other trade goods.[42] But at the end of January of 1642 these had still not been received. This led the Dutch directors at Luanda to inform their superiors in Recife that with slave dealers in West Central Africa wanting a bit of everything, including grape wine, for the human merchandise they brought to the coast and with the *pipas* of this intoxicant running dry, it was not possible to acquire the number of slaves desired.[43] Students of the slave trade carried out by the Dutch in the Atlantic have suggested that the role of alcohol in this commerce was, in general, a minor one.[44] In the specific case of Luanda during the early 1640s, however, the available evidence suggests otherwise.

---

[41] The only data available come from Governor Sousa. Towards the end of his governorship, he received a *pipa* of wine from Diogo de Brito in Lisbon to purchase one slave. However, the wine arrived in Luanda spoiled and the proceeds from its sale were not enough for Sousa to buy and to sustain a slave. See "Incumbencia de Diogo de Brito," in Heintze, *Fontes para a História de Angola*, Vol. II, p. 326.

[42] "Decisions du Conseil de Recife sur les marchandises à envoyer à Loanda," 17–10–1641, in Jadin, *L'Ancien Congo d'après les Archives Romaines*, Vol. I, p. 122.

[43] See [P.] Moortamer et [C.] Nieulaut au Gouverneur et au Conseil de Recife," 24–01–1642, and C. Nieulaut et P. Moortamer au Conseil du Bresil," May 1642, in Jadin, *L'Ancien Congo d'après les Archives Romaines*, Vol. I, pp. 197 and 294, respectively.

[44] This is the case, for example, of Postma, *Dutch in the Atlantic Slave Trade*, p. 104, who indicates that less than five percent of slaves acquired by the West Indies Company during the early 1700s were obtained with alcoholic beverages. Jones, *West Africa in the Mid-Seventeenth Century*, p. 17, also suggests that the mid-1600s Dutch slave trade involved very small amounts of intoxicants.

Conclusion

The demographic characteristics of the early European population in Luanda and the military ventures carried out therefrom against nearby African polities did not allow Paulo de Novais to develop his monopoly of the wine trade into a profitable enterprise. Following the early 1590s, however, as his successors began to acquire slaves increasingly through commercial means and less through warfare, wine imported from Portugal, as well as Spain and the Canary Islands, emerged as an item of exchange in transactions with African suppliers. One of a vast assortment of European and Asian trade goods offloaded in the colonial capital of Angola for the purpose of trade in slaves, this intoxicant did not turn into the foremost item of exchange in the growing commerce. Nevertheless, it did become an important trade good. Without relatively large amounts of imported wine in the bundles of goods offered by the Portuguese, it was rarely possible to secure slaves from their African trading partners for export.

CHAPTER FOUR

THE DOWNFALL OF BACCHUS: BRAZILIAN TRADERS, PORTUGUESE CAPITALISTS AND THE STRUGGLE FOR THE ALCOHOL TRADE AT LUANDA AND ITS HINTERLAND, c. 1650–1699

From the last quarter of the sixteenth to the mid-seventeenth centuries, European grape wine was the major, if not the only, alcoholic beverage imported in the colonial capital of Angola. The relatively significant amounts of grape wine that arrived in this seaport prior to 1650 from Portugal and Spain were first and foremost utilized to acquire the ever increasing number of slaves required by the expanding plantation economy of Brazil. After the late 1640s, however, the privileged position gained by European wine in the slave trade conducted at Luanda and throughout its hinterland, was soon overcome by the introduction of another imported alcoholic beverage, sugar cane brandy from the land of Vera Cruz. The arrival of the new intoxicant soon led to a struggle between Portuguese metropolitan merchant capitalists and Brazilian colonial traders: the former primarily using wine as a trade good to acquire part of the slaves which they alone had previously supplied to Brazil; the latter using another alcoholic beverage widely produced in their homeland in an attempt to break this monopoly. The issue of which type of intoxicant would predominate in the acquisition of slaves did not get resolved until the late seventeenth century. In the process, the effort by Brazilian colonial trading interests to wrest control of the slave trade away from merchant capitalists in Portugal brought about significant changes to the commerce.

I. *Sugar Cane Brandy, Wine, and the Luanda Slave Trade*

The occupation of Angola's colonial capital by the Dutch during the 1640s seriously perturbed the volume of slaves acquired by Brazilian merchants from Portuguese traders established in and around

Massangano.[1] With one of their major sources of enslaved labourers in enemy hands, traders in the land of Vera Cruz could not meet the ever increasing demand for slaves to work in Brazilian sugar plantations and urban centres. This quickly led them to realize that in order to secure a more regular and voluminous flow of slaves across the southern Atlantic, they had to gain control over the slave trade carried out in the largest port of West Central Africa. To bring this objective to fruition, Brazilian commercial interests implemented a two-fold course of action: first, they provided much of the capital and personnel for the various Lusitanian expeditionary fleets that from 1641 to 1648 were periodically dispatched to oust the Dutch from Angola;[2] and, second, after one of these fleets made up of fifteen vessels successfully brought this colony back under Portuguese rule in 1648, they began to forward their own trade representatives to Luanda to establish subsidiary Brazilian commercial houses.[3]

By themselves, however, these actions were far from sufficient to breach the quasi-monopoly held before 1641 by Lisbon merchant capitalists over the Luanda slave trade. A further and infinitely more important condition necessary to achieve this goal was that the Brazilian commercial agents stationed in the colonial capital of Angola had to be abundantly supplied with more advantageous items of exchange by their parent merchant houses than those traditionally utilized by the long established Portuguese slave trading community. Here Brazilian merchants turned principally to two cheap, low grade consumer goods, tobacco and sugar cane brandy or cachaça.

---

[1] Boxer, *Salvador de Sá*, pp. 171, 176–177, 199, 22, 255, and 279; Esteves, "Os Holandeses em Angola," pp. 62–64; Miller, "Slave Trade in Congo and Angola," p. 91; Birmingham, *Trade and Conflict*, pp. 104–110; and José Gonçalves Salvador, *Os Cristãos-Novos e o Comércio no Atlântico Meridional (Com enfoque nas Capitanias do Sul, 1530–1680)*. São Paulo, 1978, pp. 314–329.

[2] These expeditions are extensively discussed in: Boxer, *Salvador de Sá*; and Alencastro, *O Trato dos Viventes*, pp. 220–238 and 266–271. The residents of Rio de Janeiro alone provided 55,000 *cruzados* to outfit the fleet that forced the Dutch out of the colonial capital of Angola in 1648. See Gastão Sousa Dias, "S. Tomé e Angola," in *A Restauração e o Império Colonial Português*. Lisbon, 1940, p. 312. The *cruzado*, a Portuguese currency that circulated particularly in Brazil, was worth $400 *réis* throughout the period under consideration here.

[3] Joseph C. Miller, "The Paradoxes of Impoverishment in the Atlantic Zone," in David Birmingham and Phyllis M. Martin, eds. *History of Central Africa*. London, 1983. Vol. I, pp. 134–135; idem, "Numbers, Origins, and Destinations of Slaves," p. 87; Pardo, "Comparative Study of the Portuguese Colonies," p. 103; and Alencastro, *O Trato dos Viventes*, pp. 306–322.

From the perspective of Brazilian commercial interests, tobacco and cane brandy were particularly appropriate items of exchange to introduce into the slave trade carried out in Luanda and throughout its hinterland. First, both were amongst the few colonial products that were the object of extensive production in the land of Vera Cruz, particularly in plantations throughout the interior of Salvador and Recife.[4] Second, they were produced by enslaved labour, which significantly lowered their production costs vis-à-vis the European and Asian trade goods, including alcoholic beverages, that were used to obtain slaves at Luanda and its hinterland.[5] Third, the much shorter sailing time between Brazil and Angola's colonial capital greatly decreased their transportation costs.[6] Fourth, since Brazilian merchants had no other local items of exchange to offer, they needed to fill up the otherwise empty bowels of the vessels that they sent to trade for slaves in Angola. Here the heavy and voluminous *cachaça*, in particular, was important as ballast for ships in outgoing voyages.[7] And finally, neither of these Brazilian colonial products were found amongst the numerous items of exchange utilized prior to 1641 by the Portuguese merchants based in this West Central African seaport to procure slaves.[8] Tobacco and cane brandy thus provided merchants in the land of Vera Cruz with an opportunity to introduce radically new and lower priced items of exchange into and, thereby, attempt to gain control over the slave trade at Luanda and its interior.

---

[4] See Roberto C. Simonsen, *História Económica do Brasil (1500–1820)*. São Paulo, 1978, pp. 95–124 and 367–369; Caio Prado Jr., *The Colonial Background of Modern Brazil*. Berkeley, 1971, pp. 170–171 and 177–178; and E. Bradford Burns, *A History of Brazil*. New York, 1980, pp. 73–75 and 82.

[5] The 1680s price of Brazilian sugar cane brandy presented below, clearly suggests that its production cost was less than that of Portuguese intoxicants, especially wine.

[6] Lisbon, in another hemisphere, was months away from the colonial capital of Angola, which substantially increased the transportation costs of the trade goods dispatched there by metropolitan merchant capitalists. According to Miller, *Way of Death*, p. 322, anywhere from 90 to 120 days were necessary to sail from Lisbon to Benguela prior to the 1790s. Even more time was required if ships left Lisbon directly for Luanda. Following the 1790s, the Lisbon-Benguela sailing time was reduced to roughly 70 days. In the case of Brazilian ports, on the other hand, voyage time from Luanda and Benguela hovered around 35 days to Recife, 40 days to Salvador, and 50 to Rio de Janeiro. See A. J. R. Russell-Wood, "Ports of Colonial Brazil," in Franklin W. Knight and Peggy K. Liss, eds., *Atlantic Port Cities: Economy, Culture, and Society in the Atlantic World*. Knoxville, 1991, p. 201.

[7] Miller, *Way of Death*, p. 329.

[8] See Chapter Three above.

Precisely when Brazilian trading interests began to forward *cachaça* and tobacco to their commercial representatives in the colonial capital of Angola has not been satisfactorily established. In the case of sugar cane brandy, some scholars have stated that it began arriving sometime in the seventeenth century.[9] Others, on the other hand, have been far more specific by suggesting the year 1660.[10] But even this more precise dating is off the mark. Once bent upon gaining command over the Luanda slave trade, it is unlikely that Brazilian merchants would have waited more than a full decade before utilizing cane brandy, not to mention tobacco, to acquire slaves there. Plantation owners in the land of Vera Cruz were in desperate need of large numbers of slaves with which to quickly replenish their much depleted enslaved labour force.[11] Moreover, the first reference to sugar cane brandy being used to acquire slaves in the hinterland of Angola's colonial capital comes from the late 1650s.[12] Thus, the first tobacco and cane brandy shipments from Brazil probably arrived around 1650, or almost immediately after trade agents of Brazilian merchants started to set up shop in Luanda.[13]

Yet, in spite of similar advantages, the utilization of Brazilian tobacco and sugar cane brandy as items of exchange in the Portuguese slave trade carried out in the colonial capital of Angola and throughout its interior after 1650 developed along radically different lines. Consumers in West Central Africa preferred locally grown varieties of tobacco to the newly introduced low grade weed from Salvador and Recife.[14] Consequently, demand for Brazilian tobacco at Luanda

---

[9] See, for example: David Birmingham, "The African Response to Early Portuguese Activities in Angola," in R. H. Chilcote, ed. *Protest and Resistance in Angola and Brazil.* Berkeley, 1972, p. 24; and José Honório Rodrigues, "The Influence of Africa on Brazil and of Brazil on Africa," *Journal of African History.* Vol. III, 1962, p. 53.

[10] Douglas Wheeler and René Pélissier, *Angola.* London, 1971, p. 48; and Gerald J. Bender, *Angola Under the Portuguese: Myth and Reality.* Berkeley, 1978, p. 356.

[11] Boxer, *Salvador de Sá*, pp. 176–177, 199, 222, and 255; José Capela, *Escravatura: Conceitos; A Empresa de Saque.* Lisbon, 1974, p. 140; Esteves, "Os Holandeses em Angola," pp. 62–64; Selma A. Pantoja, *Nzinga Mbandi: Mulher, Guerra e Escravidão.* Brasília, 2000, pp. 119–120; and Alencastro, *O Trato dos Viventes*, pp. 188–247.

[12] Birmingham, *Central Africa*, p. 78.

[13] See our dicussion below.

[14] Verger, *Trade Relations*, p. 12; Joseph C. Miller, "Imports at Luanda, Angola, 1785–1823," in G. Liesegang, H. Pasch, and A. Jones, eds., *Figuring African Trade: Proceedings of the Symposium on the Quantification and Structure of the Import and Export and Long Distance Trade of Africa in the 19th Century (c. 1800–1913).* Berlin, 1986, p. 194; and idem, "Capitalism and Slaving," p. 39.

failed to grow substantially. This conclusion is clearly borne out by the number of ships partially laden with tobacco rolls that were dispatched from Salvador during the second half of the 1600s and the 1700s to supply the weak Angolan market. A mere seventeen vessels were involved in this traffic from 1681 to 1710, while from 1736 to 1800 their number suffered an important proportionate decrease to twenty-one.[15] With consumer demand low and correspondingly depressed import volumes, Brazilian tobacco could not emerge into a major item of exchange in the slave trade carried out in Luanda and its hinterland.[16] Thus, the competitive edge with which Brazilian merchants sought to cut into this traffic did not materialize in the case of tobacco.

Sugar cane brandy, on the other hand, fared significantly better. Aside from the advantages discussed above, this distilled alcoholic drink possessed two further comparative edges over its major generic competitor, European grape wine. Not only was it a brand new and lower priced beverage in Luanda and its hinterland, but its alcohol content, which ranged from eighteen to twenty-two degrees Cartier, or roughly forty-five to sixty percent,[17] was also notably higher. In a region where the exchange of slaves for imported alcohol had grown progressively since the mid-sixteenth century, this factor emerged as a significant variable and a desirable characteristic. It provided African slave suppliers with the possibility of acquiring proportionately greater quantities of a more potent alcoholic beverage for the slaves which they proposed to exchange than was the case with the more expensive and less alcoholized European grape wine. Furthermore, precisely because it was a distilled and highly alcoholized drink, sugar cane brandy resisted deterioration during shipment across the southern Atlantic and the heat of the tropics, while wine was prone to

---

[15] Verger, *Trade Relations*, pp. 4 and 578–580.

[16] By way of comparison, this same weed proved a real "hit" amongst consumers along the Bight of Benin where, during the last quarter of the 1600s, it developed into a crucial import to sustain the slave trade with Salvador: Verger, "Rôle joué par le tabac de Bahia;" and Jean-Baptiste Nardi, *O fumo brasileiro no período colonial*. São Paulo, 1996, pp. 115–125, 150, 163, and 366–369. Consumer tastes were not uniform throughout western Africa. On this point, see Richardson, "West African Consumption Patterns."

[17] The alcohol content expressed in degrees Cartier is provided by Cascudo, *Prelúdio da Cachaça*, p. 12. Its percentage equivalency is taken from Yves Renouil, *Dictionaire du Vin*. Bordeaux, 1962, p. 495.

spoilage.[18] This enabled importers in the colonial capital of Angola to lower their transportation losses and allowed African slave suppliers to keep larger supplies of alcohol within their domains for longer periods of time.

Shortly after cane brandy became available at Luanda, Brazilian slave traders established there began to forward this distilled spirit to the *feiras* that following 1648 were re-established under nominal Portuguese control in the interior. By the late 1650s, *cachaça* was already found amongst the trade goods which *pombeiros* utilized to acquire slaves directly as far east as the kingdom of Matamba.[19] How it was used in the commercial transactions that took place is not known. What is certain is that more and more of these African individuals began to ask for this distilled spirit as part and parcel of the trade goods which they sought in return for their slaves. This turn of events presumably enabled the commercial representatives of Brazilian merchant houses to acquire appreciable numbers of the 10,000 to 12,000 slaves that were annually exported from the colonial capital of Angola throughout the 1650s,[20] while the purchasing power of the agents of Lisbon merchant capitalists must have started to decrease correspondingly.

As demand for enslaved labour continued to augment in Brazil and African slave dealers in the interior of Angola's colonial capital increasingly insisted on cane brandy as part of the items offered for

---

[18] On the weak resistance which Portuguese wines had vis-à-vis transportation and heat, see Carl A. Hanson, *Economy and Society in Baroque Portugal, 1668–1703*. Minneapolis, 1981, p. 197. More than half of the wine imported at Luanda by António Coelho Guerreiro between 1684 and 1692 either arrived spoiled or turned sour while in storage. See his alcohol trading accounts in Virgínia Rau, *O "Livro de Razão" de António Coelho Guerreiro*. Lisbon, 1956, fls. 14v, 15v, 20v, 21v, and 25v. Similarly, during the late 1600s, one missionary operating in the Kingdom of Kongo complained about how quickly the wine which he and his colleagues imported from Lisbon through Angola's colonial capital went bad. See the letter of 19–03–1692 and the report dated 24–05–1692 by Fra Francesco de Monteleone in Jonghe and Simar, *Archives Congolaises*, pp. 165 and 169, respectively. On spoiled wines arriving at Luanda during the early 1700s, see the shipping and sale accounts of Francisco Pinheiro in Luis Lisanti, ed., *Negócios Coloniais: Uma Correspondência Comercial do Século XVIII*. São Paulo, 1973, Vol. IV, 431, 445–446, and 500. Only the Madeira wines, precisely because they were fortified (as they are today), escaped this generalized problem. See T. Bently Duncan, *Atlantic Islands: Madeira, the Azores and the Cape Verdes in Seventeenth-Century Commerce and Navigation*. Chicago, 1972, p. 38.

[19] Birmingham, *Central Africa*, p. 78.

[20] This slave export estimate is taken from Miller, "Slave Trade from Congo and Angola," p. 101.

their slaves, trading interests in the land of Vera Cruz responded by
dispatching ever greater quantities of this alcoholic beverage. After
1665, in particular, the volume of *gerebita*, as *cachaça* came to be
known in West Central Africa, available to the trade representatives
of Brazilian merchants reached appreciable proportions.[21] Most of
this cane brandy continued to be forwarded to slave markets in the
immediate interior of Luanda.

The growing importance gained by *gerebita* in the slave trade carried out at Luanda and throughout its interior in the late 1660s did
not escape the attention of the Conselho Ultramarino, the advisory
council of the Portuguese Crown for overseas affairs, in Lisbon. Soon
after assuming the governorship of the colony, Francisco de Tavora
informed the government in the metropole that the disinterest of the
settler population and the lack of firewood did not allow sugar plantations, and consequently cane brandy production, to be established
there. Following the receipt of this letter, the Conselho Ultramarino
promptly recommended to the Prince of Portugal that he order
Tavora to leave things as they were and, more specifically, not to
allow the local production of cane brandy. The reason given by this
advisory council for the Portuguese Crown not to permit its production was that metropolitan grape wine and *aguardente*, as well as
gerebita from Brazil, would no longer have a consumer market in
Angola.[22] In its view, these were the leading metropolitan and Brazilian
export goods for commerce in the colony. Destroying their market
would harm the export trade of Portugal and severely diminish the
number of ships that were forwarded from Salvador and Recife to
acquire slaves in Angola's colonial capital, since these almost exclu-

---

[21] Governor Aires de Saldanha de Menezes e Souza to the King, 10–07–1678,
AHU, Angola, Cx. 11, Doc. 107. The rise in *cachaça* exports to Luanda was made
possible by the fact that its production in Brazil augmented considerably during the
1660s. See Vitorino de Magalhães Godinho, "Portugal and Her Empire, 1680–1720,"
in *New Cambridge Modern History*. Vol. VI, 1970, p. 510.

[22] Cadornega, *História Geral das Guerras*. Vol. II, p. 544. This is the first time that
metropolitan *aguardente* appears in the extant documentation as an alcoholic beverage imported at Luanda. The date of its introduction in West Central Africa can
not be established. In Europe, the industrial production of "spirits" began during
the sixteenth century. See the general account of this industry in Fernand Braudel,
Capitalism and Material Life, 1400–1800. London, 1974, pp. 170–178; and Cascudo,
Prelúdio da Cachaça, pp. 1–21. It could very well be that *aguardente* was first brought
to Luanda during the late 1640s as a substitute for locally produced distillates.

sively transported *cachaça* in their holds.[23] Not wishing either of these possible developments to occur, the Portuguese Prince complied with the recommendation of the Conselho Ultramarino.

The rising importation of Brazilian sugar cane brandy in the colonial capital of Angola during the late 1660s and the first half of the 1670s and its increasing use in the procurement of slaves, however, quickly turned this alcoholic drink into a target for attack. In 1678, Governor Aires de Saldanha de Menezes e Souza wrote to Pedro II informing him that, in his view, outlawing the importation cane brandy from the land of Vera Cruz was essential. Outlining the various reasons which made its ban imperative, Menezes e Souza stated that *gerebita* was an alcoholic beverage of very low quality and, hence, was extremely prejudicial to the health of its consumers. In particular, he emphasized, the immoderate consumption of *gerebita* was directly responsible for the death of many Portuguese soldiers and African slaves in and around Luanda. Without such a prohibition, Menezes e Souza concluded, the military reinforcements regularly sent for the defense and expansion of the *conquista* or conquered territories were simply useless, while the decreasing African enslaved labour force would endanger the economic well-being of the Portuguese settlers.[24]

What influenced Governor Menezes e Souza to formulate this request is not known. As it happens, during the 1670s, slave exports from Luanda fell to an average of 9,000 per year.[25] Menezes e Souza was most probably acting on behalf of Portuguese slave traders established there and, by extension, their wine suppliers in the metropole.[26] After all, these individuals had seen their monopoly of the

---

[23] Cadornega, *História Geral das Guerras*, Vol. II, p. 544.

[24] Governor Menezes e Souza to the King, 10–07–1678, AHU, Cód. 554, fl. 21–21v.

[25] Miller, "Slave Trade in Congo and Angola," p. 101.

[26] Aires de Saldanha de Menezes e Souza was the cousin of João de Saldanha Albuquerque who, based in the metropole from 1677 to 1687, had extentive commercial dealings throughout the Atlantic World, including exporting wine to Angola to acquire slaves for sale in Brazil. See Alberto Vieira, ed., *O Público e o Privado na História da Madeira: Vol. I, Correspondência de João de Saldanha Albuquerque 1673–1694*. Funchal, 1998, pp. 14–30, 36–48, 53, 61–71, 78–79, 86–91, and 95. His preferred commercial partner was no other than Diogo Fernandes Branco in Funchal, Madeira. As we will see in Chapter VI, Branco was a major player in the wine-slave trade at Luanda.

traffic reduced by the arrival of Brazilian merchant representatives and the introduction of sugar cane brandy.

The fact that the highest ranking government official in Angola had requested a ban on the importation of *gerebita* because of its supposedly deadly effects upon the European, Luso-African, and African population of the colony led the Portuguese Crown to consider the matter seriously. Shortly upon receiving Menezes e Souza's letter, the King wrote to the *Procurador da Fazenda Real* or the Treasurer of the Crown in Angola asking him to confirm or to repudiate the allegations made by the Governor. Sometime in the beginning of 1679, the Portuguese Crown received an answer from its treasurer in Angola which corroborated every aspect of the assertions penned by Menezes e Souza.[27] Thereafter, the case was quickly forwarded to the Conselho Ultramarino for evaluation.

Given its verdict in 1670 regarding the production of sugar cane brandy in Angola, the assertions made by Governor Menezes e Souza and confirmed by the *Provedor da Fazenda Real* must have placed the Conselho Ultramarino in a somewhat awkward position. After deliberating the issue, this advisory body finally agreed to recommend to the Portuguese Crown that *gerebita* imports at Luanda should be prohibited.[28] The reasons behind this decision are not altogether clear. As already alluded to above, however, the ban on the importation of Brazilian cane brandy was not desired by Portuguese slave traders and their metropolitan suppliers because this distilled spirit was supposedly responsible for the death of numerous Portuguese colonial soldiers and African enslaved labourers. In reality, the prohibition was sought because *gerebita* was in the process of eclipsing grape wine as the major alcohol import in this port town and the most important alcoholic beverage exchanged for slaves in its hinterland.[29]

---

[27] "Parecer" of the Conselho Ultramarino dated 31–01–1679, AHU, Cód. 554, fls. 21–21v; and "Provisão" of 8–04–1679, AHU, Angola, Cx. 13, Doc. 97.

[28] "Parecer" of the Conselho Ultramarino dated 31–01–1679, AHU, Cód. 554, fls. 21–21v. An abridged version of this document is also found in AHU, Angola, Cx. 11, Doc. 107.

[29] On this point see António Pacheco de Almeida (Ouvidor Geral de Angola) to the King, 23–02–1689, AHU, Angola, Cx. 13, Doc. 97; and the "Traslado da Proposta feita ao Governador D. João de Lencastre pelos Oficiais da Câmara" of 9–02–1689, AHU, Angola, Cx. 13, Doc. 97. Nevertheless, just before the ban was to come into effect, remittances of *vinho* continued to find their way to the expanding slave mart in Kasanje. See "Registo de huma carta, que escreverão os officiais da Camara ao Sr. Governador Ayres de Saldanha," 8–03–1679, AHBML, Cód. 6, fls. 18–18v.

Moreover, compounding this development was the fact that the metropole was suffering an economic recession which created difficulties for wine producers to market their product at home.[30] Consequently, the recommendation of the Conselho Ultramarino can only be seen as a shift in colonial economic policy, favouring metropolitan viniculturalists, wine exporters in Lisbon, and Portuguese slave traders in the colonial capital of Angola at the expense of Brazilian trading interests and sugar plantation owners.

In spite of representing a major change in the economic policy of the metropole vis-à-vis the southern Atlantic, Pedro II did not hesitate to accept the recommendation of the Conselho Ultramarino. On April 8, 1679, he signed a *Provisão* or royal instruction which not only made it illegal to export *cachaça* from Brazil to Luanda, but also banned its importation in and its utilization throughout the Angolan hinterland.[31] Portuguese slave traders and their metropolitan suppliers had thus succeeded in their assault against this distilled spirit.

Once implemented in Luanda, the ban on *gerebita* imports had a number of important repercussions. Following the summer of 1679, as the volume of this distilled alcoholic drink available there began to dry up, metropolitan merchant capitalists significantly increased the amount of grape wine and *aguardente* exported to their commercial agents and private customers in this port town.[32] However, although greater volumes of alcohol imported from Lisbon soon became available once again, grape wine failed to re-emerge as and *aguardente* did

---

[30] During the late 1660s, wine production expanded appreciably throughout the mainland. See Oliveira Marques, *História de Portugal*, Vol. I, pp. 518–519. But by 1678, according to Peres, *História de Portugal*, Vol. VI, p. 403, viniculturalists from the surroundings of Lisbon were complaining of stiff competition not only between regional wines, but from foreign ones as well. Another source for the 1670s as a decade of recession for Portuguese viniculturalists is David Birmingham, *A Concise History of Portugal*, Cambridge, 1993, p. 59.

[31] "Provisão" of 8–04–1679, AHU, Angola, Cx. 13, Doc. 97. A more legible copy of this law is found in AHU, Cód. 545, fls. 20–20v.

[32] "Traslado da Proposta feita ao Governador Dom João de Lencastre pelos Oficiais da Câmara" of 12–07–1682, AHU, Angola, Cx. 12, Doc. 49; and Senado da Câmara (Senate of the Municipal Council) to the King, 12–07–1681, AHU, Angola, Cx. 12, Doc. 49. Nevertheless, the Luanda market remained extremely small for Portuguese viniculturalists in comparison to the much larger markets in Brazil and in Europe. As a result, increased wine exports to the colonial capital of Angola could hardly have been a major factor in the wine-production revival that took place in Portugal during the 1680s. On this recovery see Birmingham, *Concise History of Portugal*, p. 59.

not develop into major items of exchange in the acquisition of slaves throughout the interior. For one thing, each of these metropolitan imports was far more expensive than sugar cane brandy from Brazil. During 1688, for example, while the value of the less alcoholized grape wine and of the more spirited *aguardente* was 6$800 and 7$600 *réis*, respectively, per barrel upon arrival at Luanda, the exact same container of *gerebita* cost about 2$250 *réis*.[33] Cane brandy from the land of Vera Cruz was thus at least three times cheaper than either of the two intoxicants imported from Portugal. Furthermore, the bitter taste of grape wine and especially *aguardente* no longer satisfied the palates of African slave dealers, who had already become accustomed to the sweeter flavour of cane brandy.[34] Finally, and possibly most important of all, the larger quantities of metropolitan grape wine and *aguardente* began to arrive at a time when the volume of slaves exported was falling considerably, due to decreased demand for enslaved labour in Brazil resulting from growing competition by the Caribbean sugar plantation economies.[35] Because of their unfavourable prices and less marketable qualities, as well as the depression affecting the slave trade in the colonial capital of Angola, neither metropolitan grape wine nor *aguardente* were thus able to replace *gerebita*.

The unexpected failure of grape wine and *aguardente* to supplant Brazilian cane brandy as major commodities of exchange in the Luanda slave trade, in turn, was not without major ramifications.

---

[33] Accounts of António Coelho Guerreiro as reproduced in Rau, *"Livro de Razão"*, fls. 14v, 20v and 21v. These records show a total of twenty barrels of sugar cane brandy valued at 45$000 *réis*, one barrel of *aguardente* worth 7$600 *réis*, and eleven *pipas* of wine with a combined value of 750$500 *réis*. It is worthwhile noting here that Miller, *Way of Death*, p. 465, errs in indicating that the valuation of cane brandy and *aguardente* as found in Guerreiro's accounts were for *pipas*, as opposed to barrels. The latter held but eighty-five litres of liquid, (*ibid.*, p. 709) or roughly one-sixth of the 500 litres usually found in each *pipa*. Consequently, Miller seriously deflates the *pipa* value of both *gerebita* and *aguardente* imports. Following the barrel-*pipa* equivalency provided by Miller himself, the 1688 price of each 500 litre container of cane brandy and *aguardente* would have been around 13$000 and 45$000 *réis*, respectively.

[34] António Pacheco de Almeida to the King, 23–02–1689, AHU, Angola, Cx. 13, Doc. 97; "Resposta sobre as agoardentes escrita a Sua Magestade na era de [1]691," AHBML, Cód. 7, fls. 56v–57; and "Copia da carta escrita ao Gov.dor Aires de Saldanha na era de [1]691," *ibid.*, fls. 59v–60.

[35] Stuart B. Schwartz, "Plantations and Peripheries, c. 1580–c. 1750," in Leslie Bethell, ed., *Colonial Brazil*. Cambridge, 1987, pp. 83 and 97.

As the volume of the banned distilled spirit available in this port town decreased, demand for *gerebita* soared. This forced the price of Brazilian cane brandy to rise dramatically. In 1689, for example, it reached an impressive 50$000 to 60$000 *réis* per *pipa* at the coast and significantly more in the interior.[36] European grape wine and *aguardente* do not seem to have experienced a similar increase, although their prices remained higher than that of the prohibited *gerebita*.[37] But since imported metropolitan alcohol no longer suited the local consumer market, both in terms of taste and price, many African slave suppliers simply declined to exchange their slaves for bundles of trade goods that did not include appreciable amounts of sugar cane brandy from either Salvador or Recife.[38] Added to the soaring price of *gerebita* and its declining supplies at Luanda, these new market conditions most probably meant that fewer slaves were obtained in the interior in exchange for the Brazilian intoxicant, leading to a further decrease in the number of slaves exported across the Atlantic from the colonial capital of Angola.

The lower Brazilian demand for enslaved labourers notwithstanding, these developments created a situation where anyone capable

---

[36] "Traslado da Proposta feita ao Governador Dom João de Lencastre pelos Oficiais da Câmara" of 9-02-1689, AHU, Angola, Cx. 13, Doc. 97; António Pacheco de Almeida to the King, 23-02-1689, AHU, Angola, Cx. 13, Doc. 97; Governor João de Lencastre to the King, 23-02-1689, AHU, Angola, Cx. 13, Doc. 97; and Senado da Câmara to the King, 7-03-1609, AHU, Angola, Cx 13, Doc. 97. The unit price of a *pipa* of Brazilian cane brandy at Luanda during the late 1680s was thus not that much lower than a 500 litre container of grape wine in the mid-1660s, which sold for 60$000 *réis*. See Dionigi de Carli da Piacenza and Michel Angelo da Reggio, "A Curious and Exact Account of a Voyage to Congo in the Years 1666 and 1667," in Churchill, *Collection of Voyages and Travels*, Vol. I, p. 491.

[37] Little information exists on the price of intoxicants imported from the metropole during the early 1690s. The accounts of Guerreiro show 4 *pipas* of wine valued at a total of 193$000 *réis* in 1691, which translates to 48$250 *réis* per unit. See Rau, *"Livro de Razão"*, fl. 25v. This was less than the price of a 500 litre container of Brazilian cane brandy. But, by then, Guerreiro was preparing his return to Portugal and his trade goods were being sold at discount prices. See Miller, "Capitalism and Slaving," p. 13. This suggests that the going price of metropolitan alcoholic beverages remained in fact higher than that of *gerebita*.

[38] "Traslado da Proposta feita ao Governador Dom João de Lencastre pelos Oficiais da Câmara", 9-02-1689, AHU, Angola, Cx. 13, Doc. 97; Governor Lencastre to the King, 23-02-1689, AHU, Angola, Cx. 13, Doc. 97; António Pacheco de Almeida to the King, 23-02-1689, AHU, Angola, Cx. 13, Doc. 97; and Governor Henrique Jacques de Magalhães to the King, 13-12-1694, AHU, Angola, Cx. 15, Doc. 35.

of smuggling in the outlawed alcoholic beverage could reap significantly higher profits from the traffic than was previously possible. Within a year or so of the ban on the importation and utilization of *gerebita* at Luanda and its hinterland, there emerged an illicit but highly profitable commerce to tap the economic advantages offered by the continuously rising local demand for Brazilian cane brandy. Nearly everyone associated with the slave trade engaged in this prohibited traffic, whether by directly importing the banned alcoholic drink, by exchanging it in the hinterland for slaves, or by a combination of both of these ventures.

Perhaps the first commercial group to involve themselves in this illegal trade were the Brazilian merchant firms in Salvador and Recife. From 1680 onwards, they were actively forwarding vessels laden with cane brandy to their slave trading agents in Luanda via coastal enclaves to the north and south of this port town.[39] Given the fact that these were the commercial interests adversely affected by the 1679 *Provisão*, this measure must have been designed not only to obtain higher profits but, equally, if not more importantly, to protect the increasing share of the slave trade which Brazilian trading houses had already secured through the introduction of *gerebita*.

Another commercial group heavily engaged in this outlawed economic enterprise were the very same Portuguese slave traders in Luanda who had striven for and obtained the ban on Brazilian sugar cane brandy imports. Because neither metropolitan grape wine nor *aguardente* succeeded in supplanting *gerebita*, these individuals quickly realized that the advantages provided by the 1679 *Provisão* did not materialize. Always searching for more profitable commercial ventures and, especially, aspiring to compete on an equal footing with Brazilian slave traders, they too soon became involved in the very business which they had successfully sought to have declared illegal. The wealthier Portuguese slave traders resorted to importing cane brandy directly from commercial agents of Lisbon merchant capitalists in Salvador and Recife. As in the case of their Brazilian competitors, they introduced large quantities of the prohibited distilled spirit through coastal enclaves near the colonial capital of Angola.[40]

---

[39] Governor Lencastre to the King, 23–02–1689, AHU, Angola, Cx. 13, Doc. 97; and "Parecer" do Conselho Ultramarino, 20–10–1689, AHU, Angola, Cx. 13, Doc. 97.
[40] "Traslado da Proposta feita ao Governador Dom João de Lencastre pelos

Much, however, was also smuggled in through this port town. Thus, late in 1684, the sugar cane brandy cargoes of four vessels were effectively unloaded and thereafter openly sold to customers at the dock of Luanda.[41] Similarly, sometime in 1689, Manuel de Sousa e Benevides, an affluent local Portuguese slave trader, received an entire shipment of the banned distilled spirit.[42] Another prosperous local Portuguese merchant who also participated in this illegal commerce was João Macedo de Claris, who in 1689 received at least twenty barrels of *gerebita* from Salvador.[43] The less wealthy Portuguese slave traders, on the other hand, could not become directly involved in bootlegging cane brandy from Brazil. They possessed neither the capital necessary to outfit vessels destined to procure this alcoholic beverage in Salvador or Recife nor the business contacts in the land of Vera Cruz to have consignments of *cachaça* dispatched to them. Instead, the less prosperous Portuguese slave traders acquired the *gerebita* which they needed to continue their commercial operations from those wealthier competitors who directly imported the illegal Brazilian cane brandy. More often than not, this was done at the expense of exorbitant prices.[44]

The illicit importation of Brazilian cane brandy at Luanda could not have taken place without the compliance of low, middle, and high ranking colonial government officials who were responsible for enforcing the ban. Upon learning of the arrival of the vessels transporting *gerebita* for Sousa e Benevides in 1689, the then Governor of the colony, João de Lencastre, had the ship and its cargo immediately seized.[45] In spite of this action, the illegal shipment was nonetheless unloaded and moved to Sousa e Benevides' trading house. With

---

Oficiais da Câmara", 9–02–1689, AHU, Angola, Cx. 13, Doc. 97; António Pacheco de Almeida to the King, 23–02–1689, AHU, Angola, Cx. 13, Doc. 97; Senado da Câmara to the King, 7–03–1689, AHU, Angola, Cx. 13, Doc. 97; and King to Governor Lencastre, 4–12–1689, AHU, Cód. 545, fl. 48.

[41] Bento Teixeira de Saldanha to the King, 13–01–1687, AHU, Angola, Cx. 13, Doc. 36.

[42] Governor Lencastre to the King, 2–12–1689, AHU, Angola, Cx. 13, Doc. 102.

[43] Rau, O *"Livro de Razão"*, fl. 14v.

[44] Jerónimo da Veiga Cabral (Provedor da Fazenda de Angola) to the King, 7–11–1684, AHU, Angola, Cx. 12, Doc. 158; Governor Lencastre to the King, 23–02–1689, AHU, Angola, Cx. 13, Doc. 97; and "Parecer" of the Conselho Ultramarino, 20–10–1689, AHU, Angola, Cx. 13, Doc. 97.

[45] Jerónimo da Veiga Cabral to the King, 7–11–1684, AHU, Angola, Cx. 12, Doc. 158.

the assistance of the *Ouvidor Geral e Provedor Geral da Fazenda* or the Crown Judge and Inspector of the Royal Treasury, undoubtedly in response to a hefty payment or a cut of the sales, this Portuguese slave trader succeeded in bribing the guards placed on the ship to free its cargo.[46] How Macedo Claris managed to have his shipment of Brazilian cane brandy escape confiscation is not known. But he must have used a similar method since he also happened to be the Crown Judge and Inspector of the Royal Treasury at Luanda.[47] Last, but certainly not least, there is the case of João da Silva e Sousa, who governed the colony from 1680 to 1684. After leaving the governorship of Angola and assuming that of Pernambuco, Silva e Sousa began to export illegally significant quantities of *cachaça* to the leading slaving port in West Central Africa. On at least one occasion, one of his vessels was seized and its outlawed cargo destroyed upon orders from the succeeding Governor of Angola, Luís Lobo da Silva.[48]

Following 1681, then, appreciable amounts of *gerebita* continued to be imported at Angola's colonial capital through a variety of illegal mechanisms. Once unloaded in the port of Luanda or in neighbouring coastal enclaves, Brazilian sugar cane brandy was expanded in volume through a mixture of salted water and peppers which, although lowering its alcohol content, further increased the already high profits involved in this outlawed commerce.[49] Thereafter, this

---

[46] Governor Lencastre to the King, 6–11–1689, AHU, Angola, Cx. 13, Doc 99. The individual in question was no other than João Macedo de Claris who, aside from engaging in commerce, also occupied this important position in the colonial government of Angola. See Frédéric Mauro, "Pour une histoire de la comptabilité au Portugal: 'Le livre de Raison' de Coelho Guerreiro," *Caravelle*, Vol. 1, 1963, p. 110.

[47] This particular shipment of was forwarded by Pedro de Barros Maciel, the principal commercial connection in Salvador of António Coelho Guerreiro, who had close ties with high level administrators at Luanda. Not only did Macedo Claris exchange financial services with Coelho Guerreiro, but he was also a customer of the latter's trade goods. See Miller, "Capitalism and Slaving," p. 15.

[48] Jerónimo da Veiga Cabral to the King, 7–11–1684, AHU, Angola, Cx. 12, Doc. 158; Governor Luís Lobo da Silva to the King, 25–11–1684, in Brásio, *Monumenta Missionaria Africana*, 1st series, Vol. XIII, pp. 584–585; King to Governor Luís Lobo da Silva, 4–04–1686, AHU, Cód. 545. fl. 36v; and Bento Teixeira de Saldanha to the King, 13–01–1687, AHU, Angola, Cx. 13, Doc. 36.

[49] A Portuguese slave trader with long standing experience in Angola reports that this practice took place only before the 1679 ban. See José Barbosa Leal to the King, 10–10–1690, in Virgínia Rau and Maria F. G. da Silva, eds., *Os Manuscritos do Arquivo da Casa de Cadaval Respeitantes ao Brasil.* Coimbra, 1955, Vol. I, pp. 289–291. However, in 1688, the *Jaga* or King of Kasanje wrote the Governor of Angola informing him that the *gerebita* forwarded to his realm by Lusitanian slave traders

banned alcoholic drink was divided into *frasqueiras* or demijohns with a capacity of just over thirty-one litres and transported into the interior slave markets on the backs of enslaved or forcibly recruited African porters. By the late 1680s, at the very least, the banned cane brandy was already found in the *feira* of Kasanje, the easternmost slave market to which Lusitanian slave traders based at the coast had access.[50] Here it was directly exchanged for slaves and as a general lubricant to the slave trade.

Although higher profit margins could be gained through this illicit commerce than was the case before the late 1670s, the importation of Brazilian cane brandy did not take place without a number of drawbacks. The first lay in the illegality of the trade itself, since importers ran the risk of having their *cachaça* shipments confiscated and destroyed by responsible colonial government officials.[51] Second, because the ban significantly increased the price of this distilled alcoholic drink, proportionately fewer slaves could now be acquired and exported to Brazil in exchange for *gerebita*.[52] The third drawback rested on the fact that by outlawing the importation of Brazilian cane brandy the 1679 *Provisão* had eliminated one of the most lucrative import duties and excise taxes collected by the colonial government of Angola and by the Municipal Council of Luanda, respectively.[53] And fourth, the large profits and the bribes associated with this illegal trade rendered the prohibition practically impossible

---

was of such an extremely poor quality that it was killing his subjects. This suggests that Brazilian cane brandy continued to be adulterated at Luanda and its surroundings. See the "Parecer" of the Conselho Ultramarino dated 20–10–1689, AHU, Angola, Cx. 13, Doc. 97 or AHU, Cód. 554, fls. 60v–61.

[50] "Parecer" of the Conselho Ultramarino dated 20–10–1689, AHU, Cód. 554, fls. 60v–61 or AHU, Angola, Cx. 13, Doc. 97; "Resposta sobre as agoardentes escrita a Sua Magestade na era de [1]691," AHBML, Cód. 7, fls. 56v–57; and "Copia da carta escrita ao Gov.dor Aires de Saldanha na era de [1]691," *ibid.*, fls. 59v–60.

[51] Governor Lencastre to the King, 23–02–1689, AHU, Angola, Cx. 13, Doc. 97; and King to Governor Lencastre, 4–12–1689, AHU, Cód. 545, fl. 48.

[52] Governor Lencastre to the King, 23–02–1689, AHU, Angola, Cx. 13, Doc. 97; the "Parecer" of the Conselho Ultramarino, 20–10–1689, AHU, Angola, Cx. 13, Doc. 97; José Barbosa Leal to the King, 10–10–1690, in Rau and Silva, eds. *Os Manuscritos*, Vol. I, pp. 289–291; and Governor Magalhães to the King, 13–12–1694, AHU, Angola, Cx. 15, Doc. 35.

[53] Senado da Câmara to the King, 7–03–1689, AHU, Angola, Cx. 13, Doc. 97; the "Parecer" of the Conselho Ultramarino dated 20–10–1689, AHU, Angola, Cx. 13, Doc. 97; and "Resposta sobre as agoardentes escrita a Sua Magestade na era

to carry out.[54] As these economic issues became more evident during the 1680s to all of those affected by the 1679 *Provisão*, colonial administrators, municipal officials, and Portuguese slave traders in Luanda joined forces with Brazilian commercial, municipal, and government interests to have the anachronistic law repealed.

In 1687, the Portuguese Crown began periodically to receive representations asking that the ban on *gerebita* imports be withdrawn. Some of these petitions were penned by individual traders on both sides of the southern Atlantic.[55] But most were written under the aegis of the Municipal Councils of Salvador and Luanda, as well as by João Furtado de Mendonça (then Governor of Rio de Janeiro) and Governor Lencastre.[56] In making their arguments, colonial governmental entities and individual merchants all emphasized the various liabilities brought about by the 1679 *Provisão*: the economic risks associated with smuggling, the smaller number of slaves exported to Brazil, the dwindling colonial governmental and municipal tax revenues, and the impossibility of stopping the outlawed trade. Moreover, they suggested, the high mortality in the colony was not due to the consumption of *gerebita* but to the insalubrious climate and disease environment of the region. The King, however, found little in these complaints to warrant the re-opening of the case. Not only was the ban maintained, but orders were also sent out to the colonial administration in Angola to tighten its implementation.[57]

---

de [1]691," AHBML, Cód. 7, fls. 56v–57. On the alcohol import taxes collected by these governing bodies see Chapter Seven below.

[54] Governor Lencastre to the King, 23–02–1689, AHU, Angola, Cx. 13, Doc. 97; António Pacheco de Almeida to the King, 23–02–1689, AHU, Angola, Cx. 13, Doc. 97; Senado da Câmara to the King, 7–03–1689, Angola, Cx. 13, Doc. 97; Senado da Câmara to the King, 11–12–1794, AHU, Angola, Cx. 15, Doc. 37; and Governor Magalhães to the King, 13–12–1694, AHU, Angola, Cx. 15, Doc. 35.

[55] See, for example, José Barbosa Leal to the King, 10–10–1690, in Rau and Silva, *Os Manuscritos*, Vol. I, pp. 289–291.

[56] Charles R. Boxer, *Portuguese Society in the Tropics: The Municipal Councils of Goa, Macau, Bahia, and Luanda, 1510–1800*. Madison, 1965, pp. 123–124; Governor Lencastre to the King, n.d., in Rau and Silva, *Os Manuscritos*, p. 449; Balthazar da Silva Lisboa, *Annes do Rio de Janeiro contendo a Descoberta e Conquista deste Paiz, a Fundação da Cidade com a Historia Civil e Ecclesiastica, até a Chegada d'El-Rei Dom João VI; Além de Noticias Topographicas, Zoologicas e Botanicas*. Rio de Janeiro, 1835, Vol. 5, p. 27; Senado da Câmara de Bahia to the King, 12–08–1687, in Boxer, *Portuguese Society in the Tropics*, pp. 186–188; "Registo de uma Proposta [do Senado da Câmara de Luanda] sobre a Entrada em Angola de Aguardente do Brasil, 5–01–1689," AHBML, Cód. 12, fols. 1–3; and "Resposta [do] Governador . . . D. João de Lencastre," 9–02–1689, *ibid.*, fl. 3v.

[57] King to Governor Lencastre, 4–12–1689, AHU, Angola, Cód. 545, fl. 48.

This first setback did not put an end to the campaign led by slave traders, commercial interests, and municipal and government officials in both Luanda and Brazil to have the 1679 *Provisão* lifted. Quite the contrary, their resolve increased further still. During the early 1690s, they continued to send petitions to the Portuguese Crown bitterly denouncing the various detriments occasioned by the promulgation of the ban.[58] Moreover, to augment the pressure, they also succeeded in recruiting members of the ruling class in Lisbon to lobby the metropolitan government on their behalf.[59] Once again, however, neither their representations nor lobbying convinced the King that new arguments existed to re-examine the matter.[60]

In spite of incurring one setback after another, the Luso-Brazilian government, municipal, and commercial forces seeking the repeal of the 1679 *Provisão* nevertheless pressed on with their crusade. Late in 1694, the municipal councillors of Luanda wrote yet another lengthy petition to the Portuguese Crown. As in the case of earlier representations, this one too did not fail to point out the drawbacks brought about by the anachronistic law. But, more importantly, it also included an important argument originally made in the late 1680s and now fully backed up by three medical officers of long-standing experience in the colonial capital of Angola whom they had enlisted to analyze the contents of *gerebita* and the way it was made. According to these individuals, the high mortality found amongst the African, Luso-African, and European population in the colony was not at all due to the consumption of low quality Brazilian sugar cane brandy, as had been maintained in the late 1670s to stop its importation. Rather, they certified:

---

[58] Boxer, *Portuguese Society in the Tropics*, p. 124; "Carta para Sua Magestade sobre a aguardente do Brasil," undated, AHBML, Cód. 7, fls. 53v–54; "Resposta sobre as agoardentes escrita a Sua Magestade na era de [1]691," *ibid.*, fls. 56v–57; Copia da Carta escrita ao Conde Regedor sobre as aguardentes do Brasil na era de [1]691," *ibid.*, fl. 59; "Copia da carta escrita ao Gov.dor Aires de Saldanha na era de [1]691," *ibid.*, fls. 59v–60; King to the Oficiais da Câmara, 17–11–1692, AHU, Angola, Cód. 545, fl. 67v; "Registo de huma Carta de S. Mag.de ... sobre a geribita", 20–06–1693, AHBML, Cód. 12, fl. 67; and "Carta de Antônio Luís Gonçalves da Câmara Coutinho, governador e capitão geral do Brasil, a Mendo de Foios Pereira, secretário de Estado, sobre a conveniência ou não da proibição da aguardente em Angola," 7–12–1693, AIHGB, DL112,05.67.

[59] Boxer, *Portuguese Society in the Tropics*, p. 124.

[60] King to the Oficiais da Câmara, 17–11–1692, AHU, Cód. 545, fl. 67v.

... we find the quality [of *gerebita*] not to be harmful as has been said, but excessive quantities of it does cause prejudice, as does the drinking of too much water which is so common [here] that it results in various *thydropezias*. Having used [*gerebita*] for many years in this land, inside and outside the Hospital, we have never seen that it leads to illness. Instead, we put it to good use in many occasions as a remedy for some ailments, such as ... *hyrizypellas* from which we can infer that it results more in good than in harm.[61]

Supported by this analysis of experienced medical practitioners, the major argument of the municipal councillors was now that, with *gerebita* having been effectively shown as not constituting a detriment to the health of the population, there was no longer any reason to continue banning its importation.[62] Almost at the same time, the Governor of Angola, Henrique Jacques de Magalhães, also wrote to the King fully supporting the representation made by the Municipal Council of Luanda and informing that, since the 1679 *Provisão* had severely decreased the colonial revenue obtained from import duties, it was unthinkable to impose further taxes on Angola.[63] Both of these new issues finally forced the Portuguese Crown to re-open, after nearly a decade of similar petitions, the file on *gerebita* imports.

Soon upon receiving this new information, the King once again asked the *Provedor da Fazenda* in Angola for his views on the sworn statement made by the medical officials regarding the effects of *gerebita*. The latter expeditiously answered that:

> Brazilian cane brandy is indeed harmful, but not so much by its quality as by its quantity. And for this reason, so are *aguardente*, grape wine, and even water prejudicial to consumers. If *aguardente* is not banned, then it appears that the importation of *gerebita* should also be allowed, although with a hefty import duty in order to discourage large scale consumption.[64]

---

[61] "Certidão" by the three doctors in question, 16–12–1694, AHU, Angola, Cx. 15, Doc. 37. As in the case of most other medical conditions recognized at Luanda prior to the late 1800s, it is impossible to find specific modern equivalents for the *thydropezias* and *hyrizypellas* referred to in this document. In a personal communication, 22–05–1995, Joseph C. Miller informs that the former is apparently some form of "dropsy" and the latter probably a skin condition.

[62] Senado da Câmara to the King, 11–12–1694, AHU, Angola, Cx. 15, Doc. 37.

[63] Governor Magalhães to the King, 12–11–1694, AHU, Angola, Cx. 15, Doc. 35.

[64] "Parecer" of the Conselho Ultramarino dated 17–08–1695, AHU, Angola, Cx. 15, Doc. 37.

With such a clear cut response, the Portuguese Crown thereafter forwarded the matter to the Conselho Ultramarino for final re-consideration.

The Conselho Ultramarino met early in August of 1695 to re-evaluate the ban on Brazilian cane brandy imports at Luanda. All of the conditions which had resulted in the 1679 *Provisão* were now radically altered. First, metropolitan grape wine and *aguardente* had failed to replace *gerebita*, in terms of both the amount imported and the commercial roles to which it was put. Second, Portuguese slave traders and colonial government officials in this port town had joined forces with the local *Câmara Municipal*, or Municipal Council, as well as Brazilian commercial, government, and municipal interests, to have the ban withdrawn. And third, the supposedly deadly effects of the outlawed alcoholic drink were realized to have been no worse than those occasioned by the consumption of metropolitan *aguardente* or grape wine. Moreover, superimposed on these issues was the fact that the 1679 *Provisão* had created certain problems which could have not been foreseen by legislators in Lisbon. The ban quickly proved ineffective in stopping the importation of sugar cane brandy, con-stricted commercial transactions at the coast and in the interior, and decreased the revenue which the colonial government of Angola and the Municipal Council of Luanda required to finance their day-to-day operations and to pay the taxes imposed from the metropole. Finally, and perhaps more significantly, the economic situation in Brazil was in the process of undergoing a profound transformation. During the summer of 1695, the capital of Portugal was flooded with reports that extremely rich gold and diamond deposits had been found in Minas Gerais. This created an unprecedented demand in the land of Vera Cruz for African slaves to mine the precious metal and stones.[65] With their most advantageous trade good banned in the largest West Central African slaving port, however, Brazilian merchants could not acquire the necessary number of slaves there to supply the rapidly expanding enslaved labour requirements of Minas Gerais. In light of these changed conditions, the Conselho

---

[65] Charles R. Boxer, *The Golden Age of Brazil, 1695–1750*. Berkeley, 1962, pp. 39–60.

Ultramarino unanimously agreed to advise the Portuguese Crown that the ban on *cachaça* imports should be repealed.[66]

Once the Conselho Ultramarino concluded its re-assessment, the King lost little time in accepting the recommendation put forth by his advisory council. Sometime during the late summer or early autumn of 1695 a new *Provisão* was passed to annul that of 1679.[67] Henceforth cane brandy could once again be legally exported from Brazil to Luanda.

Although both Portuguese and Brazilian slave trading interests had been at the forefront of the campaign against the ban on *cachaça* imports, the withdrawal of the 1679 *Provisão* from the legislative books clearly favoured the latter. Brazilian trading houses were now again legally able to use this low cost consumer good, produced on a large scale in their own backyard and much sought after in the hinterland of Luanda, to acquire the large number of slaves necessary to service the enslaved labour requirements of sugar plantations inland from Salvador and Recife, as well as of the nascent mining industry in Minas Gerais. By lifting the ban on the export of cane brandy from Brazil to the colonial capital of Angola, the Portuguese Crown not only encouraged increasingly larger amounts of this distilled spirit to be imported, but also provided commercial interests in the land of Vera Cruz with a golden opportunity to further strengthen their domination of the slave trade conducted there and throughout its interior.

Brazilian commercial interests did not lose much time in seizing the advantage offered to them by the repeal of the 1679 ban. Soon after the close of 1695, cane brandy exports to Luanda began to attain the levels of the late 1660s and the 1670s. It is not possible to follow the annual flow of this increased commerce during the whole second half of the 1690s for lack of import statistics at Luanda

---

[66] "Parecer" of the Conselho Ultramarino dated 17–08–1695, AHU, Angola, Cx. 15, Doc. 37 or AHU, Cód. 554, fls. 85–85v.

[67] The date of the new instructions is not known. It was promulgated sometime between the end of August and the beginning of December of 1695. See King to the Oficiais da Câmara, 9–12–1695, AHU, Cód. 545, fls. 94v–95. Coincidentally, this development also took place soon after João de Lencastre, who laboured to have the ban lifted while Governor of Angola, had assumed the governorship of Brazil in 1694. See Ross L. Bardwell, "The Governors of Portugal's South Atlantic Empire in the Seventeenth Century: Social Background, Qualifications, Selection, Reward". Unpublished Ph. D. dissertation, University of California at Santa Barbara, 1974, p. 72.

and Brazilian export reports. Nevertheless, the extant alcohol tax accounts of the Municipal Council of Angola's colonial capital for 1699, which also list the amount of alcohol offloaded throughout that year at its port, provide a penetrating insight into this renewed legal trade at the very end of the seventeenth century. These records show a total of 685 *pipas* of intoxicants as imported in this seaport during all of 1699.[68] Of this overall amount, *cachaça* from Brazil accounted for 639.5 *pipas*, or roughly ninety-three percent. In sharp contrast, the wine and *aguardente* offloaded during the same period from Portugal represented but a combined volume of forty-five and a half *pipas*, or almost seven percent of the total alcohol imported. Thus, within a few years following the repeal of the 1679 *Provisão*, *cachaça* imports in Angola's colonial capital not only rose appreciably but almost totally displaced alcohol imports from Portugal.

Much of the increasing volume of legal cane brandy unloaded at Luanda during the second half of the 1690s continued to be forwarded to slave markets along the Kwanza River, where it was traded for slaves.[69] Because the Brazilian share of the alcohol trade in Luanda soon attained overwhelming proportions, it is reasonable to suppose, in the absence of firm data, that trading interests in the land of Vera Cruz thereby gained control over a larger part of its expanding slave trade. With grape wine and *aguardente* imports having hit rock bottom, on the other hand, the number of slaves acquired by Portuguese traders in return for metropolitan alcohol most probably shrank to the low levels of the third quarter of the seventeenth century.

As was the case prior to and, indeed, during the period in which the 1679 *Provisão* was in effect, the once again thriving legal export of sugar cane brandy to Luanda continued to be dominated by trading firms based in northeastern Brazil. Of the 639.5 *pipas* of this distilled spirit imported in the colonial capital of Angola during 1699, 561 or almost eighty-eight per cent were dispatched from two ports: Salvador was by far the most important source of this cane brandy with 393 *pipas*, representing sixty-one and a half percent of the Brazilian total; Recife, on the other hand, from where 168 *pipas* of *cachaça* originated, was a distant second with a twenty-six percent

---

[68] See Graph 2.

[69] Barbot, "Voyage to the Congo River," p. 519. Barbot also lists grape wine as another intoxicating drink used to obtain slaves in the various *feiras* found throughout the hinterland of Luanda.

share of the trade.[70] A third Brazilian port was also emerging as a supplier of the cane brandy imported at Luanda. This was Rio de Janeiro, from where 78.5 *pipas* or some twelve and a half percent of the total volume of *cachaça* imported in the colonial capital of Angola during 1699 originated.[71] Thus, even though data on the number and destination of the slaves exported from Luanda during the late seventeenth century are lacking, the overwhelming majority of those acquired in exchange for *gerebita* surely continued to have Salvador and Recife as their destination.

Conclusion

The attempt by commercial interests in northeastern Brazil to break the monopoly of metropolitan merchant capitalists over the slave trade at Luanda constitutes one of the more important chapters in the economic past of this West Central African port. It clearly shows that Brazilian colonial traders possessed a locally produced item of exchange that could be turned into an appropriate and indeed advantageous commodity for slave trading in Africa. It also explicitly demonstrates that, once the decision was made to enter the Atlantic slave trade with *cachaça*, they could effectively compete with European merchant capitalists to acquire slaves from African suppliers. As this process unfolded during the second half of the seventeenth century, the trade for slaves in Luanda and throughout its hinterland underwent a radical transformation. *Gerebita*, in particular, totally replaced intoxicants from the metropole as the most important alcoholic beverage with which slaves were procured. This, in turn, brought about a significant decrease in the alcohol commerce which merchant capitalists in Portugal had carried on with Luanda and, equally important, an end to the monopoly which they had exercised over slave trading in this port town and its interior. With such an important foothold established in the Luanda slave trade, colonial traders in the land of Vera Cruz were thereby able to wrest a growing share of the profits obtained from this lucrative commerce for themselves.

---

[70] See Graph 2.

[71] *Ibid.* Salvador, *Os Cristãos-Novos e o Comércio*, p. 351, indicates that this distillate was already an appreciable item in Rio's trade with Luanda by the second half of the 1600s, but without providing any figures or sources.

PLATES 1–11

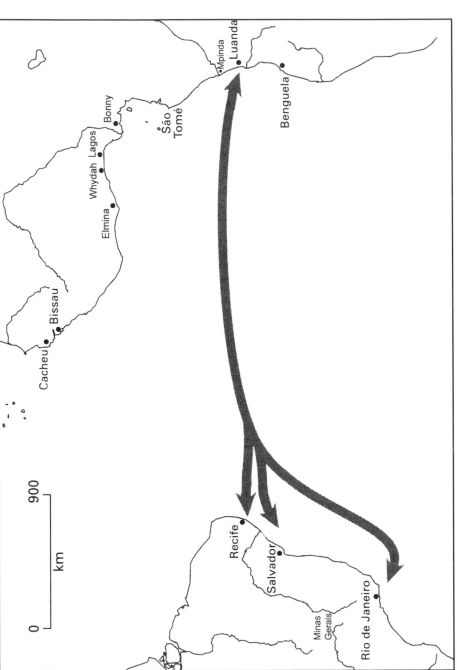

Plate 01. Luanda and Brazil. Digital Library, Harriet Tubman Resource Centre on the African Diaspora, York University.

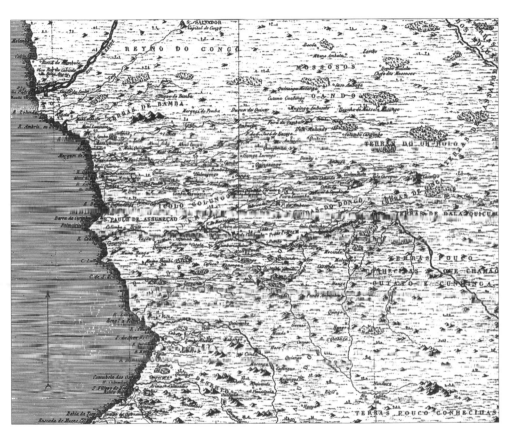

Plate 02. Luanda and its Hinterland, 1790. João C. Feo Cardoso de Castello Branco e Torres, *Memórias Contendo a Biographia do Vice Almirante Luis da Motta Feo e Torres, a História dos Governadores e Capitaes Generaes de Angola desde 1575 até 1825, e a Descripção Geográphica e Política dos Reinos de Angola e Benguella.* Paris, 1825.

Palma che fa oglio, e uino

Plate 03. Engemas in the Kingdom of Kongo. Girolamo Merolla da Sorrento, *Breve e Succunta Relatione del Viaggio nel Regno di Congo.* Naples, 1692.

Plate 04. Beer Drinking, Tamba. Jean-Baptiste Douville, *Atlas du Voyage au Congo et dans l'intérieur de l'Afrique equinoxiable, fait dans les années 1828, 1829 et 1830*. Paris, 1832.

Plate 05. Slave Coffle, Mayombe. Louis de Grandpré, *Voyage à la côte occidentale d'Afrique, fait dans les années 1786 et 1787*. Paris, 1801, Vol. 2.

Plate 06. Luanda, 1816. João C. Feo Cardoso de Castello Branco e Torres, *Memórias Contendo a Biographia do Vice Almirante Luis da Motta Feo e Torres, a História dos Governadores e Capitaes Generaes de Angola desde 1575 a é 1825, e a Descripção Geográphica e Política dos Reinos de Angola e Benguella.* Paris, 1825.

Plate 07. Slaves in the Ship's Hold. Johann M. Rugendas, *Malerische Reise in Brasilien*. Paris and Mülhausen, 1835, Part IV.

Plate 08. Slave Market, Brazil. Johann M. Rugendas, *Malerische Reise in Brasilien*. Paris and Mülhausen, 1835, Part IV.

Plate 09. Sugar Mill, Brazil 1816. Henry Koster, *Travels in Brazil*. London, 1816.

Plate 10. Loading-Unloading Casks of "Wet" Goods, Brazilian Port. Jean-Baptiste Debret, *Voyage pittoresque et historique au Brésil*. Paris, 1834-1839.

Plate 11. Ginga Drinking Rum. Jean-Baptiste Douville, *Atlas du Voyage au Congo et dans l'intérieur de l'Afrique equinoxiable, fait dans les années 1828, 1829 et 1830*. Paris, 1832.

CHAPTER FIVE

THE LONG CENTURY OF GEREBITA:
THE LUSO-BRAZILIAN ALCOHOL TRADE AT LUANDA
AND ITS HINTERLAND, c. 1700–1830

Soon after the *Provisão* banning the importation of Brazilian cane brandy at Luanda was lifted in 1695, *cachaça* imports in Angola's colonial capital began to rise appreciably once again. As was the case ever since *gerebita* had found a market in this seaport and its hinterland during the mid-1600s, most of this distilled alcohol continued to originate from two Brazilian ports: Salvador and Recife. Nevertheless, by the end of the seventeenth century, another coastal urban centre in the land of Vera Cruz, Rio de Janeiro, emerged as a third supplier of *gerebita* unloaded in the port of Angola's colonial capital. Initially quite small, the amount of *cachaça* emanating from this new source was to increase in direct proportion to the expanding gold mining industry in Minas Gerais which greatly fueled the urban economy of Rio de Janeiro and its rural sugar plantations. As demand for slaves to work in the various sectors of this booming economy augmented significantly, trading houses in Rio de Janeiro responded by exporting ever greater quantities of this intoxicant to Luanda in order to obtain the necessary number of enslaved labourers. Colonial traders in Rio de Janeiro thereby became the leading Brazilian suppliers of the *gerebita* imported in the colonial capital of Angola, a position which was to remain theirs until after the slave trade in the southern Atlantic was legally abolished in 1830. Moreover, in the process, they further enlarged the breach which commercial interests in Salvador and Recife had opened in the monopoly of the Luanda slave trade previously exercised by Portuguese merchant capitalists. The broken monopoly of the latter was never completely shattered. But the widening fissure caused by the rise of Rio de Janeiro in the Luanda alcohol trade was to enable its trading houses to gain direct control over a significant percentage of the slaves exported through the colonial capital of Angola.

I. *The Rise of Rio in the Luanda Alcohol and Slave Trades*

The first years of the eighteenth century saw the volume of *gerebita* imports at Luanda remain practically unchanged from the latter 1690s. During 1700–1703, for example, an estimated 2,807.5 *pipas* of *cachaça* were offloaded in the colonial capital of Angola.[1] This works out to an annual average of roughly 702 *pipas*, an amount just 10% higher than the 639.5 large wooden casks known to have been imported during all of 1699. In contrast, alcohol imports from the metropole seem to have undergone a sizeable increase. The estimated volume of metropolitan alcohol imports at Luanda during 1700–1703 was about 901.5 *pipas* of both *aguardente* and *vinho*.[2] This averages to roughly 225 *pipas* per year, representing a five fold increase over the forty five and a half *pipas* of metropolitan alcohol offloaded throughout 1699.

The extant documentation provides no clues as to the possible reasons behind such a substantial jump. Given that data on late seventeenth century imports are available but for one year, 1699, it is quite possible that the early eighteenth century figures are no more than a statistical anomaly. It is also just as likely that the noted increase reflects an answer on the part of metropolitan merchant capitalists to the late 1695 legalization of Brazilian cane brandy imports in the colonial capital of Angola: that is, significantly larger volumes of *aguardente* and especially *vinho* to achieve a level of competitiveness vis-à-vis *cachaça*, the major alcoholic beverage used, now once again, legally, to acquire slaves. But if this were indeed the case, it was a question of too little too late. By the close of the 1600s, Bacchus had already long surrendered to "Demon Rum." The estimated amount of alcohol imported from the metropole during 1700–1703 was but one-third of the calculated total volume of *gerebita* offloaded during the same four year period.[3] And, as the eighteenth century progressed, the ratio was only to increase in favour of *cachaça*.

---

[1] This figure has been arrived at by subtracting the 1699 import *gerebita* volumes shown in Graph 2 from the estimated aggregate total of 1699–1703 as found in Graph 3.

[2] This figure is the result of subtracting the 1699 metropolitan alcohol import volume listed in Graph 2 from the estimated aggregate total of 1699–1703 found in Graph 3.

[3] See Graph 3.

Indeed, the volume of *gerebita* imports at Luanda during the early 1700s did not remain similar to that of the late seventeenth century for long. The mid-1690s had witnessed the discovery of gold and diamonds in Minas Gerais, a captaincy in the interior of Rio de Janeiro. The nascent mining industry thereafter expanded quickly, which in turn fuelled the coastal urban economy of Rio de Janeiro and its rural sugar plantations.[4] And with these sectors of Brazil's southeastern economy booming, demand for enslaved labourers increased significantly throughout the region.[5] This led commercial houses in Rio de Janeiro to enter the slave trade conducted at Luanda, the closest and largest slave trading port across the southern Atlantic, exactly the same way as their counterparts in Salvador and Recife had done half a century before. They, too, began to forward their own commercial representatives to the colonial capital of Angola to establish subsidiary trading firms.[6] Furthermore, they also adopted *cachaça*, an increasingly important commodity produced in the expanding sugar plantations of southeastern Brazil, as the most advantageous item of exchange with which to supply their Luanda trade representatives for the purpose of acquiring slaves.

Initially, the intrusion of Rio de Janeiro into this commerce was extremely modest. In 1699, for example, only seventy-eight and a half of the 639.5 *pipas* of *gerebita* imported in the colonial capital of Angola originated from the emporium emerging behind Guanabara Bay.[7] The number of slaves acquired then at Luanda by Rio de Janeiro trading houses in exchange for this intoxicant must have thus been comparatively small. But as the Minas Gerais mining industry continued to expanded at an unrelenting pace during the early

---

[4] Rudolph W. Bauss, "Rio de Janeiro: The Rise of Late Colonial Brazil's Dominant Emporium, 1777–1808," Unpublished Ph. D. dissertation, Tulane University, 1977, pp. 17, and 23; Eulalia Maria Lahmeyer Lobo, "O Comércio Atlântico e a Comunidade de Mercadores no Rio de Janeiro e em Charleston no Século XVIII," *Revista de História*. No. 101, 1975, p. 58; and idem, "Economia do Rio de Janeiro nos Séculos XVIII e XIX," in Paulo Neuhaus, ed. *Economia Brasileira: Uma Visão Histórica*. Rio de Janeiro, 1980, pp. 127–129.

[5] Boxer, *Golden Age of Brazil*, pp. 39–60; A. J. R. Russell-Wood, "Colonial Brazil: The Gold Cycle, c. 1695–1750," in Bethell, *Colonial Brazil*, pp. 194–197; Lobo, "O Comércio Atlântico e a Comunidade de Mercadores no Rio de Janeiro," pp. 58–59; and Miller, "Slave Prices in the Portuguese Southern Atlantic," pp. 48–49.

[6] Pardo, "Comparative Study of the Portuguese Colonies," p. 103; Miller, "Numbers, Origins and Destinations of Slaves," pp. 87–88; and idem, *Way Of Death*, pp. 330–331.

[7] See Graph 2.

decades of the eighteenth century, trading houses in Rio de Janeiro begun exporting ever greater quantities of *cachaça* to Luanda so as to obtain the necessarily larger number of slaves required by their booming regional economy.

By 1727–1728, the average volume of *cachaça* unloaded at Luanda attained an estimated 2,481 *pipas* per annum.[8] This represented a staggering jump of almost 260% over the importation levels at the turn of the seventeenth century. Although data are not available to establish the specific origin of these significantly higher *gerebita* imports, indirect evidence strongly indicates that they were due to greater *cachaça* exports from Guanabara Bay. The expanding demand for enslaved labour created by Brazil's booming southeastern economy led to a significant rise in the number of slaves exported from Luanda from the late 1600s onwards. From 1710–1715 to 1718–1728 alone, the number of enslaved labourers exported through Angola's colonial capital rose from an average of 4,618.5 to 6,862 per annum, a jump of nearly 50%.[9] Moreover, by the 1720s, Rio de Janeiro had emerged from a negligible to the single most important recipient of the slaves exported from Luanda. Salvador still received almost 43.5% and Recife 10.5% of this trade: but Rio de Janeiro now dominated with a 44.5% share of the total.[10] With the volume of slaves exported from the colonial capital of Angola to Salvador and Recife declining appreciably during the first two decades of the eighteenth century, Luanda's extremely high *cachaça* imports of the late 1720s could only have originated from one predominant source: Guanabara Bay, which had become the major destination for the rising number of slaves shipped through this port.

If Luanda witnessed a substantial jump in the amount of *gerebita* imported during the late 1720s, a different trend affected its *aguardente* and *vinho* imports. Compared to 1699–1703, the volume of alcohol imported from the metropole during 1727–1728 had also risen by some 82%. Yet, the overall quantities remained rather low at an estimated average of 290 *pipas* of *vinho* offloaded in each of these two years, while *aguardente* imports amounted to a mere 54.5 large wooden casks.[11] Such comparatively small quantities of metropolitan

---

[8] See Graph 4.
[9] See Graph 5.
[10] Miller, "Numbers, Origins, and Destinations of Slaves," p. 96.
[11] See Graph 4.

alcohol probably restricted Portuguese slave traders to acquiring an equally low number of the enslaved labourers shipped during the late 1720s from Luanda in exchange of these intoxicants.

The 1727–1728 estimated volumes of *gerebita* imports at Luanda may very well have been one of the highest until the very end of the eighteenth century. The late 1720s and the early 1730s appear to have been the years when merchant firms in the land of Vera Cruz, especially those located in Rio de Janeiro, secured their highest share of the Luanda slave trade by exchanging unparalleled amounts of this distilled spirit for a similarly unprecedented number of slaves.[12] If such was the case, however, their control over the traffic was far from complete. Although possessing an extremely advantageous item of exchange in the form of *cachaça*, Brazilian trading houses lacked the most sought after consumer and luxury good of all in West Central Africa, European and Asian trade cloths.[13] From the very beginning of the slave trade, metropolitan merchant capitalists exported huge amounts of these most favourable and advantageous items of exchange to their Portuguese agents and private customers in Angola's colonial capital to trade for slaves. And the first decades of the 1700s were no exception.[14] Local Portuguese slave traders and merchant capitalists in Lisbon were thus able to maintain their overall dominance over the slave trade carried out in the interior of and from this port town in spite of the ever growing volume of *cachaça* imports.

The inability of *cachaça* to provide Brazilian trading houses with

---

[12] Miller, "Paradoxes of Impoverishment," p. 135. More recent research by Brazilian historians suggests that Rio de Janeiro merchant houses had indeed become, by this time, heavily involved in slave trading. See João L. R. Fragoso and Manolo G. Florentino, *O Arcaísmo como Projeto: Mercado Atlântico, Sociedade Agrária e Elite Mercantil no Rio de Janeiro, c. 1790–c. 1840*. Rio de Janeiro, 1993, p. 35; and Florentino, *Em Costas Negras*, p. 37.

[13] Miller, "Paradoxes of Impoverishment," p. 135.

[14] On the continued predominance of trade cloths in the Luanda slave trade during this period, see Birmingham, *Trade and Conflict*, p. 138; Miller, "Slave Trade in Congo and Angola," pp. 103–104; João Vicente dos Santos, "Lista dos generos convenientes para Angola," 1712 in Lisanti, ed., *Negócios Coloniais*, Vol. IV, pp. 412–413; the undated, but circa 1750s, report on metropolitan commerce with West Central Africa, penned by Francisco Henrique Hubens, AHU, Angola, Cx. 179, Doc. 88; and paragraph no. 72 of the "Instruções para José Gonçalo da Câmara," 1779, AHU, Angola, Cx. 62, Doc. 57. Between 1785 and 1823, cloths accounted for some 60% by value of all imports at Luanda. See Miller, "Imports at Luanda," pp. 192 and 215–222.

a greater share of the Luanda slave trade seems to have been realized precisely when the importation of this alcoholic drink there was
at an apex. Shortly after 1730, many of the trade representatives of
merchant firms in the land of Vera Cruz, especially those with
affiliation in Rio de Janeiro, began to move their operations from
Angola's colonial capital to Benguela, away from the dominance of
Portuguese slave traders and metropolitan commercial capitalists.[15]
Their physical relocation in another West Central African colonial
port town, whose interior slave markets were also still largely unex-
ploited, could be interpreted as a major defeat in the Brazilian
attempt to gain a significant share of the Luanda slave trade. However, this was far from being the case.

As argued in Chapter Four, the presence of Brazilian commercial
representatives was not the most decisive prerequisite for their parent
firms to break the monopoly which metropolitan merchant capitalists
and their trade representatives had exercised until the 1650s over
the commerce for slaves conducted in the interior of and from
Luanda. Of far greater importance was possession of and control
over an extremely advantageous item of exchange such as *cachaça*.
Produced on a large scale in their own colony, Brazilian trading
interests not only had easy access to this low cost and much sought
after consumer item, but also controlled its shipping and, hence,
export to the colonial capital of Angola.[16] In order to acquire the
ever rising number of slaves required by the sugar plantations, urban
centres, and mining industry of their colony during the 1730s and
the 1740s, they continued to forward large volumes of *cachaça* to the

---

[15] Miller, "Paradoxes of Impoverishment," p. 135.

[16] After 1640, following the destruction of much of the metropolitan merchant
navy during the era of the dual monarchy, most of the Luso-Brazilian ships plow-
ing the southern Atlantic originated from the land of Vera Cruz. See Carlos A. M.
do Couto, *Os Capitães-Mores Em Angola no Século XVIII: Subsídio para o Estudo da Sua
Actuação*. Luanda, 1972, pp. 190–191; Herbert S. Klein, *The Middle Passage: Comparative
Studies in the Atlantic Slave Trade*. Princeton, 1978, p. 41; Pardo, "Comparative Study,"
p. 103; Fernando A. Novais, *Portugal e Brasil na Crise do Antigo Sistema Colonial
(1777–1808)*. São Paulo, 1979, p. 195; Bauss, "Rio de Janeiro," p. 119; Selma A.
Pantoja, "O Encontro nas Terras de Além-Mar: Os Espaços Urbanos do Rio de
Janeiro, Luanda, e Ilha de Moçambique na era da Ilustração," Unpublished Ph.D.
dissertation, Universidade de São Paulo, 1994, p. 22; Florentino, *Em Costas Negras*,
pp. 119–120 and 194; and João L. R. Fragoso, *Homens de Grossa Aventura: acumulação e hierarquia na praça mercantil do Rio de Janeiro (1790–1830)*. Rio de Janeiro, 1992,
p. 194. The data presented in Graph 6 on the origin of vessels docking at the port
of Luanda are, in this respect, particularly revealing.

major slaving port in West Central Africa.[17] Now, however, they shipped this commodity no longer just to their own trade agents who remained there, since these were relatively few, but increasingly to the more numerous Portuguese slave traders. Having adopted cane brandy in order to effectively compete with Brazilian slave traders, the latter continued to require *gerebita* to improve the marketability of other trade goods, which were often of poor quality and more expensive, during transactions for slaves throughout the interior.[18] Consequently, the number of enslaved labourers which Brazilian merchant firms thereafter obtained for their *cachaça* exports must have remained significant. The share of the Luanda slave trade which they had gained in previous decades was thus most probably maintained.

The 1750s, on the other hand, saw the Brazilian economy begin to slow down. By the early 1760s, the decline turned into a full recession: the end of the Seven Years War and its concomitant military activities in the Caribbean appreciably reduced European demand for Brazilian sugar, while and gold and diamond production in Minas Gerais started to drop.[19] Fewer slaves were now required to work in the sugar plantations, urban centres, and mining industry of Brazil. The lower demand for enslaved labourers in the land of Vera Cruz immediately affected the export of slaves from the colonial capital of Angola. Slave exports from Luanda fell to 101,805 during the 1750s, a 3.5% decrease from the 104,406 shipped in the previous decade: but, over the course of the 1760s, they plummeted to 82,911 or by a substantial margin of 18.5%.[20] As the recession set in, Brazilian cane brandy exports to this port naturally began to fall. During 1756–1761 *gerebita* imports there decreased to an estimated average of 1,962.5 *pipas* per year.[21] This represented a significant 21% drop

---

[17] This is clearly suggested by the shipping data in Graph 6.

[18] José Ribeiro Júnior, *Colonização e Monopólio do Noreste Brasileiro: A Companhia Geral de Pernambuco e Paraíba (1759–1780)*. São Paulo, 1976, p. 125.

[19] Eulalia Maria Lahmeyer Lobo, *História do Rio de Janeiro (do Capital Comercial ao Capital Industrial e Financeiro)*. Rio de Janeiro, 1978, Vol. 1, p. 35; Bauss, "Rio de Janeiro," pp. 32 and 50–60; Boxer, *Golden Age of Brazil*, p. 302; and Simonsen, *História Econômica do Brasil*, pp. 254, 261, 278, and 298.

[20] See Graph 5.

[21] See Graph 4. One source from the late 1750s informs that "more than twelve ships leave Salvador every year for Luanda laden with European and Asian goods, *cachaça*, and other items to acquire slaves and wax." See Jozé Antonio Caldas, "Noticia Geral de toda esta Capitania da Bahia desde o Seu descobrimento até o Prezente Anno de 1759," *Revista do Instituto Geographico e Historico da Bahia*. Vol. 57,

over its 1727–1728 importation level. Even metropolitan alcohol imports suffered a parallel decline during this six year period. *Vinho* dropped to an estimated annual average of 229.3 *pipas* and *aguardente* to 43 large wooden casks.[22]

The slave based economy in the land of Vera Cruz fell to its most depressed state during the 1770s. Appropriate quantitative information is lacking to determine the volume of *cachaça* that was exported to Luanda during this decade. But the 1770s was a period during which fewer slaves were shipped from this seaport than in previous decades. Only 75,743, or almost 28% less compared to the 1760s, were exported.[23] One can thus conclude that the amount of *cachaça* exported to acquire fewer slaves had to have been necessarily lower than that of the first half of the 1700s.[24] Such an appraisal is given further weight by existing quantitative data on metropolitan alcohol exports to Angola's colonial capital. Lisbon merchant capitalists dispatched an annual average of 177 *pipas* of *vinho* from 1775 to 1777 and thirty large wooden casks of *aguardente* during 1776–1777 to this port town.[25] Compared to 1756–1761, this suggests a significant drop there of nearly one quarter in the metropole's alcohol trade. With the Brazilian economy at its lowest ebb, even Lisbon merchant capitalists found it necessary to reduce further their alcohol exports to Luanda.

In spite of decreased volumes of imported alcohol available at Luanda after 1750, Luso-Brazilian slave traders there nevertheless persisted in forwarding appreciable quantities of *gerebita* and smaller amounts of *vinho* and *aguardente* to slave markets along the Kwanza

---

1931, p. 229. This could be construed as meaning that no decline took place. But the downward trend is further suggested by the shipping data, including those which relate to Salvador, found in Graph 6. Indeed, by 1761, there was a shortage of *gerebita* at Luanda, confirming that a decrease in the cane brandy trade with Angola's colonial capital occurred. See Júnior, *Colonização e Monopólio do Nordeste Brasileiro*, p. 125.

[22] These figures are taken from Graph 4.

[23] See Graph 5.

[24] The anonymous "Discurso Preliminar, Historico, Introductivo, com Natureza de Descripção Economica da Comarca e Cidade da Bahia" *Annaes da Bibliotheca Nacional do Rio de Janeiro*. Vol. 27, 1905, p. 345, informs that only a few, small ships ladden with Brazilian colonial products left for Luanda during this decade from Salvador. Even *cachaça* exports from Rio de Janeiro to Portugal dwindled appreciably during the 1770s. See Santos, *Relações Comerciais do Rio de Janeiro*, p. 165.

[25] These totals are taken from Graph 10.

River, particularly that at Kasanje.[26] This enabled trading interests
in the land of Vera Cruz to retain much of their share of the slave
trade conducted in the colonial capital of Angola and throughout its
interior. One mid-level colonial official estimated in the early 1770s
that 81,280 slaves had been exported during the previous decade
through this town, a figure lower by only 1,631 than the cumula-
tive total known to have been actually shipped.[27] According to this
same source, the overall value of these slaves amounted to some
2,438,000$000 or 79% of the roughly 3,083,000$000 réis total exports
from Luanda throughout the decade.[28] The overall value of Brazilian
imports at Luanda and Benguela, on the other hand, is given as
amounting to 1,600,000$000 réis, primarily in the form of gerebita.[29]
Although not very precise, this last piece of information indicates
that cachaça most probably represented from half to three-quarters
in value of Brazilian imports, or 800,000$000 to 1,200,000$000 réis.[30]
Much of this gerebita landed at Angola's colonial capital, not Benguela.
Between 1798 and 1809, for example, almost 82% of the combined
Luanda-Benguela cachaça imports was offloaded at West Central
Africa's premier seaport.[31] If roughly the same percentage held true
in the 1760s, Luanda would have then imported anywhere between

---

[26] See Gastão Sousa Dias, ed., (Manoel Correia Leitão) "Uma Viagem a Cassange
nos Meados do Século XVIII," in Boletim da Sociedade de Geografia de Lisboa. Vol. 56,
1938, p. 16.

[27] "Calculo dos Effeitos que annualmente sahem de Loanda e Benguela e da
importancia da Fazenda que annualmente deve entrar nos ditos dous Portos," AHU,
Angola, Cx. 54, Doc. 28. The actual number of slaves exported throughout the
1760s was 82,911. See Graph 5.

[28] "Calculo dos Effeitos que annualmente sahem de Loanda e Benguela," AHU,
Angola, Cx. 54, Doc. 28.

[29] Ibid.

[30] During the late 1790s and early 1800s, that is after colonial traders in Brazil
began to supplement their gerebita commerce at both Luanda and Benguela with
Euro-Asian trade goods, cachaça still made up 45% in value of all of imports from
the land of Vera Cruz. This figure is taken from the combined Luanda-Benguela
values of the gerebita imported in 1798, 1802 and 1809: out of a total 1,075,250$200
réis worth of Brazilian imports, 483,549$300 were in the form of cachaça. See Graph
8 for Luanda and Curto, "Luso-Brazilian Alcohol and the Legal Slave Trade at
Benguela and its Hinterland," pp. 351–369, for Benguela. From the sources at hand,
1798, 1802, and 1809 are the first years for which such a calculation is possible.

[31] This figure is taken from the combined Luanda-Benguela cachaça import totals
of 1798, 1802, 1805 and 1809, the first years for which such a calculation is possible. Of the combined 9,882.25 pipas imported, 8,076.75 landed at Luanda and
1,805.5 at Benguela. See Graph 7 for the former and Curto, "The Luso-Brazilian
Alcohol Commerce at Benguela," for the latter.

656,000$000 and 984,400$000 *réis* worth of *gerebita*. These *cachaça* import values, in turn, would have represented between 21 and 32% of Luanda's total exports and between 27 and 40.5% of the 82,911 slaves shipped,[32] The average of these percentages translates to a ratio ranging from roughly one in three (27,640) to one in four (20,730). In short, even during the depressed 1760s, the proportion of slaves acquired in the colonial capital of Angola in exchange of *gerebita* appears to have remained significant.

And most of the *cachaça* surely continued to arrive from Rio de Janeiro. Of the 191 Brazilian ships that docked at Luanda during the 1760s, roughly 53% originated from Guanabara Bay, 24.5% came from Salvador, and 22.5% originated from Recife.[33] As it happens, these percentages mirror the major Brazilian destinations of slaves exported from this port during the 1760s: while 24.5% were bound for Recife and 20.5% for Salvador, 48.5% were shipped to Rio de Janeiro.[34] Consequently, a majority of the slaves then obtained in the colonial capital of Angola in exchange for *cachaça* continued to have the trading houses of Rio de Janeiro as its destination.

II. *The Recovery of Gerebita and the Slave Trade at Luanda*

The early 1780s saw Brazil begin to recoup from the prolonged depression which had enveloped the colony since the mid-eighteenth century, a recovery helped by the American Revolution and the serious conflicts that simultaneously took place in the Caribbean. Increasing sugar prices in Europe led to a significant expansion in the production of this commodity throughout Brazil. The cultivation of tobacco also underwent an important rise to meet expanding demand in West Africa and in Europe. Similarly, cotton production jumped substantially to supply the rapidly growing cotton textile industries of both England and France. Moreover, production of

---

[32] Miller has worked out figures for the combined Luanda-Benguela trade in 1770 which fall within these exclusively Luanda ones. Using the same source as summarized in Jean-Luc Vellut, "Le royaume de Cassange et les réseaux luso-africains (ca. 1750–1810)," *Cahiers d'études africaines*. Vol. 15, 1975, p. 134, he calculates *gerebita* imports as accounting for about 28% of all Luanda-Benguela exports and 41.7% of the value of slaves shipped. See Miller, *Way of Death*, p. 317.

[33] See Graph 6.

[34] Miller, "Numbers, Origins, and Destinations of Slaves," p. 96.

cacao and coffee also augmented greatly to satisfy the expanding
European need for these tropical consumer goods. Finally, the production of rice and wheat swelled appreciably to fill the chronic
shortages of these two foodstuffs in the metropole.[35] In short, the
first years of the 1780s were a period of resurrection for the plantation sector in the land of Vera Cruz and, by extension, for the
Brazilian economy as a whole.

The two decades preceding the 1780s had seen Brazilian slave
imports from Luanda decline to relatively low levels. Not surprisingly, the renaissance of the plantation sector in the land of Vera
Cruz created a greater need for servile labour to produce the rising
amounts of sugar, tobacco, cotton, coffee, cacao, rice, and wheat
required in Europe than was the case before.[36] To accommodate
this increased Brazilian demand, slave exports from the colonial capital of Angola rose from annual average of 7,574 during the 1770s
to 9,463 in the 1780s, a 25% jump.[37] In order to obtain part of the
larger numbers of enslaved labourers necessary for the increased production of these foodstuffs and raw materials, as well as to continue
supplying the slave labour requirements of the urban sector and the
dwindling mining industry, colonial traders in the land of Vera Cruz
naturally strove to augment their share of the slave trade in this port
town still further. A two-fold course of action was, once again, adopted
to attain this goal: first, a new wave of commercial agents was dispatched to set up shop in Luanda; and, second, these were flogged
by large amounts of the major Brazilian export commodity required
for slave trading in the colonial capital of Angola, *cachaça*.[38] And
here, as was the case before, the way was led by the trading houses

---

[35] On the revival of the Brazilian plantation economy see Dauril Alden, "Late
Colonial Brazil, 1750–1808," in Leslie Bethell, ed. *Colonial Brazil*. Cambridge, 1987,
pp. 310–336; James Lang, *Portuguese Brazil: The King's Plantation*. New York, 1979,
pp. 185–187; Caio Prado Jr., *História Econômica do Brasil*. São Paulo, 1970, pp. 79–87;
Simonsen, *História Econômica do Brasil*, pp. 363–364; and Bauss, "Rio de Janeiro,"
pp. 60 and ff.
[36] Alden, "Late Colonial Brazil," pp. 294 and 331; Lang, *Portuguese Brazil*, pp.
185–187; and Miller, *Way of Death*, p. 490.
[37] See Graph 5.
[38] Miller, *Way of Death*, p. 492. Miller adds that colonial Brazilian merchants also
began to supply their trade agents in Luanda with English manufactured goods illegally imported into the land of Vera Cruz. Nonetheless, cane brandy, one of the
few local colonial consumer items produced on a large scale and in heavy demand
throughout West Central Africa, was to remain the cornerstone of their commerce
with the colonial capital of Angola.

of Rio de Janeiro which, following the late 1770s, saw the production of cane brandy in their immediate hinterland increase substantially.[39]

Colonial traders in the land of Vera Cruz, however, were not the only ones beginning to forward rising volumes of alcohol to Luanda during the early 1780s. The increased production of sugar, tobacco, cotton, coffee, and cacao in Brazil enabled the metropolitan commercial sector to recover from the depression which had also struck the economy of Portugal during the third quarter of the eighteenth century by re-distributing larger and larger quantities of these tropical consumer goods and raw materials throughout Europe.[40] With the metropolitan commercial sector recuperating, merchant capitalists in Lisbon and Porto, too, started to augment their trade with the colonial capital of Angola.[41] As was the case before 1780, the growing metropolitan commerce there involved, amongst other trade goods, *vinho* and *aguardente*. Moreover, a variety of other European alcoholic beverages, such as beer, gin, liqueur, and Port wine, now also became part of the revived metropolitan trade in this seaport.[42]

---

[39] Production was heavily concentrated in Campos, Parati, Ilha Grande and the Guanabara Bay area, where ninety percent of all sugar and *cachaça* mills in the captaincy of Rio de Janeiro were located. See Bauss, "Rio de Janeiro," pp. 90 and 114. In 1778, according to Fragoso, *Homens de Grossa Aventura*, p. 84, Rio de Janeiro and its hinterland produced a total of 4,960.5 *pipas* of *cachaça*. The following year, according to Delso Renault, *Indústria, Escravidão, Sociedade: Uma Pesquiza Historiográfica do Rio de Janeiro no Século XIX*. Rio de Janeiro, 1976, p. 56, production in the Guanabara Bay area and its immediate surroundings was 3,969 *pipas*. These were already sizeable volumes, allowing even a total of 1,221 large wooden casks of this intoxicant to be shipped from Rio de Janeiro to Portugal in 1779. See "Memórias Públicas e Econômicas da Cidade de São-Sebastião do Rio de Janeiro para uso do Vice-Rei Luiz de Vasconcellos por Observação Curiosa dos Annos de 1779 até o de 1789," *Revista do Instituto Historico, Geographico e Ethnographico do Brasil*. Vol. XLVII, Part 1, 1884, pp. 49–51. By 1795–1797, production attained an average of 6,088 *pipas* per annum. See Corcino Medeiros dos Santos, *O Rio de Janeiro e a Conjuntura Atlântica*. Rio de Janeiro, 1993, p. 58.

[40] Simonsen, *História Económica do Brasil*, pp. 363–364; and Godinho, *Prix et Monnaies au Portugal*, pp. 258–276.

[41] Miller, *Way of Death*, pp. 607–622.

[42] Although the introduction of these "new" alcoholic beverages at Luanda can not be precisely dated, the available documentation suggests that this was during the first half of the 1780s, when intoxicants other than *gerebita*, *vinho* from Lisbon and Madeira, and *aguardente* are referred to. See article 55, no. 9 of the minutes of the instructions given to Barão de Moçâmedes upon being nominated Governor of Angola, undated, AHU, Angola, Cx. 65, Doc. 61; Queen to Governor Barão de Moçâmedes, 1–03–1784, AHU, Cód. 549, fls. 102v–103 or Cód. 556, fls. 2v–3; "Balanço da Importação, & Exportação deste Reîno de Angola desde a Anno de 1785 [. . .] até o Anno de 1794," 20–11–1797, AIHGB, DL794,28; and José Pinto

All of these new intoxicants, with the exception of beer, were also highly potent,[43] which made their belated appearance at Luanda fall within the long-standing practice of using heavily alcoholized intoxicants for slave trading purposes.

As both colonial traders in the land of Vera Cruz and metropolitan merchant capitalists exported greater and greater quantities of alcoholic beverages to Luanda, the Luso-Brazilian alcohol commerce with the colonial capital of Angola began to recover from the depressed volumes of the 1770s. From 1782 to 1784, *gerebita* imports at seaport reached 4,021 *pipas*, which averages out to some 1,340.5 large wooden casks per annum.[44] Given that the Brazilian economy had just started to recover, this was already a considerable amount, lower by only one-third in comparison to the larger quantities estimated as imported between 1756 and 1761. And, following the pattern established in the early eighteenth century, most of this distilled spirit continued to originate from just one port. A walloping 76% (3,050 *pipas*) came from Guanabara Bay,[45] the largest recorded share of Rio de Janeiro in the *gerebita* trade at Luanda. That originating from Salvador and Recife, on the other hand, represented but a combined 24% of the total *cachaça* imports.

Comparable quantitative data on the importation of metropolitan alcohol at Luanda is lacking for the early 1780s. Nevertheless, extant shipping data also points to a small rise in this commerce vis-à-vis the low import levels of the 1770s. A total of fourteen vessels originating from the metropole, thirteen from Lisbon and one from Porto, called at Angola's colonial capital between 1781 and 1784, for an

---

de Azeredo, *Ensaios sobre Algumas Enfermidades d'Angola*. Luanda, 1967 (but originally published in Lisbon in 1799), p. 74. In the specific case of Port wine, it may have been imported as early as the mid-eighteenth century. On this possibility, see Schneider, *Marquês de Pombal e o Vinho do Porto*, p. 216; and Ferreira, "Economia do Vinho e o Crescimento do Porto," p. 272.

[43] According to Pena, "Alcool na Ração Alimentar," p. 94, the alcohol content of Port wine, gin, and liqueur consumed during the early 1960s in Angola was 15.5 to 17, 28 to 50, and 50%, respectively.

[44] "Relação do Numero de Pipas de Gerebita Vindas dos Portos do Brasil," 5-01-1785, AHU, Angola, Cx. 70, Doc. 29.

[45] *Ibid*. Of the remaining 971 *pipas*, 591 or 14.7% came from Recife and 380 or 9.5% from Salvador. By way of comparison, *cachaça* exports from Rio de Janeiro to Lisbon during 1782-1784 totalled but 2,245 *pipas*. See Santos, *Relações Comerciais do Rio de Janeiro*, p. 165.

annual average of three and a half, which was exactly the same as that of the 1760s.[46] It is reasonable to assume that the growing number of metropolitan ships anchoring off this port town also transported larger quantities of *vinho* and *aguardente* in their bowels, as well as smaller amounts of beer, gin, liqueur, and/or Port wine. Yet, because the number of both Lisbon and Porto vessels engaged in trade with Luanda was modest compared to that of ships from the land of Vera Cruz, the overall volume of traditional and new European alcoholic beverages imported each year from the metropole must have been greatly below that from Brazil.

In 1784, the metropolitan government attempted to speed up the slowly recovering slave trade carried out in the colonial capital of Angola from its low ebb of the previous decades. The existing taxation system on alcoholic beverages offloaded in this seaport, the second most important item of exchange with which slaves were procured, was then altered by exempting *aguardente*, beer, *gerebita*, gin, *vinho*, liqueur, and Port wine imports destined solely for the purpose of acquiring slaves in the interior from all import and excise duties.[47] As a result, the Luso-Brazilian alcohol trade with Luanda expanded yet again.

Between 1785 and 1794, an average of 1,486 *pipas* of *cachaça* arrived per annum in the colonial capital of Angola.[48] Compared to the *gerebita* import levels of the early 1780s, this represented an increase of nearly 11%. The origin of vessels calling at Luanda during this ten-year period suggests that, even though *cachaça* imports from Salvador and Recife may have doubled, Rio de Janeiro remained the single most important source of this distilled alcohol. Ninety-four out of a total of 147 Brazilian ships came from this southern emporium, while only twenty-eight originated from Salvador and twenty-five departed from Recife.[49] Moreover, to supplement this growing commerce, colonial traders in Brazil began to periodically supply their commercial agents in Luanda with small quantities of European alcoholic drinks from their own alcohol imports. A further six and

---

[46] See Graph 6.

[47] For an analysis of alcohol import taxes at Luanda, see Chapter Seven below.

[48] "Balanço da Importação, & Exportação deste Reîno de Angola desde a Anno de 1785 [. . .] até o Anno de 1794," 20–11–1797, AIHGB, DL 794,28.

[49] See Graph 6.

a half *pipas* of liqueur were also offloaded annually from vessels originating in the land of Vera Cruz.[50]

Alcohol imports from Portugal, too, must have experienced a similar rise during this ten-year period. A total of forty-two metropolitan vessels, thirty-seven from Lisbon and five from Porto, called at
Angola's colonial capital between 1785 and 1794, for an increase of
20% over the 1760s and the early 1780s.[51] From these ships, an
average of approximately 322 *pipas* of *vinho*, sixty large wooden casks
of *aguardente*, five *pipas* of liqueur, and one and a half large wooden
casks of beer were unloaded per annum.[52] But these higher metropolitan volumes still made up only one-fifth of Luanda's total alcohol imports during 1785–1794.

The 1791 revolt in Saint-Domingue, the major sugar producing
colony of France, seriously perturbed the flow of tropical consumer
goods from the Caribbean to Europe. This development encouraged
plantation owners in the land of Vera Cruz to increase sugar production even more, thereby creating greater demand for African
enslaved labour than that which existed during the 1780s.[53] Reflecting
this higher demand, slave exports from Luanda jumped to an average of 10,260 per annum in the 1790s, a rise of 8.5% over the levels of the preceding decade.[54] In response to the increasing numbers
of African slave labourers required by the Brazilian plantation economy, larger amounts of imported alcoholic beverages were necessary
in Luanda. Moreover, towards the end of 1793, the trading community in this port town succeeded in securing from the colonial
government yet lower import duties on *gerebita*, *vinho*, and *aguardente*[55]
The Portuguese and Brazilian alcohol trade with the colonial capital of Angola consequently reached even larger proportions.

Between 1795 and 1797, a total 7,613 *pipas* of *cachaça* were offloaded

---

[50] "Balanço da Importação, & Exportação deste Reîno de Angola desde a Anno
de 1785 [. . .] até o Anno de 1794," 20–11–1797, AIHGB, DL794,28. This development was most likely in response to the introduction of "new" alcoholic beverages by metropolitan merchant capitalists.

[51] See Graph 6.

[52] "Balanço da Importação, & Exportação deste Reîno de Angola desde a Anno
de 1785 [. . .] até o Anno de 1794," 20–11–1797, AIHGB, DL794,28.

[53] Lang, *Portuguese Brazil*, pp. 185–186; Lobo, *História do Rio de Janeiro*, Vol. 1,
p. 41; Bauss, "Rio de Janeiro," p. 60 and 68–69; and Miller, "Legal Portuguese
Slaving," pp. 149–150.

[54] See Graph 5.

[55] For the a discussion of this development, see Chapter Seven below.

at Luanda.[56] Averaging almost 2,538 *pipas* per year, this was nearly a 71% increase over the annual import volume of 1785–1794. The overwhelming bulk of this distillate continued to arrive from just one port. Out of a total of sixty-one Brazilian ships calling at the colonial capital of Angola during this three year period, forty-one came from Rio de Janeiro, twelve arrived from Salvador, and eight originated from Recife.[57] Moreover, larger volumes of *cachaça* from Guanabara Bay may have been at the root of this increase, with the quantities imported from Salvador and Recife suffering a proportionate decrease. By itself, the major southern port in the land of Vera Cruz exported 2,272 *pipas* of *gerebita* to Luanda in 1796, which accounted for some 52% of its total *cachaça* exports.[58]

During this same three year period, the importation of metropolitan alcohol followed a somewhat different course. A total of slightly more than 1,309 *pipas* of *vinho* were offloaded.[59] Averaging roughly 436 large wooden casks per annum, this represented about a one-third increase over the amount of *vinho* annually imported during the previous ten years. The less important metropolitan alcohol imports, on the other hand, actually underwent a decrease: *aguardente* totalled but 120 *pipas*, while beer and liqueur amounted to just slightly over three large wooden casks, for a drop of 33% and 93%, respectively, compared to the volumes offloaded annually from 1785 to 1794.[60] Most of this alcohol originated from Lisbon, since no vessels were dispatched from Porto to Luanda in either 1796 or 1797.[61]

With most of Europe engaged in war during the late 1790s, however, demand for sugar plunged, leading the Brazilian economy into

---

[56] "Balanço da Importação e Exportação do Reîno de Angola nos Annos de 1795, 1796, e 1797," BNRJ, Divisão de Manuscritos, 15-3-33 No. 1.

[57] See Graph 6.

[58] "Mappa dos Efeitos que se Transportarão d'esta Cidade do Rio de Janeiro para os Portos Abaixo Declarados no Anno de 1796," in *Revista do Instituto Histórico e Geográfico Brasileiro*. Vol. 46, 1883, Part I, pp. 197–204. Representing 33% of all the *cachaça* produced in the captaincy of Rio de Janeiro (6,830 *pipas*), this figure was also almost double the volume of *cachaça* (1,195 *pipas*) exported from Rio de janeiro to Lisbon in 1796. See, respectively: Santos, *Rio de Janeiro e a Conjuntura Atlântica*, p. 58; and idem, *Relações Comerciais do Rio de Janeiro*, p. 165. Furthermore, data found in José J. de Andrade Arruda, *O Brasil no Comércio Colonial*. São Paulo, 1980, p. 407, indicate that slightly over 85% of all the cane brandy exported from Brazil during 1796 originated from Guanabara Bay.

[59] "Balanço da Importação e Exportação do Reîno de Angola nos Annos de 1795, 1796, e 1797," BNRJ, 15-3-33 No. 1.

[60] *Ibid.*

[61] "Balanço do Comercio do Reino de Portugal," for 1796 and 1797 in INE.

another recession.[62] This, in turn, decreased the need for new African slaves to be brought into the land of Vera Cruz. The number shipped from the colonial capital of Angola to Brazil dropped from an annual average of 10,665 in 1790–1796 to 9,014 during 1797–1800 or by 15.5%.[63] Consequently, after 1797 *gerebita* imports at Luanda fell to more stable quantities. An average of about 1,511 large wooden casks of this alcoholic beverage were unloaded both in 1798 and 1799, a quantity just slightly over that of the second half of the 1780s and the first half of the 1790s.[64] Almost all of this *cachaça* seems to have arrived from one port. From a total of twenty-three Brazilian ships calling at this seaport during this two year period, twenty originated at Rio de Janeiro, while only two came from Salvador and one arrived from Recife.[65] Both of the major coastal urban centres in northeastern Brazil thus virtually withdrew from the alcohol trade at Luanda.

Similarly, as the war ravaging much of Europe during the late 1790s threatened to spill into Portugal, metropolitan alcohol imports at Luanda also underwent a significant decline in 1798–1799. The volume of *vinho* offloaded fell to an average of 303 *pipas* each year, or almost 30% below the import levels of 1795–1797.[66] The importation of *aguardente* suffered an even sharper drop. While 120 *pipas* of this distilled spirit were unloaded from 1795 to 1797, only six large wooden casks of *aguardente* were imported during both 1798

---

[62] Miller "Legal Portuguese Slaving," p. 152.

[63] See Graph 5. According to Miller "Legal Portuguese Slaving," p. 152, this decrease was mainly due to colonial traders in Salvador and Recife greatly diminishing their slave trading at Luanda.

[64] Annual import reports in AHU, Angola: Cx. 89, Doc. 79 for 1798; and Cx. 93-A, Doc. 48 for 1799. According to Miller, *Way of Death*, p. 467, the production of *cachaça* in Rio de Janeiro during the later 1790s also decreased by half compared to the 2,477 *pipas* produced in the 1760s.

[65] See Graph 6. According to data available in Andrade Arruda, *Brasil no Comércio Colonial*, p. 407, Rio de Janeiro accounted for 87% of all the cane brandy exported from Brazil during 1798–1799.

[66] Annual import reports in AHU, Angola: Cx. 89, Doc. 79 for 1798: and Cx. 93-A, Doc. 48 for 1799. These very low volumes of *vinho* imported from the metropole continued through 1800 and 1801, since the amounts exported from Lisbon remained small. See Graph 11. This resulted in a particularly acute shortage of *vinho* at Luanda. See Governor Miguel António de Melo to Rodrigo de Sousa Coutinho, 17–08–1801, AHU, Angola, Cx. 101, Doc. 34 and Governor Fernando António de Noronha to Visconde de Anadia, 2–06–1803, *Arquivos de Angola*, 2nd series, Vol. XIX, Nos. 75–78, 1962, pp. 35–36.

and 1799.[67] Other metropolitan alcoholic beverages imported during these same two years amounted to a combined total of almost thirty-one *pipas* of beer and liqueur.[68] With no vessels dispatched to Luanda from Porto in 1798–1799, all of this alcohol must have originated from Lisbon.[69]

The late 1790s decline in the Luso-Brazilian alcohol commerce with the colonial capital of Angola, however, was but momentary. By the beginning of the nineteenth century, with peace returning to Europe, demand for tropical products was once again on the rise, leading to an increase in the number of new African slaves needed to service the plantation economy and urban centers in the land of Vera Cruz.[70] To supply this rising Brazilian demand, slave exports from the colonial capital of Angola jumped to an annual average of 12,156 during the first decade of the 1800s, an increase of 18.5% over the levels of the 1790s.[71] As a result, the volume of *cachaça* exported to Luanda correspondingly revived. From 1802 to 1804, an annual average of about 1,595 large wooden casks of *gerebita* were offloaded at Luanda, or an amount just slightly 5% higher than that of the last two years of the eighteenth century.[72] This modest increase was followed by Brazilian cane brandy imports attaining overwhelming proportions in 1805, with 3,041.5 *pipas* offloaded, or almost double the volume of the latter 1790s and the first years of

---

[67] Annual import reports in AHU, Angola: Cx 89, Doc. 79 for 1798; and Cx. 93-A, Doc. 48 for 1799.

[68] *Ibid.*

[69] "Balanço do Comercio do Reino de Portugal," for 1798 in AHMOP; and "Balanço do Comercio do Reino de Portugal," for 1799 in INE.

[70] Miller, "Legal Portuguese Slaving," p. 152.

[71] See Graph 5.

[72] See annual import reports in AHU, Angola: Cx. 106, Doc. 5 for 1802; Cx. 109, Doc. 54 for 1803; and Cx. 112, Doc. 47 for 1804. The "Receita do Rendimento do Subsidio Literário no Reino de Angola", on the other hand, presents conflicting *cachaça* import volumes during the first years of the nineteenth century: 1,387.5 *pipas* in 1800, 2,422 in 1801, 1,584.5 in 1802, and 2,383 in 1803. See, AHU, Angola, Cx. 102, Doc. 12, Cx. 105, Doc. 42, Cx. 106, Doc. 45, and Cx. 109, Doc. 25, respectively. According to this source, the amount of *gerebita* imported in 1802–1803 was 30% higher than that given in the annual import reports. It could thus very well be that the volume was much larger than the import reports indicate. But the "Receita do Rendimento Subsidio Literário" suffers from a number of drawbacks. First, 1800–1803 are the only years where the volumes of *cachaça* imports are actually presented. Second, although the small amounts of *aguardente* and liqueur offloaded are also listed, it provides no information on the larger *vinho* imports.

the nineteenth century. Moreover, 1805 also saw the arrival from the land of Vera Cruz of three *pipas* of another alcoholic beverage, liqueur.[73]

The importation of *cachaça* did not persist at such massive levels through 1806 1807. Another European recession drove demand for Brazilian colonial products and, hence, new African slave labourers in the land of Vera Cruz, downward.[74] Nonetheless, the quantities of this distilled spirit unloaded during each of these two years appear to have remained well above the amounts imported in the first half of this decade. In 1807, for example, an estimated 2,539 large wooden casks of *gerebita* were offloaded.[75] Rio de Janeiro still continued as the port from which most of the *cachaça* was imported, although both Salvador and Recife now re-entered the trade. Out of a total of 169 Brazilian vessels that called at Luanda from 1800 to 1808, one-hundred and twelve originated from this southern coastal urban centre, thirty-two arrived from Salvador, and twenty-five came from Recife.[76]

The return of peace throughout the European continent during the first decade of the 1800s, although momentary, also enabled Portugal's commerce in alcoholic beverages with the colonial capital of Angola to surpass the depressed levels of the late eighteenth

---

[73] Import report for 1805, AHU, Angola, Cx. 115, Doc. 14.

[74] On the European recession as it related to Portugal and Brazil see: Valentim Alexandre "Um Momento Crucial do Desenvolvimento Português: Efeitos Económicos da Perda do Império Brasileiro," *Ler História*. Vol. 7, 1986, p. 20; and Godinho, *Prix et Monnaies au Portugal*, p. 277. The resulting lower slave exports from Luanda are particularly noticeable after 1806. See Graph 5.

[75] See Graph 7. More conflicting data on *gerebita* imports during the early 1800s is found in Corcino M. dos Santos, "Relações de Angola com o Rio de Janeiro (1736–1738)," *Estudos Históricos*. No. 12, 1973, p. 9. Based on the number of Rio de Janeiro vessels calling at Luanda with *molhados* or "wet" goods, dos Santos lists *cachaça* imports as follows: 2,116 pipas in 1803, 2,085 in 1804, 1,815 in 1805, 2,342 in 1806, 1,732 in 1807, and 2,623 in 1808. The 1803–1804 amount of *gerebita* given here as imported from Guanabara Bay is 28% higher than all the *cachaça* imports given in the annual import reports for the same period. But, aside from being less chronologically comprehensive than the annual import report series, the data presented by dos Santos are also suspect. Alcoholic beverages were not the only type of *molhados* unloaded and, by the early 1800s, *gerebita* was no longer the only intoxicant imported from Rio de Janeiro.

[76] See Graph 6. The "Mappa de Exportação dos Produtos da Capitania da Bahia... em 1800," BNRJ, I–29, 19, 30, Doc. 02, lists only eighty *pipas* of cane brandy as exported during 1800 from Salvador to Luanda and Benguela. Rio de Janeiro, on the other hand, was responsible for almost 71% of all of the *cachaça* exported from Brazil from the beginning of 1800 until the end of 1807. See Andrade Arruda, *Brasil no Comércio Colonial*, p. 407.

century. Between 1802 and 1805, an annual average of roughly 559
pipas of *vinho*, fifteen large wooden casks of *aguardente*, and some fourteen *pipas* of beer and liqueur were offloaded.[77] This was a forty-six
per cent jump over the *vinho* and slightly more than double the beer
and liqueur importation levels of the second half of the 1790s,
although *aguardente* imports were nearly halved. After 1805, in contrast to what occurred in the case of Brazilian cane brandy, the economic recession that enveloped Europe did not adversely affect these
large metropolitan alcohol imports. To the contrary, the quantity of
alcohol offloaded at Luanda from Portugal remained quite stable. A
total of 1,093 large wooden casks of *vinho*, twenty-six *pipas* of *aguardente*,
and a small amount of liqueur were exported from the metropole
to the colonial capital of Angola during both 1806 and 1807.[78]

Lisbon merchant capitalists, however, were not at the root of these
high metropolitan alcohol import levels. During the first years of the
nineteenth century, following the tentative incursions of the 1780's
and early 1790's, merchant capitalists in Porto set out to break the
monopoly which their counterparts in Lisbon had exercised over the
metropole's alcohol trade at Luanda.[79] Between 1802 and 1807, they
exported 843 of the 2,410.4 *pipas* of wine dispatched from Portugal
to the colonial capital of Angola, or nearly one-third of the total.[80]
Thus, if the metropolitan alcohol trade in this port town expanded
significantly between 1802 and 1805 and then stabilized, as opposed
to what thereafter occurred in the case of Brazilian cane brandy, it

---

[77] Annual import reports in AHU, Angola: Cx. 109, Doc. 5 for 1802; Cx. 109,
Doc. 54 for 1803; Cx. 112, Doc. 47 1804; and Cx. 115, Doc. 14 for 1805.

[78] On *vinho* and *aguardente* exports from the metropole, see "Balanço do Comercio
do Reino de Portugal," for 1806 and 1807 in INE. On the liqueur offloaded see
the alcohol import report for the first three quarters of 1807 in AHU, Angola, Cx.
119, Doc. 48.

[79] Immediately following the late 1790s, when the volumes of *vinho* imported from
Lisbon were extremely depressed, there occurred an acute shortage of this alcoholic
beverage at Luanda. See Governor Melo to Rodrigo de Sousa Coutinho, 17–08–1801,
AHU, Angola, Cx. 101, Doc. 34. (A published version of this letter is also found
in *Arquivos de Angola*, 1st series, Vol. II, No. 15, 1936, p. 626.) The price of *vinho*
at Porto, on the other hand, was decreasing significantly from $600 *réis* in 1800 to
only $375 *réis* in 1807 per *almude*, a unit of liquid measure of about 20 litres. See
Godinho, *Prix et Monnaies au Portugal*, tables following p. 371. Porto merchant capitalists may thus have found in this conjuncture an excellent opportunity to break
the near total control which their counterparts in Lisbon exercised over the metropole's alcohol trade with the colonial capital of Angola.

[80] "Balanço do Comercio do Reino de Portugal," for 1802, 1803, 1804, 1805,
1806, and 1807 in INE.

was largely due to the intrusion made by merchant capitalists in Porto into this lucrative sector of the metropolitan overseas commerce. The monopoly which Lisbon merchant capitalists had held over the alcohol trade of Portugal with Luanda thereby came to an abrupt end.

Late in 1807, however, Portugal experienced yet another invasion by French and Spanish republican military forces which led to its occupation. This compelled the Portuguese court, most of the nobility, and many merchant capitalists to flee to Brazil.[81] Once on their way, British naval forces immediately set up a coastal blockade. Consequently, no alcoholic beverages were exported in 1808 from either Lisbon or Porto to Luanda.[82] As Napoleon's forces withdrew into the interior of the country late that same year, the British lifted their blockade, allowing Portugal's alcohol trade with the colonial capital of Angola to resume. Yet, the resumption of this commerce involved exceedingly low volumes. Only some six large wooden casks of *aguardente*, half a *pipa* of beer, and roughly seventy-six large wooden casks of *vinho* were offloaded in 1809.[83] Compared to metropolitan alcohol imports during 1802–1805, beer fell by more than 96%, *vinho* experienced a drop of over 86%, and *aguardente* decreased by 60%. The flow of alcohol from the metropole to this port was thus brought to a virtual standstill.

The impact of the late 1807 invasion and subsequent occupation of Portugal by French-Spanish military forces was not so disastrous for the Brazilian alcohol trade at Luanda. As demand for tropical products in Europe continued to fall due to the chaos generated by the Napoleonic wars, the Brazilian economy entered deeper into recession. This lowered even more the numbers of new African slaves required to be imported into Brazil. During 1808–1809, the number

---

[81] On the effects of the French-Spanish invasion in the southern Atlantic see Alexandre, "Um Momento Crucial do Desenvolvimento Português," pp. 20 and 22–41: Leslie Bethell, *The Abolition of the Brazilian Slave Trade: Britain, Brazil and the Slave Trade Question 1807–1869*. London, 1970, pp. 1–26; Godinho, *Prix et Monnaies au Portugal*, pp. 276. Lang, *Portuguese Brazil*, pp. 195–204; Alan K. Manchester, *British Preeminence in Brazil, Its Rise and Decline: A Study in European Expansion*. New York, 1964, p. 54–159; and Marques, *História de Portugal*, Vol. I, pp. 577–580.

[82] "Balança do Comercio do Reino de Portugal," for 1808 in AHMOP; and "Nota da Exportação e Preços dos Vinhos que Sahiram pelos Differentes Portos do Reino, 1796–1831," LC, Portuguese Manuscripts Collection, P–578.

[83] Import report for 1809, AHU, Angola, Cx. 121, Doc. 6.

exported from the colonial capital of Angola fell to an annual average of just slightly over 10,252. This volume, although equal to that
of the peak years of the late nineteenth century, represented a 19%
decrease vis-à-vis 1800–1807.[84] The *gerebita* trade at Luanda thus con-
tracted correspondingly. In 1809, 2,208.5 large wooden casks of cane
brandy, an amount just slightly 13% below the 1807 estimated import
volume, were offloaded in the colonial capital of Angola.[85] Furthermore,
a total of three and a half *pipas* of liqueur were also unloaded at
Luanda in 1809 from Brazilian vessels.[86] Once again, Rio de Janeiro
dominated much of this commerce, although Recife's share was on
the rise.[87] After an initial increase in the Brazilian alcohol trade with
the colonial capital of Angola, then, the immediate effects of the
metropole's occupation by Napoleon's forces were merely to com-
press the commerce.

The three decades following the extremely depressed 1770s saw
colonial traders in the land of Vera Cruz export greater quantities
of *cachaça* to Luanda so as to acquire part of the larger numbers of
slaves required by their once again expanding economy. The proportion of this exchange, although far from that of the first half of
the eighteenth century, remained appreciable. Information on the
actual value of the 1782–1784 *gerebita* imports does not exist. But it
is nevertheless known that each large wooden cask of *cachaça* was
then worth some 50$000 *réis*.[88] The 4,021 *pipas* of *gerebita* imported
during this three year period would thus have been worth around

[84] See Graph 5.
[85] Import report for 1809 in AHU, Angola, Cx. 121, Doc. 6.
[86] *Ibid.* This liqueur most probably originated from France. See Heitor Ferreira
Lima, *História Político-Econômica e Industrial do Brasil.* São Paulo, 1970, p. 137.
[87] According to Catherine Lugar, "The Merchant Community of Salvador, Bahia,
1780–1830," Unpublished Ph. D. dissertation, State University of New York (Stony
Brook), 1980, Lugar, "Merchant Community of Salvador," p. 108, Salvador in 1809
exported only 78 *pipas* of cane brandy to Luanda, Benguela, and São Tomé. Figures
available in Andrade Arruda, *Brasil no Comércio Colonial*, p. 407, on the other hand,
indicate that Rio de Janeiro accounted for at least 36% of all cane brandy exported
from Brazil during the same year. On the growing Recife commerce at Luanda
see Miller, *Way of Death*, p. 525; idem, "Legal Portuguese Slaving," p. 155; and
idem, "Numbers, Origins, and Destinations," p. 99.
[88] "Parecer" of the Desembargador Geral do Reino de Angola (Appeals Court
Judge), 5–01–1785, AHU, Angola, Cx. 70, Doc. 29. By the end of 1785, however,
the price of each *pipa* of *gerebita* had reached an exorbitant 80$000 *réis*. See the let-
ter of Governor Barão de Moçâmedes to Jozé de Seabra e Silva, 5–10–1785, in
Arquivos das Colonias. Vol. III, 1918, p. 210.

201,000$000 *réis*. At the same time, the cost of a prime slave at Angola's colonial capital was roughly 53$000 *réis*.[89] Since a total of 26,917 were then exported from this seaport,[90] their maximum value would have been in the neighbourhood of 1,426,000$000 *réis*. If *gerebita* was used exclusively in slave trading, these figures suggest that roughly 14% of the slaves exported through Luanda between 1782 and 1784 were directly acquired through this intoxicant. As it happens, the detailled data given in the extant import-export annual reports for the subsequent two and a half decades work out to almost exactly the same percentage. These sources show the overall value of alcohol imports from the land of Vera Cruz at Luanda, which were almost exclusively in the form of *cachaça*, accounting for 13.2% of the total value of items exported from Angola's colonial capital and for 14.7% of the total cost of the slaves shipped therefrom between 1785 and 1809.[91] Overall, the 1782–1784 and 1785–1809 percentages translate to a ratio of one out of seven. Consequently, of the 318,799 slaves exported through Luanda between 1780 and 1809, 45,540 were directly acquired in exchange of *gerebita*.[92]

The number of slaves obtained in exchange of all intoxicants imported from the metropole, on the other hand, was much smaller. Between 1785 and 1809, value of alcoholic beverages unloaded off vessels originating from Portugal represented 5.7% of all exports from Angola's colonial capital and 6.4% of its slave exports.[93] These percentages translate to a ratio of roughly one out of seventeen. As a result, it is unlikely that more than 19,130 of the 318,799 slaves exported through Luanda between 1780 and 1809 were acquired in exchange of intoxicants originating from the metropole.

From the early 1780s until 1810, *cachaça* thus remained the most important foreign intoxicant with which slaves were obtained at Luanda. And this exchange continued to be dominated by trading houses in Rio de Janeiro. Between 1782 and 1784, 75.8% of *gerebita* imports originated from Guanabara Bay, 14.7% came from Recife, and 9.5% arrived from Salvador.[94] During 1785–1808, of the 400

---

[89] Miller, "Numbers, Origin, and Destination," p. 67.
[90] See Graph 5.
[91] See Graphs 15, 16 and 17.
[92] The overall slave export total is taken from Graph 5.
[93] See Graphs 15, 16 and 17.
[94] See "Relação do Numero de Pipas de Gerebita Vindas dos Portos do Brazil," in AHU, Angola, Cx. 70, Doc. 29.

Brazilian vessels that docked at Angola's colonial capital, 66.7%
emanated from Rio de Janeiro, 18% came from Salvador, and 14.7%
originated from Recife.[95] Thus anywhere from two-thirds to three-
quarters of the 45,540 slaves acquired at this seaport in exchange
of *cachaça* were destinned for Guanabara Bay.

III. *The Late Gerebita and Slave Trades at Luanda, 1810–1830*

As war continued to envelop much of Europe throughout the first
half of the 1810s, demand for tropical products remained flat. The
plantation economy in the land of Vera Cruz was thereby maintained in a depressed state, forcing the number of new enslaved
labourers imported from Africa to remain correspondingly low.[96]
During 1810–1815, slave exports from Luanda averaged 10,851 per
annum or just some 6% more than the volume of 1808–1809.[97]
Cachaça imports could have been expected to remain depressed. But,
in fact, they plummeted to extremely low quantities. The amount of
gerebita offloaded at Luanda fell to almost 1,721 *pipas* in 1810 and
again to a mean of slightly over 1,410 large wooden casks in
1812–1813.[98] This represents a significant decrease of nearly one-
third when compared to the volume imported in 1809. Nonetheless,
some 70% of the *cachaça* continued to come from Rio de Janeiro,
while 23% arrived from Recife and only 7% emanated from Salvador.[99]
Consequently, the early 1810s massive downswing in the *gerebita* trade
at Luanda was equally spread out amongst the three Brazilian ports
of supply.

The beginning of the 1810s not only saw the volume of *gerebita*
imports at Luanda decline appreciably, but also witnessed a structural change in Brazil's alcohol commerce there. The arrival of the
court, most of the nobility, and many metropolitan merchant capitalists in the land of Vera Cruz during 1808 turned the colony into

---

[95] See Graph 6.
[96] Miller, "Legal Portuguese Slaving," pp. 153–154; and Florentino, *Em Costas
Negras*, p. 46.
[97] See Graph 5.
[98] Annual import reports in AHU, Angola: Cx. 121-A, Doc. 35. for 1810; Cx.
127, Doc. 1 for 1812; and Cx. 128, Doc. 26 for 1813.
[99] *Ibid.*

the centre of the Portuguese Empire. Soon thereafter, ports in Brazil were opened to international commerce, allowing traders in the land of Vera Cruz to draw increasingly upon the European and Asian goods which they had lacked to acquire slaves. This development drastically reduced the position which *cachaça* had enjoyed since the mid–1660s in the Brazilian trade with Angola's colonial capital. While *gerebita* imports made up a dominating 73% of the total value of goods imported between 1785 and 1809 at Luanda from the land of Vera Cruz, the proportion plummeted to only 15% during 1810–1823.[100] The opening of the land of Vera Cruz to "free trade" thus abruptly ended the overwhelming domination by *cachaça* of Brazil's commerce with this port town. Yet, significant as it was, this structural change failed to radically transform the fundamental roles played by *gerebita* at Luanda. Indeed, *cachaça* was to remain the most important good produced within Brazil for export to and persist as the second most significant item for slave trading purposes in the colonial capital of Angola.

The opening of Brazilian ports to international commerce was not, however, without important ramifications for Luanda's alcohol and slave trades. Although most of the foreign goods which colonial traders in the land of Vera Cruz subsequently drew upon for slave trading were in the form of cloths, these also included intoxicants such as *vinho*, *aguardente*, gin, liqueur, and beer imported from Portugal and other European countries. As early as 1810, 338 large wooden casks of *vinho*, six *pipas* of *aguardente*, nearly nine large wooden casks of gin, and four *pipas* of liqueur were further imported in the colonial capital of Angola from Rio de Janeiro and Recife.[101] Moreover,

---

[100] See Graph 8.

[101] Import report for 1810 in AHU, Angola, Cx. 121-A, Doc. 35. The point of origin of these non-Brazilian intoxicants is not known. Ferreira Lima, *História Político-Econômica*, p. 137, states that Brazil was then importing *vinho* and *aguardente* from Portugal, as well as gin and liqueur from Holland and France, respectively. Manchester, *British Preeminence in Brazil*, p. 96, further informs that wine and brandy from England was also offloaded in the land of Vera Cruz during this period. For the mid–1820s, James Birckhead and Co., *Pro-Forma Sales and Invoices of Imports and Exports at Rio de Janeiro*. Rio de Janeiro, 1827, pp. 34–35 and 48–49, lists French and Spanish brandy, gin, Port and Madeira wine, *vinho* from Lisbon and Fayal, and Spanish, particularly Catalonian, wine as being imported at Rio de Janeiro. During the late 1820s, according to Robert Walsh, *Notices of Brazil in 1828 and 1829*. London, 1830, Vol. I, pp. 517–518, the volume of Catalonian wine unloaded at Rio de Janeiro was "considerable."

an annual average of about 176 large wooden casks of *vinho* and almost twenty *pipas* of gin, beer, and liqueur were unloaded at Luanda during 1812–1813 off vessels originating from Brazil's three major seaports.[102] Given that almost 52% of these re-exported European alcoholic beverages came from Rio de Janeiro, 48% originated from Recife, and less than 1% arrived from Salvador,[103] the pattern emerging here was far different from that of the *cachaça* trade, which was under the overwhelmingly domination of Rio de Janeiro. But this is not the most salient point. Far more important is the fact that, when added to *gerebita*, the volume of these re-exported intoxicants place the total amount of alcohol imported at Luanda from ports in the land of Vera Cruz during 1810 and 1812–1813 at a level just 16% lower than that of the first decade of the nineteenth century. This overall figure, as it happens, is not too dissimilar from that representing the decline in slave exports from the colonial capital of Angola. And, by supplementing their *cachaça* commerce with re-exported European intoxicants, colonial traders in Brazil were able to further increase their grip over the alcohol and slave trades at Luanda.

Indeed, precisely at the time when the Brazilian alcohol trade with the colonial capital of Angola was diversifying and thereby maintaining itself at respectable levels, the metropole's commerce in alcoholic beverages with this port town remained in a state of paralysis due to the continuation of warfare throughout the European continent. In 1810, no *aguardente*, beer, *vinho*, gin, liqueur, or Port wine found their way to Luanda from Portugal.[104] The following year, minute amounts of alcoholic drinks originating from Lisbon and, perhaps, Porto most likely arrived, since fifty-two large wooden casks of *vinho* and thirteen *pipas* of *aguardente* were then dispatched from Portugal to all of its African colonies.[105] During 1812–1813, the

---

[102] Annual import reports in AHU, Angola: Cx. 127, Doc. 1 for 1812; and Cx. 128, Doc. 26 for 1813.

[103] See the annual import reports in AHU, Angola: Cx. 121-A, Doc. 35 for 1810; Cx. 127, Doc. 1 for 1812; and Cx. 128, Doc. 26 for 1813.

[104] Import report for 1810, AHU, Angola, Cx. 121-A, Doc. 35. According to Maria de L. Roque de Aguiar Ribeiro, *As Relações Comerciais entre Portugal e Brasil Segundo as 'Balanças de Comércio', 1801–1821.* Lisbon, 1972, p. 30, there was little *aguardente* produced throughout all of Portugal during the first half of the 1810s as a result of the late 1807 Napoleonic invasion and the resulting warfare.

[105] "Nota da Exportação e Preços dos Vinhos que Sahiram pelos Differentes Portos do Reino, 1796–1831," LC, Portuguese Manuscripts Collection, P–578.

importation of metropolitan alcohol continued with exceedingly depressed volumes. Only eleven and a half *pipas* of *vinho* were offloaded at Luanda during each of these years.[106] The amount of metropolitan alcohol imported probably increased in 1814, when a larger total of 135.5 *pipas* of *vinho* (fifty-four from Lisbon and eighty-one and a half from Porto) and 152 large wooden casks of *aguardente* were dispatched from Portugal to Africa.[107] Still, the volumes involved were but a small fraction of what they once had been. Following the 1807 Napoleonic invasion and occupation of the metropole, merchant capitalists in both Lisbon and Porto were thus compelled to withdraw from the alcohol trade at Luanda, allowing colonial traders in Brazil to virtually monopolize this commerce.

The end of warfare in Europe led to an economic recovery throughout the old continent during the second half of the 1810s. This enabled merchant capitalists in Portugal to attempt to reactivate their alcohol commerce at Luanda. In 1815, although Lisbon forwarded thirty-four and a half large wooden casks of *vinho* and Porto a further eleven *pipas* of this same alcoholic beverage to African ports, still no alcohol was brought to the colonial capital of Angola aboard metropolitan vessels.[108] But, in 1816, a total of fifty-two and a half *pipas* of *vinho*, two and a half large wooden casks of *aguardente*, and half a *pipa* of liqueur finally arrived in this seaport from the metropole.[109] The following two years saw the import volumes of metropolitan *vinho* and *aguardente* increase significantly to an annual average of about 218 large wooden casks and six and a half *pipas*, respectively.[110] However, by 1819, the importation of metropolitan alcohol at Luanda once again plummeted to seventy-one *pipas* of *vinho*, five large wooden casks of *aguardente*, and just slightly over two *pipas* of liqueur.[111] Although larger than those of the previous ten year period, the annual metropolitan alcohol import levels of 1816–1819 thus paled in comparison to those of 1802–1805. Even under better

---

[106] Annual import reports in AHU, Angola: Cx. 127, Doc. 1 for 1812; and Cx. 128, Doc. 26 for 1813.
[107] "Balança do Comercio do Reino de Portugal," for 1814 in INE.
[108] "Balança do Comercio do Reino de Portugal," for 1815 in INE.
[109] Import report for 1816 in AHU, Angola, Cx. 132, Doc. 26.
[110] Annual import reports in AHU, Angola: Cx. 133, Doc. 3 for 1817; and Cx. 134, Doc. 4 for 1818.
[111] Import report for 1819 in AHU, Angola, Cx. 138, Doc. 56.

economic circumstances, Portuguese merchant capitalists failed to restore their alcohol trade with Luanda to its former levels.[112]

In sharp contrast, the economic recovery of Europe during the second half of the 1810s stimulated the Brazilian alcohol commerce with the colonial capital of Angola to re-attain its former heights. Demand for tropical products rose appreciably once again throughout the old continent, allowing the economy in the land of Vera Cruz to recuperate from its depressed state.[113] Furthermore, the slave trade north of the equator, where Brazil had traditionally acquired large numbers of enslaved labourers in exchange for tobacco, was outlawed in 1815.[114] Both of these developments, in turn, increased the need for more slaves to be imported from West Central Africa.[115] To supply this increasing demand, slave exports from Luanda jumped to an average of 15,733 per year during the second half of the 1810s, or an increase of 45% over the previous five year period.[116] In order to acquire the increasing numbers of slaves required, colonial traders in Brazil again augmented their alcohol exports to Luanda. Between 1815 and 1819, a yearly average of slightly over 1,854 large wooden casks of *cachaça* were unloaded in this port town.[117] Furthermore, colonial traders in the land of Vera Cruz also augmented consider-

---

[112] The irregular supply of very modest quantities of wines from the metropole in the 1810s may well explain the beginning of *vinho* production at Luanda towards the end of the decade. According to Governor Luis da Motta Feo e Torres, this alcoholic drink was first produced there in April of 1817 and was destined exclusively for the holy sacrament, implying that its volume must have been rather small. See his letter to the King, dated 31–05–1817, in João C. Feo Cardoso de Castello Branco e Torres, *Memórias Contendo a Biographia do Vice Almirante Luis da Motta Feo e Torres, a História dos Governadores e Capitaes Generaes de Angola desde 1575 até 1825, e a Descripção Geográphica e Política dos Reinos de Angola e Benguella*. Paris, 1825, p. 83. A decade later, the French traveller Jean Baptiste Douville, much to his surprise, found vines being grown on a landed estate in the Bengo district that belonged to the convent of Santo António in Luanda. See his *Voyage au Congo et dans l'interieur de l'Afrique équinoxale ... 1828, 1829, 1830*. Paris, 1832, Vol. I, pp. 74–75. Presumably, the objective was also to produce small amounts of *vinho* for the holy sacrament.

[113] Alexandre "Um Momento Crucial do Desenvolvimento Português," p. 24; and Simonsen, *História Económica do Brasil*, pp. 363–383 and 431–434.

[114] Manchester, *British Preeminence in Brazil*, pp. 170–171.

[115] Robert E. Conrad, *World of Sorrow: The African Slave Trade to Brazil*. Baton Rouge, 1986, p. 62; Ferreira Lima, *História Político-Económica*, p. 202; Miller, "Legal Portuguese Slaving," p. 155; and Florentino, *Em Costas Negras*, p. 46.

[116] See Graph 5.

[117] Annual import reports in AHU, Angola: Cx. 131, Doc. 11 for 1815; Cx. 132, Doc. 26 for 1816; Cx. 133, Doc. 3 for 1817; Cx. 134, Doc. 24 for 1818; and Cx. 138, Doc. 56 for 1819.

ably their metropolitan alcohol re-exports to Luanda. An average of 367.5 *pipas* of *vinho*, sightly more than one-quarter of a wooden cask of *aguardente*, and roughly sixteen *pipas* of gin, liqueur, and beer were further imported each year from colonial traders in Brazil.[118] Overall, the annual average of alcohol offloaded from Brazilian vessels during 1815–1819 represented a 27% increase vis-à-vis the first half of the 1810s. Since metropolitan merchant capitalists failed to restore their alcohol exports, Brazilian colonial traders thereby maintained their control over the alcohol commerce at Luanda.

The beginning of the 1820s saw demand for new enslaved African labourers in the land of Vera Cruz remain very high. As one of the few ports along the western coast of Africa where these could still be legally acquired, slave exports from Luanda jumped to an average of slightly more than 18,385 per annum during the first three years of this decade, or by almost 17% over the levels of the later 1810s.[119] Consequently, the amount of alcohol from Brazil required to obtain this larger number of slaves must also have been substantial. Indeed, although annual import reports are not available for this three year period, other quantitative data suggest this to have been the case. In 1820, for example, forty vessels originating from ports in the land of Vera Cruz, or a number comparable to the annual average of the second half of the 1810s, called at Luanda.[120] Following a long-standing pattern, these ships almost certainly transported similar or, perhaps, even larger volumes of *gerebita*, *vinho*, *aguardente*, beer, gin, and liqueur in their holds.[121]

Alcohol imports from the metropole, on the other hand, must have decreased throughout this three year period. Only 156 *pipas* of

---

[118] Annual import reports in AHU, Angola: Cx. 131, Doc. 11 for 1815; Cx. 132, Doc. 26 for 1816; Cx. 133, Doc. 3 for 1817; Cx. 134, Doc. 24 for 1818; and Cx. 138, Doc. 56 for 1819.

[119] See Graph 5.

[120] Manuel dos A. da Silva Rebelo, *Relações entre Angola e Brasil, 1808–1830*. Lisboa, 1970, Table 15 following p. 206. The majority of these must have originated from Rio de Janeiro since a total of 54 vessels left this port town in 1820 for Africa. See Luis G. dos Santos, *Memórias para Servir à História do Reino do Brasil*. Rio de Janeiro, 1943, Vol. II, p. 759.

[121] This is particularly true in the case of cane brandy exported from Rio de Janeiro. During 1820–1822, for example, a total of 13,876 *pipas* of *cachaça* arrived at Guanabara Bray from its hinterland. Averaging some 4,625 *pipas* per annum, this was the single largest volume of *cachaça* entering Rio de Janeiro in any three year period since 1799. See Fragoso, *Homens de Grossa Aventura*, p. 137.

vinho and twenty-nine large wooden casks of *aguardente* were then annually exported from Portugal to its African colonies.[122] Compared to the second half of the 1810s, this was a drop of almost 8%. Slightly more than two-thirds of the *vinho* originated from Lisbon, almost 30% percent emanated from Porto, and a very small amount was dispatched from other metropolitan ports, while all of the *aguardente* was dispatched from the Portuguese capital.

In 1822, Brazil declared its independence from Portugal. Since under the royal decree of September 20, 1710, Portugal barred foreign nations from trading with its African colonies,[123] this political development should have brought Brazilian commerce at Luanda to a stop and thereby enabled metropolitan merchant capitalists to regain control over the alcohol trade there. Nothing of the kind, however, occurred. The long-standing economic inter-dependence between the colonial capital of Angola and Brazil was too well entrenched for a commercial schism to take place. For traders in the land of Vera Cruz, this seaport remained one of the important sources of slaves through which they could replenish the servile labour force in Brazil.[124] For traders in Luanda, on the other hand, Brazilian *cachaça* persisted as one of the more important items of exchange with which they could obtain slaves from the interior for export, the only notable economic activity of the colony.[125] Furthermore, Brazil continued as the premier overseas consumer market for Portuguese wine.[126] As a result, in order to keep the Brazilian market open for

---

[122] "Balança do Commercio do Reino de Portugal," for 1820 and 1822 in INE; and "Balança do Commercio do Reino de Portugal," for 1821 in AHMOP. See also "Nota da Exportação e Preços dos Vinhos que Sahiram pelos Differentes Portos do Reino, 1796–1831," LC, Portuguese Manuscripts Collection, P–578.

[123] See the "Parecer" of Francisco Joze Vieira, AHU, Angola, Cx. 161, Doc. 14; and Rebelo, *Relações entre Angola e Brasil*, p. 277.

[124] See Miller, "Legal Portuguese Slaving," pp. 155–156; idem, "Slave Trade in Congo and Angola," pp. 108–109; and Graph 5.

[125] Rebelo, *Relações entre Angola e Brasil*, pp. 273–283. Soon after 1822, the colonial administration in Luanda encouraged the creation of an Angolan sugar cane brandy industry along the banks of the River Bengo. This attempt at import substitution, however, had still not produced one drop of cane brandy by the end of 1830. See Governor Nicolau d'Abreu Castelo Branco to António Manuel de Noronha, 28–06–1827, AHU, Angola, Cx. 156, Doc. 28; the instructions of Conde de Basto to Governor Barão de Santa Comba Dão, 4–01–1830, AHU, Cód. 543, fls. 1v–2; Governor Comba Dão to Duque de Cadaval, 14–12–1830, AHU, Angola, Cx. 167, Doc. 46; and the late 1830 economic report of Governor Comba Dão, AHU, Angola, Cx. 167, Doc. 58.

[126] On the importance of the Brazilian market for Portuguese wine during the

Portuguese wine and to maintain the economic viability of Angola, government officials in both Lisbon and Luanda went out of their way not only to allow traders in the land of Vera Cruz to carry on their alcohol commerce at Angola's colonial capital, but also to maintain the pre-1822 duties on *gerebita* imports.[127]

Although Brazil was allowed to continue its alcohol trade with Luanda after 1822, the slave traffic from this port town nevertheless underwent an appreciable decline. In anticipation of new and considerably higher taxes that could be imposed at Luanda on their commerce as a result of Brazil's declaration of independence, traders in the land of Vera Cruz began to seek larger and larger numbers of enslaved labourers along the enclaves of the northern Angolan coastline, away from Portuguese colonial customs officials.[128] Thus compared to 1815–1822 when an annual average of 16,728 slaves were exported from the colonial capital of Angola, the number fell to but 11,765 per annum during 1823–1835, or an appreciable drop of roughly 30%.[129] Yet, in spite of this decrease, the volume of alcohol arriving at Luanda from Brazilian ports remained quite high. Between 1823 and 1825, a mean of 2,064 large wooden casks of *gerebita* were offloaded, or almost 11.5% more than in the second half of the 1810s.[130] Similarly, of the 3,015 *pipas* of *vinho* imported

---

late eighteenth and early nineteenth centuries see: Ribeiro, *Relações Comerciais entre Portugal e Brasil*, pp. 20–28; Alexandre, "Um Momento Crucial do Desenvolvimento Português" pp. 39–41 and 45; Andrade Arruda, *O Brasil no Comércio Colonial*, pp. 522–523; Santos, *Relações Comerciais do Rio de Janeiro*, p. 191; and "Nota da Exportação e Preços dos Vinhos, 1796–1831," LC, Portuguese Manuscripts Collection, P-578. Of the 59,634 *pipas* of *vinho* exported from Portugal in 1827, for example, 24,347, or almost 41% were dispatched to Brazil. See "Registo de Mappas: Demonstrações e Tabellas LI," AHMOP, SGC 3, fl. 17v.

[127] See the discussion in Chapter Seven below on the deliberations over taxing the now foreign *cachaça* imports at Luanda.

[128] Carlos Pacheco, *José da Silva Maia Ferreira: O Homen e a sua Época*. Luanda, 1990, pp. 87–89; Mary C. Karasch, "The Brazilian Slavers and the Illegal Slave Trade, 1836–1851," Unpublished M. A. thesis, University of Wisconsin, 1967, p. 3; and Douglas L. Wheeler, "The Portuguese in Angola 1836–1891: A Study in Expansion and Administration," Unpublished Ph. D. dissertation, Boston University, 1963, p. 4. According to Herbert S. Klein, "O Tráfico de Escravos Africanos para o Porto do Rio de Janeiro, 1825–1830," *Anais de História*. No. 5, 1973, pp. 85–101, this was especially true of merchants in Rio de Janeiro.

[129] See Graph 5.

[130] According to José J. Lopes de Lima, *Ensaios sobre a statistica das possessões portuguesas: Vol. III—Angola e Benguela*. Lisbon, 1846, pp. 70–71, *cachaça* imports at Luanda totalled 6,192 *pipas* during this three year period.

throughout this three year period,[131] a relatively significant quantity must have arrived from the land of Vera Cruz, since the volume of this alcoholic beverage exported from Lisbon and Porto to the colonial capital of Angola in both 1824 and 1825 was comparatively small.[132] Moreover, an undetermined, but much lower, amount of other alcoholic drinks, such as gin, beer, and liqueur also made its appearance aboard vessels dispatched from Brazilian ports.[133]

With traders in the land of Vera Cruz continuing to forward large quantities of cane brandy and *vinho* to Luanda, Portuguese merchant capitalists found it impossible to regain their long lost monopoly over the alcohol commerce in the colonial capital of Angola. In 1823, for example, alcohol imports from the metropole totalled but 354 *pipas* of *vinho*, seven and a half large wooden casks of *aguardente*, and fifty-one *pipas* of Port wine and liqueur.[134] The majority of this alcohol came from Lisbon since the volume of alcohol exports from Porto to Africa during 1822–1823 was extremely small.[135] Although almost a three fold increase over the average metropolitan alcohol import levels of 1816–1819, the volume of Portuguese alcoholic beverages offloaded in 1823 represented no more than a modest 16% of the total alcohol imports. The following year, alcohol imports from Portugal must have been even lower: only 416.5 *pipas* of *vinho* and seventeen large wooden casks of *aguardente* were exported from the metropole to Africa in 1823, while in 1824 their volume dispatched to Luanda amounted to a mere sixty-six and eight and a half *pipas*, respectively.[136] Once again, most of this alcohol, 382.5 large wooden casks of *vinho* in 1823 and a further fifty-four and a half *pipas* of the same alcoholic drink in 1824, was dispatched from Lisbon. The decline evidenced in Portuguese alcohol exports to Luanda immediately following the independence of Brazil was thus due mainly to

---

[131] *Ibid.*, pp. 70–71.
[132] See Graph 10.
[133] The only annual import report available for this period, that of 1823, also lists 199.75 *pipas* of *vinho* and 16 large wooden casks of other alcoholic drinks, aside from 1,948.75 *pipas* of *gerebita*, imported from the land of Vera Cruz during that year. See AHU, Angola, Cx. 144, Doc. 92.
[134] *Ibid.*
[135] Only 70 of the 546.5 *pipas* of wine that were exported during both of these years to Africa originated from Porto. See "Nota da Exportação e Preços dos Vinhos, 1796–1831," LC, Portuguese Manuscript Collection, P–578.
[136] For 1823 see *ibid.* For 1824 see Graph 10.

the withdrawal of merchant capitalists in Porto from this commerce.[137]

The inability of Portuguese merchant capitalists to surmount the alcohol commerce of their Brazilian counterparts after 1822 eventually forced the Crown to come to their assistance. Late in 1824, the existing tariffs on intoxicants exported from the metropole to Luanda were significantly reduced: *vinho* was thenceforth to pay but 25% of the previous export duty, while *aguardente*, the one Portuguese alcoholic beverage that could compete with *cachaça* in terms of alcohol content, was to pay merely 2$400 *réis* per *pipa*.[138] This was followed in May of 1825 by the concession of privileges granted to metropolitan commercial houses wishing to establish branches in the colonial capital of Angola.[139] Then in June of the same year, the Crown further lowered the export taxes on wines shipped from Porto to the colonial capital of Angola by another 33%.[140] Yet, even with these notably decreased export duties and privileges, the volume of *vinho* and *aguardente* thereafter dispatched from both Lisbon and Porto to the colonial capital of Angola failed to rise appreciably. Indeed, during 1825–1829, the volume of metropolitan *vinho* exported to Luanda totalled just 1,515.75 *pipas*, while *aguardente* amounted to only 416.5 large wooden casks,[141] or an annual average of 303 and eighty-three and a half *pipas*, respectively. Following the pattern established immediately after 1822, the majority of this alcohol, 85.5% of the *vinho* and 81.5% of the *aguardente*, originated from the Portuguese capital, with the remainder dispatched from Porto.

Although comparable quantitative data are not available on the

---

[137] During 1823–1825, merchant capitalists in Porto concentrated their South Atlantic alcohol trade on Brazil: while *vinho* exports from Lisbon to the land of Vera Cruz plummeted by roughly two-thirds, those from the second most important Portuguese urban centre rose by more than one-third. See Alexandre, "Um Momento Crucial do Desenvolvimento Português" pp. 39–40 and 45.

[138] See Rebelo, *Relações entre Angola e Brasil*, pp. 268–269; and Miller, *Way of Death*, pp. 638–639.

[139] One of the commercial houses known to have taken advantage of these privileges was that of João Paulo Cordeiro e Companhia, which dealt primarily in wine from Porto. See José Accurcio das Neves, *Considerações Politicas e Commerciaes sobre os Descobrimentos e Possessões dos Portuguêzes na Africa e na Asia.* Lisbon, 1830, pp. 240–241, and the *requerimentos* of this commercial house, dated 11–07–1825, AHU, Angola, Cx. 149, Doc. 15 and Doc. 16. Amongst the privileges granted to Cordeiro e Companhia was the preference of its *vinho* shipments and the free transportation of its directors, clerks, and servants to Luanda aboard Royal vessels.

[140] Decree of 4–06–1826, AHU, Angola, Cx. 147, Doc. 29.

[141] See Graph 10.

Brazilian alcohol commerce with Luanda during most of the second half of the 1820s, the volume of the trade most probably equalled, if it did not actually surpass, the levels of 1823–1825. Towards the end of 1825, the Portuguese central government officially dispensed *gerebita* from paying foreign duties in this seaport.[142] At the same time, demand for new enslaved labourers in the land of Vera Cruz continued very high for the rest of the decade, while the colonial capital of Angola remained one of the few West Central African ports where Brazilian traders could still legally acquire slaves.[143] Not surprisingly, Luanda saw its slave exports rise to an average of almost 12,533 per annum during 1826–1829, or 6.5% more than in 1823–1825.[144] All of these factors must have enticed traders in the land of Vera Cruz to continue exporting relatively large volumes of *cachaça*, as well as smaller amounts of *vinho* and other alcoholic beverages, to the colonial capital of Angola in order to acquire slave labour.[145]

Indeed, high alcohol exports from Brazil to Luanda persisted not only during the late 1820s, but until the very end of the legal transAtlantic slave trade. Between January and the middle of March of 1830, when the commerce was finally outlawed, a total of 8,102 slaves were shipped from the colonial capital of Angola.[146] During all of that year, however, alcohol imports from the land of Vera Cruz amounted to 1,748 large wooden casks of *gerebita* and 130 *pipas* of *vinho*,[147] most of which probably arrived from Rio de Janeiro. This was clearly a disproportionate volume vis-à-vis the lower number of slaves shipped, which Governor Barão de Santa Comba Dão

---

[142] See the Royal Decree of 7–12–1825, in AHU, Angola, Cx. 147, Doc. 3.

[143] On the continuing high demand for slaves in Brazil during the second half of the 1820s see: Bethell, *Abolition of the Brazilian Slave Trade*, pp. 27–71; Conrad, *World of Sorrow*; Lang, *Portuguese Brazil*, pp. 195–204; Manchester, *British Preeminence in Brazil*; and Florentino, *Em Costas Negras*, p. 47.

[144] See Graph 5.

[145] In 1827, Rio de Janeiro alone exported a total of 4,289.25 *pipas* of *gerebita*. See Maxwell, Wright & Co., *Commercial Formalities of Rio de Janeiro*. Baltimore, 1830, p. 44. If the percentage forwarded to Luanda remained unchanged from the late 1700s, then roughly 2,230 large wooden casks would have been dispatched to this port town. For circumstantial evidence on persisting high *cachaça* imports during the later 1820s, see AHU, Angola, Cx. 161, Doc. 14; and Rebelo, *Relações entre Angola e Brasil*, pp. 273–283, 426, and 437–441.

[146] See Graph 5.

[147] The 1830 figures come from the import summary for 1830–1832 in AHU, Angola, Cx. 176, Doc. 10.

(1829–1834) explained as resulting from the fact that "most of the trade goods imported from Brazil after the middle of March, 1830, were in payment of the extraordinary amounts of slaves exported during the last years of the slave trade."[148] In contrast, alcohol imports from the metropole were limited to a mere ninety-two large wooden casks of *vinho*, primarily originating from Lisbon.[149]

Immediately after the trans-Atlantic slave trade was legally abolished, alcohol imports from Brazil at Luanda continued to rise in volume. During 1831–1832 an annual average of 2,077.5 *pipas* of *gerebita* and 290.5 large wooden casks of *vinho* were offloaded, or an increase of almost 19 and 120.5%, respectively, over the quantities imported throughout 1830.[150] What this increase represents is not altogether clear. It may be, following Governor Comba Dão, that these larger alcohol exports from Brazil went to repay the massive number of slaves exported during the last years of legal slave trading. But they may also represent a concerted effort by Brazilian traders to fuel the illegal trans-Atlantic slave commerce that was then emerging in the colonial capital of Angola and its neighbouring coastal enclaves.[151] Alcohol imports from the metropole, on the other hand, lagged way behind, averaging but 135 large wooden casks of *vinho* and six *pipas* of *aguardente* per annum during the same time

---

[148] Governor Comba Dão to Conde de Basto, 11–11–1830, AHU, Angola, Cx. 166, Doc. 55.

[149] Import summary for 1830–1832 in AHU, Angola, Cx. 176, Doc. 10. The origin of this metropolitan alcohol can be determined from the data for 1829–1830 in Graph 10.

[150] Import summary for 1830–1832 in AHU, Angola, Cx. 176, Doc. 10.

[151] For the illegal slave trade, the best study remains Karasch, "Brazilian Slavers and the Illegal Slave Trade." Alcohol imports from Brazil persisted very high throughout this era. In 1837, for example, a total of 2,378 *pipas* of *cachaça*, 1,071 *botijas* and 41 *frasqueiras* of gin, 2,133 *garrafas* (demijohns of about 5 litres) of liqueur, almost 1,429 *canadas* (a liquid measure unit of 1.4 litres) of beer, and nearly 1,660 *pipas* of *vinho* were offloaded from vessels originating from ports in the land of Vera Cruz. See the import report for 1837, AHU, Correspondência dos Governadores de Angola, Pasta 4-A. Similarly, during the second half of 1840, Recife alone exported some 712 *pipas* of *gerebita* valued at 89,688,000 *réis* to the colonial capital of Angola. See "Mappas de Importação e Exportação MR 57 fornecidos pelos Consules de Portugal," AHMOP. Even after 1850, by which time the illegal Angolan slave trade had largely subsided, the decreasing volumes of alcohol imported from Brazil remained significant. In 1852, 790 *pipas* of *gerebita* from Rio de Janeiro alone were still offloaded at Luanda and Benguela. See João Baptista Moreira [Conselheiro, Consulado Geral de Portugal no Rio de Janeiro], "Mappas Geraes do commercio de Importação e de Exportação entre Portugal, seus dominios e Rio de Janeiro, 1852," BNL, Cód. 11490, pp. 30–32.

period.[152] Thus not even the outlawing of the trans-Atlantic slave trade enabled Portuguese merchant capitalists to supplant the alcohol trade of their Brazilian counterparts in the colonial capital of Angola.

Between 1810 and 1830, trading houses in Brazil thus exercised an almost total monopoly over the alcohol trade at Luanda. As a result, the proportion of slaves acquired at this seaport in exchange of intoxicants unloaded off vessels originating from the land of Vera Cruz underwent a notable increase. During 1810–1819, the extant annual import-export reports show the overall value of alcohol imports from Brazil at Luanda as representing 18.5% of the total value of items shipped and 20.5% of the cost of slaves exported.[153] In 1823, the only year between 1820 and 1830 for which an import report is now available, these figures jumped to 31.9% and 35.1%, respectively. Aggregate data presented by José J. Lopes de Lima on Luanda's export-import commerce during 1823–1825 indicate that this increase persisted through the mid-1820s. Throughout this three year period, total exports averaged 829,979$890 réis per year, out of which 744,705$000 réis or almost 90% were in the form of slaves, and total imports averaged 1,087,960$425 réis per annum, with the value of intoxicants reaching 318,245$000 réis or 29.3%.[154] Gerebita imports alone represented an average of 200,356$600 réis, while the volume of vinho offloaded from Brazilian vessels probably hovered around a mean of 37,290$000 réis.[155] Intoxicants arriving from the land of

---

[152] Import report for 1830–1832 in AHU, Angola, Cx. 176, Doc. 10. The amount of metropolitan alcohol unloaded continued extremely depressed throughout most of the decade. Thus, in 1837, only 58 barrels of aguardente, 936 garrafas of beer, 72 garrafas of liqueur, and 24 garrafas, 10 frasqueiras, and 145 pipas of vinho were imported from the metropole. See the import report for 1837, AHU, Correspondência dos Governadores de Angola, Pasta 4-A. But by 1840, according a merchant in the metropole, the total volume of vinho imported from Lisbon and Porto reached 1,800 pipas. See the anonymous "Memorias sobre o estado actual d'Africa Occidental, seu Commercio com Portugal e medidas que convivia adoptar-se em 1841," BSGL, Reservados, Pasta D/no. 14, p. 1.

[153] See Graphs 15, 16 and 17.

[154] Lima, Ensaios sobre a statistica das possessões portuguesas, Vol. III, pp. 70–73. Lima extracted these figures in the early 1840s from the then still extant annual Luanda import-export reports for 1823, 1824, and 1825.

[155] The estimated value of the 1823–1825 Brazilian wine imports is based on the proportion of vinho offloaded from vessels originating from the land of Vera Cruz vis-à-vis that of total vinho imports during 1823: 21,000$000 réis out of an overall 65,760$000 réis or 31.9%. This percentage, transposed onto the 1823–1825 total value of vinho imports, 350,690$400 réis, works out to an overall 111,870$000 réis worth of wine unloaded from Brazilian ships, or 37,290$000 réis per annum. For

Vera Cruz thereby accounted for some 28.5% of all exports and nearly 32% of all slaves shipped between 1823 and 1825. If these 1823–1825 percentages are taken as representative of the last ten years of legal slave trading for which annual import-export reports are not available, then the proportion of the value of alcohol imported from Brazil vis-à-vis the overall value of Luanda's exports from 1810 to the 1830 reaches 23.9%, while that in relation to the total value of slaves shipped jumps to 26.7%. This translates into a ratio of roughly one out of four. As it happens, this estimate is just barely higher than the proportion obtained for the better documented period of 1810–1819 and 1823. The extant annual import-exports reports for these years give the total value of alcohol imports from Brazil as accounting for 20% of Luanda's total exports and 25% of its slave exports. This works out to a ratio of one in four and a half. Consequently, of the 281,604 slaves exported from Luanda between 1810 and 1830, anywhere from 62,580 to 70,400 were acquired in exchange of intoxicants imported from the land of Vera Cruz.

In sharp contrast, the number of slaves acquired at Luanda between 1810 and 1830 in exchange of alcoholic beverages imported from the metropole was significantly smaller. During 1810–1819 and 1823, the value of intoxicants unloaded off vessels originating from Portugal amounted to merely 1.6% of total exports and just 1.9% of slaves shipped by value from the colonial capital of Angola.[156] Thereafter, the value percentages of metropolitan alcohol imports vis-à-vis the export commerce of Angola's colonial capital rose due to the lower alcohol export duties and other privileges secured in 1824 and 1825 by metropolitan merchant capitalists. This can, once again, be established from the 1823–1825 aggregate data presented by Lima. Throughout this three year period, metropolitan alcohol imports accounted for some 9.7% of total exports and roughly 10.8% of slaves shipped from Luanda.[157] If we use these 1823–1825 percent-

---

the 1823 import value of *vinho* from Brazil see the annual import report in AHU, Angola, Cx. 144, Doc. 92. For the combined 1823–1825 value of *vinho* imports at Luanda, see Lima, *Ensaios sobre a statistica das possessões portuguesas*, Vol. III, pp. 70–71. Note, moreover, that 1824–1825 saw Portugal export relatively small amounts of *vinho* to Luanda. See Graph 10. This further suggests that the volume, and value, of wine offloaded from Brazilian vessels persisted high.

[156] See Graphs 15, 16 and 17.

[157] Lima, *Ensaios sobre a statistica das possessões portuguesas*, Vol. III, pp. 70–71, lists 353,665$200 *réis* worth of *vinho* and *aguardente* imported at Angola's colonial capital

ages as representative of the last ten years of legal slave trading for which annual import-export reports are not available, then the proportion of the value of metropolitan alcohol imports in comparison to the overall value of Luanda's exports from 1810 to the 1830 reaches 5.6%, while that in relation to the total value of slaves shipped rises to 6%. As a result, a maximum of 16,330 of the 281,604 slaves shipped during the last twenty-one years of legal slaving would have been obtained in exchange of all intoxicants imported from Portugal, for a ratio of roughly one out of seventeen.

Alcohol imports from Brazil thus persisted as the most widely used intoxicants to acquire slaves at Luanda from 1810 to 1830. And of these, *cachaça* remained the most important. Of the overall value of intoxicants imported from Brazil at Angola's colonial capital during 1810–1819 and in 1823, *gerebita* accounted for 74.8% and 89.6%, respectively, or a combined average of 77%.[158] But given that the 1823 import report is the only one that exists for the last eleven years of legal slave trading, the percentage for 1810–1830 was certainly higher. Between 1823 and 1825, for example, *cachaça* imports accounted for an estimated 84% by value of all intoxicants unloaded off ships originating from the land of Vera Cruz.[159] If we take this estimate as representing the average of the ten years during 1820–1830 for which import reports are lacking, then the figure for the whole period increases to 80%. Consequently, we can project that between 50,065 and 56,320 of the 62,580 to 70,400 slaves acquired during 1810–1830 in exchange of alcohol imported from Brazil would have been directly obtained through *gerebita*, or one in five to five and a half of those shipped.

Moreover, commercial houses in Rio de Janeiro continued to dominate this exchange. During 1810–1819 and 1823, 58% of *cachaça* imports originated from Rio de Janeiro, 33% came from Recife, and 9% emanated from Salvador.[160] Salvador thus seems to have con-

---

between 1823–1825. In 1823, 64% of *vinho* and 100% of *aguardente* by value at Luanda originated from Lisbon and Porto. See the import report for that year in AHU, Angola, Cx. 144, Doc. 92. Transposed onto the 1823–1825 figures provided by Lima, these percentages work out to 238,820$400 *réis* worth of *vinho* and 2,974$800 *réis* worth of *aguardente* from the metropole. Combined, the value of alcohol imports from Lisbon and Porto average to 80,598$400 *réis*, which represents 9.7% and 10.8%, respectively, of Luanda's total exports and slaves shipped.

[158] These percentages are worked out from the data presented in Graph 14.

[159] Percentage based on the discussion above relating to this period.

[160] See Graph 9.

tinued exporting relatively small volumes of this intoxicant to Luanda. *Gerebita* imports from Recife, on the other hand, more than doubled during this period, indicating that merchants in this northeastern Brazilian port utilized larger volumes of this alcoholic beverage to acquire more slaves at Angola's colonial capital than was the case before. Rio de Janeiro, in turn, lost some ground. But even then, Brazil's southern emporium persisted as the port from where more than half of the *cachaça* offloaded at Luanda originated.[161] As a result, we can deduce that at least 60% of the 50,065 to 56,320 slaves obtained at Luanda between 1810 and 1830 in exchange of *gerebita* were acquired by trading houses in Rio de Janeiro.

Conclusion

The relationship between *cachaça*, particularly that emanating from Guanabara Bay, and the slave trade at Luanda during the eighteenth century and the first third of the 1800s has not always been properly understood by modern historians. Luis-Felipe de Alencastro, for example, once argued that traders in Rio de Janeiro, unlike those of Recife and Salvador, were at a disadvantage in the slave trade carried out at Angola's colonial capital because their hinterland was not a major producer of tobacco.[162] Other scholars have suggested that the rise of trading houses behind Guanabara Bay in the Luanda slave trade was primarily due to their drawing upon gold from Minas Gerais to buy most of the enslaved labourers they required.[163] Both of these arguments, however, run totally against the historical record. Brazilian tobacco, as evidenced in Chapter Four, was important only in commerce with West Africa. West Central African consumers, including those in the interior of Luanda, were not particularly fond

---

[161] In 1825, nine of the twelve Brazilian ships that docked at Luanda came from Guanabara Bay. See Silva Rebelo, *Relações entre Angola e Brasil*, Table 15, following p. 206.

[162] Alencastro, "Traite Négrière et les Avatars de la Colonisation Portugaise," p. 38. But compare with his most recent *O Trato dos Viventes*, pp. 247–325.

[163] See, for example, Affonso Escragnolle de Taunay, *Subsídios para a História do Tráfico Africano no Brasil*. São Paulo, 1941, p. 162; António Carreira, *As Companhias Pombalinas de Grão Pará e Maranhão e Pernambuco e Paraíba*. Lisbon, 1983, pp. 29–30; Pardo, "Comparative Study of the Portuguese Colonies," pp. 103 and ff.; and, especially, Bauss, "Rio de Janeiro," pp. 79–80, 225–228, 235, 247, 262–273, and 328–329.

of this imported narcotic, regardless of where it came from. The gold hypothesis, on the other hand, rests upon extremely thin historical evidence. Only one primary source from the later 1790s mentions the precious Brazilian yellow metal at all in this context.[164] Gold from the land of Vera Cruz simply did not play much of a role in the acquisition of slaves at Luanda, a point correctly highlighted by Miller.[165] Commercial houses in Rio de Janeiro neither required tobacco to enter the slave trade at Luanda, nor used gold to acquire part of the large numbers of slave labourers required by their regional economy. As the preceding pages make plain, it was *cachaça* that they primarily drew upon.

If the proponents of the gold thesis have seriously downplayed the role of *gerebita* in the Luanda slave trade, Miller's most recent appraisal greatly exagerates it. In his *magnum opus*, Miller claims "a rough correlation of ten slaves exported per *pipa* of imported Brazilian rum."[166] During 1782–1799, 1802–1805, 1809–1810, 1812–1813, 1815–1819, 1823–1825, and 1830, *gerebita* imports at Luanda amounted to an overall 61,310 large wooden casks.[167] If one *pipa* of *gerebita* imported equalled ten slaves exported, then 613,100 slaves acquired in exchange of *cachaça* would have been exported throughout this thirty-five year

---

[164] "Balanço da Importação, & Exportação deste Reîno de Angola desde a Anno de 1785 [...] até o Anno de 1794," 20–11–1797, AIHGB, DL794,28. According to the compiler of this 1797 document, the *ouvidor geral* João Alvares de Mello, "large sums of currency in gold were brought in by Brazilian *commisarios* to acquire slaves." But he found it impossible to determine exactly what these sums were. If large sums of this precious metal were in fact being brought in by Brazilians for slave trading purposes, one can only ask why the extant Angolan documentation is otherwise silent on this particular contraband trade and not others.

[165] See his *Way of Death*, p. 473. This is not to say that Brazilian gold failed to make its way to Luanda. During the late 1760s and early 1770s, for example, the slave Manoel de Salvador is known to have spent small quantities of gold coins originating from Rio de Janeiro. See "Traslado do Auto de Exame, e Corpo de Delicto, que se fes ao preto Manoel de Salvador, escravo do Tenente João da Sylva Franco," 10–07–1771, AHU, Angola, Cx. 55, Doc. 43. And in November of 1800, an unspecified number of merchants in Luanda were about to sent 25,080$000 *réis* in Brazilian gold to their metropolitan trading partners, via Rio de Janeiro. See Governor Miguel Antonio de Mello to Dom Rodrigo de Souza Coutinho, 04–11–1800, in *Arquivos de Angola*. 2nd Series, Nos. 91–94, 1966, pp. 245–246. Translating into 4% of the value of all slave exports in 1799, this was a modest sum. In neither case, however, was the context slave trading.

[166] *Ibid.*, p. 83. Note that the data and mathematical operations used to arrive at this ratio are not disclosed.

[167] See Graph 7. The import volume for 1823–1825 is taken from Lima, *Ensaios sobre a statistica das possessões portuguesas*, Vol. III, pp. 70–71.

period. In fact, however, the number of slaves known to have been shipped is only 399,682.[168] The ratio posited by Miller, translating as it does into a figure that is some 53% higher than the actual number of slaves exported, is thus grossly inflated.

The actual role of *cachaça* in the Luanda slave trade during 1700–1830 falls in between these two diametrically opposed appraisals. For the 1760s and 1780 to 1830, the documented proportion of exported slaves acquired in exchange of *gerebita* was slightly greater than one out of six. Since the first half of the 1700s saw this exchange at its height, the ratio for the whole period of 1700–1830 was surely higher. If we draw upon the 1760s maximum as representative of this earlier period, the documented 1760–1830 ratio increases to one out of four. This suggests that of the 1,181,500 slaves legally exported from the colonial capital of Angola between 1710 and 1830, some 295,375 were directly acquired in exchange for *gerebita*. And the majority of these went to the merchant houses of Rio de Janeiro, which shipped most of the *cachaça*, some 64% according to extant documentation for the 1760s and 1780–1830. But with traders behind Guanabara Bay heavily dominating this exchange from the 1720s through the 1750s, the figure for the whole period under consideration most probably ranged between 70 and 75%. In short, *gerebita*, especially that emanating from Rio de Janeiro, enabled trading houses in Brazil to directly obtain a significant portion of the slaves exported through Luanda.

---

[168] See Graph 5.

CHAPTER SIX

THE PROFITS OF LUSO-BRAZILIAN ALCOHOL IN SLAVING AT LUANDA AND ITS HINTERLAND

Once the export slave trade began at Luanda and its hinterland in the mid-sixteenth century, foreign intoxicants soon developed into major goods with which Luso-Brazilians acquired slaves there. Alcohol imports from Portugal, with *vinho* leading the way, predominated until the second half of the seventeenth century, while Brazilian *cachaça* became the single most important intoxicant imported throughout the long eighteenth century. Although direct alcohol imports from Portugal accounted for only 6% of slave exports between 1782 and 1830 in terms of value, the percentage was surely greater during previous periods, especially before the late 1600s. *Gerebita* imports, on the other hand, represented 25% in value of slave exports from 1700 to 1830. Here, foreign intoxicants were clearly a fundamental component of slave trading. How lucrative was this exchange? The question is not only important in its own right. It is also crucial to reach a comprehensive understanding of the importance of foreign alcohol in slave trading at Luanda and its hinterland.

I. *The Slippery Road to Estimating Profits*

The question at hand is not an easy one to tackle as the historiography on the broader issue of the profitability of the Luanda slave trade demonstrates. Few students of this commerce have attempted to calculate the general returns involved, let alone those arising specifically from the utilization of foreign alcohol. Moreover, those that have engaged in such an exercise have reached considerably different conclusions.[1]

---

[1] This problem is neither peculiar to Luanda's slave trade, in particular, nor to that carried out by Luso-Brazilians along the Angolan coast, in general. It is a general characteristic of much of the historiography on the Atlantic slave trade. See, for example, the debate on the profitability of the British slave trade generated

For António Carreira, the first scholar to have dealt with the issue in some detail, the Luanda slave trade definitively presented Luso-Brazilians with "high earnings."[2] Working through the extensive documentation of and on the Companhia Geral do Grão Pará e Maranhão (CGGPM), one of the Portuguese joint-stock companies involved in the Atlantic slave trade, he found that 4,551 of the slaves bought by its representatives at Luanda during 1758–1765 cost a total of 149,565$500 *réis*, including expenses for food, commissions, taxes, and baptism charges. Of these, 4,105 were exported, representing 46.1% of its overall slave shipments from Angola. And of those exported, 3,137 were landed alive in Brazil and sold for 234,291$300 *réis*. The difference in the Luanda and Brazil prices thus presented the CGGPM with a profit of 84,725$800 *réis*, or 56.6% over its initial cost.[3] With the company having lost 31% of this lot of bought slaves due to mortality and flight, this was a significant return indeed.

Joseph Miller, in turn, presents a much different appraisal. Drawing upon an impressively rich database of slave prices at Angola's colonial capital and various Brazilian ports from 1600 to 1830, he notes even larger margins. Averaging about 150–200% during the early 1600s, these rose to almost 500% in the first four decades of the eighteenth century, then declined substantially up to the 1770s before

---

since Eric Williams, *Capitalism and Slavery*. Chapel Hill, 1944, p. 30, posited that it operated at a 30% profit level: C. K. Hyde, B. B. Parkinson, and S. Mariner, "The Nature and Profitability of the Liverpool Slave Trade," *Economic History Review*. Vol. 5, 1953, pp. 368–377; Roger Anstey, "The Volume and Profitability of the British Slave Trade," in Stanley L. Engerman and Edward D. Genovese, eds. *Race and Slavery in the Western Hemisphere: Quantitative Studies*. Princeton, 1975, pp. 3–36; Robert P. Thomas and Richard N. Bean, "The Fishers of Men: The Profits of the Slave Trade," *Journal of Economic History*. Vol. 34, 1974, pp. 885–914; David Richardson, "Profitability in the Bristol-Liverpool Slave Trade," *Revue française d'histoire d'outre-mer*. Vol. 62, 1975, pp. 301–308; idem, "Profits in the Liverpool Slave Trade: The Accounts of William Davenport, 1757–1784," in Roger Anstey and P. E. H. Hair, eds. *Liverpool, The African Slave Trade, and Abolition*. Liverpool, 1976, pp. 60–90; Joseph E. Inikori, "Market Structure and the Profits of the British African Trade in the Late Eighteenth Century," *Journal of Economic History*. Vol. 41, 1981, pp. 745–776; B. L. Anderson and David Richardson, "Market Structure and Profits of the British African Trade in the Late Eighteenth Century: A Comment," *ibid.*, Vol. 43, 1983, pp. 713–721; Joseph E. Inikori, "Market Structure and Profits of the British African Trade in the Late Eighteenth Century: A Rejoinder" *ibid.*, pp. 723–728; William Darity Jr., "The Numbers Game and the Profitability of the British Trade in Slaves," *ibid.*, Vol. 45, 1985, pp. 693–703; and idem., "The Profitability of the British Trade in Slaves Once Again," *Explorations in Economic History*. Vol. 26, 1989, pp. 380–384.
 [2] Carreira, *As Companhias Pombalinas*, p. 156.
 [3] *Ibid.*, pp. 87 and 150–152.

stabilizing at 60–100% until 1830.[4] But, although such large differentials were normal, according to Miller, they did not necessarily translate into substantial gains. Indeed, he goes on to explain, these very high margins had to cover the usual costs associated with slave trading: mortality in Luanda and during the middle passage, maintenance, taxes, freight charges, and commissions. The evidence available to Miller suggests that these typical costs represented 138.5% over the price of slaves in the colonial capital of Angola during the early trade and 53.5% in the latter decades of the legal commerce. Moreover, on top of these usual expenses, there were also extraordinary costs relating to epidemics, bribes, and shipping surcharges during times of peak demand which he estimates as representing a further 100% and 25%, respectively, above the Luanda cost of slaves in the early and later periods of the trade.[5] For Miller, taking these variables into account suggests "that gains were possible in good years but turned into losses, sometimes catastrophic ones, when slave mortality rose [above expected levels], or when other unusual costs appeared."[6] This is exactly what took place, he indicates, during the 1710s and the 1720s when, in spite of price differentials being at their highest, a virulent smallpox epidemic and shipping surcharges eliminated any potential gains for Luso-Brazilian traders.

A third and equally diverging assessment has been put forth more recently by Manolo Florentino. This Brazilian scholar begins his calculations with the number of slaves known to have been exported from Luanda to Rio de Janeiro during 1810, 1812, 1815, 1817, and 1820: 36,738 slaves. Their valuation at Angola's colonial capital, 2,622,969$000 réis, is taken to represent the investment made by merchants in southern Brazil to buy them in this port. Since extant sources say little about the fate of these specific slaves, Florentino draws upon the known annual mortality rates aboard slavers arriving in Guanabara Bay from Luanda during the same years, 70.5 per thousand on average, to estimate the number of slaves landed alive: 34,216. He then multiplies this figure by the mean price of slaves in Rio de Janeiro at the time, 123$200 réis, to arrive at a total of 4,220,651$000 réis as earned from their sale. The difference

---

[4] Miller, "Slave Prices in the Portuguese Southern Atlantic," pp. 62–64.
[5] *Ibid.*, pp. 64–65.
[6] *Ibid.*, p. 65.

between investment and sales is 1,597,682$000 *réis*, which translates into a gross profit of 60.9%. Once he establishes this margin, Florentino injects other slave trading expenses, such as the cost of food for slaves and crews, wear and tear of equipment, crews' wages, taxes, and insurance, to his calculations. Based on insurance records detailing the overall valuation of Guanabara Bay slavers engaged in the commerce, he estimates these extra costs as comprising 35% over the investment made to buy slaves in West Central Africa. Added to this investment, the extra expenses result in a total investment of 3,541,008$000 *réis*. Subtracting the gross earnings from the total investment leaves a residue of 679,643$000 *réis*, which translates into a profitability rate of 19.2% net.[7] For Florentino, there is thus no question that the Luanda slave trade was an appreciably lucrative commerce for the merchants of Rio de Janeiro.

The widely varying conclusions presented by Carreira, Miller, and Florentino result not from different methodologies, but from the types of sources available. In the case of Carreira, for example, the extant documentation does not provide evidence of all of the expenses incurred by the CGGMP in its slave trading ventures from Luanda. Freight charges, crews' wages, and the cost of vessels are not covered. Consequently, the high profits he notes are not exactly net returns. Miller's calculations, on the other hand, also suffer from a lack of concrete examples relating actual slave trading ventures.[8] Moreover, his contention that epidemics and shipping surcharges necessarily reduced the very high gross margins of the 1710s and 1720s to insignificant net profits is hardly persuasive. Since slave traders were merchants who by definition sought not only reasonable, but the highest possible net profits,[9] one can only ask why Luso-Brazilians persisted in slave trading at Luanda in the early eighteenth century and, especially, during subsequent periods when net earnings were apparently even less attractive. Finally, the assessment by Florentino is similarly plagued by the non-existence of documentation evidencing most of the various slave trading operations

---

[7] Florentino, *Em Costas Negras*, pp. 154–174.

[8] These are presented later in his *magnum opus*. See Miller, *Way of Death*, pp. 478–479. Here, details are provided on eighteen ventures involving 5,556 slaves exported from Bissau, Luanda, and Benguela to Brazil. Most of these slaves were shipped aboard vessels of the CGGPM during the third quarter of the 1700s, which turns the database almost identical to that used earlier by Carreira.

[9] On this point, see Florentino, *Em Costas Negras*, p. 155.

which he deems necessary to consider. Aside from the number of slaves exported, no other direct evidence is presented on their specific fate. Their middle passage mortality rate, in particular, is estimated from sources which do not necessarily cover the same slaves. But more important is the average price of slaves in Rio de Janeiro used to determine the valuation of those estimated as landed and sold there. Taken from *post-mortem* inventories and referring only to unde-formed male Africans aged between 12 and 55 years old, this price is not only unrepresentative of the demographic make-up and med-ical condition of all slaves imported from the colonial capital of Angola,[10] but it is also lower than that found in other contempora-neous sources.[11] And, as the debate on the profitability of the British slave trade has clearly shown, one of the most sensitive variables in determining net gains is the sale price of slaves in the Americas.[12] Sources thus loom large in these appraisals, with massive sets of data required, but unavailable, to reach convincing conclusions.

Exactly the same problem arises in assessing how lucrative was the alcohol-slave trade at Luanda and its hinterland. On the Brazilian side, for example, we would need quantitative information not only on the costs of the vessels involved, their fitting out, insurance, and cargoes, but also their sales and expenses at Luanda, the number and the cost of slaves boarded, the volume of and earnings from slaves, as well as other African commodities, landed and sold in the land of Vera Cruz, and the residual value of the ships. On the Portuguese side, added to all of these components, we would fur-ther need data on freight earnings from or sale of the Brazilian pro-duce that their vessels hauled to Europe. And from the African end, we would also require quantitative information on the value of the

---

[10] On the demography and medical conditions of slave exports from Luanda, see especially: Joseph C. Miller, "Overcrowded and Undernourished: The Techniques and Consequences of Tight-Packing in the Portuguese Southern Atlantic Slave Trade," in Daget, ed. *De la Traite à l'Esclavage*, Vol. II, pp. 395–424; and Dauril Alden and Joseph C. Miller, "Unwanted Cargoes: The Origins and Dissemination of Smallpox via the Slave Trade from Africa to Brazil, c. 1560–1830," in Kenneth F. Kiple, ed. *The African Exchange: Toward a Biological History of Black People.* Durham, 1988, pp. 35–109.

[11] Miller, "Slave Prices in the Portuguese Southern Atlantic," p. 53, lists price ranges of 130$000 to 150$000 *réis* for 1810–1815 and rising thereafter. Florentino, *Em Costas Negras*, pp. 281–282, ft. 29, also indicates other higher prices.

[12] Compare, for example, Anstey, "Volume and Profitability of the British Slave Trade," with Darity Jr., "Numbers Game and the Profitability of the British Trade."

thousands of transactions that occurred in the interior of Angola's colonial capital. Such massive sets of data simply do not exit. What is available, the exhaustive set on slave exports between 1710 and 1830,[13] the nearly complete collection of import-export data for 1785–1830,[14] and the 1600–1830 set on slave prices in Brazil and Angola's colonial capital,[15] constitutes but a small fraction of the sources necessary for such a complex exercise.

As a result, other types of documentation must be drawn upon to gauge the profits involved in the exchange of alcohol for slaves. This body of data, selected through the unscientific, accidental survival of records,[16] includes sources on the various conflicts over the alcohol trades, the trade dealings of contemporaneous government officials and, especially, the merchant accounts of individual and group ventures. Too few and scattered over time to allow a comprehensive analysis of the question under consideration, they do not prove conclusively that the exchange of foreign alcohol for slaves was a lucrative venture. But, taken as a whole, they strongly indicate that the level of profitability was generally high.

II. Alcohol, Slaves, and Profits

Indeed, the evidence at hand points to the exchange of Luso-Brazilian alcohol for slaves at Luanda and its hinterland as a highly lucrative venture for nearly all who engaged in it. Once wine began to be exported from Spain to this port town, for example, it did not take long for Portuguese viniculturalists to voice their discontentment to the Crown over lower profit margins. They bitterly complained that without the colonial markets of Brazil and Angola exclusively reserved for Portuguese wine, they preferred to leave their vineyards unattended and to engage in more rewarding economic activities.[17] For

---

[13] See Miller "Legal Portuguese Slaving," pp. 135–176; idem, "Numbers, Origins, and Destinations of Slaves," pp. 77 115; and Curto, "Quantitative Re-Assessment of the Legal Slave Trade from Luanda, 1710–1830," pp. 1–25.

[14] See Miller, "Imports at Luanda"; and Chapter Five above.

[15] Miller, "Slave Prices in the Portuguese Southern Atlantic," pp. 44–67.

[16] This paraphrase comes from Joseph E. Inikori, "Market Structure and Profits of the British African Trade," p. 723.

[17] See the unsigned and undated document from the early 1600s in Felner, Angola, pp. 488–489.

exporters the wine shipped to the colonial capital of Angola was no less lucrative. In his report written *circa* 1612, Pedro Sardinha informed the Crown that wine dispatched from Lisbon and the Azores, the Canary, and Madeira islands to this seaport enabled metropolitan merchant capitalists to make as much as 500% profit.[18] Sardinha's figure may well represent an over-estimate.[19] But that high earnings were effectively realized is further illustrated by the competitive struggles over the alcohol trade at Luanda: that carried out in the name of Bacchus against *gerebita* during the second half of the 1600s[20] and that of Porto wine exporters in the early 1800s against their Lisbon counterparts.[21] Similarly, slave traders in Angola's colonial capital also reaped important gains from this commerce. The low priced slaves obtained in interior markets in exchange for cheaply imported wine, as well as other European and Asian goods, were considerably more valuable at the coast, which allowed them to increase substantially their profit margins.[22]

The significant profits derived from the utilization of imported wine in the acquisition of slaves did not fail to attract the attention of some of the more enterprising governors of the colony. A case in point is that of Manuel Pereira Forjaz, who took over the governorship of Angola in 1607. Before taking up this assignment, he concluded a partnership with João de Argomedo, a Lisbon merchant capitalist with agents spread throughout Brazil and New Spain. This partnership involved sending large quantities of *vinho* and textiles to the colonial capital of Angola, where Forjaz was to be entrusted with their distribution to Portuguese traders. In return, the latter were to provide the new Governor with slaves which he then was to forward to agents in Latin American for sale.[23] Little is known about

---

[18] "Memórias de Pedro Sardinha," *Monumenta Missionaria Africana*, 1st series, Vol. VI, pp. 105–106.

[19] Between 1603 and 1604, the price of a *pipa* of wine at Luanda is reported to have risen from 42$000 *réis* to an average of 103$333 *réis*. See "Carta do Padre Pêro de Sousa ao Padre João Álvares (18–05–1604)," in Brásio, *Monumenta Missionaria Africa*. Vol. 15, p. 393. But by the middle of 1615, according to Salvador, *Os Magnatas do Tráfico Negreiro*, p. 162, the price had fallen to but 60$000 *réis*.

[20] See Chapter Four.

[21] See Chapter Five.

[22] On this point, see the "Relação de António Dinis," *Monumenta Missionaria Africana*, 1st series, Vol. VII, p. 67.

[23] This partnership contract is found in Felner, *Angola*, pp. 427–428. For a glimpse of how it operated, see Demax to Argomedo in *ibid.*, pp. 504–519. See also Salvador,

the volume of the *vinho* dispatched by Argomedo to Forjaz or the number of slaves expedited by the latter to Brazil and New Spain. Nevertheless, after the death of Forjaz in 1611, 130 *pipas* of *vinho* (some 65,000 litres) and 600 slaves were found to be amongst his possessions.[24] Another known example is that of Luis Mendes de Vasconcelos, Governor of the colony from 1617 to 1621. According to an unsigned document from 1619, Vasconcelos had monopolized much of the European wine sold in the hinterland of Luanda. How he accomplished this feat is not divulged. Perhaps he utilized the powers associated with his office or, as in the case of Forjaz, had concluded a partnership with merchant capitalists in the metropole. Whatever the method used, however, the fact remains that the *peroleira* of *vinho* sold at the coast for 1$000 to 1$500 *réis* was sold in the interior by his agents for 5$000 to 6$000 *réis*, or four to five times its value at Luanda.[25] With such a mark up, discounting for transportation, spoilage, and other costs surely still resulted in high net returns.

Extant documentation on some of the merchants engaged in the alcohol-slave trade at Luanda also leave little doubt as to the high profits involved. One of these was João Serrão de Oliveira, a wealthy Lisbon merchant capitalist with business operations spread throughout Brazil, Africa, and northern Europe. By the middle of the 1600s, he had developed partnerships with António Fiois and Diogo de Carvalho to carry out trade in the South Atlantic.[26] During one business trip to Luanda in 1654 to acquire slaves for sale in Brazil, one of Oliveira's associates called at Madeira to buy three *pipas* of wine. Neither the cost of this alcohol, nor the number or value of the slaves obtained with it at Angola's colonial capital and sold in the land of Vera Cruz are known. Nonetheless, upon learning of his

---

Os Magnatas do Tráfico Negreiro, pp. 131–132. In 1600, Argomedo made at least one slaving trip from Angola to Cartagena as the captain of the ship São Francisco. See, Enriqueta Vila Vilar, *Hispanoamerica Y El Comercio de Esclavos*. Sevilla, 1977, Table 2.

[24] Felner, *Angola*, pp. 195–196. The 130 *pipas* of *vinho* would have had a value of about 3,432$000 *réis*, since each was then worth 26$400 *réis*. See "Inventario do Governador Manuel Pereira" [Forjaz] 1612, in *ibid.*, pp. 580–584.

[25] See document #38, dated 7–09–1619, in *ibid.*, p. 455.

[26] See the synopsis of one of Oliveira's account books in Charles R. Boxer, "The Commercial Letter-Book and Testament of a Luso-Brazilian Merchant, 1646–1656" *Boletim de Estudios LatinoAmericana e del Caribe*. Vol. 18, 1975, pp. 49–56.

associate's purchase of Madeira wine, Oliveira expected the venture to "give us handsome profits."[27]

Another merchant engaged in this trade was Diogo Fernandes Branco. Based in Funchal, Madeira, Branco was part of a network of merchant capitalists in Lisbon, London, Bordeaux, La Rochelle, the major Brazilian port towns, and the colonial capital of Angola. One of Branco's principal business dealings was to forward Madeira wine to this port town to be exchanged for slaves who were then shipped to Brazil and exchanged for sugar.[28] The sugar thus obtained was thereafter transported to Funchal where, once processed, it was exported to his business contacts throughout Europe. Between 1649 and 1652, he exported, both on his own account and as an agent of his business partners, a total of 3,339 *pipas* of Madeira wine: of these, no less than 1,368, or 41%, went to the major slave trading port in West Central Africa.[29] Averaging 342 *pipas* per year, this made Branco a major player in the alcohol-slave trade at Luanda, a fact from which we can infer reasonable earnings.

The accounts of Francisco Pinheiro, another Lisbon merchant capitalist with business operations spread throughout most of Portugal's overseas possessions, are even more revealing. The first third of the eighteenth century saw Pinheiro actively forwarding European and Asian goods to his trade representatives at Angola's colonial capital to acquire slaves destined for Brazil. During these decades, a total of 33% by value of all the trade goods he sent to his commercial agents in this port town were in the form of metropolitan alcoholic beverages.[30] Late in 1711, he dispatched a vessel laden with European and Asian goods worth 4,241$460 *réis* to Luanda, which included 12.5 *pipas* of *vinho* valued at 292$160 *réis* and 11 barrels of *aguardente* priced at 196$200 *réis*. Early in the following year, this cargo was sold for 6,310$847 *réis*, with 12 *pipas* of *vinho* fetching 1,491$000 *réis* and 7 barrels of *aguardente* retailing for 335$000 *réis*.[31] While non-

[27] João Serrão de Oliveira to António Frois, 30–04–1654, in "1646–1656 Portugal History MSS. Portuguese Commercial Letterbook," Lilly Library, Indiana University, fl. 140.
[28] Alberto Vieira, ed. *O Público e o Privado na História da Madeira: Vol. I, Correspondência Particular do Mercador Diogo Fernandes Branco*. Funchal, 1996, pp. 10–11.
[29] *Ibid.*, *Vol. I*, pp. 13–14.
[30] Lisanti, ed., *Negócios Coloniais*, Vol. I, p. CDLXXVI.
[31] For all of the information pertaining to this cargo see *ibid.*, p. CCCXCI; and João Vicente dos Santos to António Pinheiro Neto, 25–02–1712, in *ibid.*, Vol. IV, pp. 416–418 and 428–446.

alcoholic goods were sold at a price merely 18.6% over their original cost, *vinho* and *aguardente* were sold for an impressive 274% above their Lisbon price. In 1717, Pinheiro dispatched another shipment of 12 *pipas* of *vinho* valued at 216$000 *réis* to his trade representatives in Luanda. It, too, was retailed for a substantially higher amount: 770$000 *réis*, or 256.5% over its original value.[32] Expenses incurred in both Lisbon and Angola's colonial capital with commissions, freight costs, export-import taxes, storage, etc., obviously reduced the gross profits which Pinheiro reaped from both of these alcohol shipments. The *vinho* and *aguardente* cargo of 1711–1712, for example, had an outlay of 114$115 *réis*, while the *vinho* shipment of 1717 had an expense tag of 306$400 *réis*.[33] Consequently, Pinheiro was still able to net a profit of 1,223$525 *réis* or 250.5% in 1712 and 254$600 *réis* or 114.6% in 1717.

Duarte Sodré Pereira, a contemporary of Pinheiro with a similarly extensive trade network that stretched across both sides of the Atlantic, was also involved in this commerce. During the early 1700s, Pereira was dispatching *vinho* and especially *aguardente* to the colonial capital of Angola. Part was destined for his commercial agent there, José da Rocha Freire.[34] Other, undetermined amounts were destined for private customers. One of these was a certain Inacio da Silva Medela who, in 1711 received from Pereira a shipment of *vinho* and *aguardente* aboard the Nossa Senhora do Monte e S. João Baptista valued at 961$560 *réis*.[35] The priests of the Companhia de Angola also periodically received cargoes of metropolitan alcohol from this same merchant.[36] It is not possible to determine the profits, if any, made by Pereira from these shipments. But, in each and every case, what he sought in exchange was slaves for sale in Rio de Janeiro,[37]

---

[32] Detailed information on this shipment is found in Lisanti, ed., *Negócios Coloniais*, Vol. I, p. CCCXCII and Vol. IV, pp. 499–500.

[33] The first figure represents 11.3% of the expenses incurred with the 488$360 *réis* worth of wine/*aguardente* in Lisbon plus 9.2% of the outlay with the same alcoholic drinks valued at 1,826$000 *réis* in Luanda during 1711–1712 and the second relates to 39.8% of the total expenses assumed with the exportation of 770$000 *réis* of wine/*aguardente* to the colonial capital of Angola in 1717. See *ibid.*, Vol. I, pp. CCCXCII–CCCXCIII.

[34] Silva, *Fidalgos-Mercadores no Século XVIII*, pp. 226–227.

[35] *Ibid.*, p. 263.

[36] *Ibid.*, pp. 224–225.

[37] *Ibid.*, pp. 107, 224–225, 226–227, and 374.

presumably in order to cash in on the anticipated large returns which then could be made from selling them there.

Yet another merchant who appears to have reaped lucrative gains from this trade was Manuel Monteiro da Rocha. Sometime during the early 1730s, he was selling 84.5 litre barrels of *vinho* for an extravagant 168$000 *réis* each.[38] The cost of the same volume of this alcoholic drink in the colonial capital of Angola was 26$333 *réis* in 1712 and a substantially lower 12$833 *réis* in 1717.[39] It is unlikely that the price of wine would have more than doubled within the two following decades.[40] Consequently, even after the deduction of expenses related to the importation of the wine, we can speculate that Rocha still netted a considerable profit.

To be sure, not all of those who engaged in Luanda's alcohol-slave trade succeeded in securing considerable gains. This was true, for example, of the Companhia Geral do Grão Pará e Maranhão. In 1764, it forwarded two vessels, the Nossa Senhora da Conceição and the São Lázaro, to Luanda. Although each of these vessels transported a variety of trade goods in their holds, *vinho* and *aguardente* made up a large part of their cargoes. The Nossa Senhora da Conceição and the São Lázaro hauled a combined total of 74 barrels of *vinho* (some 9,250 litres) and 762 frasqueiras of *aguardente* (about 23,812 litres).[41] The proceeds from the sale of the trade goods carried by both vessels were utilized to acquire slaves. The Nossa Senhora da Conceição purchased 457 slaves at a cost of 16,718$772 *réis*. Of these, 277 survived the transatlantic crossing and were sold in Pará

---

[38] "Parecer" of the Conselho Ultramarino dated 7–11–1750, AHU, Angola, Cx. 37, Doc. 66.

[39] See Lisanti, ed., *Negócios Coloniais*, Vol. I, pp. CCCXCI–CCCXCII, and Vol. IV, pp. 416, 428 and 499–500.

[40] *Vinho* prices at Luanda seem to have remained relatively stable from the 1610s to the 1710s, at the very least. Its mid–1615 value of 60$000 *réis* per *pipa* was exactly the same as that reported for the mid–1660s and for the middle of 1713. See, respectively: Salvador, *Os Magnatas do Tráfico Negreiro*, p. 162; Carli da Piacenza and Angelo da Reggio, "Curious and Exact Account of a Voyage to Congo," p. 491; and P. Evaristo Gatti, ed. *Sulle Terre e Sui Mari*. Parma, 1935 (2nd edition), p. 113. Nevertheless, short and medium term fluctuations were sometimes impressive. Thus, during times of scarcity, the price of a *pipa* of wine could jump to as high as 200$000 *réis*. On this point, see P. Guiseppe Manari da Modena in Gatti, *Sulle Terre et Sui Mari*, p. 113.

[41] Manuel Nunes Dias, *Fomento e Mercantalismo: A Companhia Geral do Grão Pará e Maranhão*. São Paulo, 1971, Vol. I, pp. 510–511.

for 21,126$980 *réis*.[42] The São Lázaro, on the other hand, bought 551 slaves at a cost of 18,682$230 *réis* and retailed the 407 that survived the voyage across the southern Atlantic for 31,372$900 *réis*, also in Pará.[43] With both slave trading ventures based on the sale of large volumes of metropolitan alcohol, the Nossa Senhora da Conceição thus provided the CGGPM with an interesting profit of 26% and the São Lázaro with a far more attractive 68%. But since the accounts of this joint-stock company do not cover all of the costs related to slave trading, as we have seen, the net earnings derived from each of these ventures, were undoubtedly lower.

Moreover, there were times when profits just did not materialize. A case in point is that of António Coelho Guerreiro, one of the few individuals in Luanda not heavily engaged in slave trading. His accounts show that, from 1684 to 1692, he imported no less than twenty-eight and a half *pipas* of *vinho*.[44] If sold at the usual price of around 40$000 *réis* each, these would have netted roughly 1,150$000 *réis*, making *vinho* the third most important trade good imported by Coelho Guerreiro. However, fifteen and a half of the *pipas* either arrived spoiled or spoiled during storage, forcing him to subsequently sell them off for a mere 141$600 *réis*, or almost 80% below their usual market value.[45] The remaining *pipas* were retailed for 535$000 *réis*.[46] The return for all of the *vinho* known to have been sold by Coelho Guerreiro was thus nearly 33% less than what he could have expected under better circumstances. Consequently, although he may have broken even in this portion of his business, Coelho Guerreiro most likely suffered a loss.

Information on the exchange of Brazilian *cachaça* for slaves in Angola's colonial capital is significantly less comprehensive than that available for *vinho* and *aguardente*. Nonetheless, what does exist also points to substantial returns made by those involved in this commerce. For José Barbosa Leal, a metropolitan trader with some twenty-four years experience in Luanda, *gerebita* "was the most lucrative item" exported by Brazilian merchants to this seaport during

[42] Carreira, *As Companhias Pombalinas*, p. 156.
[43] *Ibid.*, p. 156.
[44] Rau, *O "Livro de Razão"*, fls. 14v, 15v, 20v, 21v, and 25v.
[45] *Ibid.*, fls. 15v and 21v.
[46] *Ibid.*, fls. 14v, 15v, 20v, and 21v.

the late 1600s.[47] Here, as long as abundant supplies of this imported intoxicant were available, a *pipa* was then valued between 40$000 and 45$000 *réis*. But, in Massangano, a town used by traders at the coast as a springboard to attain slave marts further in the interior, the same volume of *gerebita* sold for 68$000 to 70$000 *réis*.[48] The merchants of Salvador, who thereafter shipped but relatively low quantities of *cachaça* to Luanda, seemingly continued to obtain appreciable returns from this trade.[49] Similarly, the Companhia Geral de Pernambuco e Paraíba (CGPP), another Portuguese joint-stock company involved in the Atlantic slave trade, secured relatively impressive returns on the trade goods, one of the more important of which was *gerebita*, that it exported during the mid-1760s to the colonial capital of Angola for the purpose of acquiring slaves. According to one of its officials, despite low earnings from the sale of slaves in Brazil, the commerce of the CGPP with Luanda remained "always a lucrative business" because "the trade goods it sends [there] result in a return of 40% or higher."[50] And for the colonial traders behind Guanabara Bay who dispatched most of Brazil's *cachaça* to Luanda throughout the long eighteenth-century, profits appear to have even greater.[51] How could it have been otherwise when, by the later decades of legal slave trading, they were securing significantly higher earnings from this commerce than metropolitan merchants through *aguardente* and *vinho*. While the Lisbon-Luanda average price differential of *aguardente* was only 29% and that of *vinho* a more significant 66% during 1798–1823, the Rio de Janeiro-Luanda average value margin of *gerebita* between 1799 and 1819 was a substantially higher 138.1%.[52]

It was considerable price margins such as this one, not to mention those highlighted by Carreira, Miller, and Florentino on both

---

[47] José Barbosa Leal to the King of Portugal, 10–10–1690, in Rau and Silva, *Os Manuscriptos*, Vol. I, pp. 289–291.

[48] "Copia da carta escrita ao Gov.dor Aires de Saldanha na era de [1]691," AHBML, Cód. 7, fls. 59v–60.

[49] Marieta Alves, "O Comércio Marítimo e Alguns Armoradores do Século XVIII na Bahia," *Revista de História* (São Paulo), Vol. 31, 1965, p. 137.

[50] Júnior, *Colonização e Monopólio do Nordeste Brasileiro*, p. 125. From 1760 to 1787, this joint-stock company purchased 44,155 slaves in Angola for export to Brazil. See Carreira, *As Companhias Pombalinas*, p. 233.

[51] Pardo, "Comparative Study," pp. 118–129.

[52] See Graphs 18 and 19.

sides of the southern Atlantic, that turned the utilization of Luso-Brazilian alcohol in the Luanda slave trade into such an important and profitable enterprise. Francisco Pinheiro, as we have seen, secured net profits of 250.5% and 114.6%, respectively, from the *aguardente* and *vinho* he exported to Angola's colonial capital in 1712 and 1717 to acquire slaves. From their sale in Brazil, he could have expected gross earnings in the order of some 470%.[53] Even if we halve this figure to take into account normal and extraordinary expenses related to his slave trading operations, the exchange of alcohol for slaves remained highly profitable. Similar potential earnings were accessible to colonial traders in Rio de Janeiro, who enjoyed gross price margins of 138.1% from the *cachaça* they exported to Luanda during the early 1800s for the acquisition of slaves. Sold in their hometown, these slaves would have then produced gross gains of almost 100%.[54] Halving these percentages, once again, to account for expenses related to both legs of the commerce, the result is still more than appreciable net gains.

The lucrative sums obtained from Luso-Brazilian alcohol in Luanda's export slave trade commerce with Angola's colonial capital, however, were not just limited to metropolitan merchant capitalists or Brazilian colonial traders. Similar hefty profits were also made by their Portuguese, Brazilian, and Luso-African commercial partners in Luanda involved in forwarding *vinho* and, later, *aguardente* and especially *gerebita* to the *feiras* spread throughout the hinterland of Luanda for the acquisition of slaves. These were secured through two different, although symbiotic, mechanisms. First, slave traders at Angola's colonial capital liberally expanded through a mixture of water and peppers the volume of the fortified and highly potent alcoholic beverages imported,[55] a technique which produced significantly more limited

[53] Average margin taken from Miller, "Slave Prices in the Portuguese Southern Atlantic," p. 63.
[54] *Ibid.*, p. 63.
[55] See the "Parecer" of the Conselho Ultramarino dated 20–10–1689, AHU, Cod. 554. fls. 60v–61; José Barbosa Leal to the King, 10–10–1690, in Rau and Silva, eds. *Os Manuscriptos*, Vol. I, pp. 289–291; Luis de Pina, ed., "Tractado [de Francisco Damião Cosme] das Queixas Endemicas e Mais Fataes Nesta Conquista (Loanda 14 Agosto 1770)" *Studia*. Nos. 20–22, 1967, pp. 173, 180–181, 219, 224, and 266–268; "Negociantes de molhados multados em 16–12–1784," AHU, Angola, Cx. 69, Doc. 20; Azeredo, *Ensaios sobre Algumas Enfermidades*, pp. 54–55, 74–76 and 82–83; "Edital do Senado da Camara, 19–01–1785," in José de Almeida Santos, *Luanda d'Outros Tempos*. Luanda, 1970, p. 80; Governor Melo to Rodrigo de Sousa

results when applied to dry goods such as cloths. Second, as with other trade goods, they increased the price of the *vinho, aguardente,* and *gerebita* dispatched to the interior slave markets by 100%.[56] But, as we have seen in the case of Governor Vasconcelos in the late 1610s, the mark up for imported alcohol could be as high as 500%. Accordingly, expanding the volume and augmenting the price of imported alcoholic drinks destined for the hinterland enabled Luso-Brazilian slave traders to make, at the very least, a significant profit of 200% (less transit and other expenses) over their cost in Luanda.[57] This was particularly true of *cachaça,* since its price at the coast was the lowest, its alcoholic content was extremely high, and its volume forwarded to the hinterland was the largest of all alcoholic drinks imported.

The profitable earnings acquired by the commercial partners of Portuguese merchant capitalists and Brazilian colonial traders in Luanda through the exchange of *cachaça* for slaves did not end here. According to José Barbosa Leal, *gerebita* was also the item of exchange which allowed these individuals to reap the largest profits from trading for slaves.[58] Slaves in the interior could be procured in exchange for this inexpensive Brazilian distillate, its volume increased at the coast and given a markup of 100% or more, at a very low cost.[59]

Coutinho, 29–08–1801, *Arquivos de Angola,* 2nd series, Vol. XXVI, Nos. 103–109, 1969, p. 64; and Governor Melo to Municipal Council of Luanda, 26–08–1801, in Santos, *Luanda d'Outros Tempos,* p. 94.

[56] This was a generalized practice with all imported trade goods. See, in particular: Couto, *Os Capitães-Mores em Angola,* p. 227 for the 1730s; King to Governor António de Vasconcelos, 14–11–1761, AHNA, Cód. 439-A, fl. 6v; Rodrigo de Sousa Coutinho to Governor Melo, 22–10–1799, AHU, Angola, Cx. 93, Doc. 70; Governor Melo's "Observações sobre os Mappas . . . para as noticias annuaes do estado da Povoação, Agricultura e Commercio des Reino," 14–04–1800, AHU, Angola, Cx. 95, Doc. 42.

[57] This figure does not take into account the expenses which Luso-Brazilian slave traders incurred as a consequence of dispatching imported alcoholic beverages into the hinterland of Luanda. These costs clearly reduced net profits. By how much, however, remains to be determined, since quantitative information on expenses involved with the porterage system has not yet come to light.

[58] José Barbosa Leal to the King of Portugal, 10–10–1690, in Rau and Silva, eds. *Os Manuscriptos,* Vol. I, pp. 289–291.

[59] See, for example, "Tomo que Mandaram Fazer os Oficiais do Senado da Câmara Sobre o Parecer do Povo Sobre as Aguardentes Neste Reino," 23–01–1689 and "Traslado da Proposta Feita ao Governador D. João de Lencastre pelos Oficiais da Câmara Sobre a Entrada das Aguardentes," 9–02–1689, both in AHU, Angola, Cx. 13, Doc. 97. See also the evidence on interior slave prices presented in Joseph C. Miller, "Quantities and Currencies: Bargaining for Slaves on the Fringes of the

And the value of the slaves thus obtained in the interior roughly doubled upon their arrival at Luanda.[60] Even allowing for operating expenses in the order of 50%, this must have further increased the returns which Portuguese, Brazilian, and Luso-African traders eventually secured from the acquisition of slaves in the hinterland of Luanda through their investment in *gerebita*.

Finally, the exchange of alcohol for slaves was an equally lucrative enterprise for Africans in the interior who engaged in this commerce. Even though the foreign alcohol which they received for slaves was adulterated and much more expensive than at the coast, the costs incurred with the production of slaves were minimal. Behind the colonial capital of Angola, as elsewhere throughout much of the continent, slaves were "produced" through three major mechanisms:[61] one was through warfare carried out by African polities against neighbours for political reasons, which generated the by-product of prisoners, another, but economic in nature, was through African political authorities and wealthy entrepreneurs attacking their neighbours exclusively for slaves; and the third was in the form of taxes exacted by African political authorities from their subjects, refugees flocking to their side in time of warfare and climatic disasters, conversion of criminals and other undesirable elements of society into outcasts for sale and exile, compensation received from debtors, kidnapping, and their own slaves deemed expendable.[62] These schemes involved

---

World Capitalist Economy." Unpublished paper presented at the Congresso Internacional sobre a Escravidão, São Paulo, June 7–11, 1988, Table III. I am indebted to Prof. Miller for providing a copy of this important paper, the results of which have been only partially published in his "Slave Prices in the Portuguese Southern Atlantic."

[60] A comparison of selected slave prices in the interior and at Luanda between the 1620s and 1830, shows a differential in the order of 110%. See Miller, "Quantities and Currencies," especially Table III and Table IV.

[61] Some of the major studies surveying the issue include: Curtin, *Economic Change in Precolonial Africa*; Claude Meillassoux, ed. *l'Esclavage en Afrique précoloniale*. Paris, 1975; Suzanne Miers and Igor Kopytoff, eds. *Slavery in Africa: Historical and Anthropological Perspectives*. Madison, 1977; Joseph E. Inikori, ed., *Forced Migration: The Impact of the Export Slave Trade on African Societies*. London, 1981; Lovejoy, *Transformations in Slavery*; Patrick Manning, *Slavery and African Life*. Cambridge, 1990; and Alberto da Costa e Silva, *A Manilha e o Libambo: A África e a Escravidão de 1500 a 1700*. Rio de Janeiro, 2002.

[62] See John K. Thornton, "The Art of War in Angola, 1575–1680," *Comparative Studies in Society and History*. Vol. 30, 1988, pp. 360–378; idem, "Kingdom of Kongo, ca. 1390–1678," pp. 334–335; idem, *Kingdom of Kongo*, pp. 28–55 and ff.; David Birmingham, *The Portuguese Conquest of Angola*. London, 1965. pp. 25–41; Beatrix

negligible social costs of production.[63] To be sure, expenses related to their maintenance augmented the cost of the slaves. But even then, the price of slaves sold by African political authorities and wealthy entrepreneurs throughout the interior slave markets remained, as we have seen, extremely low. Consequently, the exchange of such a low-cost commodity for foreign alcohol was almost certainly a lucrative undertaking.

Conclusion

Assessing the profitability of the exchange of Luso-Brazilian alcohol for slaves at Luanda and its hinterland is a complex exercise requiring large sets of databases that are rarely available. The extant evidence presented above is clearly too meagre, fragmented over time and, in some cases, circumstantial for such an exercise. Although not proving conclusively that the exchange was a lucrative one for Portuguese merchant capitalists and Brazilian colonial traders, their commercial partners at Luanda, and African slave dealers in the interior, it strongly indicates high levels of profits were attainable for nearly all of those who engaged in the commerce.

Heintze, "Angola nas Garras do Tráfico de Escravos: As Guerras Angolanas do Ndongo (1611–1630)," *Revista Internacional de Estudos Africanos.* Vol. 1, 1984, pp. 11–59; "Memorial do Bispo D. Luiz Simões Brandão a El Rey," 02–11–1715, Biblioteca Pública de Évora, Secção dos Reservados, Cód. CXVI/2–15, No. 15-i, fls. 73–76; Dias, "Viagem a Cassange nos Meados do Século XVIII," pp. 14 and 19–20; Elias Alexandre da Silva Correia, *História de Angola.* Lisbon, 1937, Vol. II, p. 61; Luis António de Oliveira Mendes, *Memória a Respeito dos Escravos e Trafico da Escravatura entre a Costa d'Africa e o Brazil.* Porto, 1977, pp. 39–41; Governor Melo to Rodrigo de Sousa Coutinho, 03–02–1800, *Arquivos de Angola,* 2nd series, Vol. XXIII, Nos. 91–94, 1966, p. 93; Alfredo de Albuquerque Felner, ed. *Angola: Apontamentos Sobre a Colonização dos Planaltos e Litoral do Sul de Angola, Documentos.* Lisbon, 1940, Vol. 2, p. 14; Miller, "Central and Southern Angola to c. 1840,"; idem, *Kings and Kinsmen,* pp. 95–111; idem, "Significance of Drought, Disease and Famine,"; idem, *Way of Death,* pp. 105–139; Florentino, *Em Costas Negras,* pp. 82–103; Jean-Luc Vellut, "Notes sur le Lunda et la frontière luso-africaine (1700–1900)," *Études d'histoire africaine.* Vol. 3, 1972, pp. 77–78; idem, "Royaume de Cassange et les réseaux luso-africains," pp. 129–131; Susan H. Broadhead, "Slave Wives, Free Sisters: Bakongo Women and Slavery, c. 1700–1850" in Claire C. Robertson and Martin A. Klein, eds. *Women and Slavery in Africa.* Madison, 1983, p. 167; Jeffrey J. Hoover, "The Seduction of Ruwej: Reconstructing Ruund History (The Nuclear Lunda: Zaire, Angola, Zambia," Ph.D. Dissertation, Yale University, 1978, p. 105; and Thomas Reefe, *The Rainbow and the Kings: A History of the Luba Empire to 1891.* Berkeley, 1981, p. 85.

[63] Miller, *Way of Death,* pp. 105–139; and Florentino, *Em Costas Negras,* pp. 100–103.

A few other, but immeasurable factors lend further weight to this conclusion. Without the ballast provided by large quantities of cheap alcoholic beverages aboard Luso-Brazilian slavers on their way to Angola's colonial capital, the cost of slave trading ventures would have certainly been higher. Similarly, the lack of the expandable *vinho*, *aguardente*, and *gerebita*, would have led slave traders at Luanda to exclusively draw upon the less elastic and comparatively more expensive dry goods. And, as we will see in the following chapter, a number of invisible profits also accrued from the utilization of Luso-Brazilian alcohol throughout the interior to smooth trading operations and to further the flow of slaves to the coast. In short, the exchange of Luso-Brazilian alcohol for slaves at Luanda and its hinterland also produced earnings that are not always manifest in balance sheet accounts.

CHAPTER SEVEN

UNDERPINNING THE SLAVE TRADE: OTHER USES
OF LUSO-BRAZILIAN ALCOHOL IN LUANDA AND
ITS HINTERLAND, c. 1575–1830

The *aguardente, gerebita,* and *vinho* offloaded at Luanda until 1830 was, first and foremost, used to acquire slaves. This, however, was not their only function. Indeed, Luso-Brazilian intoxicants played a variety of other roles in the colonial capital of Angola and throughout its hinterland. Some of these were associated with slave trading. The leaders of caravans sent to the interior of Luanda in search of slaves drew upon imported alcohol to pay the toll and business taxes imposed by the African authorities of the lands where they operated. While high-level colonial officials utilized *aguardente, gerebita,* and *vinho* as gifts to entice African political leaders to provide large numbers of slaves for sale, mid-level colonial administrators used them to extort slaves from the African rulers of territories under their control. Moreover, both the central government in Lisbon and the Angolan colonial government drew upon *aguardente, gerebita,* and *vinho* imports to enact fiscal policies designed to foster slave exports from Luanda. And foreign intoxicants also developed into major trade goods which Luso-Brazilian slave traders utilized to effectively compete against European interlopers along the coast of Angola. Other functions of *aguardente, gerebita,* and *vinho,* however, had no direct relation to the infamous commerce. These alcohol imports provided sorely needed revenues through taxes to both the colonial government of Angola and the Municipal Council of Luanda. They also became the principal consummeable goods around which the population of Angola's colonial capital spent much of its leisure time and socialized in the many, but notorious, taverns found throughout this seaport. Foreign intoxicants were further used by the colonial administration of Angola as "payment" to Africans whom it forced to work on governmental projects, while the merchants of Luanda utilized them to acquire agricultural produce from African peasants inland whenever food was scarce at the coast. Lastly, European missionaries drew upon Luso-Brazilian alcohol to encourage the process of conversion in the interior of Angola's colonial capital. Beyond the direct acquisition of slaves, the multifaceted roles played by *aguardente*, *gerebita*, and *vinho*, whether directly associated with slaving and or not, all served to underpin the slave export trade, Luanda's only economic activity of note.

1. *Imported Alcohol in Roles associated with Slave Trading*

One of the more important roles played by Luso-Brazilian alcohol in association with slave trading was in the form of transit and business taxes which African political rulers inland from Luanda levied on caravans seeking to trade for slaves in their *feiras* and/or territories. Once Portuguese merchants in the colonial capital of Angola began to dispatch caravans into the interior in search of slaves, it quickly became customary for their *pombeiro* leaders to pay African political authorities a toll to pass through and a business tax to conduct trade negotiations within the territory under their jurisdiction.[1] Initially, these duties were paid with *malavu* obtained from the abundant palm trees that were found throughout the hinterland of Luanda. After the 1620s, they were increasingly disbursed in the form of various European and Asian trade goods, including *vinho*.[2] By the 1780s, these taxes were being primarily paid with Luso-Brazilian alcohol, especially *gerebita*,[3] a process which must have began following the mid-1600s introduction of this less costly and more readily available intoxicant from the land of Vera Cruz.

Should payment of these taxes not be made, caravan leaders were neither allowed access to the domains of African rulers nor permitted to conduct trade within their confines. Early in 1782, for example, one trader from Luanda, who had sailed up to the northern coast of Angola to acquire slaves on his own account, had to provide the local gentry with liberal amounts of imported intoxicants before conducting any business: the administrator of Ambriz got one *ancoreta* of *gerebita*, the Prince of Nsoyo received eight similar casks

---

[1] Undated report of Governor Fernão de Sousa in Heintze, *Fontes para a História de Angola*, Vol. I, pp. 281–282.

[2] Undated reports of Governor Sousa in *ibid.*, Vol. I, pp. 121 and 281–282; and Cadornega, *História Geral das Guerras*, Vol. III, p. 359.

[3] See, for example, Governor Moçâmedes to José de Seabra e Silva, 28–03–1786, AHU, Cód. 1642, fls. 32v–33.

of the same intoxicant and two *frasqueiras* of *aguardente*, the elite of Cabinda obtained twenty *ancoretas* of *cachaça*, and the rulers of Loango were offered six *ancoretas* of *gerebita* and two *frasqueiras* of *aguardente*.[4] Only then was he allowed to carry on his slave trading venture.

But the alcohol toll and business taxes were not always paid. Periodically, Luso-African traders attempted to avoid disbursing them so as to lower their operating costs. Whenever this occurred, African authorities rarely hesitated to appropriate the trade goods transported by their caravans. This is what seems to have happened during the early 1750s at Kasanje, the most important *feira* in the interior of Luanda, as *pombeiros* there saw their imported intoxicants and cloths confiscated.[5] Similarly, towards the end of the 1820s, the leaders of caravans dispatched from Ambaca fell into the practice of failing to pay the toll and business taxes in the kingdom of Matamba. This, once again, brought about an immediate response from the local political authorities. Their expeditions, imported cloths, intoxicants, and all, were plundered in retribution.[6] Although Luso-Brazilian slave traders sometimes bitterly complained to the Angolan colonial administration against the collection of these duties, it was thus in their self-interest to have their *pombeiros* comply.

Another function of imported intoxicants was as diplomatic presents offered by the governors of Angola to potentates in the interior of Luanda who supplied the slave export trade.[7] In 1620, for example, Garcia M. Castelo Branco wrote to the Portuguese Crown suggesting that it would be wise to forward annually three large wooden casks of *vinho* to Imbangala political leaders. Such a gift, he assured, would not prove very costly since the Imbangala would produce significantly more value in the slaves procured through warfare and raids than the 1,500 or so litres of *vinho* were worth.[8] It is not known if the governors of Angola were subsequently instructed to act favourably upon Castelo Branco's suggestion. Nonetheless,

---

[4] The account of this trading expedition, dated 15–08–1782, is found in AHU, Angola, Cx. 65, Doc. 64, fls. 2–11.

[5] See Sousa Dias, "Uma Viagem a Cassange," p. 16.

[6] See the petition of a group of 49 traders in Ambaca, 13–09–1830, AHU, Angola, Cx. 167, Doc. 57.

[7] Felner, *Angola*, p. 301.

[8] Garcia M. Castelo Branco to the King, 16–01–1629, in Cordeiro, *Viagens, Explorações e conquistas dos Portugueses: Colecção de Documentos—Da Mina ao Cabo Negro, 1574–1620*, pp. 16–17.

during his stay *circa* 1660 in the capital of the newly founded Imbangala kingdom, Kasanje, Cavazzi de Montecúccolo found relatively large amounts of this intoxicant in the possession of local political authorities.[9] Much of this *vinho* was most certainly obtained from caravan leaders who had previously visited or passed by the *feira* of Kasanje to acquire slaves. But precisely because Kasanje had by the early 1650s emerged into a major slave market, some may also have been provided by the governors of Angola to encourage Imbangala rulers to continue procuring and offering large numbers of slaves for trade with Portuguese merchants and/or their commercial representatives.

The leaders of the Imbangala, however, were not the only African political authorities with whom this practice was established. Another known beneficiary of these gifts was the much acclaimed Queen Nzinga of Matamba. When not at war with the Portuguese, she was also one of the main suppliers of the slaves that were exported through the colonial capital of Angola.[10] The price Queen Nzinga requested to maintain her *feira* open with considerable numbers of slaves for trade with the caravans dispatched to her realm from the coast by Portuguese merchants was "good" *vinho*, in particular, and other European and Asian trade goods. When these were not forthcoming from the governors of the colony, as occurred on one occasion

---

[9] Cavazzi de Montecúccolo, *Descrição Histórica dos Três Reinos*, Vol. I, p. 188.

[10] A good, general analysis of her reign is found in Joseph C. Miller, "Nzinga of Matamba in a New Perspective," *Journal of African History* Vol. XVI, No. 2, 1975, pp. 201–216. Nevertheless, subsequent research has greatly added to our knowledge and understanding of this important Angolan Queen. See, for example: Ibrahima B. Kaké, *Anne Zingha: Reine d'Angola, première résistante à l'invasion portugaise*. Paris, 1975; Roy A. Glasgow, *Nzinga: Resistencia africana à investida do colonialismo português em Angola, 1582–1663*. São Paulo, 1982; Fernando Campos, "A data da morte da Rainha Jinga D. Verónica I," *Africa* (Universidade de São Paulo), no. 4, 1981, pp. 79–103, no. 5, 1982, pp. 72–104, and no. 6, 1983, pp. 89–128; Adriano A. T. Parreira, "A Rainha Angolana Jinga: Para Além das Leis Normativas de Parentesco," *História* (Lisbon), No. 123, 1989, pp. 59–67; idem, *Economia e Sociedade em Angola na Época da Rainha Jinga, Século XVII*. Lisbon, 1990; Rosa M. M. da Cruz e Silva, "Njinga Mbandi e o Poder," Unpublished paper presented at the Canadian Association of African Studies Annual Meeting, Montreal, 13–16 May, 1992; Cathy Skidmore-Hess, "Bones and Baptism: Symbols and Ideology in the Career of Nzinga," Unpublished paper presented at the Canadian Association of African Studies Annual Meeting, Montreal, 13–16 May, 1992; idem, "Soldiers and Smallpox: The 1626 Portuguese Campaign against Njinga of Matamba in Angola," in Robert H. Harms, Joseph C. Miller, David S. Newbury, and Michele D. Wagner, eds., *Paths Towards the Past: African Historical Essays in Honor of Jan Vansina*. Atlanta, 1994, pp. 395–413; John K. Thornton, "Legitimacy and Political Power: Queen Njinga, 1624–63," *Journal of African History*. Vol. 32, 1991, pp. 25–40; and Pantoja, *Nzinga Mbandi*.

during the administration of Governor Fernão de Sousa, she did not
hesitate to seek her due from middle-level Portuguese colonial officials
nearby.[11]

But situations such as these seem to have been rare during Sousa's
governorship. When the *Ngola* of Ndongo sent an embassy to Luanda
to have one of his sons baptized, for example, Governor Sousa did
not neglect to include an unspecified amount of *vinho* amongst the
presents offered to his guests.[12] Similarly, in 1628, he dispatched six
peroleiras or some 100 litres of this imported alcoholic drink from his
own private stock, as well as a few other consumer and luxury items,
to the *sova* or chief of Ndala Quissuva in Ndongo, so as to cement
the allegiance which this potentate had recently proclaimed vis-à-vis
the Portuguese Crown.[13] With the *Ngola* ruling over an area that
supplied substantial numbers of slaves for the export trade and the
sova of Ndala Quissuva administering one of the major *feiras* in his
realm, these *vinho* presents were almost certainly intended to renumerate
indirectly African political authorities for services rendered in the
slave trade.

Yet another known example of the utilization of intoxicants in this
role comes from the Ndembu chieftainship of Kakulo Kahenda.
During the first half of the 1700s, and beyond, this polity was considered by the governors of Angola as one of the more important
chieftainships in the hinterland of Luanda, since it commanded the
western approaches to the large Ndembu *feira* at Kisoza and controlled
the north-south trade routes which channelled slaves from Kongo to
the colonial capital of Angola. Having become vassals of the Portuguese
Crown in the late seventeenth century, the *sovas* of Kakulo thereafter rendered numerous services to the Angolan colonial administration, particularly against their Ndembu rivals who controlled the
eastern approaches to Kisoza. Around 1736, Governor Rodrigo Cesar
de Menezes forwarded at least one 85 litre barrel of *gerebita* to its
chief, Dom Sebastião Francisco Cheque.[14] In 1743, Governor João

---

[11] See the letter of Queen Nzinga to Bento Banha Cardoso, dated 03–03–1625
[sic], as quoted in Skidmore-Hess, "Soldiers and Smallpox," p. 398.
[12] See the 1627 report written by Governor Sousa to the Portuguese Crown in
Brásio, *Monumenta Missionaria Africana*, 1st series, Vol. VII, p. 524.
[13] Governor Sousa to Francisco Castro, 8–04–1628, in *ibid.*, 1st series, Vol. VII,
p. 550.
[14] Almeida, "Relações com os Dembos," p. 33; and Cascudo, *Prelúdio da Cachaça*,
p. 23.

Jacques de Magalhães imitated his predecessor: he too sent one barrel of *aguardente* to the same *sova*.[15] Moreover, the governors of the colony were not the only ones forwarding these types of presents to Dom Cheque. At about the same time, a certain Manuel Vilário from Luanda, most probably a slave trader, also sent Dom Cheque a gift in the form of one *ancoreta* of *gerebita* and "remained at his disposal for whatever he wished."[16] Similarly, when Angola's colonial government established direct diplomatic links with the new King of Matamba in 1772, another important source of slaves, the Portuguese missionary entrusted with this task provided him with four small glass jars of *aguardente* and one 36 litre *ancoreta* of *gerebita*.[17]

Over time, offering imported intoxicants to African political leaders supplying the export slave trade not only became a standard practice, but by the early 1780s at the latest it was specifically recommended by the central government in Lisbon.[18] Thus, when the Portuguese sought to persuade the ruler of Cabinda in 1782 to allow the construction of a fort to reduce foreign competition in the slave trade carried out along the northern coast of Angola, Governor José Gonçalo da Câmara was explicitly advised by the Minister responsible for Portugal's colonies, Martinho de Melo e Castro, to provide him with presents which were to be mainly made up of sufficient quantities of *cachaça*.[19] Whether this recommendation was followed or not remains to be ascertained. Nevertheless, subsequent colonial authorities in Angola did make liberal use of Luso-Brazilian alcohol as part of the presents which they gave to African potentates to further diplomatic undertakings associated with slave trading.

One of the better known was Governor Manuel de Almeida e Vasconcelos. Late in 1790, he received an ambassador from the *Jaga* or ruler of Kasanje to continue the ongoing, but then particularly

[15] Almeida, "Relações com os Dembos," pp. 33–34.

[16] *Ibid.*

[17] Fr. João de S. Lucas to the Governor of Angola, 1–05–1772, *Arquivos de Angola*, 1st series, Vol. III, Nos. 30–33, 1937, p. 432.

[18] Such a policy may well date from the early eighteenth century when the Crown of Portugal instructed Governor D. Lourenço de Almada that much prudence was required in dealing with the Jaga Kasanje "so as to never break with him." See ANRJ, Negócios de Portugal/59, Cód. 543, fl. 82.

[19] Martinho de Melo e Castro to Governor José Gonçalo da Câmara, 20–09–1782, AHU, Cód. 549, fls. 64v–65.

thorny negotiations for a new commercial treaty on the *feira* there.[20] In gratitude, Vasconcelos forwarded a present to the *Jaga* which included two *ancoretas* of *gerebita* and one *frasqueira* of *aguardente*.[21] Following the arrival of two ambassadors in February and August of 1794, this time from the *Mani* Kongo, the Governor again responded with at least one *frasqueira* of fine liquers and one *ancoreta* of *aguardente*.[22] Then, early in August of 1795, upon receiving a letter from the *sova* of Musulo along with two slaves in the form of tribute, Almeida e Vasconcelos sent him, amongst other items, two *ancoretas* of *aguardente*, one *frasqueira* of fine liquers, and four *ancoretas* of *geribita*.[23] Similarly, when later that same year, he wrote *Jaga* Kalandula to destroy a *quilombo* or community composed of army deserters, fugitive slaves, and rebels that was hampering commerce passing near the Ambaca hills, accompanying his request were, amongst other presents, one *frasqueira* of *aguardente*, another of liquer from Rio de Janeiro, and ten *ancoretas* of *gerebita*.[24] Finally, just before his governorship came to an end, Almeida e Vanconcelos recompensed a Ndembu *sova* on two separate occasions with one *frasqueira* of *aguardente*, one *ancoreta* of *gerebita*, one *frasqueira* of liquer, and cloths for having accepted, after years of rebellion, Portuguese suzerainty.[25] Perhaps because of his liberal use of imported alcohol to further diplomatic efforts related to slave trading, Governor Almeida e Vasconcelos' successor would later complain that the only reason why the African potentates of

---

[20] For a discussion of these negotiations see Vellut, "Le royaume de Cassange," pp. 117–136.

[21] Governor Almeida e Vasconcelos to Jaga of Kasanje, 17–11–1790, AHU, Cód. 1627, fls. 24v–25v. A copy of the same letter found in AHNA, Cód. 84, fl. 35v, however, lists but the one *frasqueira* of *aguardente*.

[22] Governor Almeida e Vasconcelos to King of Kongo, 9–02–1794, AHNA, Cód. 87, fl. 22, with an undisclosed volume of fine liquers; and idem to Prince D. Garcia de Agoa Rozada, 15–08–1794, AHU, Cód. 1630, fls. 222v–224v. The second ambassador received another *ancoreta* of *gerebita*.

[23] Governor Almeida e Vasconcelos to Marques do Mussulo, 4–08–1795, AHU, Cód. 1631, fls. 157–157v; and "Rellação do Prezente . . . ao Marquez do Mossul," 4–08–1795, AHNA, Cód. 88, fls. 141–141v.

[24] Governor Almeida e Vasconcelos to Jaga Calandula, 2–11–1795, AHU, Cód. 1631, fls. 202v–203v. A copy of the same letter found in AHNA, Cód. 88, fls. 198–198v, lists the exact same volume of liquer and *aguardente*, but only four *ancoretas* of *gerebita*.

[25] Governor Almeida e Vasconcelos to Ndembu Nambuangongo, 22–02–1796, AHNA, Cód. 89, fl. 261; and idem to idem, 21–06–1797, AHU, Cód. 1632, fls. 291–292.

slave supplying areas nominally under Portuguese control ever both-
ered to write to him was to request *gerebita* and other gifts.[26]

But Almeida e Vasconcelos was not the only Governor to indulge
in such endeavours. Even more lavish was António de Saldanha da
Gama who, while governing the colony from 1807 to 1810, engaged
upon this practice in no less than sixteen occasions. On two separate instances, one in 1807 while relations with Kasanje over the
feira were extremely strained and another towards the end of his
term in 1810, Gama sent a total of 59 litres of *gerebita* and 56 litres
of *aguardente* for the *Jaga*'s personal consumption and some 30 litres
of *gerebita* to be shared amongst by latter's councillors.[27] Another
beneficiary of Gama's largesse was *sova* Ndala Kabassa, who in the
middle of 1808 was presented with 24 litres of *gerebita*, while his
councillors divided 2 litres of the same intoxicant amongst themselves.[28] But Gama's extravagant use of imported booze to further
diplomatic ties related to slave trading was overwhelmingly concentrated upon one specific group of African potentates: the Ndembu.
The *sova* of Kakulo Kahenda constituted by far his target of choice.
Over an eleven month period between 1807 and 1808, Gama forwarded on four different occasions at least 153 litres of *gerebita* directly
to this African ruler and some 30 litres of the same spirit to his
councillors and ambassadores.[29] The *sova* of Kaboko, another Ndembu
chief loyal to the Portuguese, was in the middle of 1807 recompensed by Governor Gama with three *ancoretas* of *gerebita* and six bottles of fine liquer after having successfully followed orders emanating
from Luanda to "hammer" neighbouring rebel chiefs.[30] Similarly,
once the *sova* of Mufuke Akitupa became a vassal of the Portuguese
crown, Gama did not fail to forward, on two separate instances,
some 100 litres of *gerebita* for his own personal consumption, while
a further 31 and 20 litres of this same beverage were destinned for

---

[26] Governor Melo to Rodrigo de Sousa Coutinho, 12–08–1798, *Arquivos de Angola*.
2nd series. Vol. III, Nos. 13–14, 1946, p. 143.
[27] Governor António de Saldanha da Gama to Jaga of Kasanje, 14–09–1807,
AHNA, Cód. 240, fl. 56; and idem to idem, 31–03–1810, *Ibid.*, fls. 74v–75.
[28] Governor Gama to *sova* Ndala Kabassa, 11–06–1807, AHNA, Cód. 240, fls.
65v–66.
[29] Governor Gama to Ndembu Kakulo Kahenda, 9–06–1807, AHNA, Cód. 240,
fls. 50v–51; idem to idem, 28–09–1807, *Ibid.*, fls. 57–57v; idem to idem, 8–06–1808,
Ibid., fl. 65; and idem to idem, 21–01–1808, *ibid.*, fl. 68.
[30] Governor Gama to Ndembu Kaboko, 28–07–1807, AHNA, Cód. 240, fls. 54.

the latter's councillors and porters, respectively.[31] Yet another Ndembu *sova* who became the recipients of Gama's lavishness was that of Ngombe Amukiama: on two different occasions, he too received a total of some 40 litres of *gerebita*, while his councillors got two jars of this same elixir.[32] Finally, four other Ndembu potentates also came to enjoy the pleasures provided by the extravagant distribution which Governor Gama made of *gerebita*: the *sova* of Mutimo Akigongo was sent three *ancoretas*, one of which was destinned for his councillors; that of Nambuangongo received some 27 litres; the *sova* of Ndambi Ngongwe obtained 24 litres; and the councillors of Kigengo had to content themselves with 12 litres.[33] For Gama, the lavish use of imported intoxicants thus became an extremely important tool to further diplomatic relations related to slaving.

A third role played by Luso-Brazilian alcohol in association with slave trading was in the extortion of tribute from *sovas* under the yoke of the Portuguese colonial administration. Ever since the Portuguese began to expand the territory under colonial rule from the coast, it became necessary for administrative purposes to organize the newly conquered lands into districts and *presídios* or larger administrative-military territorial units. These inland districts and *presídios* were administered by *capitães-mores* or captains-major who ruled the areas under their jurisdiction with despotic zeal.[34] As in the case of the governors of the colony, the *capitães-mores* were also poorly compensated for their services, which led them to seek additional sources of revenue. Along with other Lusophone individuals established in the interior, it was not uncommon for the *capitães-mores* to fill their private purses by exacting tribute from local African chiefs. One of the most prominent ways in which this was done was through a process known as *ocamba*. Fernão de Sousa has left us a vivid description of how this process functioned:

---

[31] Governor Gama to Ndembu Mufuke Akitupa, 29–07–1807, AHNA, Cód. 240, fl. 54v; and idem to idem, 5–09–1807, *ibid.*, fls. 55–55.

[32] Governor Gama to Ndembu Ngombe Amukiama, 19–09–1807, AHNA, Cód. 240, fl. 56v; and idem to idem, 4–07–1807, *ibid.*, fl. 66v.

[33] Governor Gama to Ndembu Mutimo Akigongo, 11–11–1807, AHNA, Cód. 240, fls. 58v; idem to Ndembu Nambuangongo, 28–09–1807, *ibid.*, fl. 58; idem to Ndembu Ndambi Ngongwe, 6–07–1808, *ibid.*, fl. 67v; and idem to Ndembu Kigengo, 21–11–1808, *ibid.*, fl. 68v.

[34] This group of colonial administrators is extensively analyzed in Couto, *Os Capitães-Mores em Angola*.

Ocamba is the Captain of the *Presídio* or any other Portuguese individual sending the *sovas* of his district . . . one *peroleira* of *vinho*, cloth, or other textiles with the intention of having the chiefs pay [for these items] expeditiously with feigned friendliness; and the *sovas* sometimes refusing [these goods], the captains and other Portuguese individuals force them to accept unwillingly by leaving [the said items] in [their] homes; and if the *sovas* delay payment, the captains and other Portuguese individuals order the debt to be collected in the form of slaves valued at three or four times the price of the items left behind.[35]

Once acquired in this fashion, the slaves were marched to Angola's colonial capital and sold to Portuguese merchants. A small part of the proceeds obtained from these transactions were thereafter utilized to buy more *vinho* and textiles with which to exact more slaves from other African chiefs. During his governorship, Sousa attempted to dissuade the *capitães-mores* and other Portuguese individuals from engaging in such deceitful practices, which often resulted in strained relations between African political authorities and the colonial government.[36] But his efforts were in vain. The *ocamba* was too important a source of additional revenue for the *capitães-mores* and other Portuguese individuals established in the interior to stop extorting *sovas* throughout the districts and *presídios* of the colony.

A fourth function played by imported alcohol in connection with slaving was as a trade good with which slave traders in Luanda could effectively compete against English and French interlopers, who offered better quality and lower priced consumer and luxury items for the numerous slaves exchanged by African suppliers in enclaves to the north and south of Angola's colonial capital. This was particularly true of *gerebita*. Indeed, following its introduction in the mid-1600s, this cheap, sharp, and highly alcoholized intoxicant soon became one of the few goods which provided Luso-Brazilian slave traders in Luanda with a competitive edge against European interlopers. Not a few high-ranking colonial administrators periodically exalted the virtues of *cachaça* in this role. According to Governor Francisco

---

[35] "Declaração dos Tributos que se Pedem aos Sovas," in Felner, *Angola*, p. 472. This type of extortion is also mentioned in the letter of Governor Sousa to the Conselho da Fazenda, 7–12–1631, in Heintze, *Fontes para a História de Angola*, Vol. I, p. 381.

[36] *Ibid.*

Inocêncio de Sousa Coutinho, for example, "if the English and French at Cabinda and Loango could sell [slave suppliers around the mouth of the Zaire River] our *gerebita*, the only trade good strengthening our commerce, they would for sure completely ruin us . . ."[37] Two decades later, Barão de Moçâmedes, then Governor of the colony, also informed his sovereign that "in the case of *gerebita* and *aguardente*, foreigners could not compete against the Portuguese."[38] Similarly, while writing to the central government in Lisbon about the northernmost *presídio* of Encoge, Governor António Miguel de Melo in 1798 informed that Africans there found more variety, less fraud, and more trade goods amongst European interlopers to satisfy their needs than amongst Luso-Brazilian traders: the only two exceptions were "*gerebita*, which they always prize and want, and salt, which they can not do without."[39] His successor, Governor Fernando António de Noronha further highlighted this important function of *cachaça*. In 1803, he wrote the central government in Lisbon that the Kongo supplying slaves at the River Loje were becoming increasingly "convinced that our commerce is more advantageous" partly because "we provide them with good *gerebita*, for them the most precious intoxicant."[40] Not surprisingly, as late as 1829, the central administration in Lisbon was still praising *cachaça* in this context.[41] Without it, the Luso-Brazilian slave traders based at Luanda were unable to have their caravan leaders attract the business of African slave suppliers who would otherwise illegally seek the better quality and lower priced goods provided by their English and French competitors.

Finally, beginning with the early 1780s, imported alcohol came to play yet another role in association with slaving as part and parcel of fiscal policies designed by both the central government in Lisbon

[37] Governor Sousa Coutinho to Mendonça Furtado, 23–09–1764, BNL, Cód. 8553, fl. 93.
[38] Governor Barão de Moçâmedes to the Queen, 5–01–1785, AHU, Cx. 70, Doc. 29. See also, in the same vein, Governor Barão de Moçâmedes to José de Seabra e Silva, 28–03–1786, *Arquivo das Colónias*. Vol. III, No. 8, 1918, p. 259.
[39] Governor Melo to Rodrigo de Sousa Coutinho, 24–04–1798, AHU, Angola, Cx. 87, Doc. 65. Similar comments on the competitive edge provided by *gerebita* are found in António Joseph Manzoni de Castro to Governor of Angola, 17–07–1798, AHU, Angola, Cx. 88, Doc, 34.
[40] Governor Noronha to Rodrigo de Sousa Coutinho, 30–07–1803, *Arquivos de Angola*. 2nd series, Vol. XIX, Nos. 75–78, 1962, p. 53.
[41] See the "Parecer" of the Conselho Ultramarino, 21–01–1829, AHU, Angola, Cx. 161, Doc. 14. It is published in Rebelo, *Relações entre Angola e Brasil*, pp. 437–441.

and the colonial government of Angola to foster the export of slaves from Luanda, the only notable economic activity of this port town. Following the extremely depressed 1770s, the Portuguese Crown attempted to speed up the recovery of slave trading in the colonial capital of Angola from its depressed volumes of the previous decades by radically modifying the existing tax structure on the alcohol imports, the second most important trade good after Indian cloth imports with which slaves were obtained.[42] Soon after Barão de Moçâmedes arrived at Luanda early in 1784 to assume the governorship of the colony, he was instructed to exempt alcohol imports destined exclusively for the acquisition of slaves in the interior from paying import duties.[43] The alcohol offloaded for consumption within this seaport, on the other hand, was to remain taxed at the existing rate to defray the salaries of instructors teaching at its only school.[44] With *gerebita* by far the most voluminous of the intoxicants imported and the sole alcoholic drink extensively used for slave trading in the hinterland of Angola's colonial capital, this policy was clearly designed to increase slave exports by favouring Brazilian colonial traders at the expense of metropolitan merchant capitalists. Indeed, *cachaça* imports rose by almost 11% during 1785–1794 over the levels of the previous three years, whereas slave exports grew by a slightly higher margin of 11.5%.[45]

Although the amount of *gerebita* unloaded and slaves shipped both increased after 1784, it did not take too long for traders at Luanda

---

[42] This decision appears to have been made around 1782, since the instructions written for the governorship of Barão de Moçâmedes (1784–1790) already make reference to it. See the minutes of these undated instructions in AHU, Angola, Cx, 65, Doc. 61.

[43] This directive was written on 1–03–1784. See Melo e Castro to Governor Barão de Moçâmedes, 6–03–1784, AHU, Cód. 549, fls. 81v; Queen to Governor Barão de Moçâmedes, AHU, Cód. 549, fls. 102v–103; Prince to Governor Melo, 4–11–1799, AHU, Cód. 550, fls. 49–50; AHU, Cód. 556, fls. 2–3; Governor Barão de Moçâmedes to the Queen, 5–01–1785, AHU, Cx. 70, Doc. 29; Melo e Castro to the Queen, 7–02–1795, AHU, Angola, Cx. 81, Doc. 12; and "Regimento da Alfandega da Cidade de São Paulo d'Assumpção Capital do Reino de Angola, 21–10–1799," *Arquivos de Angola*, 1st series, Vol. II, No. 12, 1936, pp. 425–428.

[44] This was the *subsídio literário*, a tax originally introduced throughout the Lusophone colonies by the Marquês de Pombal during the third quarter of the 1700s. In Brazil, this occurred at the beginning of the 1770s, while the Marquês do Lavradio was Vice-Roy (1769–1779). See Pantoja, "Encontro nas Terras do Além-Mar," p. 36. In Angola, the date of its introduction remains obscure. But see our discussion below.

[45] See Graphs 5 and 7.

to become dissatisfied with the new structure of alcohol import taxes. By the early 1790s, they were complaining to both the colonial government of Angola and the Portuguese Crown that their alcohol trade had suffered a drop of 25% in spite of the 1784 exemption.[46] Then late in 1794, they succeeded in obtaining from Governor Almeida e Vasconcelos an agreement which significantly lowered the *subsídio literário* from 1$600 to a mere $450 *réis* per *pipa* of alcohol imported.[47] Should the sums collected from the reduced tax be insufficient to pay the teachers' salaries, the slave traders committed themselves to defray the difference.

The reasons why Governor Almeida e Vasconcelos consented to this new arrangement are not altogether clear. What is known is that he was a strong advocate of greater alcohol imports as a means of increasing the number of slaves exported from the colonial capital of Angola.[48] Consequently, Governor Almeida e Vasconcelos may well have seen the 1794 agreement as a mechanism that, under the guise of alcohol offloaded solely for the Luanda market, allowed far larger quantities of intoxicating beverages to be imported for the acquisition of greater numbers of slaves in the interior. Indeed, subsequent developments lend weight to this explanation. The post-1794 *subsídio literário* proved inadequate to defray the teachers' wages and the slave traders failed to pool their financial resources to make up the balance.[49] Yet, the volume of alcohol imports augmented significantly. The amount of *gerebita* unloaded, in particular, jumped 43% during 1795–1799 over the previous ten year period, while alcohol imports from the metropole experienced a rise of roughly 5%.[50] Given that the latter were destined primarily for consumption at Luanda, the disproportionate increase in the amount of *cachaça*

---

[46] Governor Almeida e Vasconcelos to Melo e Castro, 7–02–1795, AHU, Cód. 1633, fl. 124; and Melo e Castro to the Prince, 7–02–1795, AHU, Cx. 81, Doc. 12. Whether this decrease actually took place can not be determined, since the extant documentation for 1785–1794 does not provide import data on an annual basis. See Graph 13.

[47] "Termo da Covenção [20–12–1794]," AHU, Angola, Cx. 88, Doc. 34.

[48] Governor Almeida e Vasconcelos to Paulo José do Loreiro (Director of the slave market at Kasanje), 12–04–1791, AHU, Cód. 1627, fls. 129–129v.

[49] See Antonio José Manzoni de Castro (Controller of the Royal Treasury Board) to Governor Melo, 17–07–1798, AHU, Angola, Cx. 88, Doc. 34; and the 1795–1797 figures of this tax in Graph 22.

[50] These figures are worked out from the data in Graphs 7 and 11. The 1794 agreement was finally abolished by the Crown five years later. See Prince to Governor Melo, 4–11–1799, AHU, Angola, Cx. 93–1, Doc. 5.

offloaded was surely destined for slave trading in the interior. If this was in fact the case, however, the intent of Governor Almeida e Vasconcelos backfired, as the international economic conjuncture in the second half of the 1790s forced slave exports from this port downwards by nearly 10% vis-à-vis the first half of the decade.[51] The voluminous growth in *gerebita* imports, on the other hand, enabled colonial traders in Brazil to augment the proportion of slaves acquired at Luanda in exchange for this intoxicant from about 12% in 1785–1794 to 16% in 1795–1799, or roughly one-third,[52] suggesting that it was they who spurred Governor Almeida e Vasconcelos to further lower the *subsídio literário*.

Another episode where alcohol imports were again intrinsically linked with governmental policy to increase slave exports from Luanda took place during the second half of the 1820s. Following Brazil's independence, customs officials in the colonial capital of Angola continued not only to allow the importation of *gerebita*, but they did so under the rate of 1$488 *réis* per *pipa* in place prior to 1822. In an attempt to resolve this anachronistic situation, the Portuguese Crown concluded in August of 1825 a treaty with the Emperor of Brazil with a provision stipulating that *cachaça* imports at Luanda would suffer no more than a 15% duty.[53] Since the value of each large wooden cask of *gerebita* then hovered around 100$000 *réis*, this new import tax was almost ten times higher that previously in effect.[54] Fearing reprisals against Portuguese alcohol imports in Brazil and slavers from the land of Vera Cruz sailing exclusively for duty free coastal enclaves north of the colonial capital of Angola to acquire enslaved labourers in exchange of their *cachaça*, however, the Portuguese Crown did not have the new duty implemented. Instead, less than four months later, it passed a Royal Decree which again allowed *gerebita* to be imported at Luanda under the old 1$488 *réis* tax.[55]

This immediately led Portuguese merchant capitalists to clamour for the total exclusion of Brazilian trade in this seaport in the hope

---

[51] See Graph 5.

[52] See Graphs 15, 16 and 17.

[53] Manchester, *British Preeminence in Brazil*, p. 202; and Rebelo, *Relações entre Angola e Brasil*, p. 271.

[54] Lima, *Ensaios sobre a statistica das possessões portuguesas*, Vol. III, pp. 70–71.

[55] A copy of this decree, dated 7–12–1825, is found in AHU, Angola, Cx. 147, Doc. 29.

of seeing alcohol from the metropole replace that unloaded off vessels originating from the land of Vera Cruz.[56] Soon thereafter, various governmental units began to ponder the issue. Their deliberations not only procrastinated, but proved confusingly inconclusive as well.[57] The matter was finally taken up by the Conselho Ultramarino some-time in 1828. In the view of this counselling body, banning *cachaça* imports would force Brazilian slavers to conduct their business north of Angola's colonial capital, thereby ensuring the destruction of its slave export-based economy and reducing unnecessarily its import-export revenues. Furthermore, it added, metropolitan alcohol could not substitute *gerebita*, the latter being cheaper and preferred by West Central African consumers. As a result, the Conselho Ultramarino recommended early in 1829 that the most cautious course to adopt was to continue permitting *cachaça* to be offloaded in this port town under the duty in effect.[58]

The recommendation was not accepted by the Crown. Later in 1829, the new Governor of the colony, Barão Comba Dão, was in-structed to impose the 15% duty per *pipa* of *gerebita* imported. Nevertheless, whether or not by design, the new tax came into effect only towards the end of 1830: that is, after the trans-Atlantic slave trade was legally abolished.[59] Following Brazil's independence, both the central government in Lisbon and the colonial government in Luanda thus succeeded in maintaining low duties on *cachaça* imports so as to sustain the slave export based economy of Angola until the very end of the legal traffic.

II. *Imported Alcohol in Non-Slave Trading Roles*

If imported alcohol played a number of other important functions in association with slave trading, the same was also true in the case of roles that were not directly tied to this commerce. Of these, one of the better documented is that as a source of tax revenue for the

---

[56] See document # 81 published in Rebelo, *Relações entre Angola e Brasil*, pp. 421–425.

[57] The diverging conclusions of these governmental units are adequately sum-marized in Rebelo, *Relações entre Angola e Brasil*, pp. 273–279.

[58] See the "Parecer" of the Conselho Ultramarino, 21–01–1829, AHU, Angola, Cx. 161, Doc. 14; also in AIHGB, DL31,02.28, fls. 109v–110.

[59] Governor Comba Dão to Conde de Basto, 11–11–1830, AHU, Cx. 166, Doc. 35.

colonial government. In his report to the Portuguese Crown c. 1612, Pedro Sardinha proposed that a duty of 2$000 *réis* per *pipa* be imposed on *vinho* imports at Luanda to defray the expenses involved with the defence of the colony.[60] Sardinha's suggestion, however, appears to have been shelved. A similar proposal was penned by António Dinis in 1622 when he suggested to the central government in Lisbon that, since significant profits were made from the sale of *vinho* and other European merchandise unloaded in this seaport, the Portuguese trading community established there could most certainly pay an import duty on these items.[61] This later suggestion seems to have fallen on more receptive ears, for the next individual dispatched to govern Angola, Fernão de Sousa, was soon instructed by the Portuguese Crown to impose a tax on the *vinho* imported at Luanda to help subvent the costs of fortifying the colonial capital.[62] After consulting with representatives from the Municipal Council and merchants based in the colonial capital of Angola during the first half of 1626, Governor Sousa enacted a $500 *réis* levy on each *pipa* of *vinho* offloaded at Luanda, a substantially lower amount than that recommended earlier by Sardinha.[63] During the late 1640s, Governor Salvador C. de Sá e Benevides, who had led the Brazilian expeditionary force that ousted the Dutch, increased this import tax to an unknown amount.[64] Most likely this was done to assist in paying the costs incurred with the recapture of the colony from the Protestant invaders. With much of the imported *vinho* then finding its way into the interior for the purpose of trade, financing the fortification of Luanda and the recapture of Angola through the import duty on this intoxicant thus created

---

[60] "Memórias de Pedro Sardinha," in Brásio, *Monumenta Missionaria Africana*, 1st series, Vol. VI, pp. 105–106.

[61] "Relação de António Dinis," in *ibid.*, 1st series, Vol. VII, p. 67.

[62] King to Governor Sousa, 14–11–1624, in Heintze, *Fontes para a História de Angola*, Vol. II, pp. 49.

[63] See the letter of Fernão de Sousa, 20–10–1632, in Pombo, *Annais de Angola (1630–1635)*, p. 30; "Carta do Governador Geral de Angola," 8–03–1687, in Brásio, *Monumenta Missionaria Africana*, 1st series, Vol. XIV, p. 49; and Delgado, *História de Angola*, Vol. III, p. 119. Governor Sousa's own correspondence provides conflicting information on this tax. On one occasion he states that it amounted to 2$000 *réis* and on another to 1$000 *réis*. See Governor Sousa to the central government, 8–07–1626, and idem to the King, 29–08–1628, in Heintze, *Fontes para a História de Angola*, Vol. II, pp. 161–162 and 207, respectively.

[64] Delgado, *História de Angola*, Vol. III, p. 119. Mauro, *Le Portugal, le Brésil et l'Atlantique*, p. 417, maintains that the duty collected on *vinho* imports at Luanda was still lower than that in effect in the ports of Brazil.

a situation whereby African consumers partially subsidized their own exploitation by the Portuguese.

The increased *vinho* import duty imposed by Governor Benevides appears to have remained unaltered until the late seventeenth century. Whether *aguardente* and *cachaça* imports were also taxed during this period still remains to de determined.[65] But, once the 1679 ban on the importation of *gerebita* was withdrawn, a more comprehensive fiscal policy on alcoholic beverages offloaded at the colonial capital of Angola quickly emerged. In 1695, the King of Portugal imposed an import duty of 1$600 *réis* per *pipa* on *cachaça* imports in this seaport.[66] The amount of the import duties on *vinho* and *aguardente*, on the other hand, appears to have been left up to the discretion of the Governor of the colony, Henrique Jacques de Magalhães, to fix. Indeed, later in 1695, Governor Magalhaes followed the royal decree establishing the import duty on *gerebita* with the imposition of a steep 6$000 *réis* per *pipa* of *aguardente* and an even higher 8$000 *réis* per large wooden cask of *vinho* to help defray military expenses.[67] This action clearly favoured Brazilian trading interests over representatives of metropolitan merchants, who immediately secured the assistance of officials in the Municipal Council of Luanda to forward a petition to the Portuguese Crown denouncing the exorbitant import taxes on *vinho* and *aguardente* imposed by the Governor. Upon reception of this petition, the King lost little time in writing to Governor Magalhães reprimanding him for the unjustified high duties on *vinho* and *aguardente* imports and, more importantly, ordering that the new taxes placed on these alcoholic beverages be instantly reduced by half, to 3$000 *réis* and 4$000 *réis* per *pipa*, respectively.[68] The newly implemented *vinho* and *aguardente* import duties were, nevertheless, still significantly higher than that imposed on the importation of *cachaça*. As a result, the fiscal policy elaborated in Lisbon persisted in favouring the low cost *gerebita* over the more expensive *vinho* and *aguardente*.

---

[65] Given the appreciable volume of *cachaça* imports during this period, it is unlikely that this intoxicant would have escaped the imposition of import duties.

[66] King to Oficiais da Câmara, 9–12–1695, AHU, Cód. 545, fls. 94v–95.

[67] King to Governor Magalhães, 4–09–1696, AHU, Angola, Cx. 33, Doc. 93.

[68] *Ibid.*; King to Oficiais da Câmara, 4–09–1696, AHU, Cód. 545, fls. 100–100v; and "Registo de hua carta de sua Mag.de," 4–09–1696, AHBML, Cód. 12, fl. 86v.

The import duty rates placed on *cachaça* in 1695 and on *vinho* and *aguardente* in 1696 remained in place until the early 1770s.[69] The colonial administration in Angola, however, did not have the organizational capacity required to collect these taxes from the owners or the captains of vessels that docked at Luanda with cargoes of *gerebita*, *vinho*, and *aguardente*. Consequently, from 1696 onwards, the collection of the alcohol import duties were the object of contracts which the colonial government of Angola farmed out to local individuals in exchange for fixed sums.[70] Although there were times when bids for these contracts failed to materialize, they could nevertheless be extremely profitable. Manuel Sanches dos Campos secured a three-year alcohol import duty contract on the 3rd of July, 1699, in exchange for 3,300$000 *réis*. While this contract was in effect, he succeeded in collecting a total of 6,782$750 *réis* from all of the *aguardente*, *vinho*, and *cachaça* imported.[71] The cost of collection not withstanding, this provided Campos with a hefty profit of slightly over 100%.

The alcohol import duty contracts at Luanda provided the government of the colony with sufficient sums of income to cover part of the expenses incurred by the defence and expansion of the *conquista*. During 1722–1730, 1732–1733, 1742, 1755, 1762, and 1764–1765, for example, they represented an average of some 3.5% of the total revenue that the colonial administration in Angola secured for the Portuguese Crown.[72] Although this a low figure, the alcohol import contracts were consistently the second most important source of income produced in the colony for the Portuguese Crown.[73] Overall, their role in generating royal income was only superseded by the

---

[69] In the early 1760s, Governor António de Vasconcelos proposed to levy a further tax (1$000 *réis* per *pipa*) on alcoholic beverages imported at Luanda to finance the digging of a canal that would bring fresh water from the Kwanza River to the colonial capital of Angola. See Vasconcelos to the King, 9–07–1762, AHU, Angola, Cx. 45, Doc. 64. The proposed increase in alcohol import duties was not implemented, however, because the project did not materialize.

[70] King to Oficiais da Câmara, 9–12–1695, AHU, Cód. 545, fls. 94v–95; King to Governor Magalhães, 4–09–1696, AHU, Angola, Cx. 33, Doc. 93; and the petition of Bento Fernandes Lobo, Balthazar dos Reis, and António Moreira, 12–06–1752, AHU, Angola, Cx. 37, Doc. 81.

[71] See the financial appraisal of this contract provided by Rodrigo da Costa da Almeida (Provedor da Fazenda Real de Angola) to the King, 5–08–1703, AHU, Angola, Cx. 17, Doc. 52.

[72] This figure is based on the quantitative data supporting Graph 21.

[73] *Ibid.* Only in 1740 did the alcohol import contract fall to the third major source of revenue.

taxes imposed on the slaves exported from this port town, which made up the overwhelming majority of all of the revenue accumulated in the colony for the Portuguese Crown.

In spite of the relatively appreciable sums of revenue collected from 1696 until the late 1760s by farming out the alcohol import duties to the highest bidder, alcohol import contracts nonetheless came to an abrupt end in 1769, when they were abrogated as part of the policy adopted by the Portuguese Crown to abolish the whole contract system in Angola.[74] Thereafter, responsibility for the direct collection of the taxes on *gerebita*, *vinho*, and *aguardente* imports at Luanda reverted back to the colonial administration of Angola. Soon after the transfer took place, the then Governor of the colony, Sousa Coutinho, readjusted their value. On the 24th of April, 1771, he reduced the alcohol tariffs on each *pipa* of alcohol imported: the 1$600 *réis* duty on *cachaça* was lowered by 7% to 1$488 *réis*, while the 3$000 *réis* tax on *vinho* and the 4$000 *réis* impost on *aguardente* were both decreased by 5% to 2$850 and 3$800 *réis*, respectively.[75] Whether Sousa Coutinho was specifically instructed by the Crown to implement these lower duties or whether he acted on his own can not be determined, since all of the sources relating to the new tax structure are dated well after his governorship.

What did the 1771 tax structure on alcohol imports represent? Implemented during a period of recession in both Brazil and Angola, it may have been designed to stimulate the export of alcohol from the land of Vera Cruz and the metropole to Luanda and, thereby, encourage larger number of slaves acquired in exchange of *aguardente*, *vinho*, and *gerebita* to be shipped from this seaport. But the downward readjustment was too modest to have had much of an impact. A more likely hypothesis is that this lower tax represented the *subsídio literário*, the impost on alcohol imports to defray the salaries of instruc-

---

[74] The royal decree which brought the contract system to an end in Angola, dated 5–08–1769, is found in AHU, Cód. 1252, fls. 29–31. For a lengthy discussion of the reasons behind its abolition, see Miller, *Way of Death*, pp. 590–597.

[75] "Relação dos Rendimentos que tem a Fazenda Real do Reino de Angola," 1772, AHU, Angola, Cx. 57, Doc. 40; "Regimento de Alfândega da Cidade de São Paulo da Assumpção, Capital do Reino de Angola, 21–10–1799," *Arquivos de Angola*, 1st series, Vol. II. No. 12. 1936. pp. 425–427; Governor Melo to President of the Erário Régio, 14–08–1802, AHU, Sala 12, Maço # 858; and "Relatorio do Governador Fernando António de Noronha, 2–01–1806," *Arquivos de Angola*, 1st series, Vol. II, No. 15, 1936, p. 660.

tors teaching at the only school of Luanda. Sousa Coutinho was the Governor of Angola through which the Marquês de Pombal, the enlightened, despotic, and *de facto* ruler of Portugal from 1750 to 1777, implemented his most important reforms.[76] Given that it was during Pombal's reign that the *subsídio literário* was introduced elsewhere in the Lusophone overseas world, it makes sense that its implementation in the colonial capital of Angola should have taken place while Sousa Coutinho was the Governor.[77]

The alcohol import tax structure established by Sousa Coutinho did not remain in place for too long. In 1784, as we have seen above, intoxicants imported for consumption exclusively within Luanda became the only alcohol upon which taxes were collected. Then, late in 1794, the duties on all alcoholic beverages imported for consumption in this port town were decreased to a mere $450 *réis* per *pipa*. In both cases, the sums collected were destined to pay teachers' wages. Moreover, following the arrival of a new Governor in 1797, António Miguel de Melo, high-ranking colonial officials began to mount a campaign against the new *subsídio literário* with allegations that it was not only inadequate to pay the teachers' wages, but that the Luanda trading community never pooled its financial resources to cover the difference.[78] Upon consideration of these charges, the Portuguese Crown was finally moved late in 1799 to annul both the 1784 import duty exemption on alcohol destined for slave trading and the 1794 agreement which traders in Luanda had concocted with Governor Almeida e Vasconcelos. In their place, the Crown decided to re-introduce the more comprehensive and onerous alcohol import taxes initially imposed by Governor Sousa Coutinho, with the amounts collected remaining allocated for the *subsídio literário*.[79]

---

[76] See Ralph Delgado, "O Governo de Sousa Coutinho em Angola," *Studia*. No. 6, 1960, pp. 19–56; No. 7, 1961, pp. 49–87; and No. 10, 1962, pp. 7–47.

[77] As it happens, the first school in this port town was founded during the governorship of Sousa Coutinho. See António Brásio, "Descripção dos Governos dos Ill.mos e Ex.mos Snr.es António de Vasconcellos, e D. Francisco Innocencio de Souza Coutinho," *Studia*. Nos. 41–42, 1979, p. 208.

[78] Antonio Joseph Manzoni de Castro to Governor Melo, 17–07–1798, AHU, Angola, Cx. 88, Doc. 34, fls. 4–4v.

[79] Principe to Governor Melo, 4–11–1799, AHU, Angola, Cx. 93–1, Doc. 5. Other copies of this *Carta Régia* are found in: AIHGB, DL76,02.02, fls. 10–11v; AHU, Cód. 550, fl. 50; and *Arquivos de Angola*, 1st series, Vol. III, No. 24, 1937, pp. 222–223. See also Governor Melo to Rodrigo de Sousa Coutinho, 30–05–1801, AHU, Cx. 100, Doc. 31 and AHU, Sala 12, Maço # 858.

The allegations made by high-ranking colonial officials, however, were pure fabrications. Indeed, although the sums obtained under the new *subsídio literário* fell appreciably from an annual average of almost 3,661$000 *réis* in 1792–1794 to an average of 1,143$285 *réis* per annum during 1795–1798, they were still more than enough to cover the total annual salaries, 880$000 *réis*, required for the five teaching positions existing at the turn of the eighteenth century.[80] Provided by no other than Governor Melo himself, the Portuguese Crown must have been well aware of this information.

During the 1790s, on the other hand, revenue secured from the colony of Angola by the Portuguese Crown was falling precipitously. Royal duties and excise taxes on slave exports from Luanda, in particular, which made up more than 90% of its total revenue in Angola, fell from 104,161$500 *réis* in 1792 to 81,009$000 *réis* in 1797, or by slightly more than one-quarter.[81] Such a drastic drop led the Crown to command Governor Melo to finally establish the long projected customs house at Luanda so as to better control the only Angolan colonial economic activity of note, the import-export trade, and thereby increase royal revenue. The replacement of the 1784 and 1794 alcohol import duty structures by that of 1771 became part and parcel of the *Regimento* or instructions written up in 1799 for the customs house. As a result, it clearly fell within the new policy of augmenting royal revenue through greater administrative control over commerce. Indeed, within a short period of time, the re-imposition of the much higher alcohol import taxes originally introduced by Governor Sousa Coutinho again became the Crown's second leading source of revenue.[82] Although the available data indicate that, on the average, 3.6% of the total royal revenue obtained from the colony of Angola between 1802 and 1823 derived from the new alcohol import duties, the sums involved were still significantly more than enough to defray teachers' salaries, with the remainder presumably going to the coffers of the Portuguese Crown.

---

[80] See Graph 22 for the *subsídio literário* during 1792–1797. The salaries allocated for the teaching positions at Luanda in the late 1790s are provided by Governor Melo in "Angola no Fim do Século XVIII: Documentos," *Boletim da Sociedade de Geografia de Lisboa*, Vol. 6, 1886, p. 292.

[81] See Graph 22.

[82] Governor Melo to Presidente do Erário Régio, 14–08–1802, AHU, Angola, Cx. 104, Doc. 28 (also in AHU, Sala 12, Maço # 858, fls. 9v–10); and "Relatório do Governador Fernando António de Noronha," 2–01–1806, *Arquivos de Angola*, 1st series, Vol. II, No. 15, 1936, p. 660.

The colonial government, however, was not the only administrative body which collected taxes on the alcoholic beverages that were imported at Luanda. The *Câmara Municipal* or Municipal Council of Angola's colonial capital, which was established shortly after Novais arrived in West Central Africa to found the colony, also required tax revenues to finance its day-to-day operations. At an undetermined date, it too began to levy an excise tax on intoxicants, as well as other European and Asian items, imported through its port. Little is known about the early history of this excise impost on alcohol imports. In 1649, for example, the Municipal Council collected a total of 352,034 *réis* from its excise tax on European and Asian consumer and luxury goods offloaded in its port. According to the source that compiled these data, much of this revenue came from the Municipal Council's tax on *vinho* imports,[83] then still the major intoxicant imported. By the turn of the 1670s, the Municipal Council was levying an excise duty of $500 *réis* on every *pipa* of *cachaça*, *vinho*, and *aguardente* offloaded in its port.[84]

The 1670 *Provisão* banning *gerebita*, however, severely decreased the revenue which the *Câmara Municipal* collected from its excise tax on legal alcohol imports. In order to recuperate some of this lost income, it quickly moved in the middle of 1681 to seek from the Governor of the colony a 400% increase in its excise impost on *vinho*, then the major intoxicant legally unloaded in its dock,[85] Sometime during the following two years, Governor João da Silva e Sousa partially acquiesced to this proposition. Without official instructions from the Portuguese Crown, he unilaterally raised the excise tax collected by the Municipal Council on *vinho* imports to 1$500 *réis* per *pipa* or by 300%.[86]

---

[83] "Registo da Segunda Informação, em Execussam da Provizam Regia, que Acompanha o Segundo Mappa, na Forma da Mesma," 4–04–1805, *Arquivos de Angola*, 1st series, Vol. I, No. 2, 1933, unpaginated.

[84] "Proposta do Senado da Câmara ao Governador Geral de Angola," 12–07–1681, AHU, Angola, Cx. 12, Doc. 49. A few years later, Governor Luís Lobo da Silva erred in indicating that this excise tax was collected only on *vinho*. See "Carta do Governador Geral de Angola," 8–03–1687, in Brásio, *Monumenta Missionaria Africana*, 1st series, Vol. XIV, p. 50.

[85] "Proposta do Senado da Câmara ao Governador Geral de Angola," 12–07–1681, AHU, Angola, Cx. 12, Doc. 12.

[86] "Carta do Governador Geral de Angola," 8–03–1687, in Brásio, *Monumenta Missionaria Africana*, 1st series, Vol. XIV, p. 50. Two years later officials of the Municipal Council of Luanda misleadingly informed the Crown that this amount

Despite a substantial increase in its excise duty on *vinho* imports, the *Câmara Municipal* of Luanda was not satisfied with the action taken by Governor Silva e Sousa. At an undetermined date in the mid-1680s, it forwarded a petition to the Portuguese Crown pleading that the request made in 1681 to the Governor of the colony be granted on the grounds that its revenues were still too low to finance its daily operations. The Conselho Ultramarino was entrusted with the matter and thereafter asked the new Governor, Luis Lobo da Silva, for his views on the matter. Lobo da Silva promptly answered the Crown's advisory body that:

> ... [An] excise duty of 2$000 *réis* on each *pipa* of *vinho* ... is a very high tariff [that] ... is neither appropriate to burden the people with nor to further add to their hardships. [Instead] ... the Crown should establish the excise duty on *vinho* imports at 1$000 *réis*.[87]

The Conselho Ultramarino concurred with this assessment and on the 31st of March, 1688, advised the King of Portugal to pass a decree to abolish the old excise tax rate on *vinho* imported at Angola's colonial capital and replace it with a lower rate of 1$000 *réis* on each large wooden cask.[88]

If and when a royal *Provisão* establishing a new and lower excise tax on *vinho* imports was indeed enacted can not be determined from the extant contemporaneous sources. Existing fiscal data from 1699 suggests that an excise duty of $500 *réis* per *pipa* was then being collected by the Municipal Council on the *cachaça* offloaded in its port.[89] Another document from the late 1720s informs that the same amount was still being levied by the administration of the municipality not only on *gerebita*, but on *vinho* and *aguardente* imports, as well.[90] This

---

was collected prior to the 1679 ban on *cachaça* imports. See the "Petição" of the Municipal Council, 7–03–1689, AHU, Angola, Cx. 13, Doc. 97.

[87] "Carta do Governador Geral de Angola," 8–03–1687, in Brásio, *Monumenta Missionaria Africana*, 1st series, Vol. XIV, p. 50.

[88] "Consulta do Conselho Ultramarino Sobre a Moeda de Cobre," 31–03–1688, in *ibid.*, 1st series, Vol. XIV, pp. 117–118.

[89] This is inferred from the quantitative data found in Graph 20 by dividing the total amount of alcohol import taxes which each Brazilian vessel that arrived at Luanda paid, 319$750 *réis*, by the overall volume of *cachaça* which they offloaded, 639.5 *pipas*, as reported in "Accounts of the Procurador of the Senate of Luanda for the Year 1699," in Boxer, *Portuguese Society in the Tropics*, pp. 209–218.

[90] The source in question is not signed, but appears to be a petition from the *Senado da Câmara*. It is dated 17–04–1728 and is located in AHU, Angola, Cx. 24, Doc. 37.

implies that the Portuguese Crown did not follow the recommendation put forth by the Conselho Ultramarino in 1688, but rather subsequently re-enacted the $500 *réis* excise impost in effect at the turn of the 1670s on every *pipa* of alcohol imported.

Whatever amount was settled upon as an excise tax on the Brazilian and metropolitan alcoholic beverages offloaded in the port of Luanda after the late 1680s, the fact remains that the sums collected by the administration of the municipality between 1650 and 1769 on these consumer goods were relatively appreciable. According to the source upon which the quantitative data found in Graph 23 is based, most of the revenue obtained by the *Câmara Municipal* during this period was produced through the excise duty on *gerebita, vinho,* and *aguardente* imports.[91] Thus, of the 462$500 *réis* of income secured in 1699, 342$500 *réis* or 74% were produced through its excise tax on imported alcoholic beverages.[92] Furthermore, of the total alcohol import tax levied in 1699, an overwhelming sum of 319$750 *réis* or almost 94% was collected solely on *cachaça*.[93] The close connection between the revenue of this civic body and the importation of alcoholic beverages, particularly *gerebita*, could hardly be more straightforward.

Indeed, most of the fluctuations evidenced in the revenue of the Municipal Council of Angola's colonial capital between 1650 and 1779 may be partially explained as resulting from changes in the volume of *cachaça* imported. From an annual average of 473$022 *réis* in the 1650s, the income of the municipal administration rose throughout the second half of the seventeenth century, reaching an average per annum of 679$845 *réis* during the first decade of the 1700s. This significant growth of nearly 44% coincided with a period of increasingly greater *gerebita* imports. During the 1730s, the revenue acquired by *Câmara Municipal* again jumped to an average of 937$339 *réis* per annum or an equally substantial 39% over its earnings in the first decade of the eighteenth century. This, too, was a decade during

---

[91] António Gonçalves Pinheiro (Escrivão do Senado da Câmara), "Registo da Segunda Informação, em Execussam da Provizam Regia, que Acompanha o Segundo Mapa, na Forma da Mesma," 4–04–1805, *Arquivos de Angola*, 1st series, Vol. I, No. 2, 1933, unpaginated.

[92] The total revenue is taken from Graph 21, while the overall amount collected from the alcohol import excise tax is taken from "Accounts of the Procurador of the Senate of Luanda for the Year 1699," in Boxer, *Portuguese Society in the Tropics*, pp. 209–218.

[93] See ft. 89.

which ever larger amounts of *cachaça* were unloaded at Luanda. The 1750s saw the income of this civic body augment further still to a yearly average of 1,726$248 *réis* or by an impressive 84% over its level in the 1730s. As seen above, however, an important downward trend in the importation of *gerebita* began in the mid-eighteenth century. The imposing increase in the revenue secured by the Municipal Council throughout this decade can not, therefore, be explained by a rise in the importation volume of this distilled spirit. During the 1760s and the 1770s, on the other hand, its earnings levelled off at an annual average of 1,786$983 and 1,816$750 *réis*, respectively. Not surprisingly, these were decades of significantly reduced *cachaça* imports.[94] The revenues from alcohol imports collected by the Municipal Council remained flat during the early 1780s at an average of 1,793$290 *réis* per annum. But with the alcohol import trade at Luanda rebounding from its depressed state, they increased between 1785 and 1794 to a yearly mean of 2,235$765 *réis*, or a jump of almost 25% compared to the early 1780s. From 1795 to 1799, the Municipal Council's revenues from alcohol imports rose again to an annual average of 2,703$734 *réis*, or nearly 21%. And during 1800–1804, they climbed to a yearly mean of 3,210$435 *réis*. This is the highest recorded figure. As it happens, 1800–1804 was also a period when *gerebita* imports were particularly high.

Early in the nineteenth century, the Municipal Council was levying an impost of $475 *réis* per *pipa* on all alcoholic beverages offloaded in its port.[95] This represented a small decrease of $025 *réis* vis-à-vis the same tax during the late 1600s and early 1700s.[96] Nevertheless, according to the Crown Judge Felix Correa Araujo, the larger part of municipal revenues still originated from this one source.[97] Indeed, as the data in Graph 23 reveal, the municipal levy on alcohol imports between 1785 and 1804 averaged an estimated 40% of the Council's

---

[94] The decennial fiscal data presented in this paragraph are based on the annual revenue of the Municipal Council of Luanda as found in Graph 23.

[95] Felix Correa de Araujo to Visconde de Anadia, 05–05–1803, AHU, Angola, Cx. 106, Doc. 27; and António Gonçalves Pinto, "Registo da Certidão ... sobre o Rendimento do Senado da Câmara," 30–03–1805, *Arquivos de Angola*, 1st series, Vol. I, No. 2, 1933, unpaginated.

[96] The date of the introduction of this lower municipal tax on alcohol imports remains to be determined.

[97] António Gonçalves Pinto, "Registo da segunda Informação, em Execussam da Provizão Regia, que acompanha o Segundo Mapa," 4–04–1805, *Arquivos de Angola*, 1st series, Vol. I, No. 2, 1933, unpaginated.

total revenues. With this governing body chronically underfunded, the impost on imported alcoholic beverages thus contributed significantly to the revenues that it sorely required to engage in public works (construction and repair of stone-paved streets, water wells, prisons, etc.), hold public festivities, and pay its officials.[98] This in spite of the fact that the amounts obtained therefrom were relatively small.

Moreover, the tax on imported alcoholic beverages levied by the Municipal Council of Luanda was not the only fiscal area where this governing body sought to augment its precarious finances by drawing upon foreign intoxicants. A second was in the form of municipal licenses granted upon payment of an annual fee to owners of the numerous taverns within its jurisdiction. As of 1784, if not before, these were already being sold at $560 réis apiece.[99] However, sometime after 1805, the municipal impost on imported alcohol appears to have been abolished.[100] In order to compensate for the loss of this important source of revenue, the *Senado da Câmara* then considerably augmented the value of its tavern licenses. By 1814 their cost had risen more than fivefold to 3$200 réis.[101] Yet, the objective failed to materialize: from 1814 to 1817, the sale of tavern licences generated an annual average of 448$800 réis, or only 11.75% of the Municipal Council's total revenues; nearly twenty years later, following the ban on legal slave trading in the South Atlantic, which temporarily forced Luanda into an economically depressed state, tavern license sales averaged 468$800 réis, representing a slightly higher 15% of the

[98] On this perennial problem, see de Araujo to Visconde de Anadia, 05–05–1803, AHU, Angola, Cx. 106, Doc. 27; Pinto, "Registo da segunda Informação, em Execussam da Provizão Regia, que acompanha o Segundo Mapa," 4–04–1805, *Arquivos de Angola*, 1st series, Vol. I, No. 2, 1933, unpaginated.

[99] "Requiremento dos Vendedeiros de Molhados," 14–08–1784, AHU, Angola, Cx. 69, Doc. 20. In 1805, the scribe of the Municipal Council, António Gonçalves Pinto, incorrectly stated that these licenses were originally introduced in 1798. See his "Registo da Certidão . . . sobre o Rendimento do Senado da Câmara," 30–03–1805, *Arquivos de Angola*, 1st series, Vol. I, No. 2, 1933, unpaginated.

[100] None of its extant financial reports from the mid–1810s record the collection of such an impost. See "Receita do Senado da Câmara:" 1814 in AHU, Angola, Cx. 130, Doc. 39; 1815 and 1816 in AHU, Angola, Cx. 131, Doc. 61; and 1817 in AHU, Angola, Cx. 134, Doc. 43. The precise circumstances under which this tax was rescinded are not known.

[101] This amount is derived from the "Receita do Senado da Câmara" for 1814 in AHU, Angola, Cx. 130, Doc. 39, which lists 400$000 réis originating from the sale of licenses to 125 tavern-owners.

municipality's income.[102] The previously important role played by alcohol in the finances of the *Senado da Câmara* was thus much reduced after 1805.

A second function played by imported intoxicants in non-slave trading roles was as a consumer good around which the population of Luanda spent its leisure time. Throughout the third quarter of the seventeenth century, if not before and after, the inhabitants of this port town were accustomed to attending regular festivals on the Island of Luanda, where the cool shade provided by its coconut and date palms offered excellent surroundings for this type of recreational activity. Relatively large quantities of Madeira wine and *vinho* from the Caparica region immediately south of Lisbon were consumed by those who took part in these events in order to cheer up and fortify their hearts. Without the consumption of generous amounts of these intoxicants, Cadornega, the chronicler of Angola's wars informs us, the festivals organized on the island were hardly enjoyable.[103] And the same was also most problably true during the religious feasts that were held within the port town itself from at least the late 1610s onwards, especially Corpus Christi, Lent, and civic holidays like that which after 1648 celebrated the restoration of the colony to Portuguese rule.[104]

Far larger quantities of imported intoxicants were consumed, however, in the drinking establishments of Luanda. From its very foundation in 1575, this port town became endowed with more than a

---

[102] See Graph 25.

[103] Cadornega, *História Geral das Guerras*, Vol. III, p. 36.

[104] Information on the early religious feasts, including an extremely detailed account of that celebrating the canonization of Saint Francis Xavier in 1620, comes from "Relação das Festas que a Residençia de Angolla Fez na Beatificação do Beato Padre Franco de Xavier da Companhia de Jesus," Felner, *Angola*, pp. 531–344. This feast bears such close resemblance to Luanda's modern Carnival that it may well have been its precursor. See David Birmingham, "Carnival at Luanda," *Journal of African History*. Vol. 29, 1988, pp. 93–103. However, the earliest accounts of the Carnival in the colonial capital of Angola, another occasion during which much alcohol was also consumed, date only from the latter 1800s. See Ruy Duarte de Carvalho, *Ana a Manda: Os Filhos da Rede*. Lisbon, 1989, pp. 235–236. Further information on festivals and on heavy drinking at Luanda is provided below by Governor António de Vasconcelos for the late 1750s. For later eighteenth century festivities, see Governador António de Lencastre to Câmara da Cidade, 16–02–1778, AHBML, Maço 3; and Governor Melo to Câmara Municipal, 13–08–1797, *Ibid*. For early 19th-century feasts, see the order of Governor Luiz da Mota Feo, 12–01–1818, AHU, Angola, Cx. 134, Doc. 6; and "Conta do Rendimento da Câmara em . . . 1833," AHU, Angola, Correspondência dos Governadores, 2a Secção, Pasta 2.

fair number of taverns.[105] These drinking establishments were part and parcel of the commercial houses found throughout this seaport, most of which were owned and operated by Portuguese and Brazilian traders. Which came first, the taverns or the trading houses, can not be ascertained. Be that as it may, setting up a tavern in Luanda was one of the preferred ways with which Luso-Brazilian immigrants sought to quickly get rich and then enjoy the good life. While Fernão de Sousa was Governor of Angola (1624–1630), even one of his servants operated such an establishment.[106] By the 1780s, according to the other major chronicler of Angola's past, Elias Alexandre da Silva Correia, it was not uncommon to see recently arrived Lusophone settlers begin their ascension of the colonial socio-economic ladder through this method and then, once their initial capital significantly increased, become members of the *Senado da Câmara*.[107]

The quick and substantial returns which Luso-Brazilian immigrants obtained from operating their drinking establishments were predicated upon two major factors, adulterated alcohol and rigged liquid measures. As we have seen, much of the *vinho* unloaded at the port of Luanda possessed a greater alcoholic content than regular wine.

---

[105] See, for example, "Relatorio e listas de todos os gastos que se fazem nos Reinos de Angola e Congo," 28-01-1612, *Arquivos de Angola*, 1st series, Vol. III, No. 19, 1937, p. 85; Fernão de Sousa's undated report to the Crown in Heintze, *Fontes para a História de Angola*, Vol. I, p. 224; the directive of Governor António de Vasconcelos, 30-10-1759, AHU, Angola, Cx. 42, Doc. 88; Governor Francisco Inocêncio de Sousa Coutinho to Conde Copeiro Mor, 10-08-1766, BNL, Cód. 8742, fl. 61; Governor Sousa Coutinho to Municipal Council, 23-10-1769, BNL, Cód. 8743, fls. 57–58; the "Bando" or governmental order of 17-10-1771, AHU, Cx. 56, Doc. 4; "Negociantes de Molhados Multados em 16-12-1784," AHU, Angola, Cx. 69, Doc. 20; "Edital do Senado da Câmara," 19-01-1785, in Santos, *Luanda d'Outros Tempos*, p. 80; Azeredo, *Ensaios sobre Algumas Enfermidades*, pp. 54–55; Governor Melo to Souza Coutinho, 17-08-1801, *Arquivos de Angola*, 1st series, Vol. II, No. 36, 1936, p. 626; "Representação da Câmara," 15-04-1815, AHU, Angola, Cx. 130, Doc. 49; the 13-07-1816 and 17-07-1817 orders given by Governor Branco e Torres, *Memórias Contendo a Biographia do Vice Almirante Luis da Motta Feo e Torres*, pp. 60 and 79–80, respectively; and Douville, *Voyage au Congo*. Vol. I, pp. 44 and 54. Short analyses of this institution are found in José Carlos Venâncio, *A Economia de Luanda e Hinterland no Século XVIII: Um Estudo de Sociologia Histórico*. Lisbon, 1996, pp. 70–72, and 151; Miller, *Way of Death*. pp. 84, 296, 389, 397, and 465; Ilídio do Amaral, "Descrição da Luanda Oitocentista através de uma Planta de 1755," *Garcia de Orta*. Vol. 9, 1961, p. 417; and Pantoja, "Encontro nas Terras do Além-Mar," p. 46. Here, Luanda was hardly atypical from most other seaports. See Popham, "Social History of the Tavern."

[106] Undated report of Governor Sousa to the Crown in Heintze, *Fontes para a História de Angola*, Vol. I, p. 224.

[107] Silva Correia, *História de Angola*, Vol. I, p. 40.

And, in the case of intoxicants introduced after c. 1650, particularly *aguardente* and *gerebita*, their alcohol levels were even higher. This enabled tavern-owners to expand the volume of the unadulterated intoxicants unloaded at Luanda through a mixture of river or salt water and peppers to increase the ardor of the tampered alcoholic drinks.[108] One *pipa* of *vinho, aguardente* or *cachaça* offloaded at the port was thus quickly transformed into two. Moreover, the legal measures used by the tavern-owners to determine the amount of alcohol served to any one patron were also usually rigged.[109] Consequently, added to the 50% mark up normally placed on the imported goods,[110] expanding the volume of *vinho, aguardente,* and *gerebita* with a mixture of water and peppers and doctoring the liquid measures enabled the owners of Luanda's taverns to make consumers pay dearly for the bad alcoholic beverages they guzzled down.

Yet, in spite of adulterated alcohol and rigged measures, the fact remains that the taverns of Luanda were the only places where most of the population of this seaport could spend whatever leisure time they had and socialize. Aside from the festivals periodically held,

---

[108] On adulterated alcohol see the "Parecer" of the Conselho Ultramarino dated 20–10–1689, AHU, Cód. 554, fls. 60v–61; José Barbosa Leal to the King, 10–10–1690, in Rau and Silva, eds. *Os Manuscriptos*, Vol. I, pp. 289–291; Silva Correia, *História de Angola*, Vol. I, p. 40; "Negociantes de molhados multados em 16–12–1784," AHU, Angola, Cx. 69, Doc. 20; "Edital do Senado da Câmara, 19–01–1785," in Santos, *Luanda d'Outros Tempos*, p. 80; Azeredo, *Ensaios sobre Algumas Enfermidades*, pp. 54–55; Governor Melo to Rodrigo de Sousa Coutinho, 29–08–1801, *Arquivos de Angola*, 2nd series, Vol. XXVI, Nos. 103–109, 1969, p. 64; and Governor Melo to Municipal Council of Luanda, 26–08–1801, in Santos, *Luanda d'Outros Tempos*, p. 94. The adulterated intoxicants were so bad that at least two *físicos-mores* or physicians-major at Luanda constantly prescribed good alcoholic drinks for a number of ailments and sicknesses: Francisco Damião Cosme during the 1760s and José Pinto de Azeredo during the 1790s. See, respectively, Luis de Pina, ed., "Tractado [de Francisco Damião Cosme] das Queixas Endemicas e Mais Fataes Nesta Conquista (Loanda 14 Agosto 1770)" *Studia*. Nos. 20–22, 1967, pp. 173, 180–181, 219, 224, and 266–268; and Azeredo, *Ensaios sobre Algumas Enfermidades*, pp. 74–76 and 82–83.

[109] See "Sobre uma Queixa contra os Taberneiros," 12–01–1689, AHBML, Cód. 12, fl. 1; "Negociantes de Molhados Multados em 16–12–1784," AHU, Angola, Cx. 69, Doc. 20; "Edital do Senado da Câmara, 19–01–1785," in Santos, *Luanda d'Outros Tempos*, p. 80; Silva Correia, *História de Angola*, Vol. I, p. 40; and Governor Melo to Rodrigo de Sousa Coutinho, 29–08–1801, *Arquivos de Angola*, 2nd series, Nos. 103–109, 1969, p. 64.

[110] Rodrigo de Sousa Coutinho to Governor Melo, 22–10–1799, AHU, Angola, Cx. 93, Doc. 70; and Governor Melo's "Observaçoens sobre os Mappas que . . . forão remetidos para servirem de modelo para as noticias annuaes do estado da Povoação, Agricultura e Commercio deste Reino," 14–04–1800, AHU, Angola, Cx. 95, Doc. 42.

whether they were of a religious or civic nature, the colonial capital of Angola did not begin to offer other forms of public distraction and recreation until well after the Atlantic slave trade was legally abolished. Its well-to-do residents compensated for this lacuna by holding private or semi-private social events. During the boom of the late 1820s, for example, dinner for the rich of Luanda was a veritable festive occasion: every evening they sat down amongst good company to plenty of food and large amounts of the best Port and Lisbon wines.[111] There were also the odd parties like that given in 1825 by the garrison of the capital for the officers of the British naval ship in which W. F. W. Owen arrived at Luanda.[112] Moreover, by the turn of the 1830s, the governors of the colony further held Sunday balls in their palace for Africans, Luso-Africans, and Europeans alike.[113] But the lower class of Luso-Africans and Africans never got an invitation to such events. As a result, frequenting drinking establishments to consume *vinho*, *aguardente*, and *gerebita* was one of the rare social pastimes available to the unprivileged who made up the majority of Luanda's population.[114] Even slaves were known to rob their owners so that they could afford to drink in the taverns of this seaport.[115]

[111] Douville, *Voyage au Congo*, Vol. I, p. 52.
[112] W. F. W. Owen, *Narrative of Voyages to Explore the Shores of Africa, Arabia, and Madagascar*. London, 1833, Vol. II, p. 336.
[113] See Gustav Tams, *Visit to the Portuguese Possessions in South Western Africa*. New York, 1969 (trans. by H. Evans Lloyd, but originally published in 1845), Vol. I, pp. 272–274.
[114] "Relatorio e listas de todos os gastos que se fazem nos Reinos de Angola e Congo," 28–01–1612, *Arquivos de Angola*, 1st series, Vol. III, No. 19, 1937, p. 85; Fernão de Sousa's undated report to the Crown in Heintze, *Fontes para a História de Angola*, Vol. I, p. 224; Jerónimo da Veiga Cabral (Provedor da Fazenda de Angola) to the King, 7–11–1684, AHU, Angola, Cx. 12, Doc. 158; the directive of Governor António de Vasconcelos, 30–10–1759, AHU, Angola, Cx. 42, Doc. 88; Governor Sousa Coutinho to Conde Copeiro Mor, 18–08–1766, BNL, Cód. 8742, fl. 61; Governor Sousa Coutinho to Municipal Council, 23–10–1769, BNL, Cód. 8743, fls. 57–58; the "Bando" or governmental order of 17–10–1771, AHU, Cx. 56, Doc. 4; and Douville, *Voyage au Congo*, Vol. I, p. 54. Exactly the same situation was found in Rio de Janeiro. There, "[f]or amusement the rich enjoyed receptions at the viceroy's palace or performances at the opera. The middle and lower classes contented themselves in the large number of taverns. Smugglers, gamblers, prostitutes, and others attracted by *cachaça* actively supported these establishments." See Bauss, "Rio de Janeiro," pp. 2–3.
[115] "Traslado do Auto de Exame, e Corpo de Delicto, que se fes ao preto Manoel de Salvador, escravo," 10–07–1771, AHU, Angola, Cx. 55, Doc. 43; and Silva

And the unprivileged residents of Luanda could choose from a large number of drinking establishments. During the 1780s, according to Silva Correia, taverns were found in two-thirds of the buildings in the municipality, some displaying no more than one *pipa* of *gerebita*.[116] Although surely exaggerated, this figure nonetheless points to the importance that drinking establishments gained for the social life of Luanda's poorer residents. Indeed, from 1814 to 1817, this seaport had an average of one tavern for every thirty-four inhabitants.[117] This was an extremely high ratio. It surpassed, and by far, that of two other contemporaneous colonial urban centers also known for their large number of drinking establishments: Mexico City and Rio de Janeiro. At the beginning of the nineteenth century, Mexico City had one legal tavern per fifty-six persons over the age of fifteen.[118] Rio de Janeiro, on the other hand, had an even lower ratio. During 1779–1780, for example, there was roughly one tavern for every 200 civilians.[119] Some twenty years later, the emporium behind Guanabara Bay still boasted only one legally registered tavern for every 130 civilians in 1799.[120] In Luanda, taverns were clearly an extremely important social institution.

These drinking establishments stayed open seven days a week until the early hours of the morning. This allowed the residents of Angola's

Correia, *História de Angola*, Vol. II, p. 168. This problem was not peculiar to Luanda. In Portugal, during the late 1400s and early 1500s, some slaves also frequented taverns and paid for the alcohol which they consumed with stolen goods. See A. C. de C. M. Saunders, *A Social History of Black Slaves and Freedmen in Portugal, 1441–1555*. Cambridge, 1982, p. 124. The same situation also persisted in the island of Madeira during the sixteenth century. See Vieira, *Escravos no Archipélago da Madeira*, pp. 187 and 204.

[116] Silva Correia, *História de Angola*, Vol. I, p. 40.

[117] See Graph 26.

[118] Michael C. Scardaville, "Alcohol Abuse and Tavern Reform in Late Colonial Mexico City," *Hispanic American Historical Review*. Vol. 60, 1980, p. 646.

[119] The "Memórias públicas e econômicas da cidade de São Sebastião do Rio de Janeiro ... dos anos de 1779 até o de 1789," pp. 44–45, lists a total of 196 taverns; and the "Mappa geral das cidades, villas e freguezias que formão o corpo interior da capitania do Rio de Janeiro [em 1780], com declaração do numero de seus templos, fogos, etc.," *Revista do Instituto Histórico e Geográfico Brasileiro*. Vol. 47, 1884, p. 27, gives the total civilian population as 38,707. According to Bauss, "Rio de Janeiro," p. 127, this implies "one [tavern] on nearly every block [of the city]."

[120] Antonio Duarte Nunes, "Almanaque Histórico da Cidade de S. Sebastião do Rio de Janeiro para o Anno de 1799," *Revista do Instituto Histórico e Geográfico Brasileiro*. Vol. 267, 1965, p. 198 lists 334 taverns; and "Resumo Total da População que existia no anno de 1799, comprehendidas as quatro Freguezias da Cidade do Rio de Janeiro ..." *Revista do Instituto Histórico e Geográfico Brasileiro*. Vol. 21, 1858, p. 288, gives the total civilian population as 43,376.

colonial capital, particularly the less privileged Africans and Luso-Africans, to consume appreciable quantities of low priced *gerebita* and, for those who could afford it, smaller amounts of the more expensive *vinho* and *aguardente* after a day's work. During the 1780s, for example, it was not unusual for these consumers to rapidly imbibe the *cachaça* cargoes of small incoming vessels.[121] Coupled with long operating hours, the heavy consumption of alcohol in the taverns of Luanda, even if diluted, resulted in many of their patrons becoming drunk. And inebriated patrons often engaged in all kinds of disturbances, particularly fighting, both inside and outside of their drinking establishments.

At least three governors are known to have tackled this situation. The first was Governor António de Vasconcelos who, on the 30th of October, 1759, implemented the following:

> Because it is evident that the primary origin of all disorders, fights, and wounds frequently occurring between Blacks and ordinary people, stems from the large amounts of alcoholic beverages they so senselessly imbibe, which facilitates not only the extraordinary multiplicity of Taverns throughout the whole City, but the patronization of the ambitious industry of tavern-owners; because, on top of maintaining the taverns open for a large part of the night to reach this goal, their owners also keep them open even in days forbidden by the Church . . . on the pretext of providing food for the common people; and because it is necessary to deal with such a scandalous style, so that the disorders in question are avoided whenever possible, I order: that from this date on all tavern-onwers, irrespective of the types of alcoholic drinks they sell, will be required to close their establishments at seven o'clock at night, after which they can no longer sell intoxicants to anyone, regardless of status or social condition; And I order further that on Sundays, Holy days, and days in which public processions are held, whether for Lent or other festive occasions, taverns must also remain closed and no intoxicants shall be sold from them to anyone . . .[122]

The second to deal with this issue was Governor Moçâmedes. Sometime between 1784 and 1790, he too ordered that taverns close their

---

[121] Silva Correia, *História de Angola*, Vol. I, p. 41. *Cachaça* was also the preferred alcoholic drink of the common people in Rio de Janeiro, particularly those of African descent, both free and enslaved. See Ernst Ebel, *O Rio de Janeiro e Seus Arredores em 1824*. São Paulo, 1972, p. 96; Robert Walsh, *Notices of Brazil in 1828 and 1829*. London, 1830, Vol I, pp. 517–518; Mary C. Karasch, *Slave Life in Rio de Janeiro, 1808–1850*. Princeton, 1987, pp. 143, 333, and 364; Pantoja, "Encontro nas Terras de Além-Mar," p. 28; and Bauss, "Rio de Janeiro," pp. 2–3.

[122] This governmental order is found in AHU, Angola, Cx. 42, Doc. 88.

doors not only at eight in the evenings, but also on Sundays and religious holidays.[123] And the third was Governor Luiz da Motta Feo e Torres. In the middle of 1816, he decreed that Luanda's drinking establishments close at sundown.[124] The fact that more than one attempt was made to reduce the operating hours of the taverns and thereby the disturbances resulting from heavy drinking therein clearly indicates the extent of the problem. But it also shows that each of these measures was relatively ineffective. In spite of their rowdy, if not outright dangerous, environment, the numerous drinking establishments found throughout the capital continued to be heavily frequented by the poorer folk in order to break the monotony of their daily lives.[125]

Another non-slave-trading role played by imported intoxicants, particularly *gerebita*, was as part of the "wages" paid to forced labourers in the interior of Luanda. When this practise began remains to be established, but by the middle of the eighteenth century it was already an acceptable mode of payment from the point of view of employers. In 1762, as noted earlier, Governor António de Vasconcelos planned to build a canal that would bring fresh water from the Kwanza River to Luanda. To ensure that the forcibly recruited African labourers would not escape from the job site, he proposed to sustain them primarily with generous amounts of *cachaça*.[126] Ten years later, Governor Francisco Inocêncio de Sousa Coutinho dispatched a shipment of this distilled beverage to the *capitão-mor* of Encoje, Feliciano Pinto da Costa Vianna, that was to be distributed among the African workers erecting a church within the fort of this *presídio*.[127] At the turn of the eighteenth century, when a new iron foundry was being

---

[123] Silva Correia, *História de Angola*, Vol. II, p. 168.

[124] See the directive of Governor da Motta Feo e Torres, dated 13–07–1816, in Branco e Torres, *Memórias Contendo a Biographia do Vice Almirante Luis da Motta Feo e Torres*, p. 60; and idem to Conde da Barca, 12–08–1817, *Arquivos de Angola*. Vol. XVIII, Nos. 71–74, 1961, p. 124.

[125] In 1844, for example, there was still one tavern for roughly every 50 inhabitants. Lima, *Ensaios sobre a statistica das possessões portuguesas*, Vol. III, p. 4-A, lists the total population of Luanda as 5,605. The "Estatistica da Cidade de Loanda em 1845," *Annaes Maritimos e Coloniaes*. (Parte Official) No. 12, 1845, p. 234, gives the total number of establishments that sold dry and wet goods, especially *aguardente*, as 107.

[126] See the letter of 9–07–1762 by Governor António de Vasconcelos AHU, Angola, Cx. 45, Doc. 64. Whether Vasconcelos or his immediate successors went ahead with this form of payment is not known.

[127] Governor Sousa Coutinho to Feliciano Pinto da Costa Vianna, 21–01–1772, *Arquivos de Angola*, 1st series, Vol. III, No. 29, 1937, p. 391.

established in Ilamba, northeast of Muxima, Governor Melo also dispatched six *ancoretas* of *gerebita* to its administrator, José Alvares Maciel, for use as part payment to the labourers who were going to work there.[128] Even larger amounts of this intoxicant were utilized in this role as the Kwanza-Luanda canal was being dug during the mid-1810s. A group of 130 forced labourers received no less than 1,167 *canadas* from the middle of 1813 through 1814 and another group numbering 391 obtained at least 540 *canadas* from the beginning of 1815 through the middle of 1816.[129] Work on the canal was thereafter suspended due to the drought and famine prevailing throughout the region. Nevertheless, a plan soon devised to finish the canal within a 280 day period listed 360 *canadas* of *gerebita* for a further 332 forced labourers who would be required to complete the work.[130] Given that forced labour was loathed by those pressed into it and that conscripted workers rarely ever received their real wages,[131] the *cachaça* which they obtained in exchange for their daily sweat may well have been an important factor in keeping them from deserting their jobs. And the colonial government of Angola was not alone in using imported intoxicants in this role. In the immediate hinterland of Luanda, the Africans periodically pressed by traders to transport trade goods into the interior received part of their remuneration in the form of daily rations of *cachaça*.[132] Similarly, when the landed

---

[128] Governor Melo to José Alvares Maciel, 4-11-1799, *Arquivos de Angola*, 1st Series, Vol. IV, Nos. 52–54, 1939, pp. 271–272; Governor Melo to Rodrigo de Sousa Coutinho, 7–11–1799, AHU, Angola, Cx. 93-A, Doc. 13. The first group of labourers to work in this new foundry numbered 134. See José Alvares Maciel to Governor Melo, 2–03–1800, *Arquivos de Angola*, 1st Series, Vol. IV, Nos. 52–54, 1939, pp. 283–293.

[129] "Memoria sobre o encanamento do Rio Quanza," August 1816, AHU. Angola, Cx. 131, Doc. 89.

[130] *Ibid.*

[131] On the problem of forced labourers deserting their jobs see: Governor Moçâmedes to José de Seabra e Silva, 28–93–1786, AHU, Cód. 1642, fls. 32v–33; Governor Melo to Rodrigo de Sousa Coutinho, 8–03–1800, *Arquivos de Angola*, 2nd series, Vol. XXIII, Nos. 91–94, 1966, p. 166; "Representação da Meza da Sancta Caza da Mizericordia de Loanda à Rainha, 21–07–1798," AHU, Angola, Cx. 106, Doc. 42; and "Memoria sobre o encanamento do Rio Quanza," August 1816, AHU, Angola, Cx. 131, Doc. 89: On the non-payment of wages to forced workers see: José Alvares Maciel to Governor Melo, 2–03–1800, *Arquivos de Angola*, 1st series, Vol. IV, Nos. 52–54, 1939, p. 284; and António de Saldanha da Gama (Governor of Angola during 1807–1810), *Memória sobre as Colónias de Portugal, situadas na Costa Occidental d'Africa.* Belem, 1839 (but written in 1814), p. 20.

[132] Silva Correia, *História de Angola*, Vol. I, pp. 12–20 and 80. The best survey

Luso-African residents of Luanda reviewed their *arimos* or agricultural estates in the Dande and Icollo e Bengo districts, they divided at least one *ancoreta* of *gerebita* amongst their workers, many of whom happened to be enslaved.[133]

Imported intoxicants, primarily *cachaça*, once again, were also utilized in the interior behind Luanda as an exchange item to acquire foodstuffs. From the very beginning, the population of this port town was periodically faced with food shortages.[134] To alleviate this problem, Lusophone merchants sometimes exchanged the inexpensive *gerebita* to secure maize flour produced by African agriculturalists nearby. This occurred during the governorships of Francisco de Tavora (1669–1676), António de Vasconcelos (1758–1764), and Francisco Inocêncio de Sousa Coutinho (1764–1772).[135] In the mid-1810s, one particularly intense food shortage resulted in excessively high prices for manioc flour. Although the value of one *canzonguel* (a local unit of dry measure equal to about 14 litres) of this foodstuff was officially fixed at $800 *réis*, merchants in the colonial capital of Angola were selling it for 1$900 *réis* or more than double its legal price.[136] This led them to set aside relatively large numbers of *pipas* of *cachaça* for transportation to Massangano, where their content was to be exchanged for the manioc flour produced by neighbouring Africans at a rate of three and a half *cazongueis* of this foodstuff for one *canada* of *gerebita* valued at $200 *réis*. One *cazonguel* of manioc flour obtained in this fashion thus cost $057 *réis*, transportation expenses excluded.[137] Compared to its cost near Massangano, the official price of this foodstuff at Luanda was consequently fourteen times higher, while the unofficial price was slightly more than thirty-three times greater. Clearly,

on porters in Angola up to the late 1800s remains Alfredo Margarido, "Les Porteurs: forme de domination et agents de changements en Angola (XVIIe–XIXe siècles," *Revue française d'histoire d'outre-mer*. Vol. LXV, 1978, pp. 377–399.

[133] Silva Correia, *História de Angola*, Vol. I, p. 113.

[134] Miller, "Significance of Drought, Disease and Famine," pp. 17–61.

[135] Reports on *gerebita* traded for maize flour during these periods are provided by Gaspar da Silva Reis to the King, 27–04–1702, AHU, Angola, Cx. 18, Doc. 14; Governor Vasconcelos to the King, 24–04–1762, AHU, Angola, Cx. 45, Doc. 23; and Governor Sousa Coutinho to Conde da Cunha, 9–09–1766, BNL, Cód. 8742, fls. 61–62.

[136] Prices taken from Governor Feo e Torres to Tomás António de Vila Nova Portugal, 18–08–1817, as summarized in Carlos D. Coimbra, *Ofícios para o Reino (1801–1819): Códices 7, 8, 9 e 10*. Lisbon, 1965, p. 61.

[137] "Memoria sobre o encamento do Rio Quanza," August 1816, AHU, Angola, Cx. 131, Doc. 89.

such large price differentials were more than enough to offset transportation costs in both directions and, more importantly, to provide merchants in the colonial capital of Angola with significant profit margins. Indeed, the exchange of *cachaça* for food in the interior was carried out under such lucrative terms that even the director of the iron foundry being established in Ilamba used this intoxicant early in 1800 to buy fish from local fishermen for part of the rations provided to its 134 workers.[138]

Finally, imported alcohol was also used to facilitate the process of conversion in the hinterland of Luanda. Around 1650, for example, a group of Capuchin missionaries attempting to convert the ruling elite of Matamba drew upon the *vinho* which their carriers transported to further the cause.[139] Similarly, when the Portuguese attempted to baptise the King of Matamba in 1772, the friar entrusted with the mission did not hesitate to send him four glass containers of *aguardente* and one *ancoreta* of *gerebita* as an inducement.[140] But unlike Kongo, where the conversion of Africans took place on a wider scale, the missionary effort in the interior of Angola's colonial capital was but half-hearted. As a result, the number of episodes during which missionaries provided imported intoxicants to African rulers was limited.

Conclusion

The Luso-Brazilian alcohol unloaded at Luanda up to 1830, first *vinho* and, following the mid-1600s, especially *gerebita*, played an impressive variety of functions other than the direct acquisition of slaves. These other roles of foreign intoxicants have rarely been noted in modern historical reconstructions of the colonial capital of Angola and its hinterland.[141] But, as the preceding pages make clear, their importance can not be ignored. While those functions related to slave trading furthered the flow of slaves to Luanda and smoothed the

---

[138] José Alvares Maciel to Governor Melo, 2–03–1800, *Arquivos de Angola*, 1st series, Vol. IV, Nos. 52–54, 1939, p. 284.

[139] Cavazzi de Montecúccolo, *Descrição Histórica dos Três Reinos*, Vol. I, p. 365.

[140] Frei João de S. Lucas to the Governor of Angola, 01–05–1772, *Arquivos de Angola*, 1st series, Vol. III, Nos. 30–33, 1937, p. 432.

[141] The one exception is Miller, who has sketched out the function of alcohol imports in generating tax revenues. See his, *Way of Death*, pp. 465–469, 629, and 637–641.

operations of the commerce, roles not related to this trade provided both levels of government in Luanda with much needed revenues, allowed the residents of Angola's colonial capital to escape the monotony of their daily lives and to lessen their hunger during periods of famine, and reduced the chance of forced labourers deserting their jobs. In each and every case, such multifaceted roles sustained the region's slave trading economy. And in the process, they further insinuated foreign intoxicants into the social fabric of the population of Luanda and its hinterland.

CONCLUSION

THE IMPACT OF PORTUGUESE AND BRAZILIAN INTOXICANTS

Following the mid-1500s, first *vinho* and then *gerebita* successively emerged as crucial items of exchange in the slave trading that took place at Luanda and its hinterland. Few of the transactions that generated thousands of captives for export in any given year could be concluded without these foreign intoxicants. Overall, of the 1,181,500 slaves legally exported through the colonial capital of Angola from 1710 to 1830, an estimated 25% were directly secured in exchange of *gerebita*. Extrapolating the 1785–1830 proportion of slave exports from Luanda obtained through *vinho*, *aguardente*, and additional intoxicants, a further 8% can be calculated to have been acquired there between 1710 and 1830 in exchange of these other alcohol imports. Here, Luso-Brazilian alcoholic drinks were clearly important trade goods in slave trading.

Used first and foremost to acquire slaves, Luso-Brazilian intoxicants nevertheless played a variety of other notable roles. *Vinho*, later supplanted by *gerebita* and, to lesser extent, *aguardente*, were utilized by Portuguese colonial officials as offerings to African political authorities to expand and to facilitate slave trading operations, a practice that was also employed by the *sertanejo* and *pombeiro* agents of Luso-Brazilian slave traders based in Luanda. European missionaries, in turn, bestowed these alcoholic beverages upon local African rulers to further the process of proselytization. *Gerebita*, in particular, was also used by Portuguese colonial administration to secure forced labourers for its "industrial" enterprises immediately behind the coast, to dispense a cheap form of payment for their labour, and to reduce the chance of them deserting their jobs. And, last but not least, all of the imported alcoholic beverages provided the colonial government of Angola and the Municipal Council of Luanda with much needed revenues, while they also allowed the residents of this port town to escape the monotony of their daily lives and to lessen their hunger during periods of famine. The importance of Luso-Brazilian intoxicants thus went far beyond the direct acquisition of slaves.

Given the significant roles played by Luso-Brazilian alcoholic drinks in commercial and non-commercial settings, what was their impact? Not a few of the scholars of pre-1830 colonial Angola have painted a gloomy picture. According to Douglas L. Wheeler, one of the first modern historians of this colony:

> All the shades of color were said to drink heavily. Silva Correa's accounts picture the native caravans' addiction to rum as habitual and long-standing. White society died off as much through over-drinking as through climate.[1]

The authors of the first, and still only comprehensive history of Angola published in English, in turn, remarked that:

> African consumption of . . . *gerebita* . . . was especially important in the period 1660–1830. Its effects were readily appreciated by observers in Angola: the ruin and degradation and sometimes death by poisoning of many Africans who consumed it and the discouragement of a rum industry in Angola.[2]

Gerald J. Bender, who penned one of the most influential books on the more recent Angolan past, similarly affirmed that:

> For over half a century and a half (1660–1830) rum was the most important commodity imported into Angola. While many officials complained of the ruin and even death which the alcohol trade brought to the African population, . . . there was little they could do to curb this invidious commercial activity.[3]

And more recently, in his *magnum opus* on the Angolan slave trade, Joseph Miller claims that:

> Increased quantities of European brandies and American rums at first enhanced the powers of lords and elders to contact ancestors or other spirits they engaged on behalf of the communities they represented. Later these beverages presumably helped the new men grown wealthy by trade to imitate the supernatural abilities of their predecessors. It made little sense to trade without also drinking and distributing alcohol in the large quantities commensurate with their status. By the nineteenth century, still greater quantities of imported inebriants had cheapened these beliefs, noble in their origins and acceptable then for the selectivity of their application, into the valueless dependence into

---

[1] Wheeler, "The Portuguese in Angola 1836–1891," p. 62.
[2] Wheeler and Pélissier, *Angola*, p. 48.
[3] Bender, *Angola Under the Portuguese*, p. 145.

which the fallen heirs of these men sank, left behind by further economic and political changes as the stereotyped drunken sots, sitting alone in their deserted compounds and condemned by temperate Victorians. Nobles who had managed human relations with otherwordly forces had lost out to successors possessing more mundane contacts with guns and in the trade of later eras. In the meanwhile, pipe after pipe of rum, *eau de vie*, and brandy, their sharp taste sometimes enhanced by the addition of hot American peppers, had burned the throats of African men who thus ardently aspired to greatness. Lesser folk, cast off from changing societies and abandoned to humble lives in the towns of the Europeans, concealed their failures by mimicking the drinking habits of their superiors in taverns in the seaports.[4]

These assertions are not new. Ever since the Victorian era, Africans have been portrayed by explorers, missionaries, government officials, and medical practitioners as consumers of prodigious amounts of foreign intoxicating drinks, resulting in their social, economic, and political degradation.[5] Does the evidence support such a portrait for the period under consideration here?

---

[4] See his *Way of Death*, p. 84.

[5] A representative list of works portraying this view includes: Frederick W. Lugard, "The Liquor Traffic in Africa," *The Nineteenth Century*. November, 1897, pp. 766 784; J. T. Darragh, "The Liquor Problem in the Transvaal," *Contemporary Review*. July, 1901, pp. 124–135; A. Kermorgant, "l'Alcoolisme dans les colonies françaises," *Bulletin de la Société de Pathologie Éxotique et de ses Filiales*. Vol. 2, 1909, pp. 330 340; Joseph du Teil, "La prohibition de l'alcool de traite en Afrique," *Revue Indigène*. Vol. 4, 1909, pp. 1 12; Harry H. Johnston, "Alcoholism in Africa," *The Nineteenth Century*. September, 1911, pp. 476–494; Comte de Penha Garcia, *La lutte contre l'Alcool aux Colonies Portugaises*. Geneva, 1911; B. Cleaver, "The Drink Traffic on the Gold Coast," *Sierra Leone Messenger*. No. 87, 1914, pp. 275–279; Henri A. Junod, "l'Alcoolisme Africain," *Bibliothèque Universelle et Revue de Genève*. July-December, 1930, pp. 384–397; Bureau International pour la défense des indigènes, "l'Alcoolisme en Afrique et la Convention de St. Germain-en-Laye," *International Zeitschrift Alkoholismus*. Vol. 38, 1930, pp. 208–216; H. A. Wyndham, "The Problem of West African Liquor Traffic," *Journal of the Royal Institute of International Affairs*. Vol. 9, 1930, pp. 801–818; A. L. Saffery, "The Liquor Problem in Urban Areas," *Race Relations*. Vol. 7, 1940, pp. 89–91; Norton de Matos, *Memórias e Trabalhos da Minha Vida*. Lisbon, 1944, Vol. III, pp. 260–275; Emmanuel La Gravière, "The Problem of Alcohol in the Colonies and Territories South of the Sahara," *International Review of Missions*. Vol. 46, 1957, pp. 290–298; H. H. Ferreira, "The Campaign Against Alcoholism on the Copperbelt," *Central African Journal of Medicine*. Vol. 3, 1957, pp. 71–73; António da Silva Rego, *Alguns Problémas sociológico-missionários da África Negra*. Lisbon, 1960, pp. 68–70; M. Gelfand, "Alcoholism in Contemporary African Society," *ibid.*, Vol. 12, 1966, pp. 12–13; L. S. Gillis, J. B. Lewis, and M. Slabbert, "Alcoholism amongst the Cape Coloureds," *South African Medical Journal*. Vol. 47, 1973, pp. 1374–1382; A. Anumonye, N. Omoniwa, and H. Adaranijo, "Excessive Alcohol Use and Related Problems in Nigeria," *Drug and Alcohol Dependence*. Vol. 2, 1977, pp. 23–30; J. Finlay and R. K. Jones, "Alcohol Consumption and the Nature of Alcohol Related Problems

It is not difficult to find references amongst the extant primary documentation indicating that Africans consumed significant quantities of Luso-Brazilian alcohol. In the late 1610s, for example, the Bishop of Kongo and Angola informed the King of Portugal that the *Mani Kongo* and his entourage were greatly given to *vinho*.[6] Some six decades later, in 1680, Cadornega described the society of Luanda and the leaders of African social formations in the hinterland of this port town as a brotherhood worshipping Bacchus, the Classical deity of wine. The resident historian of seventeenth century Angola noted that the inhabitants of Angola's colonial capital were greatly fond of *vinho*, particularly during the religious and public festivals held in their port town.[7] If wine was not available, as happened when they fled to Massangano in 1641, they "invented" a number of brandies from local produce "to console themselves," which distilled "only when in the receptacle of their stomachs."[8] And, further inland, the political leaders of Matamba and Kasanje were "such good friends of and so inclined towards *vinho*," Cadornega added, that whenever trade slaves were unavailable, they drew upon their own domestic slaves just to drink the European intoxicant.[9]

Even more ample, not to mention trenchant, evidence is available on heavy drinking of Luso-Brazilian alcohol following the late seventeenth century, when import levels were at their highest. In the late 1750s, Governor António de Vasconcelos characterized both Africans and lower class non-Africans as imbibing such large amounts of imported alcohol that the inebriety resulting therefrom was the major reason for the disorders, fights, and wounds that occurred in Luanda.[10]

---

in Botswana: A Preliminary Report," *Pula*. Vol. 3, 1983, pp. 1–13; J. D. Rainhorn, "l'Alcoolisme: ce fléau moderne de l'Afrique," *Developpement et Santé*. No. 43, 1983, pp. 22–28; A. Kher, "Montée préoccupante de l'alcoolisme dans le Tiers Monde," *Afrique Santé*. August 8, 1982, pp. 1–7; and S. W. Acuda, "International Review Series: Alcohol and Alcohol Problems, Research. 1. East Africa," *British Journal of Addiction*. Vol. 80, 1985, pp. 121–126. For a fuller bibliography, see: Gessesse and Molamu, *Alcohol and Alcoholism in Africa: A Bibliography*; and Curto, "Alcohol in Africa: A Preliminary Bibliography of the Post-1875 Literature". The best work on the attitudes of Victorians to alcoholic beverages and drinking remains Brian Harrison, *Drink and the Victorians: The Temperance Question in England, 1815–1872*. London, 1971.

[6] "Relação do Bispo do Congo a El-Rei," 7–09–1619, in Felner, *Angola*, p. 473.
[7] Cadornega, *História Geral das Guerras*, Vol. III, p. 36.
[8] *Ibid.*, Vol. I, pp. 488–489.
[9] *Ibid.*, Vol. II, pp. 79–80, and 223–234, and Vol. III, pp. 135–136, 226.
[10] See his order, dated 30–10–1759, in AHU, Angola, Cx. 42, Doc. 88.

The same official thereafter described the *gerebita, vinho,* and *aguardente* offloaded in the colonial capital of Angola as sustaining the cravings of Luso-Brazilian "alcoholics and the *gentio*" or common people of African descent.[11] Governor Sousa Coutinho, on the other hand, later depicted Luanda as a relatively uneventful town, save for the "occasional discords which *vinho* and *gerebita* fomented upon seamen that went ashore."[12] But this situation, which may well have resulted from the reduced hours of operation imposed by Vasconcelos in 1759 on taverns, was a temporary one.[13] Testimonials subsequent to the governorship of Governor Sousa Coutinho portray continued heavy drinking styles by the population of this port town. In the 1780s, Silva Correia, the resident historian of eighteenth century Angola, indicated that Luanda's horde of drinkers "drained in one instant the [*gerebita*] cargo of a small Brazilian vessel.[14] And a decade later, the chief physician José Pinto de Azeredo considered the abuse of imported alcohol important enough to account for a significant portion of the mortality that occurred in the colonial capital of Angola.[15] Heavy consumption of Luso-Brazilian alcohol appears to have abated again following the 1816 decree of Governor Motta Feo e Torres that forced Luanda's drinking establishments to close at sundown.[16] Yet, this situation too did not last long. By 1821, according to Governor Manoel Vieira de Albuquerque e Tovar, the "vice of inebriety was [again] very common in this town," resulting in a variety of disorders.[17] And, in the late 1820s, Jean Baptiste Douville found the inhabitants of this seaport similarly guzzling prodigious amounts of imported alcohol.[18]

The post-1700 evidence on heavy drinking of Luso-Brazilian alcoholic beverages, however, is not limited to the multicultural society of Luanda. In 1700, Lorenzo da Lucca found the Prince of Nsoyo and his subjects already quite partial to *eau-de-vie* which, in this case,

---

[11] Governor Vasconcelos to the King, 9–07–1762, AHU, Angola, Cx. 45, Doc. 64.
[12] Sousa Coutinho to Conde Copeiro Mor, 18–08–1766, BNL, Cód. 8742, fl. 61.
[13] See, for example, "Traslado do Auto de Exame, e Corpo de Delicto, que se fes ao preto Manoel de Salvador, escravo" 10–07–1771, AHU, Angola, Cx. 55, Doc. 43.
[14] Silva Correia, *História de Angola*, Vol. I, p. 41.
[15] Azeredo, *Ensaios sobre Algumas Enfermidades*, pp. 55–57.
[16] Motta Feo e Torres to Conde da Barca, 12–08–1817, AHU, Cx. 133, Doc. 37.
[17] Albuquerque e Tovar to Conde dos Arcos, 9–02–1821, AHU, Angola, Cx. 140, Doc. 21.
[18] Douville, *Voyage au Congo*, Vol. I, pp. 52–54.

probably meant either *aguardente* or, especially, *gerebita*.[19] Soon afterward, an anonymous slave trader observed further north in Cabinda that without *"cachaça,* the soul of conversation," it was "very difficult to reach a deal with Africans."[20] Governor Sousa Coutinho, in the early 1770s, was much impressed by the "great affection" which Africans in the interior had for *gerebita*.[21] Count de Capellis, on the other hand, commented in 1784 that Africans along the Angolan coast "spent their days getting drunk with *eau-de-vie . . .* until [it] lasted."[22] Silva Correia, in turn, described African societies inland as constituting, with that of the colonial capital of Angola, a veritable brotherhood of Bacchus, just like de Cadornega a century before, but with the Brazilian distillate now their drink of choice.[23] He noted that because those who dealt in slaves seldom accepted to conduct their business without generous portions of *gerebita*, coastal traders had found it "best to have the inclination of the [indigenous] inhabitants in one's favour."[24] Africans, accordingly, imbibed considerable amounts of Brazilian cane brandy, which turned their palates "extremely callused" due to its highly adulterated form.[25] For the Appeals Court Judge of Rio de Janeiro who visited the colony of Angola at the beginning of the nineteenth century, the "barbarous" Africans were similarly "greatly impassioned" with *gerebita*.[26] The same characterization was left by António de Saldanha da Gama, some thirty years after his term as Governor of Angola in 1807–1810, when he still referred to this intoxicant as that "fascinating liquid . . . so dear to savage people."[27] And Douville portrayed not a few of the societies he visited during 1828–1830 in the hinterland of Benguela as also heavy consumers of Brazilian cane brandy. While in Kambaka

---

[19] Cuvelier, *Relations sur le Congo du Père Laurent de Lucques*, p. 46.

[20] Ferrez, "Diário Anônimo de uma Viagem às Costas d'Africa (1702–1703)," p. 8.

[21] See his report on the trade of Angola, undated, but certainly from the early 1770s, in AHU, Angola, Cx. 59, Doc. 59, fls. 1–1v.

[22] François Gaulme, "Un document sur le Ngoyo et ses voisins en 1784: l'Observation sur la navigation et le commerce de la côte d'Angole du comte de Capellis," *Revue française d'histoire d'outre-mer*. Vol. 64, 1977, pp. 368–369.

[23] Silva Correia, *História de Angola*, Vol. I, pp. 39–41.

[24] *Ibid.*, Vol. I, p. 40.

[25] *Ibid.*

[26] See the report of this official, Francisco de Sousa Guerra Araujo Godinho, 23-10-1804, in AHU, Cx. 111, Doc. 28.

[27] Saldanha da Gama, *Memória sobre as Colónias de Portugal, situadas na Costa Occidental d'Africa*, p. 111.

"men drank *gerebita* like water from a source," he wrote, prodigious amounts of this imported beverage were guzzled down in Tamba without the people however becoming intoxicated.[28] But, in Mbailundu and neighbouring polities, the population were nothing less than "consummate drunks."[29]

The qualitative proof for post-1600 heavy drinking patterns of imported Luso-Brazilian alcohol is thus substantial. The multicultural societies of the colonial port towns, particularly Luanda, and the African social formations behind them are all generally depicted as consuming large amounts of alcohol imports. The assertions made by modern scholars appear to have been substantiated. Let us now turn our attention to the quantitative evidence.

Miller has suggested that roughly 2,000 *pipas* of *gerebita*, the most voluminous of the alcohol imports and the most utilized in slave trading roles, were offloaded at Luanda per year during the 1700s.[30] The paucity of import reports for the colonial capital of Angola prior to the early 1780s can only put this quantitative statement into question. Our estimated import volumes for 1727–1728 and 1756–1761, added to the known import volumes of 1699–1703 and 1782–1799, work out to an annual average of 1,603.5 *pipas*,[31] an amount 20% lower than that suggested by Miller. For the better documented period between 1782 and 1830, our data show 1,751.5 *pipas* of *cachaça* as unloaded at Luanda on average each year, with a further 468.5 *pipas* of other intoxicants imported annually during 1785–1830.[32] In the case of Benguela, the only other port town for which import reports exist, data indicate that an average of 388 *pipas* of Brazilian cane brandy and 77 *pipas* of other alcoholic beverages were unloaded there between 1798 and 1828.[33] If the Benguela figures are projected backwards to the early 1780s, the combined Luanda-Benguela alcohol imports during the last five decades of the legal slave trade amounts to 2,140 *pipas* of *gerebita* and 545 *pipas* of other intoxicants per annum, for an overall total of 2,685 *pipas*.

[28] Douville, *Voyage au Congo*, Vol. II, pp. 29 and 86.
[29] *Ibid.*, Vol. II, p. 105.
[30] Miller, *Way of Death*, p. 446.
[31] Graphs 3, 4, and 7.
[32] Graph 7.
[33] See Curto, "The Luso-Brazilian Alcohol Commerce at Benguela and its Hinterland."

The volume was, for the period, considerable. Each *pipa* of Luso-Brazilian alcohol then probably still contained some 500 litres.[34] This translates into 1,070,000 litres of *cachaça* and 272,500 litres of other intoxicants, or a total of 1,342,500 litres, imported per annum at both Luanda and Benguela during 1782–1830. These two ports alone imported nearly one-half and one-third, respectively, of the total volume of foreign alcohol estimated as offloaded along the entire western coast of Africa in 1780s and in 1820s.[35]

What was the consumption rate per capita? Statistics on the population of West Central Africa or, for that matter, any other part of the continent, generally do not exist until we cross the threshold of the late nineteenth century. Nevertheless, in the case of the colony of Angola, a large body of demographic data is available for the pre-1830 period during which the volume of alcohol imported through Luanda and Benguela is relatively well documented.[36] Let us concentrate on two specific chronological points, the late 1770s-early 1780s and the later 1820s.

In 1777–1778, two successive censuses were carried out in the colony of Angola. John Thornton, the first historical demographer to have seriously analyzed these documents, suggests that:

> [W]e cannot know exactly what part of Angola was counted. Presumably the censuses included the core areas of Portuguese conquest and settlement: the area between the Dande River on the north and the

---

[34] The volume of the *pipa* fluctuated over time. According to Brásio, *Monumenta Missionaria Africana*, 1st series, Vol. III, p. 451, this large wooden container held 500 litres of liquid in the early 1600s. Its volume appears to have shrunk to about 435 litres later in the seventeenth century. But, by the early 1730s, it had increasing again to some 535 litres. See the document attached to the petition of Manoel Monteiro da Rocha, dated 28–08–1731, in AHU, Angola, Cx. 25, Doc. 115. For the later 1810s, Johan B. von Spix and C. F. P. von Martius, *Travels in Brazil, in the Years 1817–1820: Undertaken by Command of His Majesty the King of Prussia*. London, 1824, Vol. I, p. 205, report the volume of a *pipa* of Brazilian cane brandy as averaging nearly 475 litres. But Maxwell, Wright & Co., *Commercial Formalities of Rio de Janeiro*, p. 44, list its 1827 volume as 140 US gallons, or some 535 litres, exactly the same amount as in the 1730s. We have consequently retained the early seventeenth century volume suggested by Brásio for the last half century of the legal slave trade. Fluctuating volumes notwithstanding, the issue has no bearing at all on the development of our argument, as we shall see below.

[35] See Eltis and Jennings, "Trade between Western Africa and the Atlantic World," p. 955.

[36] For the whole corpus, as found in the AHU, see José C. Curto, "Sources for the Pre-1900 Population History of Sub-Saharan Africa: The Case of Angola, 1773–1845," *Annales de démographie historique*. 1994, pp. 319–338.

Kwanza on the south, inland as far as the Lukala River, and from the central coast around the modern towns of Benguela and Lobito inland to the eastern fringes of the great central plateau . . . Given the relatively large number of people recorded in the censuses it seems likely that the population in a number of surrounding districts which had nominally accepted Portuguese suzerainty and had resident Portuguese traders or missionaries were also counted, possibly including the powerful kingdoms of Matamba and Kasange.[37]

For Thornton, then, the 1777–1778 enumerations covered the population of two of the three major areas in West Central Africa that supplied slaves for the Atlantic Slave Trade, with only that of the kingdom of Kongo and its northern neighbours not included. These censuses show the population of Luanda, Benguela and their respective hinterlands as numbering 474,117 individuals in 1777 and 487,358 persons in 1778.[38] Prior to the great drought and famine that struck West Central Africa during 1785–1794,[39] it is doubtful that this population experienced any significant increase or decrease. Let us assume that it numbered 500,000 individuals in 1782 and that this population consumed all of the alcohol estimated then as imported through Luanda and Benguela, 1,342,500 litres. The mean per capita consumption rate works out to 2.7 litres. Doubling the volume of imported intoxicants to account for the adulteration that took place along the coast, the average consumption rate rises to 5.4 litres per person.

Let us now turn towards the very end of our period. In 1826, the colony of Angola was the object of yet another census. Its geographical coverage, however, fell far short of the 1777–1778 censuses. Included were Luanda and Benguela, the *presidios* of Caconda, Novo Redondo, Muxima, Massangano, Cambambe, Pungo Andongo, Ambaca, and Encoge, as well as the districts of Dande, Icollo e Bengo, Zenza e Quilengues, Dembos, Golungo, Calumbo, and

---

[37] John K. Thornton, "The Slave Trade in Eighteenth Century Angola: Effects on Demographic Structures," *Canadian Journal of African Studies*. Vol. 14, 1980, pp. 418–419.

[38] See the "Mappa de todos os Moradores e Habitantes deste Reyno de Angola, e suas conquistas tirado no fim do anno de 1777, em q. entrão os Dembos, Potentados e Sovas Vassalos," and the "Mappa de todos os Moradores e Habitantes deste Reyno de Angola, e suas conquistas tirado no fim do anno de 1778, em q. entrão os Dembos, Potentados e Sovas Vassalos," both in AHU, Angola, Cx. 62, Doc. 67. Versions of these censuses have been published as "População de Angola, 1778," *Arquivos das Colonias*. Vol. 3, 1918, p. 176; and "População de Angola, 1779," in *ibid.*, p. 178.

[39] Miller, "Significance of Drought, Disease and Famine," pp. 21, 29, and 51–54.

Quilengues south of Benguela. In other words, this enumeration covered exclusively the areas under Portuguese control. The kingdom of Kongo, its northern neighbours, and the kingdoms of Matamba and Kasanje were excluded. The 1826 census shows a total of 255,257 individuals as residing within this reduced geographical zone.[40] If they alone consumed all of the 1,342,500 litres of alcohol estimated as imported, the average per capita rate translates to 5.3 litres.[41] And doubling the volume to account for adulteration, the mean consumption rate increases to 10.6 litres per person.

Dividing the amount of estimated alcohol imports by successively smaller numbers of people than the total population who would have had access to these intoxicants, still clearly establishes that per capita consumption rates were low.[42] Far higher quantities of intoxicants were consumed, by way of comparison, in the Continental Colonies just before and after they became the United States. Here, according to one estimate, an annual average of 14.2 litres of alcoholic beverages, mostly New England rum, were imbibed per person during the 1760s.[43] Another places the mean per capita consumption rate of rum alone in 1770 at 16.1 litres amongst whites and 3.8 litres amongst slaves.[44] The average rate of distilled spirit consumption appears to have climbed to 17.7 litres by 1810, before peaking to some 19.3 litres in 1830.[45] In spite of the impressive volumes of

---

[40] See "Mappa da População do Reino de Angolla, 20–06–1827," in AHU, Angola, Cx. 156, Doc. 16. Although dated from 1827, this census surely refers to the previous year. See, Curto, "Sources for the Pre-1900 Population History of Sub-Saharan Africa;" and Curto and Gervais, "The Population of Luanda during the Late Trans-Atlantic Slave Trade."

[41] Note that using the mid-1820s alcohol imports figures does not significantly change this rate. During 1823–1825, Luanda imported an average of 3,074 *pipas* of alcohol, or 1,537,000 litres. See Lima, *Ensaios sobre a statistica das possessões portuguesas*, Vol. III, pp. 70–71. Benguela, on the other hand, imported a mean 534.75 *pipas*, or 267,375 litres, in 1825 and 1828. See Curto, *Álcool e Escravos*, Table XXXI, p. 364. The 1826 overall total of Luso-Brazilian alcohol imports would have thus amounted to some 1,804,375 litres, or 25% higher than the 1782–1830 estimate, which works out to a mean consumption rate of 7.1 litres of unadulterated foreign intoxicants per person.

[42] It is impossible to determine total alcohol consumption rates since quantitative data on the local, lower alcoholized, beverages do not exist.

[43] W. J. Rorabaugh, *The Alcoholic Republic: An American Tradition*. New York, 1979, pp. 7–8.

[44] McCusker, *Rum and the American Revolution*, Vol. 1, pp. 476–477.

[45] Rorabaugh, *The Alcoholic Republic*, p. 8. And, according to Ron Roizen, Rorabaugh's figures are way too low! See Ron Roizen <rroizen@ix.netcom.com> to Alcohol and Temperance History Group <athg@miamiy.acs.muohio.edu>, 4 September 1996 17:47:56 EST "Re: US Alcohol Consumption rates."

Luso-Brazilian alcohol offloaded at Luanda and Benguela, these were just not enough to turn the population of the region into generalized "consummate drunks," as Douville and others, both before and after him, would have us believe.

Yet, if the consumption rates of Luso-Brazilian alcohol were generally low, there is no doubt that the impact of these intoxicants upon the drinking patterns of certain population segments was significant. Not everyone imbibed equal amounts of *vinho, aguardente, gerebita* or other foreign alcohol imports. The first to have access to these alcoholic beverages were the multicultural populations who inhabited the coastal towns. We do not know how much of the alcohol imported was consumed there. But the qualitative evidence presented above on drinking patterns at Luanda must be given its due weight. After all, the colonial capital of Angola was the place where most of our sources had considerable first hand experience. Here, indeed, whites, Luso-Africans, and Africans, slaves included, all drank heavily. Extant police records, though for a later period, indicate the nature of the problem. Between 1857 and 1878, out of some 28,140 incarcerations involving Luso-Africans and Africans, 11% were allegedly due to drunkenness.[46] This was the second most common reason, behind the corollary of creating disorders, for which free and enslaved Luso-Africans and Africans went to jail. As we have seen, this situation was not new at Luanda.

A second group of people who were avid consumers of Luso-Brazilian alcohol lived in and around the various slave markets of the interior, where a large percentage of the imported intoxicants were destined to for slave trading. Expanded in volume through adulteration at the coast, the volume of *vinho, aguardente,* and especially after the mid-1600s, *gerebita* that reached the *feiras* may well have equalled, if it did not surpass, the quantities actually offloaded at Luanda and Benguela. This enabled Africans in and around the slave marts to indulge in imbibing large portions of these diluted intoxicants. Such heavy drinking did not escape the attention of Governor Almeida e Vasconcelos. Early in the 1790s, while referring to the *feira* in Kasanje, the largest of the slave markets in West Central Africa, he remarked:

---

[46] These figures represent an as yet rough calculation of the incarceration data found in the weekly police reports of the *Boletim Oficial do Governo Geral da Província de Angola* for the time period in question.

> [W]hat does it matter for us, if Africans in the backlands inebriate themselves [with our] . . . *vinho, aguardente,* and *cachaça.* [T]he more they acquire this taste, the more they will come to the slave markets with what to satisfy their appetite. [T]hose that do wrong will be punished and treated following the terms negotiated [with the Jaga]. [O]ne of [our] principal objectives is to attempt to please those with whom we live and from whom we wish to take advantage, making them successively more dependent and passionate for our booze . . .[47]

And lower stratum, slave-dealing Africans were not the only ones who drank heavily the Luso-Brazilian alcohol circulating in the slave marts.

The political authorities ruling over the *feiras* did the same with the alcohol imports secured through presents, taxes, and direct slave-trading. During the late 1820s, as was the case since the mid-seventeenth century, the warehouses of the *Jaga* of Kasanje were reportedly full of *gerebita,* amongst other items, guarded day and night by his soldiers.[48] Sometime in 1804–1805, in particular, the then *Jaga* created a diplomatic incident with the representatives of Luanda's slave-trading community established in his *feira* during one of his "inebriety sessions."[49] In Ambaca, by the late 1820s, neighbouring African political authorities had even resorted to pooling their finances to acquire barrels of *gerebita,* "because experience had shown them that by buying wholesale the price was lower."[50] A Ndembu chief, who preferred imported *cachaça* to *walo,* the local beer, apparently told Douville one day:

> Why is there no God of liquor, to give it to us when we want? What pleasure we experience when drunk! I forget my troubles; I then no longer remember that I have enemies, I only see the pleasure of the moment.[51]

According to this Frenchman, *gerebita* was the "foodstuff" of African political authorities and, as a result, they used the expression "I am hungry" to ask for a drink.[52]

Two other groups of Africans also appear to have engaged in drinking relatively significant amounts of Luso-Brazilian intoxicants.

---

[47] Governor Almeida e Vasconcelos to Paulo Joze de Loreiro (Director of the *feira* in Kasanje), 12–05–1791, AHNA, Cód. 84, fls. 178v–179.
[48] Douville, *Voyage au Congo,* Vol. II, p. 350.
[49] Vellut, "Le royaume de Cassange," p. 124.
[50] Douville, *Voyage au Congo,* Vol. II, p. 314.
[51] *Ibid.,* Vol. I, pp. 287–288.
[52] *Ibid.,* Vol. II, p. 29.

One was the labourers who were conscripted to work in the various enterprises of the colonial government. Joseph Miller has recently calculated that, during the early 1810s, workers in the sulphur mine south of Benguela were allocated a daily average of seven centilitres, or a little over two fluid ounces, of *gerebita*.[53] But on one occasion, the administrator of the colonial "industries" behind this seaport noted that the labourers working in the white-wash factory in 1800 had become addicted to *gerebita*, drinking "a whole *ancoreta*" or some thirty-six litres of this intoxicant within twenty-four hours.[54] And another group who periodically indulged in heavy drinking was the bearers upon whose backs all of the Luso-Brazilian alcohol circulating in the interior of the Angolan coast was transported.[55]

Inhabitants of the coastal port towns, regardless of the colour of their skin or social status, and African political authorities, slave dealers, and workers engaged in colonial enterprises were thus the groups who, identifiably, consumed most of the intoxicants imported at Luanda and Benguela. In each and every case, they were directly tied to the Luso-Brazilian slave trading economy in the South Atlantic. These groups obviously constituted a minority of the population. How was the majority affected by Luso-Brazilian alcohol?

Many other Africans also consumed imported intoxicants. But they did so only occasionally and in much smaller amounts than those directly tied to the slave trading economy. It was customary for ruling elites to distribute part of the Luso-Brazilian alcohol which they acquired to their nobles and their subjects.[56] In the mid-1600s, for

---

[53] Miller, *Way of Death*, p. 697.

[54] Pedro Roiz Bandeira to Jozé Mauricio Roiz (Governor of Benguela), 13–11–1800, in Delgado, *Ao Sul do Cuanza*, Vol. I, p. 546.

[55] Silva Correia, *História de Angola*, Vol. I, pp. 12–20 and 80.

[56] Exactly the same practice was observed by West African potentates with their foreign intoxicants. See, in particular, Akinjogbin, *Dahomey and Its Neighbours 1708–1818*, p. 75; Daaku, *Trade and Politics on the Gold Coast, 1600–1720*, pp. 64–65 and 98–99; Donnan, *Documents Illustrative of the History of the Slave Trade*, Vol. II, p. 403; and Ryder, *Benin and the Europeans*, p. 207. Sharing alcoholic beverages, whether local or foreign, had and still has great symbolic value for Africans. See Beidelman, "Beer Drinking and Cattle Theft in Ukaguru, pp. 534–549; Eguchi, "Beer Drinking and Festivals amongst the Hide," pp. 69–90; Hellman, "Importance of Beer-Brewing in an Urban Native Yard," pp. 39–60; Karp, "Beer Drinking and Social Experience in an African Society, pp. 83–119; Krige, "The Social Significance of Beer among the Balobedu," pp. 343–357; MacGaffey, *Custom and Government in the Lower Congo*, pp. 110–111; Netting, "Beer as a Locus of Value among the West African Kofyar," pp. 375–384; Ngokwey, "Varieties of Palm Wine among the Lele of the Kasai," pp. 113–121; Parkin, *Palms, Wine, and Witnesses*, p. 42; Platt, "Traditional Alcoholic

example, Queen Nzinga sometimes provided portions of her *vinho* to labourers involved in state projects.[57] At the end of the seventeenth century, Caltanisetta witnessed, much to his surprise, the local ruler of Nsonso share two small glasses of *vinho* which he had given him with more than twenty of his subjects.[58] Similarly, a slave trader from Luanda in the early 1780s saw the Princess of Nsoyo divide eight *ancoretas* of *gerebita* and two *frasqueiras* of *aguardente*, some 350 litres in all, that were offered to her in the form of a business tax, among twenty to thirty of her male subjects.[59] And Douville found exactly the same practice nearly everywhere he went. Of two bottles of *gerebita* and one of *vinho* that he gave to a chief in Golungo Alto, one bottle of the Brazilian distillate was drunk with his nobles.[60] African political authorities in Ndembu, from chiefs to the lower nobility, always gave part of the *gerebita* which Douville offered them to their subjects.[61] In the specific case of the inhabitants of Tamba, he noted that:

> The[y] share everything they have. If there are two hundred of them together, they pass from one to another a single glass of *gerebita* given to them. Each is content with wetting his lips, so that there will be enough for the others.[62]

Etiquette clearly called African ruling elites to share a portion of this intoxicant with their less fortunate subjects.

Another way through which lower class Africans gained access to Luso-Brazilian alcohol imports was during public feasts. During the mid-1600s, according to Cavazzi de Montecúccolo:

> Amongst the Imbangala, [whether they are] poor or rich, it is customary to mutually invite themselves to eat and drink together, following their possibilities. During these banquets, every type of food and beverage, especially European wine and a local drink *quilunda* is served.[63]

Beverages and their Importance," pp. 115–124; Sangree, "The Social Functions of Beer Drinking in Bantu Tiriki," pp. 6–21; Saul, "Beer, Sorghum and Women," pp. 746–764; and Umunna, "Drinking Culture of a Nigerian Community," pp. 529–537.

[57] Cavazzi de Montecúccolo, *Descrição Histórica dos Três Reinos*, Vol. II, p. 147.

[58] Bontinck, *Diaire Congolais de Fra Luca da Caltanisetta*, p. 177.

[59] See the report of this slave trading venture, dated 15–08–1782, in AHU, Angola, Cx. 65, Doc. 64, fl. 4.

[60] Douville, *Voyage au Congo*, Vol. I, pp. 156 and 158.

[61] *Ibid.*, Vol. I, pp. 229–230 and 265.

[62] *Ibid.*, Vol. II, p. 87.

[63] See his *Descrição Histórica dos Três Reinos*, Vol. I, p. 188.

In Tamba, at the end of the 1820s, the alcoholic beverage of choice for consumption during these occasions had long become *gerebita*. Here, Douville recounts, a chief one day sought to hold a feast and needed the Brazilian distillate. Although there "was no other way of procuring it than by selling some slave," at the time there was not a single *pombeiro* or *sertanejo* within his domains. Consequently, the organizer of the feast turned to Douville,[64] who was always well stocked with barrels of *gerebita*.

Other occasions also presented themselves for African masses to do more than just "wet their lips" with Luso-Brazilian intoxicants. Amongst these were rituals and marriage contracts. When Queen Nzinga died in 1663, the many *peroleiras* of *vinho* then sent to Matamba were liberally consumed with "much largesse," a rite that her subjects observed following funerals.[65] Inebriating amounts of *eau-de-vie* (most likely *gerebita*) were similarly used in Mbamba in a variety of rituals as early as the 1710s.[66] In and around Luanda, during the 1790s, the ceremonials followed subsequent to the death of Africans were "always accompanied by much wine, [w]ulo, and Brazilian cane brandy."[67] And, last but not least, by the 1820s, a bottle of *gerebita* was already part of the bride price required by father-in-laws in the central highlands.[68]

The impact of Luso-Brazilian alcohol, although not commensurate in its spacial and socio-economic distribution, was thus more than a trivial phenomenon. The minority of the population directly tied to the South Atlantic slave trading economy constituted the most avid drinkers of the imported intoxicants.[69] African political authorities significantly expanded their traditional drinking habits with the

---

[64] Douville, *Voyage au Congo*, Vol. II, pp. 77 and 87.

[65] Cadornega, *História Geral das Guerras*, Vol. II, pp. 223–224. This same source also mentions wine (p. 224) as offered by the Imbangala to ancestors in their place of rest. But is it not evident here if the reference is to palm or grape wine.

[66] See Francesco de Massafra au préfet Giuseppe de Modena, 1–01–1723, in Jadin, "Clergé Séculier et les Capucins du Congo et d'Angola aux XVIe et XVIIe Siècles," p. 350.

[67] Azeredo, *Ensaios sobre Algumas Enfermidades*, pp. 54–55.

[68] Douville, *Voyage au Congo*, Vol. II, p. 364.

[69] During the era of "legitimate commerce," the socio-economic groups most closely tied to the Atlantic economy still consumed the bulk of the foreign alcohol imported. For the case of West Africa, see: Ayandele, *Missionary Impact on Modern Nigeria, 1872–1914*, pp. 307–327; Dumett, "Social Impact of the European Liquor Trade on the Akan, pp. 69–101; and Olorunfemi, "Liquor Traffic Dilemma in British West Africa, pp. 229–241.

greater quantities of the adulterated *vinho, aguardente,* and *gerebita* they secured, which still remained far more alcoholized than any of the locally produced drinks. In and around the *feiras,* the transformed drinking patterns of the region's ruling elites were quickly mimicked by African slave dealers. And, in the coastal towns, freed and enslaved Africans and Luso-Africans soon adopted the heavy drinking modes of resident Europeans. The majority of the population, the average persons not directly involved in the slave trading economy, only occasionally indulged their palates with *vinho, aguardente,* and *gerebita* as these foreign intoxicants became part and parcel of their customs and rituals.[70] Yet, even though the amounts of Luso-Brazilian alcohol consumed during these occasions were comparatively small, the masses thereby also acquired a taste for the more alcoholized foreign intoxicants.

This development was to prove decisive. Between the 1830s and the early 1910s, the Portuguese, taking full advantage of this acquired taste, established hundreds of sugar cane plantations throughout Angola with one specific objective: to produce cane brandy, which became the major industrial activity of the colony.[71] Thereafter, Angola was turned into an exclusive dumping ground for the fortified wines of Portugal until it secured its independence in 1974.[72] As these processes coalesced, alcoholism emerged into a serious socioeconomic and health problem for increasing numbers of Angolans.

---

[70] By the second half of the nineteenth century, foreign alcohol imports had also become important an element in the marriage, burial, and religious rites of coastal societies in West Africa. See, in particular, Ayandele, *Missionary Impact on Modern Nigeria, 1872–1914,* pp. 307–327; and Dumett, "Social Impact of the European Liquor Trade on the Akan, pp. 69–101.

[71] See the sketch of this industry in Gervase Clarence-Smith, "The Sugar and Rum Industries in the Portuguese Empire, 1850–1914," in B. Albert and A. Graves, eds., *Crisis and Change in the International Sugar Economy, 1860–1914.* Edinburgh, 1984, pp. 227–349. See also idem, *Slaves, Peasants, and Capitalists in Southern Angola (1840–1926).* Cambridge, 1979, pp. 24–25, 49, and 50–51; idem, *The Third Portuguese Empire, 1825–1975: A Study in Economic Imperialism.* Manchester, 1985, pp. 38, 49, 75, 105, 120, and 134; and Bender, *Angola Under the Portuguese,* pp. 145–146.

[72] Though impressionistic, Capela, *O Vinho para o Preto,* provides much information on this important shift. See also: Clarence-Smith, *Third Portuguese Empire, 1825–1975,* pp. 5, 7–8, 11–14, 18, 24, 44, 68, 92–94, 120–122, 160–166, 200–201, and 220; Pirio, "Commerce, Industry and Empire," especially Chapter 7—"The Political Economy of Alcohol in the Portuguese Empire," pp. 234–302; and Bender, *Angola Under the Portuguese,* pp. 146–147. As Capela, Clarence-Smith, Pirio and, more recently, Jeanne M. Penvenne, *African Workers and Colonial Racism: Mozambican Strategies and Struggles in Lourenço Marques, 1877–1962.* Portsmouth, 1995, pp. 40–43, show, this development also took place in Mozambique.

At the onset of the twentieth century, António D. Ramada Curto, who governed the colony during 1904–1906, Ayres Kopke, one of the founding professors of the School of Tropical Medicine in Lisbon, and Count de Giraul, a colonial army doctor subsequently appointed as the director of the health services of Angola and São Tomé, could still confidently argue:

> We can say that the consumption [of foreign intoxicants] is, in general, more considerable in urban and commercial centres, [but] diminishes progressively, until it becomes almost nill, in the small villages of the interior, where trade is not directly concluded with the European.[73]

But as Bender realised in the late 1960s: "It was not uncommon to find, especially in the south, entire villages drunk on Portuguese wine. [A]lcoholism [had become] one of Angola's principal social problems."[74] Only then was the circle was complete.

---

[73] António D. Ramada Curto, Ayres Kopke, and Visconde de Giraul, *l'Alcoolisme dans les colonies portugaises*. Lisbon, 1910, p. 13.

[74] Bender, *Angola Under the Portuguese*, p. 146. Elsewhere, as studies on Mozambique, the Rand, and other areas of Southern Africa have clearly shown, comparable developments produced similar results. See Capela, *O Vinho para o Preto*; Pirio, "Commerce, Industry and Empire," pp. 234–302; Penvenne, *African Workers and Colonial Racism*, pp. 40–43; Onselen: "Randlords and Rotgut, 1886–1903," pp. 32–89; Charles Ambler and Jonathan Crush, "Alcohol in Southern African Labor History," in Ambler and Crush, *Liquor and Labor in Southern Africa*, pp. 1–55; and other case studies found in this last volume.

GRAPHS

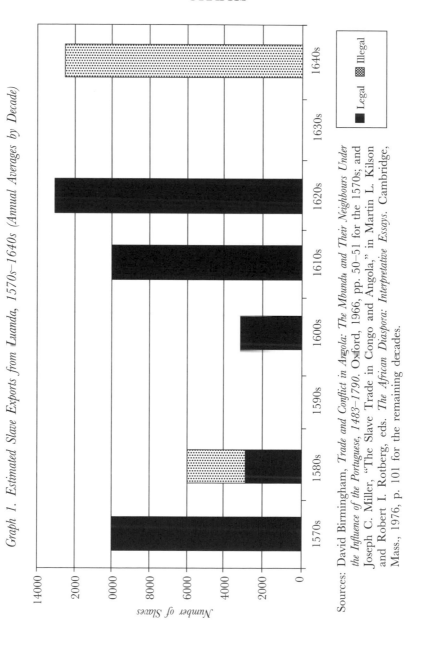

Graph 1. Estimated Slave Exports from Luanda, 1570s–1640s (Annual Averages by Decade)

Sources: David Birmingham, *Trade and Conflict in Angola: The Mbundu and Their Neighbours Under the Influence of the Portuguese, 1483–1790.* Oxford, 1966, pp. 50–51 for the 1570s; and Joseph C. Miller, "The Slave Trade in Congo and Angola," in Martin L. Kilson and Robert I. Rotberg, eds. *The African Diaspora: Interpretative Essays.* Cambridge, Mass., 1976, p. 101 for the remaining decades.

Graph 2. Alcohol Imports at Luanda by Volume and Port of Origin, 1699

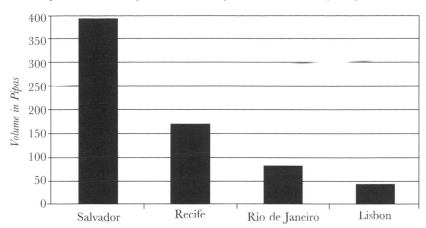

Source: "Accounts of the Procurador of the Senate of Luanda for the Year 1699,"
in Charles R. Boxer, *Portuguese Society in the Tropics: The Municipal Councils of
Goa, Macau, Bahia, and Luanda, 1510–1800.* Madison, 1965, pp 209 218.

Graph 3. Alcohol Imports at Luanda by Volume and Type, 1699–1703

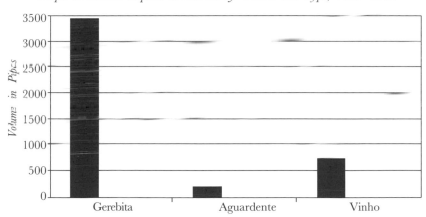

Source: AHU, Angola, "Contrato de 1699–1702" and "Contrato de 1703", n.d.
and n.s., Cx. 17, Doc. 55.

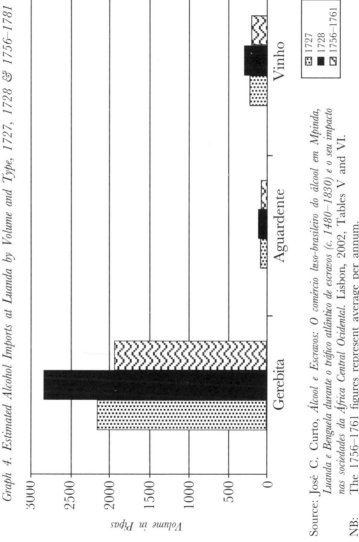

Graph 4. Estimated Alcohol Imports at Luanda by Volume and Type, 1727, 1728 & 1756–1781

Source: José C. Curto, *Álcool e Escravos: O comércio luso-brasileiro do álcool em Mpinda,*
  Luanda e Benguela durante o tráfico atlântico de escravos (c. 1480–1830) e o seu impacto
  nas sociedades da África Central Ocidental. Lisbon, 2002, Tables V and VI.

NB: The 1756–1761 figures represent average per annum.

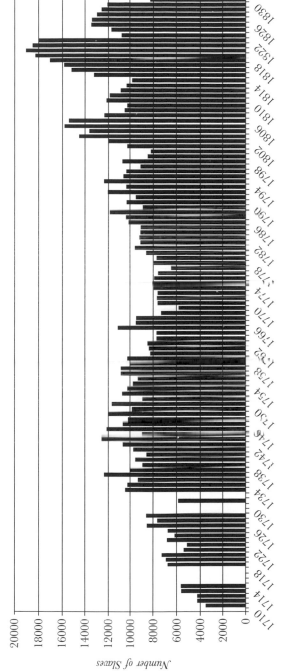

Graph 5. *Legal Slave Exports from Luanda, 1710–1830*

Source: José C. Curto, "A Quantitative Re-Assessment of the Legal Slave Trade from Luanda, 1710–1830," *African Economic History*. Vol. 20, 1992, pp. 1–25.

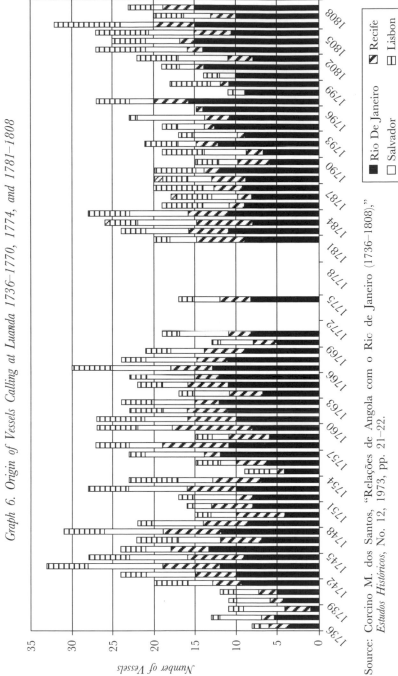

Graph 6. Origin of Vessels Calling at Luanda 1736–1770, 1774, and 1781–1808

Source: Corcino M. dos Santos, "Relações de Angola com o Ric de Janeiro (1736–1808)," *Estudos Históricos*, No. 12, 1973, pp. 21–22.

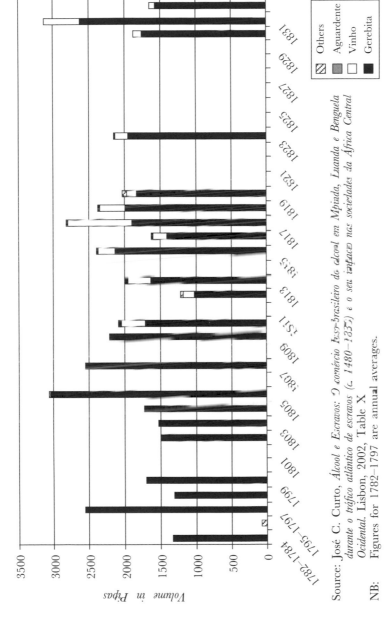

Graph 7. Alcohol Imports at Luanda from Brazil by Volume, 1782–1832

Source: José C. Curto, Álcool e Escravos: O comércio luso-brasileiro do álcool em Mpinda, Luanda e Benguela durante o tráfico atlântico de escravos (c. 1480–1830) e o seu impacto nas sociedades da África Central Ocidental. Lisbon, 2002, Table X

NB: Figures for 1782–1797 are annual averages.

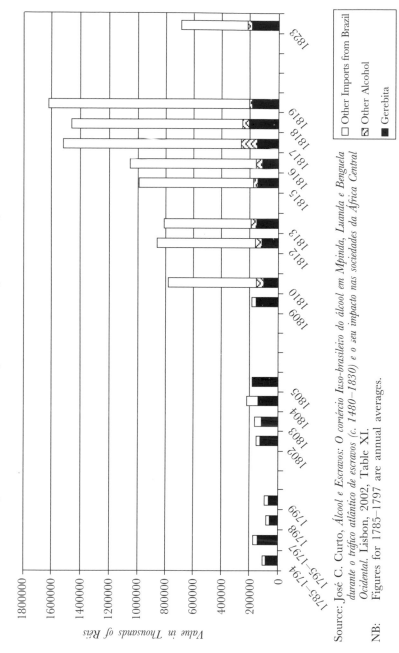

Graph 8. Alcohol & Other Imports at Luanda from Brazil by Value, 1785–1823

Source: José C. Curto, *Álcool e Escravos: O comércio luso-brasileiro do álcool em Mpinda, Luanda e Benguela durante o tráfico atlântico de escravos (c. 1480–1830) e o seu impacto nas sociedades da África Central Ocidental.* Lisbon, 2002, Table XI.

NB: Figures for 1785–1797 are annual averages.

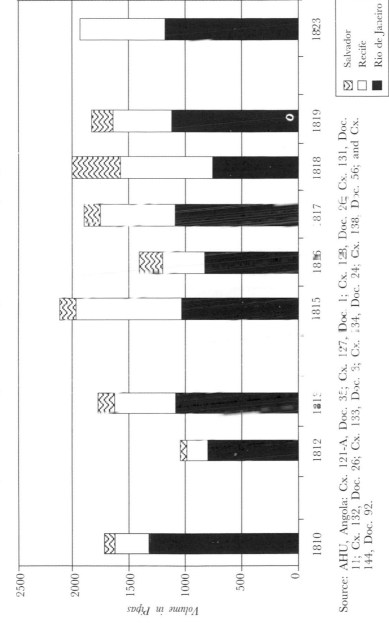

Graph 9. *Gerebita Imports at Luanda by Volume and Port of Origin 1810–1823*

Source: AHU, Angola: Cx. 121-A, Doc. 35; Cx. 127, Doc. 1; Cx. 128, Doc. 26; Cx. 131, Doc. 11; Cx. 132, Doc. 26; Cx. 133, Doc. 3; Cx. 134, Doc. 24; Cx. 138, Doc. 56; and Cx. 144, Doc. 92.

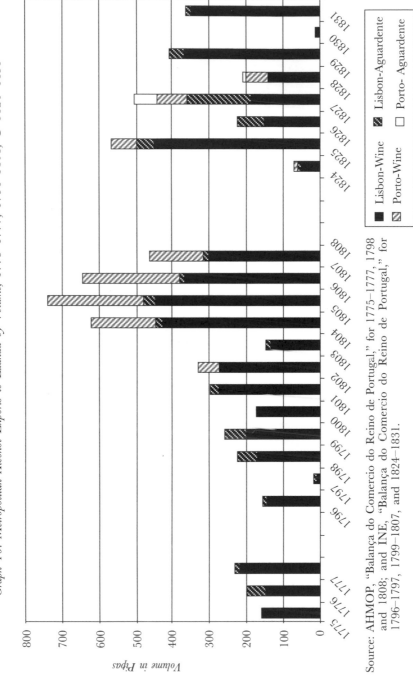

Graph 10. Metropolitan Alcohol Exports to Luanda by Volume, 1775–1777, 1796–1808, & 1824–1831

Source: AHMOP, "Balança do Comercio do Reino de Portugal," for 1775–1777, 1798 and 1808; and INE, "Balança do Comercio do Reino de Portugal," for 1796–1797, 1799–1807, and 1824–1831.

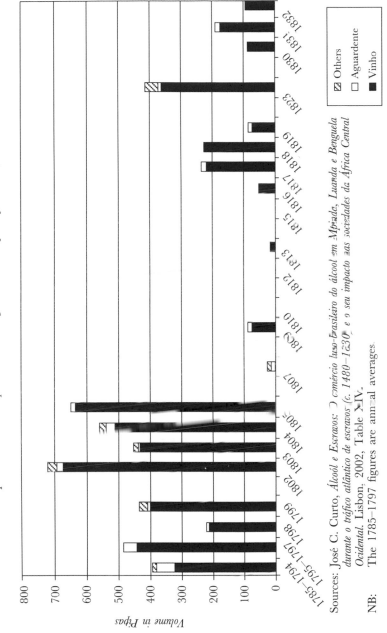

Graph 11. Alcohol Imports at Luanda from the Metropole by Volume, 1785–1832

Sources: José C. Curto, Álcool e Escravos: O comércio luso-brasileiro do álcool em Mpinda, Luanda e Benguela durante o tráfico atlântico de escravos (c. 1480–1830) e o seu impacto nas sociedades da África Central Ocidental. Lisbon, 2002, Table XIV.

NB: The 1785–1797 figures are annual averages.

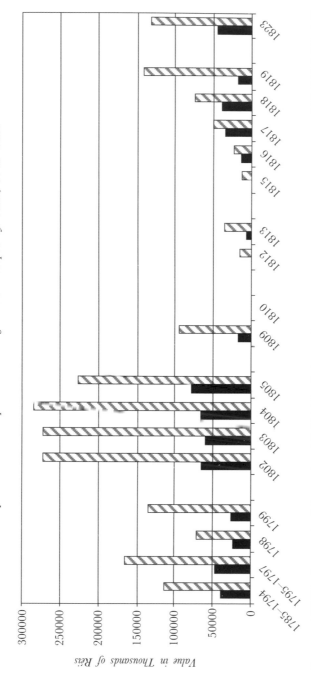

Graph 12. Alcohol Imports at Luanda from the Metropole by Value, 1785–1823

Sources: AIHGB, Secção dos Manuscritos, D.794,28, "Balanço da Importação, & Exportação deste Reíno de Angola desde a Anno de 1785 [. . .] até o Anno de 1794"; BNRJ, Divisão dos Manuscritos, 15–3–33 Nos, 1-8, "Balanço da Importação e Exportação do Reíno de Angola nos Annos de 1795, 1796, e 1797"; and, for 1798–1823, AHU, Angola: Cx. 89, Doc. 79; Cx. 93-A, Doc. 48; Cx. 106, Doc. 5; Cx. 109, Doc. 54; Cx. 112, Doc. 49; Cx. 115, Doc. 28; Cx. 121, Doc. 6; Cx. 121-A, Doc. 35; Cx. 127, Doc. 1; Cx. 128, Doc. 26; Cx. 131, Doc. 11; Cx. 132, Doc. 26; Cx. 133, Doc. 3; Cx. 134, Doc. 24; Cx. 138, Doc. 56; and Cx. 144, Doc. 92.

NB: The figures for 1785–1797 are annual averages.

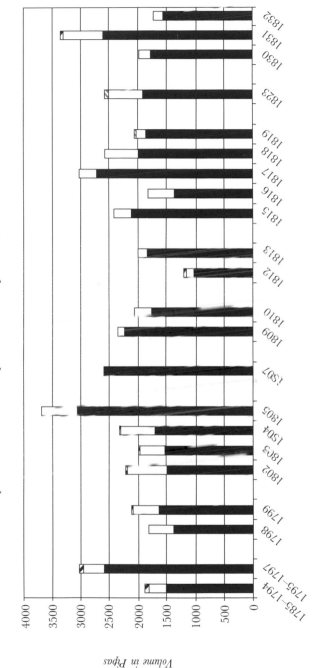

Graph 13. Total Alcohol Imports at Luanda by Volume, 1785–1832

Volume in Pipas

Sources: AIHGB, Secção dos Manuscritos. DL794,28, "Balarço da Importação, & Exportação deste Reíno de Angola desde a Anno de 1785 [. . .] até o Anno de 1794"; BNRJ Divisão dos Manuscritos, 15–3–33 Nos. 1–8, "Balanço da Importação e Exportação do Reíno de Angola nos Annos de 1795, 1796, e 1797"; and, for 1798–1823, AHU, Angola: Cx. 89, Doc. 79; Cx. 93-A, Docc. 48; Cx. 106, Doc. 5; in Cx. 109, Doc. 54; Cx. 112, Doc. 49; Cx. 115, Doc. 28; Cx. 121, Doc. 6; Cx. 127, Doc. 1; Cx. 128, Doc. 26; Cx. 131, Doc. 11; Cx. 132, Doc. 26; Cx. 133, Doc. 3; Cx. 124, Doc. 24, Cx. 138, Doc. 56; Cx. 144, Doc. 92; and Cx. 176, Doc. 10.

NB: Figures for 1785–1797 are annual averages.

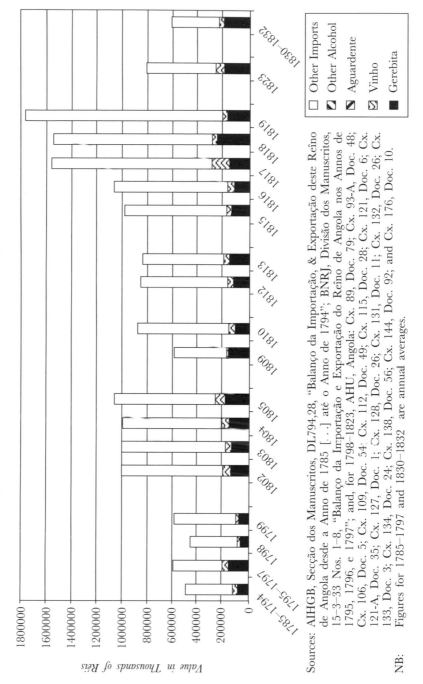

Graph 14. Alcohol and Other Imports at Luanda by Value, 1785–1832

Value in Thousands of Réis

Sources: AIHGB, Secção dos Manuscritos, DL794,28, "Balanço da Importação, & Exportação deste Reîno de Angola desde a Anno de 1785 [. . .] até o Anno de 1794"; BNRJ, Divisão dos Manuscritos, 15–3–33 Nos. 1–8, "Balanço da Importação e Exportação do Reîno de Angola nos Annos de 1795, 1796, e 1797"; and, for 1798–1823, AHU, Angola: Cx. 89, Doc. 79; Cx. 93-A, Doc. 48; Cx. 106, Doc. 5; Cx. 109, Doc. 54; Cx. 112, Doc. 49; Cx. 115, Doc. 28; Cx. 121, Doc. 6; Cx. 121-A, Doc. 35; Cx. 127, Doc. 1; Cx. 128, Doc. 26; Cx. 131, Doc. 11; Cx. 132, Doc. 26; Cx. 133, Doc. 3; Cx. 134, Doc. 24; Cx. 138, Doc. 56; Cx. 144, Doc. 92; and Cx. 176, Doc. 10.

NB: Figures for 1785–1797 and 1830–1832 are annual averages.

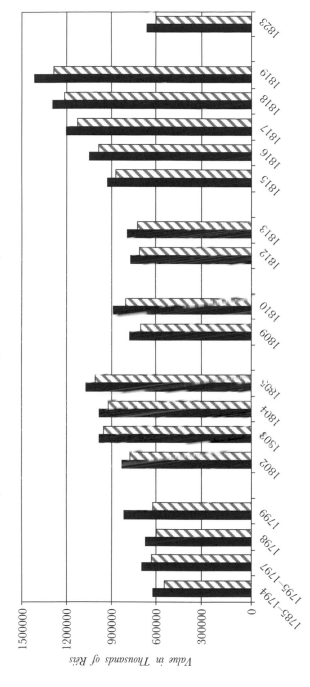

Graph 15. Total and Slave Exports from Luanda by Value, 1785–1823

Sources: AIHGB, Secção dos Manuscritos, DL794,28, "Balanço da Importação, & Exportação deste Reino de Angola desde a Anno de 1785 [. . .] até o Anno de 1794"; ENRJ, Divisão dos Manuscritos, 15–3–33 Nos. 1–8, "Balanço da Importação e Exportação do Reino de Angola nos Annos de 1795, 1796, e 1797"; and, for 1798–1823, AHU, Angola: Cx. 39, Doc. 7; Cx. 93-A, Doc. 48; Cx. 106, Doc. 5; Cx. 109, Doc. 54; Cx. 112, Doc. 49; Cx. 115, Doc. 28; Cx. 121, Doc. 6; Cx. 121-A, Doc. 35; Cx. 127, Doc. 1; Cx. 128, Doc. 26; Cx 131, Doc. 11; Cx. 132, Doc 26; Cx. 133, Doc. 3; Cx. 134, Doc. 24; Cx. 138, Doc. 56; Cx. 144, Doc 92; and Cx. 155, Doc. 10.

NB: Figures for 1785–1797 are annual averages.

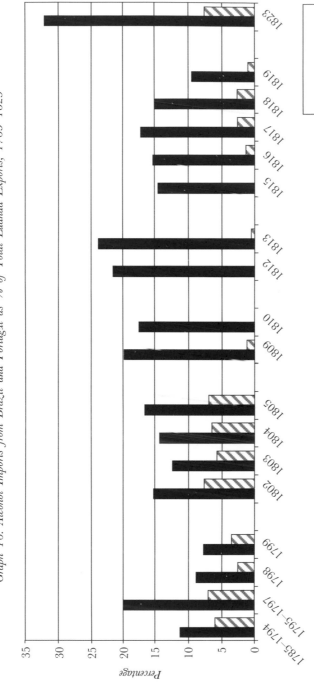

Graph 16. Alcohol Imports from Brazil and Portugal as % of Total Luanda Exports, 1785–1823

Legend:
- ■ Alcohol Imports from Brazil
- ▨ Alcohol Imports from Portugal

Sources: AIHGB, Secção dos Manuscritos, DL794,28, "Balanço da Importação, & Exportação deste Reino de Angola desde a Anno de 1785 [. . .] até o Anno de 1794"; BNRJ, Divisão dos Manuscritos, 15–3–33 Nos. 1–8, "Balanço da Importação e Exportação do Reíno de Angola nos Annos de 1795, 1796, e 1797"; and, for 1798–1823, AHU, Angola: Cx. 89, Doc. 79; Cx. 93-A, Doc. 48; Cx. 106, Doc. 5; Cx. 109, Doc. 54; Cx. 112, Doc. 49; Cx. 115, Doc. 28; Cx. 121, Doc. 6; Cx. 121-A, Doc. 35; Cx. 127, Doc. 1; Cx. 128, Doc. 26; Cx. 131, Doc. 11; Cx. 132, Doc. 26; Cx. 133, Doc. 3; Cx. 134, Doc. 24; Cx. 138, Doc. 56; Cx. 144, Doc. 92; and Cx. 176, Doc. 10.

NB:　　　Figures for 1785–1797 are annual averages.

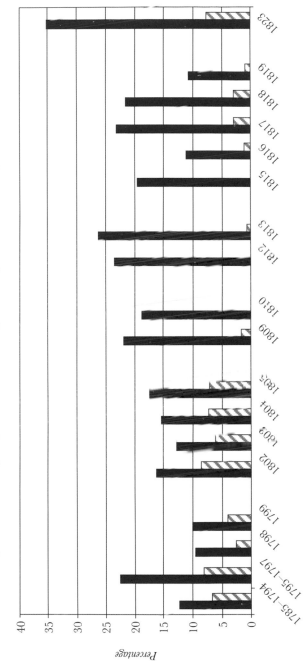

Graph 17. Alcohol Imports from Brazil and Portugal as % of Luanda's Slave Exports, 1785–1823

Sources: AIHGB, Secção dos Manuscritos, DL794.28. "Balanço da Importação, & Exportação deste Reino de Angola desde a Anno de 1785 [...] até o Arro de 1794"; BNRJ, Divisão dos Manuscritos, 15-3-33 Nos. 1–8, "Balanço da Importação e Exportação do Reino de Angola nos Annos de 1795, 1796, e 1797"; and, for 1798–1823, AHU, Angola: Cx. 89, Doc. 7; Cx. 93-A, Doc. 48; Cx. 106, Doc. 5; Cx. 109, Doc. 54; Cx. 112, Doc. 49; Cx. 115, Doc. 23; Cx. 121, Doc. 6; Cx. 121-A, Doc. 35; Cx. 127, Doc. 1; Cx. 128, Doc. 26; Cx. 131, Doc. 11; Cx. 132, Doc. 26; Cx. 133, Doc. 3; Cx. 134, Doc. 24; Cx. 138, Doc. 56; Cx. 144, Doc. 92; and Cx. 176, Doc. 10.

NB: Figures for 1785–1797 are annual averages.

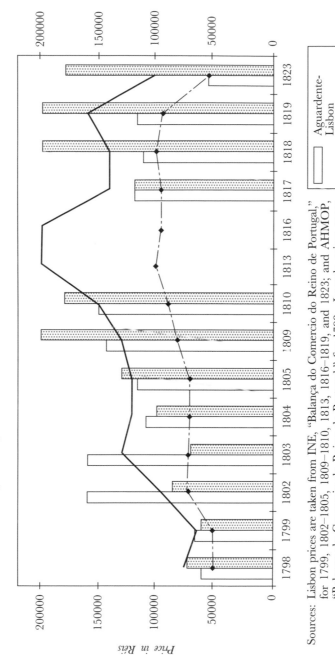

Graph 18. Aguardente and Vinho Prices at Lisbon & Luanda, 1799–1823

Sources: Lisbon prices are taken from INE, "Balança do Comercio do Reino de Portugal," for 1799, 1802–1805, 1809–1810, 1813, 1816–1819, and 1823; and AHMOP, "Balança do Comercio do Reino de Portugal," for 1798. Luanda prices come from the 1798–1823 import reports in AHU, Angola: Cx. 89, Doc. 79; Cx. 93-A, Doc. 48; Cx. 106, Doc. 5; Cx. 109, Doc. 54; Cx. 112, Doc. 49; Cx. 115, Doc. 28; Cx. 121, Doc. 6; Cx. 121-A, Doc. 35; Cx. 127, Doc. 1; Cx. 128, Doc. 26; Cx. 131, Doc. 11; Cx. 138, Doc. 56; and Cx. 144, Doc. 92.

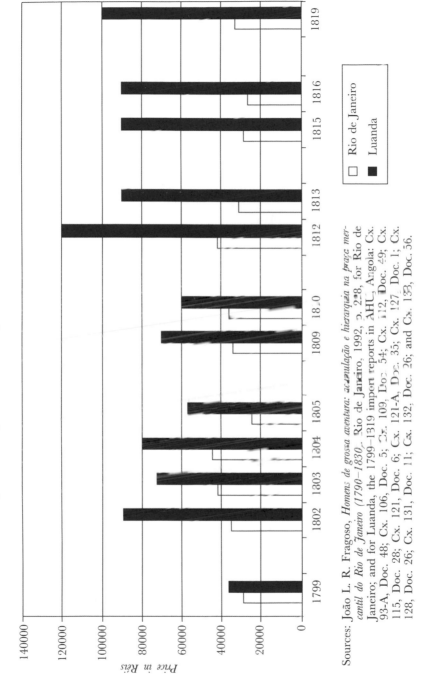

Graph 19. Cacheça Prices at Rio de Janeiro and Luanda, 1799–1819

Sources: João L. R. Fragoso, Homens de grossa aventura: acumulação e hierarquia na praça mercantil do Rio de Janeiro (1790–1830). Rio de Janeiro, 1992, p. 228, for Rio de Janeiro; and for Luanda, the 1799–1819 import reports in AHU, Angola: Cx. 93-A, Doc. 48; Cx. 106, Doc. 5; Cx. 109, Doc. 54; Cx. 112, Doc. 49; Cx. 115, Doc. 28; Cx. 121, Doc. 6; Cx. 121-A, Doc. 35; Cx. 127, Doc. 1; Cx. 128, Doc. 26; Cx. 131, Doc. 11; Cx. 132, Doc. 26; and Cx. 133, Doc. 36.

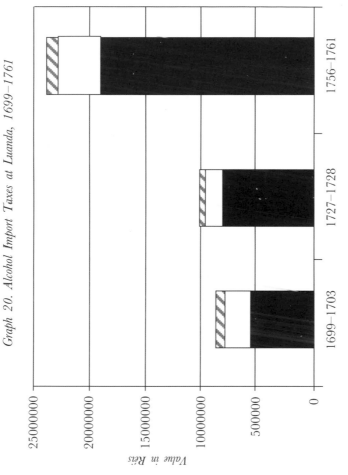

Graph 20. Alcohol Import Taxes at Luanda, 1699–1761

Source: José C. Curto, *Álcool e Escravos: O comércio luso-brasileiro do álcool em Mpinda, Luanda e Benguela durante o tráfico atlântico de escravos (c. 1480–1830) e o seu impacto nas sociedades da África Central Ocidental.* Lisbon, 2002, Table XXI.

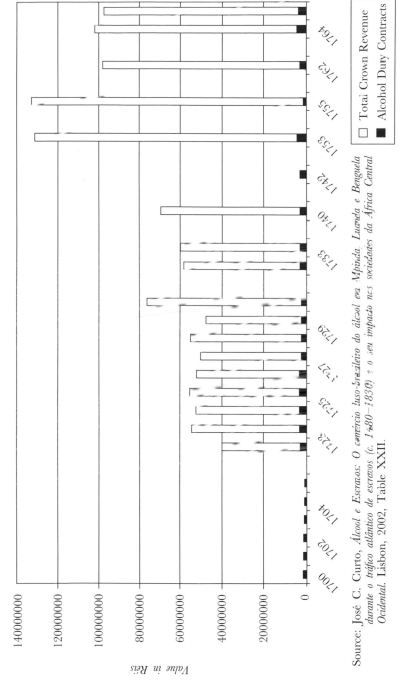

Graph 21. Alcohol Duty Contracts and Total Crown Revenues at Luanda, 1700–1765

Source: José C. Curto, Álcool e Escravos: O comércio luso-brasileiro do álcool em Mpinda, Luanda e Benguela durante o tráfico atlântico de escravos (c. 1480–1830) e o seu impacto nas sociedades da África Central Ocidental. Lisbon, 2002, Table XXII.

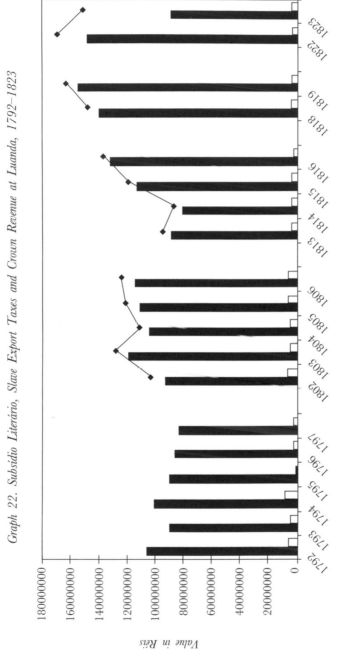

Graph 22. Subsídio Literário, Slave Export Taxes and Crown Revenue at Luanda, 1792–1823

Sources: AHU, Angola; "Conta do Rendimento do Subsídio dos Molhados e do Rendimento dos Direitos Reais e Subsídios dos Escravos Exportados," for 1792-1797 in Cx. 88, Doc. 34; "Receita da Alfândega de Luanda," for 1803 in Cx. 109, Doc. 37, 1804 in Cx. 112, Doc. 47, 1805 in Cx. 115, Doc. 28, 1806 in Cx. 118, Doc. 21, 1813 in Cx. 128, Doc. 26, 1814 in Cx. 130, Doc. 22, 1815 and 1816 in Cx. 133, Doc. 3, 1818 in Cx. 136, Doc. 1, and 1819 in Cx. 138, Doc. 39; and "Receita da Tesouraria de Luanda," for 1822 and 1823 in Cx. 141, Doc. 102.

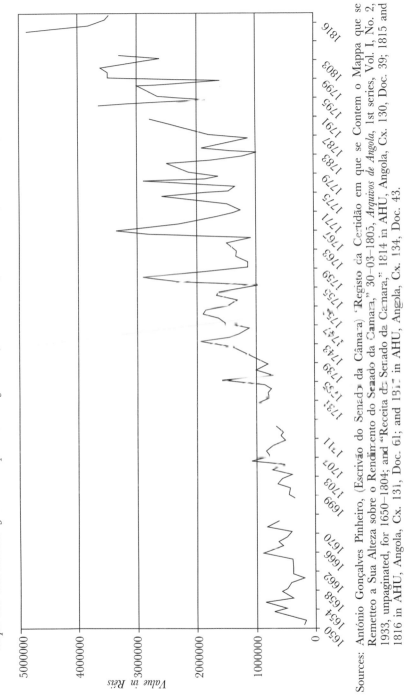

Graph 23. Tax Revenue of the Municipal Council of Luanda, 1650–1672, 1698–1713, 1730–1804, and 1814–1817

Sources: António Gonçalves Pinheiro, (Escrivão do Senado da Câmara) "Registo da Certidão em que se Contem o Mappa que se Remetteo a Sua Alteza sobre o Rendimento do Senado da Camara," 30-03-1805, *Arquivos de Angola*, 1st series, Vol. I, No. 2, 1933, unpaginated, for 1650–1804; and "Receita do Serado da Camara," 1814 in AHU, Angola, Cx. 130, Doc. 39; 1815 and 1816 in AHU, Angola, Cx. 131, Doc. 61; and 1817 in AHU, Angola, Cx. 134, Doc. 43.

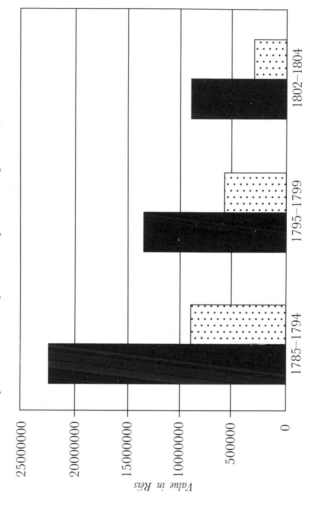

Graph 24. Total and Alcohol Import Tax Revenue of the Municipal Council of Luanda, 1785–1799 & 1802–1804

Sources: The total tax revenues are taken from António Gonçalves Pinto, (Escrivão do Senado da Câmara) "Registo da Certidão em que se Contem o Mappa que se Remetteo a Sua Alteza sobre o Rendimento do Senado da Camara," 30–03–1805, *Arquivos de Angola*, 1st series, Vol. I, No. 2, 1933, unpaginated. The alcohol import tax was estimated by multiplying the annual volumes of alcoholic beverages offloaded by $475 *réis*.

*Graph 25. Tavern Licence and Total Revenues of the Municipal Council of Luanda,
1814–1817 & 1833–1834*

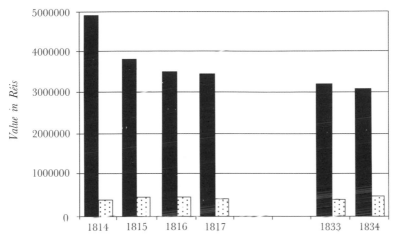

Sources: "Receita do Senado da Camara," 1814 in AHU, Angola, Cx. 130, Doc. 39; 1815 and 1816 in AHU, Angola, Cx. 131, Doc. 61; and 1817 in AHU, Angola, Cx. 134, Doc. 43.

■ Total Revenue
◻ Tavern Licences

Graph 26. Taverns and Total Population of Luanda, 1814–1817

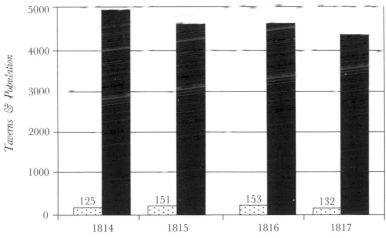

Sources: The number of taverns is based on the annual tavern licence revenue of the Municipal Council as presented in Graph 25, divided by 3$200 *réis*, the value of a tavern license in 1814. The population figures are taken from José C. Curto and Raymond R. Gervais, "The Population History of Luanda During the Late Atlantic Slave Trade, 1781–1844," *African Economic History*, Vol. 29, 2001, pp. 1–59.

◻ Taverns
■ Total Population

BIBLIOGRAPHY

I. *Unpublished Primary Sources*

1. Arquivo Histórico Ultramarino (AHU), Lisbon.
   a) *Caixas de Angola*: Cx. 1 (1602–1619) to Cx. 181 (n.d.).
   b) *Códices de Angola*: 400, 407–409, 472, 481, 542–556, 1252–1253, 1269, 1481, 1483, 1627–1636, and 1641–1642.
   c) *Maços de Angola*: *Sala* 12, # 858.
   d) *Correspondência dos Governadores de Angola*: Pastas 2 and 4–A.
2. Instituto Nacional de Estatística (INE), Lisbon.
   Balanças do Comercio do Reino de Portugal: 1796–1797, 1799–1807, 1809–1820, and 1822–1831.
3. Arquivo Histórico do Ministério das Obras Publicas (AHMOP), Lisbon.
   a) *Balanças do Comercio do Reino de Portugal*: 1776, 1777, 1783, 1789, 1798, 1808, and 1821.
   b) *Registo de Mappas: Demonstrações e Tabellas*, 1825–1827. SG3.
   c) "Mappas de Importação e Exportação MR 57 fornecidos pelos Consules de Portugal": 1840.
4. Biblioteca Nacional de Lisboa (BNL), Lisbon, *Secção dos Manuscritos.*
   Códice 8553, 8742, 8743, and 11490.
5. Biblioteca da Sociedade de Geografia de Lisboa (BSGL), Lisbon, *Reservados.*
   Anonymous, "Memorias sobre o estado actual d'Africa Occidental, seu Commercio com Portugal e medidas que convivia adoptar-se em 1841," Pasta D/no. 14.
6. Biblioteca Pública de Évora (BPE), Évora, *Secção dos Reservados.*
   "Memorial do Bispo D. Luiz Simões Brandão a El Rey," 02–11–1715, Cód. CXVI/2–15, No. 15–i, fls. 73–76.
7. Arquivo do Instituto Histórico e Geográfico Brasileiro (AIHGB), Rio de Janeiro, *Secção dos Manuscritos.*
   DL112,05.67 "Carta de Antônio Luís Gonçalves da Câmara Coutinho, governador e capitão geral do Brasil, a Mendo de Foios Pereira, secretário de Estado," 7–12–1693.
   DL794,28 "Balanço da Importação, & Exportação deste Reîno de Angola desde o Anno de 1785 em que Teve Prîncîpîo o Estabelecîmento da Alfandega, até o Anno de 1794, Incluzîve" (João Álvares de Melo), 20–11–1797.
   DL76,02.02 "Carta régia do príncipe regente d. João para d. Miguel Antônio de Melo, governador e capitão general do Reino de Angola," 10–11–1799.
   DL31,02.28 "Parecer do Conselho Ultramarino ao rei [d. Miguel I] sobre o envio das contas da Junta da Real Fazenda do Reino de Angola à Secretaria de Estado dos Negócios da Fazenda de Portugal," 21–01–1829.
8. Biblioteca Nacional do Rio de Janeiro (BNRJ), Rio de Janeiro, *Divisão de Manuscritos.*
   15–3–33, No. 1 "Balanço da Importação e Exportação deste Reîno de Angola em 1795, 1796, e 1797."
   I–29, 19, 30, Doc. 02 "Mappa de Exportação dos Produtos da Capitania da Bahia . . . em 1800."
9. Arquivo Nacional do Rio de Janeiro (ANRJ).
   Negócios de Portugal/59, Códice 543.

10. Library of Congress (LC), Washington.
    Portuguese Manuscript Collection: P-578, "Nota de exportação, e preços dos
    vinhos, que sahiram dos differentes portos do reino, para as nossas possessões
    do Ultramar, e para paises estrangeiros, nos annos abaixo mencionados (1796–
    1831)."
11. Lilly Library, Indiana University.
    "1646–1656 Portugal History MSS. Portuguese Commercial Letterbook."
12. Arquivo Histórico Nacional de Angola (AHNA), Luanda.
    Códice 84, 87, 88, 89, 240, and 439–A.
13. Arquivo Histórico da Biblioteca Municipal de Luanda (AHBML), Luanda.
    Códice 6, 7, and 12.
    Maço 3.

II. *Published Primary Sources*

Almeida, António de. "Relações com os Dembos: Cartas do Dembado de Kakulu-
    Kahenda," in 1º *Congresso da História da Expansão Portuguesa no Mundo: 4ª Secção—
    Africa*. Lisbon, 1938, Vol. 3, pp. 3–98 and 151–179.
"Angola no Fim do Século XVIII: Documentos," *Boletim da Sociedade de Geografia de
    Lisboa*. Vol. 6, 1886, pp. 274–304.
Anonymous, "Discurso Preliminar, Historico, Introductivo, com Natureza de Descripção
    Economica da Comarca e Cidade da Bahia" *Annaes da Bibliotheca Nacional do Rio
    de Janeiro*. Vol. 27, 1905, pp. 281–348.
Arquivos de Angola. 1st series, Nos. 1–54, 1933–1999, 2nd series, Nos. 1–107, 1943–1979.
Arquivos das Colónias. Vol. III, 1918.
Azeredo, José P. de. *Ensaios sobre Algumas Enfermidades d'Angola*. Luanda, 1967 (orig-
    inally published in Lisbon, 1799).
Bal, Willy. ed. *Le Royaume du Congo aux XVᵉ et XVIᵉ Siècles: Documents d'histoire*
    Léopoldville, 1963.
Barbot, Jean. "Voyage to the Congo River or the Zaire in the Year 1700," John
    Churchill, ed. *A Collection of Voyages and Travels*. London, 1732. Vol. V, pp. 497–522.
Birckhead, James and Co. *Pro Forma Sales and Invoices of Imports and Exports at Rio de
    Janeiro*. Rio de Janeiro, 1827.
Blake, John W. Trans. and ed. *European Beginnings in West Africa, 1450–1560*, London,
    1942. 2 Vols.
Boletim Official do Governo Geral de Angola. 1057–1787 and 1891.
Bontinck, François. ed. *Diaire Congolaise de Fra Luca da Caltanisetta (1690–1701)*.
    Louvain, 1970.
Bowdich, T. Edward. *An Account of the Discoveries of the Portuguese in the Interior of Angola
    and Mozambique*. London, 1824.
Brásio, António. ed. *Monumenta Missionaria Africana: Africa Occidental*. 1st Series. 15
    Vols. Lisbon, 1952–1988.
———. ed. *História do Reino do Congo*. Lisbon, 1969.
Cadornega, António de Oliveira de. *História Geral das Guerras Angolanas*. Lisbon, 1972.
    3 Vols. (Edited by José Matias Delgado and Manuel Alves da Cunha).
Caldas, Jozé Antonio. "Noticia Geral de toda esta Capitania da Bahia des o Seu
    Descobrimento até o Prezente Anno de 1759," *Revista do Instituto Geographico e
    Historico da Bahia*. Vol. 57, 1931, pp. 1–444.
Castello Branco e Torres, João C. Feo Cardoso de. *Memórias Contendo a Biographia
    do Vice Almirante Luis da Motta Feo e Torres, a História dos Governadores e Capitaes
    Generaes de Angola desde 1575 até 1825, e a Descripção Geográphica e Política dos Reinos
    de Angola e Benguella*. Paris, 1825.

228   BIBLIOGRAPHY

Cavazzi de Montecúccolo, Giovanni António. *Descrição Histórica dos Três Reinos do Congo, Matamba e Angola*. Lisbon, 1965. 2 Vols. (Translated and edited by Graziano Maria da Legguzzano).

Coimbra, Carlos D. *Ofícios para o Reino (1801–1819): Códices 7, 8, 9 e 10*. Lisbon, 1965.

Cordeiro, Luciano. ed. *Viagens, Explorações e Conquistas dos Portugueses: Collecção de Documentos*. Lisbon, 1881. 6 Vols.

Cuvelier, Jean. ed. *Relations sur le Congo du Père Laurent de Lucques, 1700–1717*. Brussels, 1953.

——. and Jadin, Louis. eds. *L'Ancien Congo d'après les Archives Romaines, 1518–1640*. Brussels, 1954.

Dapper, Olifert. *Description de l'Afrique contenant les noms, la situation & les confins de toutes les parties, leurs rivieres, leurs villes & leur habitations, leurs plantes & leurs animaux; les mouers, les coûtumes, la langue, les richesses, la religion & le gouvernement de ses peuples*. Amsterdam, 1686.

Delgado, Ralph. ed. *Ao Sul do Cuanza: Ocupação e Aproveitamento do Antigo Reino de Benguela, 1483–1942*. Lisbon, 1944. 2 Vols.

"Descoberta de Angola e Congo: Relações de Angola, Tiradas do Cartorio do Collegio dos Padres da Companhia," *Boletim da Sociedade de Geografia de Lisboa*. Vol. 4, 1883, pp. 300–386.

Dias, Gastão Sousa. ed. *Relações de Angola (Primordios da Ocupação Portuguesa) Pertencentes ao Cartorio do Colégio dos Padres da Companhia de Luanda, e Transcritas do Codice Existent na Biblioteca Nacional de Paris*. Coimbra, 1934.

——. ed. (Manoel Correia Leitão) "Uma Viagem a Cassange nos Meados do Século XVIII," *Boletim da Sociedade de Geografia de Lisboa*. Vol. 56, 1938, pp. 3–30.

Donnan, Elizabeth. ed., *Documents Illustrative of the History of the Slave Trade to America*. New York, 1965. 4 Vols.

Douville, Jean Baptiste. *Voyage au Congo et dans l'intérieur de l'Afrique équinoxale . . . 1828, 1829, 1830*. Paris, 1832. 3 Vols.

Ebel, Ernst. *O Rio de Janeiro e Seus Arredores em 1824*. São Paulo, 1972. (Translated by Joaquim de Sousa Leão Filho).

"Estatistica da Cidade de Loanda em 1845," *Annaes Maritimos e Coloniaes*. (Parte Official) No. 12, 1845, p. 234.

Felner, Alfredo de Albuquerque. *Angola: Apontamentos Sobre a Ocupação e Inicio do Estabelecimento dos Portugueses no Congo, Angola e Benguela (extraidos de documentos históricos)*. Coimbra, 1933.

——. ed. *Angola: Apontamentos Sobre a Colonização dos Planaltos e Litoral do Sul de Angola, Documentos*. Lisbon, 1940. 3 Vols.

Ferrez, Gilberto. "Diário Anônimo de uma Viagem às Costas d'Africa e às Indias Espagnholas: O Tráfico de Escravos (1702–1703)" *Revista do Instituto Histórico e Geográfico Brasileiro*. Vol. 267, 1967, pp. 3–42.

Gama, António de Saldanha da. *Memória sobre as Colónias de Portugal, situadas na Costa Occidental d'Africa*. Belem, 1839.

Gatti, P. Evaristo. ed. *Sulle Terre e Sui Mari*. Parma, 1935 (2nd edition).

Gaulme, François. "Un document sur le Ngoyo et ses voisins en 1784: l'Observation sur la navigation et le commerce de la côte d'Angole du comte de Capellis," *Revue française d'histoire d'outre-mer*. Vol. 64, 1977, pp. 350–375.

Godinho, Vitorino de Magalhães. ed. *Documentos sôbre a Expansão Portuguesa*. Lisbon, 1943–1956. 3 Vols.

Heintze, Beatrix. ed. *Fontes para a História de Angola do Século XVII: Memórias, Relações, e outros Manuscriptos da Colectânea Documental de Fernão de Sousa, 1622–1635*. Stuttgart, 1985. Vol. I.

——. ed. *Fontes para a História de Angola do Século XVII: Cartas e Documentos da Colectânea Documental de Fernão de Sousa, 1622–1635*. Stuttgart, 1988. Vol. II.

Imperial y Gomes, Claudio Miralles de. *Angola en Tiempos de Felipe II y de Felipe III*. Madrid, 1951.

Jadin, Louis. "Rivalités luso-néerlandaise au Soyo, Congo, 1600–1675," *Bulletin de l'Institut Historique Belge de Rome*. Vol. XXXVII, 1966, pp. 137–359.

——. "Pero Tavares, missionaire jésuite, ses travaux apostoliques au Congo et en Angola, 1629–1635," *Bulletin de l'Institut Historique Belge de Rome*. Vol. XXXIX, 1967, pp. 271–401.

——. "Relations sur le Congo et l'Angola tirées des archives de la Compagnie de Jésus, 1621–1631," *Bulletin de l'Institut Historique Belge de Rome*. Vol. XXXIX, 1968, pp. 333–453.

——. "Andrea da Pavia au Congo, à Lisbonne, à Madère: Journal d'un missionaire capucin, 1685–1702" *Bulletin de l'Institut Historique Belge de Rome*. Vol. XLI, 1970, pp. 375–592.

——. ed. *L'Ancien Congo et l'Angola, 1639–1655, d'après les Archives Romaines, Portugaises, Neerlandaises, et Espagnoles*. Rome, 1975. 3 Vols.

Jobson, Richard. *The Golden Trade: Or, a Discovery of the River Gambra, and the Golden Trade of the Aethiopians*. London, 1968 (originally published in 1623).

Jones, Adam. ed. *Brandenburg Sources for West African History 1680–1700*. Stuttgart, 1985.

——. ed. and trans. *West Africa in the Mid-Seventeenth Century: An Anonymous Dutch Manuscript*. Atlanta, 1995.

Jonghe, E. de, and Simar, Th. *Archives Congolaises*. Brussels, 1919.

Lacerda, Paulo Martins Pinheiro de. "Noticia da Cidade de S. Filippe de Benguella, e dos Costumes dos Gentios Habitantes daquelle Sertão, 1797," *Annaes Maritimos e Coloniaes* (Parte Não Official). 1845, No. 11, pp. 486–491.

Lisanti, Luis. ed. *Negócios Colôniais: Uma Correspondencia Commercial do Século XVIII São Paulo*, 1973. 5 Vols.

Manso, Visconde Paiva. ed. *História do Congo (Documentos) 1492–1772*. Lisbon, 1877.

Monod, Th., da Mota, A. Teixeira, and Mauny, Raymond. *Description de la Côte Occidentale d'Afrique (Sénégal au Cap de Monte, Archipels), par Valentim Fernandes, 1505–1510*. Bissau, 1951.

"Mappa dos Efeitos que se Transportarão d'esta Cidade do Rio Janeiro para os Portos abaixo Declarados no anno de 1796," *Revista do Instituto Histórico e Geográfico Brasileiro*. Vol. 46, 1883, Part I, pp. 107–204.

"Mappa geral das cidades, villas e freguezias que formão o corpo interior da capitânia do Rio de Janeiro [em 1780], com declaração do numero de seus templos, fogos, etc.," *Revista do Instituto Histórico e Geográfico Brasileiro*. Vol. 47, 1884, pp. 27–29.

"Memórias públicas e econômicas da cidade de São Sebastão do Rio de Janeiro para uso do vice-rei Luis de Vasconcellos por observação curiosa dos anos de 1779 até o de 1789," *Revista do Instituto Histórico e Geográfico Brasileiro*. Vol. 48, Part 1, 1884, pp. 25–51.

Nunes, Antonio Duarte, "Almanaque Histórico da Cidade de S. Sebastião do Rio de Janeiro para o Anno de 1799," *Revista do Instituto Histórico e Geográfico Brasileiro*. Vol. 267, 1965, pp. 93–214.

Oliveira Mendes, Luis António de. *Memória a Respeito dos Escravos e Trafico da Escravatura entre a Costa d'Africa e o Brazil*. Porto, 1977. (Edited and with preface by José Capela).

Owen, W. F. W. *Narrative of Voyages to Explore the Shores of Africa, Arabia, and Madagascar*. London, 1833. 2 Vols.

Pereira, Duarte Pacheco. *Esmeraldo de Situ Orbis*. London, 1937. (Translated and edited by G. H. T. Kimble).

Piacenza, Dionigi de Carli da, and Reggio, Michel Angelo da, "A Voyage to Congo in the Years 1666 and 1667," in Churchill, *Collection of Voyages and Travels*, Vol. I, pp. 485–519.

Pigafetta, Filippo and Lopes, Duarte. *Description du Royaume de Congo et des Contrées Environantes (1591)*. Louvain, 1965, 2nd edition (translated and annotated by Willy Bal).

Pina, Luis de. ed. "Tractado [de Francisco Damião Cosme] das Queixas Endemicas e Mais Fataes Nesta Conquista (Loanda 14 Agosto 1770)" *Studia*. Nos. 20–22, 1967, pp. 119–268.

Pombo, Padre Ruela. *Anais de Angola (1630–1635), Epoca de Decadencia no Governo de D. Manuel Pereira Coutinho: Fontes Documentais e Narrativas com Indicações, Comentários e Notas*. Lisbon, 1944.

"População de Angola, 1778," *Arquivos das Colonias*. Vol. 3, 1918, p. 176.

"População de Angola, 1779," *ibid.*, p. 178.

Ramos-Coelho, José. ed. *Alguns Documentos do Archivo Nacional da Torre do Tombo acerca das Navegações e Conquistas Portuguesas*. Lisbon, 1892.

Rau, Virginia. *O "Livro de Razão" de António Coelho Guerreiro*. Lisbon, 1956.

——, and da Silva, Maria F. G. eds. *Os Manuscritos do Arquivo da Casa de Cadaval Respeitantes ao Brasil*. Coimbra, 1955. 2 Vols.

Ravenstein, E. G. ed. *The Strange Adventures of Andrew Battell of Leigh in Angola and the Adjoining Regions*. London, 1901.

"Resumo Total da População que existia no anno de 1799, comprehendidas as quatro Freguezias da Cidade do Rio de Janeiro . . ." *Revista do Instituto Histórico e Geográfico Brasileiro*. Vol. 21, 1858, p. 288.

Rome, Jean-François de. *La Fondation de la Mission des Capucins au Royaume de Congo (1648)*. Louvain, 1964. (Edited by François Bontinck).

Salmon, P. "Mémoires de la relation de voyage de M. de Massiac a l'Angola et a Buenos-Aires," *Bulletin des Sceances de l'Académie Royal des Sciences d'Outre-Mer*. Vol. 6, 1960, pp. 586–604.

Silva Correia, Elias Alexandre da. *História de Angola*. Lisbon, 1937. 2 Vols. (Introduction and notes by Dr. Manuel Murias).

Silva Marques, João M. da. ed. *Descobrimentos Portugueses: Documentos para a Sua História*. Lisbon, 1971. 3 Vols.

Sorrento, Girolamo Merolla da. "A Voyage to Congo and Several Other Countries Chiefly in Southern Africa," in Churchill, *Collection of Voyages and Travels*, Vol. I, pp. 525–616.

Spix, Johan B. von, and Martius, C. F. P. von. *Travels in Brazil, in the Years 1817–1820: Undertaken by Command of His Majesty the King of Prussia*. London, 1824. 2 Vols.

Tams, Gustav. *Visit to the Portuguese Possessions in South-Western Africa*. New York, 1969 (trans. by H. Evans Lloyd, originally published in 1845). 2 Vols.

Toso, Carlo. ed. *L'Anarchia Congolese nel sec. XVII. La relazione inedita di Marcellino d'Atri*. Genoa, 1984.

Vasconcelhos, Alexandre José Botelho de. "Descripção da Capitania de Benguella, suas Provincias, Povos, Rios . . . Anno de 1799," *Annaes Maritimos e Coloniaes* (Parte Não Official). No. 4, 1844, pp. 147–161.

Vieira, Alberto. ed. *História do Vinho da Madeira: Documentos e Textos*. Funchal, 1993.

——. ed. *O Público e o Privado na História da Madeira: Vol. I, Correspondência Particular do Mercador Diogo Fernandes Branco*. Funchal, 1996.

——. ed. *O Público e o Privado na História da Madeira: Vol. II, Correspondência de João de Saldanha Albuquerque 1673–1694*. Funchal, 1998.

Walsh, Robert. *Notices of Brazil in 1828 and 1829*. London, 1830. 2 Vols.

Zurara, Gomes Eanes da. *Crónica da Guiné*. Barcelos, 1973.

III. *Published Secondary Sources*

Acuda, S. W. "International Review Series: Alcohol and Alcohol Problems, Research. 1. East Africa," *British Journal of Addiction*. Vol. 80, 1985, pp. 121–126.

Adams, W. I. *Nubia: Corridor to Africa*. London, 1984.

Adandé, A. "Le Vin de Palme chez les Diola de la Casamance," *Notes Africaines.* No. 61, 1954, pp. 4–6.

Adriaens, E. L. "Contribution à l'étude des vins de palme au Kwango," *Bulletin des Sceances de l'Institut Royale Colonial Belge.* Vol. 22, 1951, pp. 334–350.

Africae Monumenta. Vol. I—A Apropriação da Escrita pelos Africanos (edited by Ana P. Tavares and Catarina M. Santos) Lisbon, 2002.

Alden, Dauril. "Late Colonial Brazil, 1750–1808," in Leslie Bethell, ed. *Colonial Brazil.* Cambridge, 1987, pp. 284–343.

———. and Miller, Joseph C. "Unwanted Cargoes: The Origins and Dissemination of Smallpox via the Slave Trade from Africa to Brazil, c. 1560–1830," in Kenneth F. Kiple, ed. *The African Exchange: Toward a Biological History of Black People.* Durham, 1988, pp. 35–109.

Akinjogbin, I. A. *Dahomey and its Neighbours 1708–1818.* London, 1967.

Akyeampong, Emmanuel K. *Drink, Power, and Cultural Change: A Social History of Alcohol in Ghana, c. 1800 to Recent Times.* Portsmouth, NH, 1996.

———. "What's in a Drink? Class Struggle, Popular Culture and the Politics of *Akpeteshie* (Local Gin) in Ghana, 1930–1967," *Journal of African History.* Vol. 37, 1996, pp. 215–236.

———, and Pashington Obeng, "Spirituality, Gender and Power in Asante History," *International Journal of African Historical Studies.* Vol. 28, 1995, pp. 481–508.

Alencastro, Luiz-Felipe de. *O Trato dos Viventes: Formação do Brasil no Atlântico Sul.* São Paulo, 2000.

———. "La Traite Négrière et les Avatars de la Colonisation Portugaise au Brésil et en Angola (1550–1825)," *Cahiers du Centre de Recherches Ibériques et Ibéro-américaines de L'Université de Rouen.* Vol. 1, 1981, pp. 9–76.

Alexandre, Valentim. "Um Momento Crucial do Desenvolvimento Português: Efeitos Económicos da Perda do Império Brasileiro," *Ler História.* Vol. 7, 1986, pp. 3–45.

Alpern, Stanley B. "What Africans Got for Their Slaves: A Master List of European Trade Goods," *History in Africa.* Vol. 22, 1995, pp. 5–43.

Alves, Marieta. "O Comércio Marítimo e Alguns Armoradores do Século XVIII na Bahia," *Revista de História* (São Paulo). Vol. 31, 1965, pp. pp. 133–142.

Amaral, Ilídio do. *O Reino do Congo. Os Mbundu (ou Ambundos), o Reino dos 'Ngola' (ou de Angola) e a Presença Portuguesa, de Finais do Século XV a Meados do Século XVI.* Lisboa, 1996.

Amaral, Ilídio do. "Descrição da Luanda Oitocentista através de uma Planta de 1755," *Garcia de Orta.* Vol. 9, 1961, pp. 409–420.

———, and Ana Amaral, "A Viagem dos pombeiros angolanos Pedro Baptista e Amaro José entre Mucari (Angola) e Tete (Moçambique), em princípios do século XIX, ou a história da primeira travessia da África central," *Garcia de Orta, Série Geográfica.* Vol. 9, 1984, pp. 17–58.

Amaral Lapa, José R. da. *A Bahia e a Carreira da Índia.* São Paulo, 1968.

Ambler, Charles H. *Alcohol and Disorder in Precolonial Africa.* African Studies Center, Boston University, Working Papers # 126, 1987.

———. "Alcohol, Racial Segragation and Popular Politics in Northern Rhodesia," *Journal of African History.* Vol. 31, 1990, pp. 295–313.

———. "Drunks, Brewers and Chiefs: Alcohol Regulation in Colonial Kenya, 1900–1939," in Susanna Barrows and Robin Room, eds. *Drinking: Behavior and Belief in Modern History.* Berkeley, 1991, pp. 165–183.

———, and Jonathan Crush, eds. *Liquor and Labor in Southern Africa.* Athens, 1992.

Anderson, B. L. and Richardson, David. "Market Structure and Profits of the British African Trade in the Late Eighteenth Century: A Comment," *Journal of Economic History.* Vol. 43, 1983, pp. 713–721.

Andrade Arruda, José Jobson de. *O Brasil no Comércio Colonial.* São Paulo, 1980.

Anstey, Roger. "The Volume and Profitability of the British Slave Trade," in Stanley L. Engerman and Edward D. Genovese, eds. *Race and Slavery in the Western Hemisphere: Quantitative Studies*. Princeton, 1975, pp. 3–36.

Anumonye, A., Omoniwa, N., and Adaranijo, H. "Excessive Alcohol Use and Related Problems in Nigeria," *Drug and Alcohol Dependence*. Vol. 2, 1977, pp. 23–30.

Arner, Robert D. "Politics and Temperance in Boston and Philadelphia: Benjamin Franlin's Journalistic Writings on Drinking and Drunkenness," in J. A. Leo Lemay, ed. *Reappraising Benjamin Franklin: A Bicentennial Perspective*. Newark, Del., 1993, pp. 52–77.

Assadourian, Carlos S. *El Tráfico de Esclavos en Córdoba de Angola a Potosí siglos XVI–XVII*. Córdoba, 1966.

Ayandele, Emmanuel A. *The Missionary Impact on Modern Nigeria, 1872–1914*. London, 1966.

Azevedo, Thales de. *Povoamento da Cidade do Salvador*. São Paulo, 1955.

Balandier, Georges. *La vie quotidienne au Royaume de Kongo du XVIᵉ au XVIIIᵉ Siècle*. Paris, 1965.

Ballong-wen-Mewuda, J. Bato'ora. *São Jorge da Mina, 1482–1637: La vie d'un comptoir portugais en Afrique occidentale*. Lisbon, 1993. 2 Vols.

Beidelman, Thomas. "Beer Drinking and Cattle Theft in Ukaguru: Intertribal Relations in a Tanganyika Chiefdom," *American Anthropologist*. Vol. 63, 1961, pp. 534–549.

Bender, Gerald J. *Angola Under the Portuguese: Myth and Reality*. Berkeley, 1978.

Bennet, Judith M. *Ale, Beer, and Brewsters in England: Women's Work in a Changing World, 1300–1600*. New York, 1996.

Bennett, Norman R. "The Golden Age of the Port Wine System, 1781–1807," *International History Review*. Vol. 12, 1990, pp. 221–248.

——. "The Vignerons of the Douro and the Peninsular War," *Journal of European Economic History*. Vol. 21, 1992, pp. 7–29.

——. "The Wine Growers of the Upper Douro, 1780–1800," *Portuguese Studies Review*. Vol. 2, 1992–1993, pp. 28–45.

——. "The Port Wine System in the 1890s," *International History Review*. Vol. 16, 1994, pp. 251–266.

——. "Port Wine Merchants: Sandeman in Porto, 1813–1831," *Journal of European Economic History*. Vol. 24, 1995, pp. 239–269.

Bergeret, B. "Note préliminaire à l'étude du vin de palme au Cameroun," *Médecine Tropicale*. Vol. 6, 1957, pp. 901–904.

Bernard, Joel. "The Transit of 'Small, Merry' Anglo-American Culture: Sir John Barley-Corne and Sir Richard Dum (Captain Whiskey)," *Proceedings of the American Antiquarian Society*. Vol. 100, 1990, pp. 81–136

Bernier, G., and A. Lambrechts, "Étude sur les Boissons Fermentées Indigènes du Katanga," *Problèmes Sociaux Congolais*. No. 48, 1960, pp. 6–41.

Bethell, Leslie. *The Abolition of the Brazilian Slave Trade: Britain, Brazil and the Slave Trade Question, 1807–1869*. Cambridge, 1970.

Birmingham, David. "The Date and Significance of the Imbangala Invasion of Angola," *Journal of African History*. Vol. VI, 1965, pp. 143–152.

——. *The Portuguese Conquest of Angola*. London, 1965.

——. *Trade and Conflict in Angola: The Mbundu and their Neighbours Under the Influence of the Portuguese, 1483–1790*. Oxford, 1966.

——. "The African Response to Early Portuguese Activities in Angola," R. H. Chilcote, ed. *Protest and Resistance in Angola and Brazil*. Berkeley, 1972, pp. 11–28.

——. *Central Africa to 1870: Zambezia, Zaire, and the South Atlantic*. Cambridge, 1981.

——. "Carnival at Luanda," *Journal of African History*. Vol. 29, 1988, pp. 93–103.

——. *A Concise History of Portugal*. Cambridge, 1993.

Bontinck, François. "Un mausolée pour les Jaga," *Cahiers d'Études Africaines*. Vol. 20, 1979, pp. 387–389.

Bowers, John M. "'Dronkennesse is Ful of Stryvyng': Alcoholism and Ritual Violence in Chaucer's *Pardoner's Tale*," *English Literary History*. Vol. 57, 1990, pp. 757–784.

Boxer, Charles R. *Salvador de Sá and the Struggle for Brazil and Angola, 1602–1686*. London, 1952.

——. ed., *The Tragic History of the Sea: 1589–1622: Narratives of the Shipwrecks of the Portuguese East Indiamen* São Thome *(1589)*, Santo Alberto *(1593)*, São João Baptista *(1622)*, *and the Journeys of the Survivors in South East Africa*. Cambridge, 1959.

——. *The Golden Age of Brazil, 1695–1750*. Berkeley, 1962.

——. *Portuguese Society in the Tropics: The Municipal Councils of Goa, Macao, Bahia and Luanda, 1580–1800*. Madison, 1965.

——. *The Portuguese Seaborne Empire, 1415–1825*. London, 1969.

——. "The Commercial Letter-Book and Testament of a Luso-Brazilian Merchant, 1646–1656" *Boletim de Estudios LatinoAmericana e del Caribe*. Vol. 18, 1975, pp. 49–56.

——. *From Lisbon to Goa, 1500–1750: Studies in Portuguese Maritime Enterprise*. London, 1984.

Bradford, Helen. "'We Are Now Men': Beer Protests in the Natal Countryside, 1929" in Belinda Bozzoli, ed. *Class, Community and Conflict: South African Perspectives*. Johannesburg, 1987, pp. 292–323.

——. "'We Women Will Show Them': Beer Protests in the Natal Countryside, 1929," in Ambler and Crush, *Liquor and Labor in Southern Africa*, pp. 208–234.

Brásio, António. "Descripção dos Governos dos Ill.mos e Ex.mos Snr.es António de Vasconcellos, e D. Francisco Innocencio de Souza Coutinho," *Studia*. Nos. 41–42, 1979, pp. 205–225.

Braudel, Fernand. *Capitalism and Material Life, 1400–1800*. London, 1974. (Translated by Miriam Kochan).

——. *The Structures of Everyday Life: The Limits of the Possible. Civilization & Capitalism 15th–18th Century, Vol. 1*. (Translated and revised by Siân Reynolds) New York, 1982.

Brennan, Thomas. *Public Drinking and Popular Culture in Eighteenth Century Paris*. Princeton, 1988.

Broadhead, Susan H. "Slave Wives, Free Sisters: Bakongo Women and Slavery, c. 1700–1850" in Claire C. Robertson and Martin A. Klein, eds. *Women and Slavery in Africa*. Madison, 1983, pp. 160–181.

Brooks, George E. "Kola Trade and State Building: Upper Guinea Coast and Senegambia, 15th–17th Centuries," *Working Paper no. 38*, African Studies Center, Boston University, 1980.

Bryceson, Deborah Fahy ed. *Alcohol in Africa: Mixing Business, Pleasure, and Politics*. Portsmouth, NH, 2002.

Bureau International pour la défense des indigènes. "l'Alcoolisme en Afrique et la Convention de St. Germain-en-Laye," *International Zeitschrift Alkoholismus*. Vol. 38, 1930, pp. 208–216.

Burns, E. Bradford. *A History of Brazil*. New York, 1980.

Campos, Fernando. "A data da morte da Rainha Jinga D. Verónica I," *África* (Universidade de São Paulo). No. 4, 1981, pp. 79–103, no. 5, 1982, pp. 72–104, and no. 6, 1983, pp. 89–128.

Capela, José. *O Vinho para o Preto: Notas e Textos Sobre a Exportação do Vinho para a África*. Lisbon, 1973.

——. *Escravatura: Conceitos, A Empresa de Saque*. Porto, 1974.

Carlsson, Jerker. "Brazilian Trade with West Africa and Angola within the Portuguese Colonial Empire, 1500–1850: The Dialectics of South-South Exchange," in Jerker Carlsson and Timothy M. Shaw, eds. *Newly Industrialized Countries and the Political Economy of South-South Relations*. London, 1988, pp. 151–183.

Carpenter, Edmund S. "Alcohol in the Iriquois Dream Quest," *American Journal of Psychiatry*. Vol. 116, 1959, pp. 148–151.

Carreira, António. *As Companhias Pombalinas de Grão-Pará e Maranhão e Pernambuco e Paraíba*. Lisbon, 1983 (2nd edition).

Carvalho, Ruy Duarte de. *Ana a Manda: Os Filhos da Rede*. Lisbon, 1989.

Cascudo, Luis da Camâra. *Prelúdio da Cachaça: etnografia, história e sociologia da aguardente no Brasil*. Rio de Janeiro, 1968.

Chaunu, Pierre and Huguette. *Seville et l'Atlantique, 1504–1650*. Paris, 1955–1960. 8 Vols.

Childs, Gladwyn M. *Umbundu Kinship & Character*. London, 1949.

Christian, David. *'Living Water': Vodka and Russian Society on the Eve of Emancipation*. Oxford, 1990.

Clark, Peter. *The Alehouse: A Social History, 1200–1830*. London, 1983.

——. "The 'Mother Gin' Controversy in the Early Eighteenth Century," *Transactions of the Royal Historical Society*. 5th Series, Vol. 38, 1988, pp. 63–84.

Clarence-Smith, Gervase. *Slaves, Peasants, and Capitalists in Southern Angola (1840–1926)*. Cambridge, 1979.

——. "The Sugar and Rum Industries in the Portuguese Empire, 1850–1914," in B. Albert and A. Graves, eds., *Crisis and Change in the International Sugar Economy, 1860–1914*. Edinburgh, 1984, pp. 227–349.

——. *The Third Portuguese Empire, 1825–1975: A Study in Economic Imperialism*. Manchester, 1985.

Cleaver, B. "The Drink Traffic on the Gold Coast," *Sierra Leone Messenger*. No. 87, 1914, pp. 275–279.

Cobley, Alan G. "Liquor and Leadership: Temperance, Drunkenness and the African Petty Bourgeoisie in South Africa," *South African Historical Journal*. Vol. 31, 1994, pp. 128–148.

Coelho, Virgílio. "Em Busca de Kábàsà: Uma Tentativa de Explicação da Estrutura Político-Administrativa do Reino de Ndongo, in *Actas do Seminário Encontro de Povos e Culturas em Angola: Luanda, 3 a 6 de Abril de 1995*. Lisbon, 1997, pp. 443–477.

Coffey, T. G. "Beer Street, Gin Lane: Some Views of Eighteenth-Century Drinking," *Quaterly Journal of Studies on Alcohol*. Vol. 27, 1966, pp. 669–692.

Colson, Elizabeth and Thayer Scudder, *For Prayer and Profit: The Ritual, Economic and Social Importance of Beer in the Gwembe District, Zambia, 1950–1982*. Stanford, 1988.

Conrad, Robert E. *World of Sorrow: The African Slave Trade to Brazil*. Baton Rouge, 1986.

Conroy, David W. "Puritans in Taverns: Law and Popular Culture in Colonial Massachusets, 1630–1720," in Susanna Barrows and Robin Room, eds. *Drinking: Behavior and Belief in Modern Times*. Berkeley, 1991, pp. 29–60.

Costa e Silva, Alberto da. *A Manilha e o Libambo: A África e a Escravidão de 1500 a 1700*. Rio de Janeiro, 2002.

Coughtry, Jay. *The Notorious Triangle: Rhode Island and the African Slave Trade 1700–1807*. Philadelphia, 1981.

Couto, Carlos A. M. de. *Os Capitães-Mores em Angola no Século XVIII: Subsídio para o Estudo da Sua Actuação*. Luanda, 1972.

Crothers, T. D. "Inebriety in Ancient Egypt and Chaldea," *Quarterly Journal of Inebriety*. Vol. 25, 1903, pp. 142–150.

Curtin, Philip D. *Economic Change in Precolonial Africa: Senegambia in the Era of the Slave Trade*. Madison, 1975.

Curto, António D. Ramada, Kopke, Ayres, and Visconde de Giraul, *l'Alcoolisme dans les colonies portugaises*. Lisbon, 1910.

Curto, José C. *Álcool e Escravos: O comércio luso-brasileiro do álcool em Mpinda, Luanda e Benguela durante o tráfico atlântico de escravos (c. 1480–1830) e o seu impacto nas sociedades da África Central Ocidental*. Lisbon, 2002.

——. "Luso-Brazilian Alcohol and the Legal Slave Trade at Benguela and its Hinterland, c. 1617–1830," in Hubert Bonin and Michel Cahen, eds. *Négoce Blanc en Afrique Noire: L'évolution du commerce à longue distance en Afrique noire du 18ᵉ au 20ᵉ siècles.* Paris, 2001, pp. 351–369.

———. "The Anatomy of a Demographic Explosion: Luanda, 1844–1850," *International Journal of African Historical Studies.* Vol. 32, 1999, 381–405.

———. "Vinho verso Cachaça: A Luta Luso-Brasileira pelo Comércio do Álcoól e de Escravos em Luanda, 1648–1703," in Selma Pantoja and José F. S. Saraiva, eds. *Angola e Brasil nas Rotas do Atlântico Sul.* Rio de Janeiro, 1999, pp. 69–97.

———. "Sources for the Pre-1900 Population History of Sub-Saharan Africa: The Case of Angola, 1773–1845," *Annales de démographie historique.* 1994, pp. 319–338.

———. "A Quantitative Re-assessment of the Legal Portuguese Slave Trade from Luanda, Angola, 1710–1830," *African Economic History.* Vol. 20, 1992, pp. 1–25.

———. "Alcohol in Africa: A Preliminary Bibliography of the Post-1875 Literature," *A Current Bibliography on African Affairs.* Vol. 21, 1989, pp. 3–31.

———. "The Angolan Manuscript Collection of the Arquivo Historico Ultramarino, Lisbon: Toward a Working Guide," *History in Africa.* Vol. 15, 1988, pp. 163–189.

———. and Gervais, Raymond R. "The Population History of Luanda During the Late Atlantic Slave Trade, 1781–1844," *African Economic History.* Vol. 29, 2001, pp. 1–59.

Cuvelier, Jean. *L'Ancien Royaume de Congo.* Brussels, 1946.

Daaku, Kwame Y. *Trade and Politics on the Gold Coast, 1600–1720: A Study of the African Reaction to European Trade.* Oxford, 1970.

Dailey, R. C. "The Role of Alcohol among North American Indian Tribes as Reported in the *Jesuit Relations*," *Anthropologica.* Vol. 10, 1968, pp. 45–59.

Darity Jr., William. "The Numbers Game and the Profitability of the British Trade in Slaves," *Journal of Economic History.* Vol. 45, 1985, pp. 603–709.

— —. "The Profitability of the British Trade in Slaves Once Again," *Explorations in Economic History.* Vol. 26, 1989, pp. 380–384.

Darragh, J. T. "The Liquor Problem in the Transvaal," *Contemporary Review.* July, 1901, pp. 124–135.

d'Assumpção, Lino. "Exploração á Africa nos Ineditos da Bibliotheca de Evora," *Boletim da Sociedade de Geografia de Lisboa.* Vol. 6, 1885, pp. 350–370.

Davidson, Basil. *The African Slave Trade: Precolonial History, 1450–1850.* Boston, 1961.

Davison, Lee. "Experiments in the Social Regulation of Industry: Gin Legislation, 1729–1751," in Lee Davidson, et al., *Stilling the Grumbling Hive: Responses to Social and Economic Problems in England, c. 1869–1750.* London, 1992, pp. 25–48.

Davies, K. G. *The Royal African Company.* New York, 1970.

Delgado, Ralph. *História de Angola.* Benguela, 1948–1955. 4 Vols.

———. "O Governo de Sousa Coutinho em Angola," *Studia.* No. 6, 1960, pp. 19–56; No. 7, 1961, pp. 49–87; and No. 10, 1962, pp. 7–47.

Dias, Gastão Sousa. "S. Tomé e Angola," *A Restauração e o Império Colonial Português.* Lisbon, 1940, pp. 257–321.

Dias, Manuel Nunes. *Fomento e Mercantalismo: A Companhia Geral do Grão Pará e Maranhão (1755–1778).* São Paulo, 1971. 2 Vols.

Diduk, Susan. "European Alcohol, History, and the State in Cameroon," *African Studies Review.* Vol. 36, 1993, pp. 1–42.

Dike, K. Onwuka. *Trade and Politics in the Niger Delta, 1830–1885: An Introduction to the Economic and Political History of Nigeria.* London, 1956.

Dumett Raymond E. *Merchants versus moralists: the impact of the liquor trade in the Gold Coast and Asante in the late nineteenth century.* Waltham, Mass., 1970.

———. "The Social Impact of the European Liquor Trade on the Akan of Ghana (Gold Coast and Asante), 1875–1910," *Journal of Interdisciplinary History.* Vol. 1, 1974, pp. 69–101.

Duncan, T. Bently. *Atlantic Islands: Madeira, the Azores and the Cape Verdes in Seventeenth-Century Commerce and Nagivation.* Chicago, 1972.

Edwards, A. C. *The Ovimbundu under Two Sovereignties: A Study of Social Control and Social Change among a People of Angola.* London, 1962.

Edwards, D. N. "Sorghum, Beer, and Cushite Society," *Norwegian Archaeological Review.* Vol. 29, 1996, pp. 65–77.

Eguchi, P. K. "Beer Drinking and Festivals amongst the Hide," *Kyoto University African Studies.* Vol. 9, 1975, pp. 69–90.

Eltis, David and Lawrence C. Jennings, "Trade between Western Africa and the Atlantic World in the Precolonial Era," *American Historical Review.* Vol. 93, 1988, pp. 936–959.

David Eltis and David Richardson, "West Africa and the Transatlantic Slave Trade: New Evidence and Long-Run Trends," *Slavery and Abolition.* Vol. 18, 1997, pp. 16–35.

Esteves, Maria L. "Os Holandeses em Angola: Decadência do comércio externo e soluções locais adoptadas," *Studia.* No. 52, 1994, pp. 49–82.

Ferraz, Maria de Lurdes de F. "O vinho da Madeira no século XVIII: produção e mercados internacionais," in *Actas do I Colóquio Internacional de História da Madeira 1986.* Funchal, 1990, Vol. 2, pp. 935–965.

Ferreira, H. H. "The Campaign Against Alcoholism on the Copperbelt," *Central African Journal of Medicine.* Vol. 3, 1957, pp. 71–73.

Ferreira, J. A. Pinto. "A Economia do Vinho e o Crescimento do Porto, nos Séculos XVII ao XIX," in Joaquim V. Serrão, ed. *O Vinho na História Portuguesa, Séculos XIII–XIX.* Porto, 1983, pp. 241–317.

Finlay, J., and Jones, R. K. "Alcohol Consumption and the Nature of Alcohol Related Problems in Botswana: A Preliminary Report," *Pula.* Vol. 3, 1983, pp. 1–13.

Florentino, Manolo G. *Em Costas Negras: Uma História do Tráfico Atlântico de Escravos entre a Africa e o Rio de Janeiro (Séculos XVIII e XIX).* São Paulo, 2002, 2nd edition.

Fragoso, João L. R. *Homens de Grossa Aventura: acumulação e hierarquia na praça mercantil do Rio de Janeiro (1790 1830).* Rio de Janeiro, 1992.

Fragoso, João L. R., and Florentino, Manolo G. *O Arcaísmo como Projeto: Mercado Atlântico, Sociedade Agrária e Elite Mercantil no Rio de Janeiro, c. 1790–c. 1840.* Rio de Janeiro, 1993.

Gelfand, M. "Alcoholism in Contemporary African Society," *Central African Journal of Medicine.* Vol. 12, 1966, pp. 12–13.

Gessesse, Kebede, and Louis Molamu. *Alcohol and Alcoholism in Africa: A Bibliography.* National Institute of Development Research and Documentation, University of Botswana, 1988, Working Bibliography no. 15.

Gildrie, Richard P. "Taverns and Popular Culture in Essex County Massachusetts, 1678–1686," *Essex Institute Historical Collections.* Vol. 124, 1988, pp. 158–185.

Gillis, L. S., Lewis, J. B., and Slabbert, M. "Alcoholism amongst the Cape Coloureds," *South African Medical Journal.* Vol. 47, 1973, pp. 1374–1382.

Gilmore, Thomas B. "James Boswell's Drinking," *Eighteenth-Century Studies.* Vol. 24, 1991, pp. 337–357.

Glasgow, Roy A. *Nzinga: Resistencia africana à investida do colonialismo português em Angola, 1582–1663.* São Paulo, 1982.

Godinho, Vitorino de Magalhães. *Prix et Monnaies au Portugal, 1750–1850.* Paris, 1955.

——. "Portugal and Her Empire, 1660–1720," *New Cambridge Modern History.* Vol. VI, 1970, pp. 509–539.

——. *Os Descobrimentos e a Economia Mundial.* Lisbon, 1982. 4 Vols.

Goodman, Jordan., Lovejoy, Paul E., and Sherrat, Andrew. *Consuming Habits: Drugs in History and Anthropology.* New York, 1995.

Gordon, David. "From Rituals of Rapture to Dependence: The Political Economy of Khoikhoi Narcotic Consumption, c. 1487–1870," *South African Historical Journal.* Vol. 35, 1996, pp. 62–88.

Gravière, Emmanuel La. "The Problem of Alcohol in the Colonies and Territories South of the Sahara," *International Review of Missions.* Vol. 46, 1957, pp. 290–298.

Greenlee, William Brooks. *The Voyage of Pedro Alvares Cabral to Brasil and India from Contemporary Documents and Narratives.* London, 1938.

Haggblade, Steven J. "The Shebeen Queen and the Evolution of Botswana's Sorghum Beer Industry," in Ambler and Crush, *Liquor and Labor in Southern Africa,* pp. 395–413.

Hambly, Wilfrid D. *The Ovimbundu of Angola.* Chicago, 1934.

Hanson, Carl A. *Economy and Society in Baroque Portugal, 1668–1703.* Minneapolis: University of Minnesota Press, 1981.

Harms, Robert W. *River of Wealth, River of Sorrow: The Central Zaire Basin in the Era of the Slave and Ivory Trade, 1500–1891.* New Haven, 1981.

Harrison, Harrison. *Drink and the Victorians: The Temperance Question in England, 1815–1872.* London, 1971.

Hauenstein, Alfred. "L'Ombala de Calumquembe," *Anthropos.* Vol. 58, 1963, pp. 47–120.

Heap, Simon. "'We Think Prohibition is a Farce': Drinking in the Alcohol-Prohibited Zone of Colonial Northern Nigeria," *International Journal of African Historical Studies.* Vol. 31, 1998, pp. 23–52.

——. "Before 'Star': The Import Substitution of Western Style Alcohol in Nigeria, 1870–1970," *African Economic History.* Vol. 24, 1996, pp. 69–89.

——. "Alcohol in Africa: A Supplementary List of Post-1875 Literature," *Current Bibliography on African Affairs.* Vol. 26, 1994–95, pp. 1–14.

Hedlund, M., and Lundahl, M. "The Economic Role of Beer in Rural Zambia," *Human Organization.* Vol. 43, 1984, pp. 61–65.

Heintze, Beatrix. "Angola nas Garras do Tráfico de Escravos: As Guerras Angolanas do Ndongo (1611–1630)," *Revista Internacional de Estudos Africanos.* Vol. 1, 1984, pp. 11–59.

——. "Traite de «Pièces» en Angola: Ce Qui N'est pas Dit dans Nos Sources" Serge Daget, ed. *De la Traite à l'Esclavage, du XVe au XVIIIe Siècle: Actes du Colloque International sur la Traite des Noirs.* Paris, 1988, Vol. I, pp. 147–172.

Hellman, Ellen "The Importance of Beer-Brewing in an Urban Native Yard," *Bantu Studies.* Vol. 8, 1934, pp. 39–60.

Henige, David. *Oral Historiography.* New York, 1982.

Henriques, Isabel C. *Percursos da Modernidade em Angola: Dinâmicas comerciais e transformações sociais no século XIX.* Lisbon, 1997.

Herlehy, Thomas J. "Ties that Bind: Palm Wine and Blood Brotherhoods at the Kenya Coast during the 19th Century," *International Journal of African Historical Studies.* Vol. 17, 1984, pp. 285–308.

Heusch, Luc de. *Le Roi Ivre ou l'origine de l'État.* Paris, 1972.

Hildebrand, P. *Le Martyr Georges de Geel et les Débuts de la Mission du Congo (1645–1652).* Anvers, 1940.

Hilton, Anne. "Reconsidering the Jaga," *Journal of African History.* Vol. 22, 1981, pp. 191–202.

——. *The Kingdom of Kongo.* Oxford, 1985.

Howay, F. W. "The Introduction of Intoxicating Liquors Amongst the Indians of the Northwest Cost," *British Columbia Historical Quarterly.* Vol. 6, 1942, pp. 157–169.

Hudson, Harris G. *A Study of Social Regulations in England under James I and Charles I: Drink and Tobacco.* Chicago, 1933.

Hyde, C. K., Parkinson, B. B., and Mariner, S. "The Nature and Profitability of the Liverpool Slave Trade," *Economic History Review.* Vol. 5, 1953, pp. 368–377.

Inikori, Joseph E. "Market Structure and the Profits of the British African Trade in the Late Eighteenth Century," *Journal of Economic History.* Vol. 41, 1981, pp. 745–776.

——. ed. *Forced Migration: The Impact of the Export Slave Trade on African Societies.* London, 1981.

——. "Market Structure and Profits of the British African Trade in the Late Eighteenth Century: A Rejoinder" *Journal of Economic History.* Vol. 43, 1983, pp. 723–728.

Isnard, Hildebert. *La Vigne en Algérie.* Gap, 1951–1954. 2 Vols.

Jadin, Louis. "Le Congo et la secte des Antoniens: Restauration du Royaume sous Pedro IV et la «sainte Antoine» congolaise (1694–1718)," *Bulletin de l'Institut Historique Belge de Rome.* Vol. XXXIII, 1961, pp. 411–615.

——. "Rivalité luso-néerlandaises au Sohio, Congo, 1600–1675," *Bulletin de l'Institut Historique Belge de Rome.* Vol. XXXVII, 1966, pp. 136–359.

Janzen, John M. *Lemba, 1650–1930: A Drum of Affliction in Africa and the New World.* New York, 1982.

Jhue-Beaulaton, Dominique. "La diffusion du maïs sur les Côtes de l'Or et des Esclaves aux XVIIᵉ et XVIIIᵉ siècles," *Revue française d'histoire d'outre-mer.* Vol. 77, 1990, pp. 177–198.

Johnson, Hugh. *The Story of Wine.* London, 1988.

Johnston, Harry H. "Alcoholism in Africa," *The Nineteenth Century.* September, 1911, pp. 476–494.

Junod, Henri A. "l'Alcoolisme Africain," *Bibliothèque Universelle et Revue de Genève.* July–December, 1930, pp. 384–397.

Kaké, Ibrahima B. *Anne Zingha: Reine d'Angola, première résistante à l'invasion portugaise.* Paris, 1975.

Karasch, Mary C. *Slave Life in Rio de Janeiro, 1808–1850.* Princeton, 1987.

Karp, Ivan. "Beer Drinking and Social Experience in an African Society: An Essay in Formal Sociology," in Ivan Karp and C. S. Bird, eds. *Explorations in African Systems of Thought.* Bloomington, 1980, pp. 83–119.

Kermorgant, A. "l'Alcoolisme dans les colonies françaises," *Bulletin de la Société de Pathologie Éxotique et de ses Filiales.* Vol. 2, 1909, pp. 330–340.

Kher, A. "Montée préoccupante de l'alcoolisme dans le Tiers Monde," *Afrique Santé.* August 8, 1982, pp. 1–7.

Klein, Herbert S. "The Portuguese Slave Trade from Angola in the 18th Century," *Journal of Economic History.* Vol. XXXII, 1972, pp. 849–918.

——. "O Tráfico de Escravos Africanos para o Porto do Rio de Janeiro, 1825–1830," *Anais de História.* No. 5, 1973, pp. 85–101.

——. *The Middle Passage: Comparative Studies in the Atlantic Slave Trade.* Princeton, 1978.

Krige, Jensen E. "The Social Significance of Beer among the Balobedu," *Bantu Studies.* Vol. 4, 1932, pp. 343–357

La Hausse, Paul. *Alcohol, the Ematsheni and Popular Struggle in Durban: The Origins of the Beer Hall in South Africa, 1902–08.* Cape Town (University of Cape Town, Centre for African Studies), 1983.

——. *The Struggle for the City: Alcohol, the Ematsheni and Popular Sulture in Durban, 1902–1936.* Durban, 1984.

——. *Brewers, Beerhalls and Boycotts: A History of Liquor in South Africa.* Johannesburg, 1988.

Lang, James. *Portuguese Brazil: The King's Plantation.* New York, 1979.

Langton, Marcia. "Rum, Seduction, and Death: 'Aboriginality' and Alcohol," *Oceania.* Vol. 63, 1993, pp. 195–206.

Lasko, L. H. *King Tut's Wine Celar.* Berkeley, 1977.

Law, Robin. *The Oyo Empire c. 1600–1836: A West African Imperialism in the Era of the Atlantic Slave Trade.* Oxford, 1977.

——. *The Slave Coast of West Africa, 1550–1750: The Impact of the Atlantic Slave Trade on an African Society.* Oxford, 1991.

Leipoldt, C. Louis. *300 Years of Cape Wine.* Cape Town, 1974.

Lender, Mark E., and Martin, James K. *Drinking in America: A History*. New York, 1982.

Levine, Harry G. "The Vocabulary of Drunkenness," *Journal of Studies on Alcohol*. Vol. 42, 1981, pp. 1038–1051.

———. "The Discovery of Addiction: Changing Conceptions of Habitual Drunkenness in America," *Journal of Studies on Alcohol*. Vol. 39, 1978, pp. 143–174.

Lima, Heitor F. *História político-econômica e industrial do Brasil*. São Paulo, 1970.

Lima, José J. Lopes de, *Ensaios sobre a statistica das possessões portuguesas: Vol. III— Angola e Benguela*. Lisbon, 1846.

Lima, Mesquitela. *Os Kyaka de Angola*. Lisbon, 1988. 3 Vols.

Lisboa, Balthazar da Silva. *Annes do Rio de Janeiro contendo a Descoberta e Conquista deste Paiz, a Fundação da Cidade com a Historia Civil e Ecclesiastica, até a Chegada d'El-Rei Dom João VI; Além de Noticias Topographicas, Zoologicas e Botanicas*. Rio de Janeiro, 1835. 7 Vols.

Lobo, Eulalia Maria Lahmeyer. "O Comércio Atlântico e a Comunidade de Mercadores no Rio de Janeiro e em Charleston no Século XVIII," *Revista de História*. No. 101, 1975, pp. 49–106.

———. *História do Rio de Janeiro (do Capital Comercial ao Capital Industrial e Financeiro)*. Rio de Janeiro, 1978. 2 Vols.

———. "Economia do Rio de Janeiro nos Séculos XVIII e XIX," in Paulo Neuhaus, ed. *Economia Brasileira: Uma Visão Histórica*. Rio de Janeiro, 1980, pp. 123–159.

Lovejoy, Paul E. *Caravans of Kola: The Hausa Kola Trade, 1700–1900*. Ibadan, 1980.

———. *Transformations in Slavery: A History of Slavery in Africa*. New York, 1983.

———. *Salt of the Desert Sun: A History of Salt Production and Trade in the Central Sudan*. Cambridge, 1986.

Lugard, Frederick W. "The Liquor Traffic in Africa," *The Nineteenth Century*. November, 1897, pp. 766–784.

Machado, Herlander Alves. *O Vinho na Economia Portuguesa: Alguns Aspectos*. Lisbon, 1967.

Mancall, Peter C. *Deadly Medicine: Indians and Alcohol in Early America*, Ithaca, NY, 1995.

Manchester, Alan K. *British Preeminence in Brazil, Its Rise and Decline; A Study in European Expansion*. New York, 1964.

Manning, Patrick. *Slavery and African Life*. Cambridge, 1990.

Margarido, Alfredo. "Les Porteurs: forme de domination et agents de changements en Angola (XVIIe–XIXe siècles," *Revue française d'histoire d'outre mer*. Vol. LXV, 1978, pp. 377–399.

Martin, A. Lynn. *Alcohol, Sex, and Gender in Late Medieval and Early Modern Europe*. New York, 2001.

Matos, Norton de. *Memórias e Trabalhos da Minha Vida*. Lisbon, 1944. 4 Vols.

Mauro, Frédéric. *Le Portugal, le Brésil, et l'Atlantique au XVII Siècle*. Paris, 1983.

———. *L'Expansion Européene (1600–1870)*. Paris, 1967.

———. "L'Atlantique Portugais et les Esclaves (1570–1670)," *Revista da Faculdade de Letras da Universidade de Coimbra*. Vol. 22, 1966, pp. 5–55.

———. "Pour une histoire de la comptabilité au Portugal: `Le livre de Raison' de Coelho Guerreiro," *Caravelle*. Vol. 1, 1963, pp. 85–110.

———. "Économie et Budget à Madère (1591–1641)," *Annales économiques, sociales et culturelles*. Vol. VII, 1952, pp. 504–507.

Maxwell, Wright & Co. *Commercial Formalities of Rio de Janeiro*. Baltimore, 1830.

McAllister, Patrick A. "Indigenous Beer in Southern Africa: Functions and Fluctuations," *African Studies*. Vol. 52, 1993, pp. 71–88.

———. *Bulding the Homestead: Agriculture, Labour and Beer in South Africa's Transkei*. Aldershot, 2001.

McFall, Daniel F. *Africa in Time-Perspective: A Discussion of Historical Reconstruction from Unwritten Sources*. New York, 1970.

McCusker, John J. *Rum and the American Revolution: The Rum Trade and the Balance of Payments of the Thirteen Colonies*. New York, 1989. 2 Vols.

McGaffey, Wyatt. *Custom and Government in the Lower Congo*. Berkeley, 1970.

Medick, Hans. "Plebeian Culture in the Transition to Capitalism," in Raphael Samuel and Gareth S. Jones, eds. *Culture, Ideology and Politics: Essays for Eric Hobsbawn*. London, 1982, pp. 84–113.

Meillassoux, Claude. ed. *l'Esclavage en Afrique précoloniale*. Paris, 1975.

Mello, A. Brandão de. *Angola: Monographie Historique, Géographique et Économique de la Colonie Destinée à l'Exposition Coloniale Internationale de Paris de 1931*. Luanda, 1931.

Metcalfe, George. "A Microcosm of Why Africans Sold Slaves: Akan Consumption Patterns in the 1770s," *Journal of African History*. Vol. 28, 1987, pp. 377–394.

Mezza Cuadra, G. "Le pisco, eau de vie du Pérou," *Premier Symposium International sue les eaux-de vie traditionnelles d'origine viticole*. Paris, 1991, pp. 28–31.

Miers, Suzanne and Kopytoff, Igor. eds. *Slavery in Africa: Historical and Anthropological Perspectives*. Madison, 1977.

Miller, Joseph C. "Angola central e sul por volta de 1840," *Estudos Afro-Asiáticos*. Vol. 32, 1997, pp. 7–34.

———. "The Numbers, Origins, and Destinations of Slaves, in the Eighteenth Century Angolan Slave Trade" in Joseph. E. Inikori and Stanley L. Engerman, eds. *The Atlantic Slave Trade: Effects on Economies, Societies, and Peoples in Africa, the Americas, and Europe*. Durham, NC, 1992, pp. 77–115.

———."Overcrowded and Undernourished: The Techniques and Consequences of Tight-Packing in the Portuguese Southern Atlantic Slave Trade," in Daget, ed. *De la Traite à l'Esclavage*, Vol. II, pp. 395–424.

———. *Way of Death: Merchant Capitalism and the Angolan Slave Trade, 1730–1830*. Madison, 1988.

———. "Slave Prices in the Portuguese Southern Atlantic, 1600–1830," in Paul E. Lovejoy, ed. *Africans in Bondage: Studies in Slavery and the Slave Trade*. Madison, 1986, pp. 43–77.

———. "Capitalism and Slaving: The Financial and Commercial Organization of the Angolan Slave Trade, According to the Accounts of Antonio Coelho Guerreiro (1684–1692)," *International Journal of African Historical Studies*. Vol. 17, 1984, pp. 1–57.

———. "Imports at Luanda, Angola 1785–1823," in G. Liesegang, H. Pasch, and A. Jones, eds. *Figuring African Trade: Proceedings of the Symposium on the Quantification and Structure of the Import and export and Long Distance Trade of Africa in the 19th Century (c. 1800–1913)*. Berlin, 1983, pp. 163–246.

———. "The Paradoxes of Impoverishment in the Atlantic Zone," in David Birmingham and Phyllis Martin, eds. *History of Central Africa*. London, 1983, Vol. I, pp. 118–159.

———. "The Significance of Drought, Disease and Famine in the Agriculturally Marginal Zones of West-Central Africa," *Journal of African History*. Vol. XXIII, 1982, pp. 17–61.

———. "Introduction: Listening for the African Past," in Joseph C. Miller, ed. *The African Past Speaks: Essays on Oral Tradition and History*. Folkestone, 1980, pp. 1–60.

———. "Some Aspects of the Commercial Organization of Slaving at Luanda, Angola, 1760–1830," in Henry A. Gemery and Jan S. Hogendorn, eds. *The Uncommon Market: Essays in the Economic History of the Atlantic Slave Trade*. New York, 1979, pp. 77–106.

———. "Thanatopsis," *Cahiers d'études africaines*. Vol. XVIII, 1978, pp. 229–231.

———. "The Slave Trade in Congo and Angola," in Martin L. Kilson and Robert I. Rotberg, eds. *The African Diaspora: Interpretive Essays*. Cambridge, 1976, pp. 75–113.

———. *Kings and Kinsmen: Early Mbundu States in Angola*. Oxford, 1976.

———. "Nzinga of Matamba in a New Perspective," *Journal of African History*. Vol. XVI, 1975, pp. 201–216.

——. "Legal Portuguese Slaving from Angola: Some Preliminary Indications of Volume and Direction, 1760–1830," *Revue française d'histoire d'outre-mer*. Vol. LXII, 1975, pp. 135–176.

——. "Requiem for the "Jaga", *Cahiers d'études africaines*. Vol. XIII, 1973, pp. 121–149.

——. "A Note on Jean-Baptiste Douville," *Cahiers d'études africaines*. Vol. XIII, 1973, pp. 150–153.

——. "The Imbangala and the Chronology of Early Central African History," *Journal of African History*. Vol. XIII, 1972, pp. 549–574.

Mills, Wallace G. "Cape Smoke: Alcohol Issues in the Cape Colony in the Nineteenth Century," *Contemporary Drug Problems*. Vol. 12, 1985, pp. 1–12.

——. "The Roots of African Nationalism in the Cape Colony: Temperance, 1865–1898," *International Journal of African Historical Studies*. Vol. 13, 1980, pp. 197–213.

Miracle, Marvin P. *Maize in Tropical Africa*. Madison, 1966.

Mora de Tovar, G. *Aguardiente y Conflictos Sociales en la Nueva Grenada durante el Siglo XVIII*. Bogotá, 1988.

Moreno, M. "Aguardientes y alcoholismo en el Mexico colonial," *Cuadernos hispano-americanos*. Vol. 52, 1985, pp. 81–96.

Munro, William B. "The Brandy Parliament of 1678," *Canadian Historical Review*. Vol. 2, 1921, pp. 172–189.

Netting, Robert McC. "Beer as a Locus of Value among the West African Kofyar," *American Anthropologist*. Vol. 66, 1964, pp. 375–384.

Neves, José Accurcio das. *Considerações Politicas e Commerciaes sobre os Descobrimentos e Possessões dos Portuguêzes na Africa e na Asia*. Lisbon, 1830.

Newbury, Colin W. *The Western Slave Coast and its Rulers: European Trade and Administration among the Yoruba and Adja-speaking Peoples of South-Western Nigeria, Southern Dahomey and Togo*. London, 1961.

Ngokwey, Ndolamb. "Varieties of Palm Wine among the Lele of the Kasai," in Mary Douglas, ed. *Constructive Drinking: Perspectives on Drink from Anthropology*. Cambridge, 1987, pp. 113–121.

Niehaus, Charles J. G. "The Birth of our Wine Industry on the 2nd of February 1659," *Wine and Spirit*. Vol. 15, 1946, pp. 11–15.

Novais, Fernando A. *Portugal e Brasil na Crise do Antigo Sistema Colonial (1777–1808)*. São Paulo, 1979.

Obenga, Théophile. "Histoire du Monde Bantu," in Théophile Obenga and Simão Souindoula, eds. *Racines Bantu/Bantu Roots*. Libreville, 1991, pp. 121–150.

Oliveira Marques, A. H. de. *Daily Life in Portugal in the Late Middle Ages*. Madison, 1971. (Translated by S. S. Wyatt)

——. *História de Portugal*. Lisbon, 1978. 2 Vols.

——. *Ensaios de História Medieval*. Lisbon, 1965.

Olorunfemi, A. "The Liquor Traffic Dilemma in British West Africa: The Southern Nigerian Example, 1895–1918," *International Journal of African Historical Studies*. Vol. 17, 1984, pp. 229–241.

Olukoju, Ayodeji. "Race and Acces To Liquor: Prohibition as Colonial Policy in Northern Nigeria, 1919–45," *Journal of Imperial and Commonwealth History*. Vol. 24, 1996, pp. 218–243.

——. "Prohibition and Paternalism: The State and the Clandestine Liquor Traffic in Northern Nigeria, c. 1889–1918," *International Journal of African Historical Studies*. Vol. 24, 1991, 349–368.

Onselen, Charles van. "Randlords and Rotgut, 1886–1903," *History Workshop*. Vol. 2, 1976, pp. 32–89.

Pacheco, Carlos. *José da Silva Maia Ferreira: O Homen e a sua Época*. Luanda, 1990.

Pan, Lynn. *Alcohol in Africa*. Helsinki, 1975.

Pantoja, Selma A. *Nzinga Mbandi: Mulher, Guerra e Escravidão*. Brasília, 2000.

Parkin, David J. *Palms, Wine, and Witnesses: Public Spirit and Private Gain in an African Farming Community.* San Francisco, 1972.
Parreira, Adriano A. T. *Dicionário Glossográfico e Toponímico da Documentação sobre Angola, Séculos XV–XVII.* Lisbon, 1990.
——. *Economia e Sociedade em Angola na Época da Rainha Jinga, Século XVII.* Lisbon, 1990.
——. "A Rainha Angolana Jinga: Para Além das Leis Normativas de Parentesco," *História* (Lisbon), No. 123, 1989, pp. 59–67.
——. "Primórdios da presença militar portuguesa em Angola: O tráfico de escravos: 1483–1643" in *Portugal no Mundo.* Lisbon, 1989, pp. 214–236.
——. *The Kingdom of Angola and Iberian Interference: 1483–1643.* Uppsala, 1985.
Pena, Antero J. "O Alcool na Ração Alimentar," *Boletim do Instituto de Angola.* No. 21, 1965, pp. 91–101.
Penha Garcia, Comte de. *La lutte contre l'Alcool aux Colonies Portugaises.* Geneva, 1911.
Penvenne, Jeanne M. *African Workers and Colonial Racism: Mozambican Strategies and Struggles in Lourenço Marques, 1877–1962.* Portsmouth, 1995.
Peres, Damião. ed. *História de Portugal.* Barcelos, 1929–1935. 9 Vols.
Pinson, A. "The New England Rum Era: Drinking Styles and Social Chande in Newport, R. I., 1720–1770," *Alcoholism* (Zagreb). Vol. 16, 1980, pp. 26–42.
Platt, B. S. "Some Traditional Alcoholic Beverages and their Importance in Indigenous African Communities," *Proceedings of the Nutrition Society.* Vol. 14, 1955, pp. 115–124.
Polanyi, Karl (in collaboration with Abraham Rotstein). *Dahomey and the Slave Trade: An Analysis of an Archaic Economy.* Seattle, 1966.
Popham, Robert E. "The Social History of the Tavern," in Israel, Y., Glaser, F. B., Kalant, H., Popham, R. E., Schmidt, W., and Smart, R. G. eds. *Research Advances in Alcohol and Drug Problems: Vol. 4.* New York, 1978, pp. 225–302.
Postma, Johannes M. *The Dutch in the Atlantic Slave Trade, 1600–1815.* Cambridge, 1990.
Prado Jr., Caio. *The Colonial Background of Modern Brazil.* Berkeley, 1971. (Translated by Suzette Macedo).
——. *História Econômica do Brasil.* São Paulo, 1970.
Purseglove, J. W. "The Origins and Migrations of Crops in Tropical Africa," in J. R. Harlan, Jan de Wet, and A. B. L. Stemler, eds. *Origins of African Plant Domestication.* The Hague, 1976.
Rainhorn, J. D. "l'Alcoolisme: ce fléau moderne de l'Afrique," *Developpement et Santé.* No. 43, 1983, pp. 22–28.
Randles, W. G. L. *L'Ancien royaume du Congo des origines à la fin du XIXe siècle.* Paris, 1968.
Rawley, James A. *The Transatlantic Slave Trade: A History.* New York, 1981.
Rebelo, Manuel dos Anjos da Silva. *Relações entre Angola e Brasil (1808–1830).* Lisbon, 1970.
Redding, Sean. "Beer Brewing in Umtata: Women, Migrant Labor, and Social Control in a Rural Town," in Ambler and Crush, *Liquor and Labor in Southern Africa,* pp. 325–251.
Reefe, Thomas. *The Rainbow and the Kings: A History of the Luba Empire to 1891.* Berkeley, 1981.
Rego, António da Silva. *Alguns Problémas sociológico-missionários da Africa Negra.* Lisbon, 1960.
Renault, Delso. *Indústria, Escravidão, Sociedade: Uma Pesquiza Historiográfica do Rio de Janeiro no Século XIX.* Rio de Janeiro, 1976.
Renouil, Yves. *Dictionnaire du Vin.* Bordeaux, 1962.
Ribeiro, Maria de L. Roque de Aguiar. *As Relações Comerciais entre Portugal e Brasil Segundo as 'Balanças de Comércio', 1801–1821.* Lisbon, 1972.

Ribeiro Júnior, José. *Colonização e Monopólio do Nordeste Brasileiro: A Companhia Geral de Pernambuco e Paraíba (1759–1780)*. São Paulo, 1976.
Rice, M. "Wine and Brandy Production in Colonial Peru," *Journal of Interdisciplinary History*. Vol. 27, 1998, pp. 455–479.
Richardson, David. "West African Consumption Patterns and Their Influence on the Eighteenth-Century English Slave Trade," Gemery and Hogendorn, eds *Uncommon Market*, pp. 303–330.
——. "Profits in the Liverpool Slave Trade: The Accounts of William Davenport, 1757–1784," in Roger Anstey and P. E. H. Hair, eds. *Liverpool, The African Slave Trade, and Abolition*. Liverpool, 1976, pp. 60–90.
——. "Profitability in the Bristol-Liverpool Slave Trade," *Revue française d'histoire d'outre-mer*. Vol. 62, 1975, pp. 301–308.
Rorabaugh, William. *The Alcoholic Republic: An American Tradition*. New York, 1979.
Rodney, Walter. *A History of the Upper Guinea Coast, 1545 to 1800*. New York, 1980.
Rodrigues, José H. "The Influence of Africa on Brazil and of Brazil on Africa," *Journal of African History*. Vol. III, 1962, pp. 49–67.
Rude, George. "'Mother Gin' and the London Riots of 1736," *Guildhall Miscellany*. Vol. 10, 1959, pp. 53–63.
Russell-Wood, A. J. R. *A World on the Move: The Portuguese in Africa, Asia, and America, 1415–1808*. Manchester, 1992.
——. "Ports of Colonial Brazil," in Franklin W. Knight and Peggy K. Liss, eds., *Atlantic Port Cities: Economy, Culture, and Society in the Atlantic World*. Knoxville, 1991, pp. 196–223.
——. "Colonial Brazil: The Gold Cycle, c. 1695–1750," in Bethell. *Colonial Brazil*, pp. 190–243.
Ryder, Allen F. C. *Benin and the Europeans, 1485–1897*. New York, 1969.
Saffery, A. L. "The Liquor Problem in Urban Areas," *Race Relations*. Vol. 7, 1940, pp. 89–91.
Salvador, José Gonçalves. *Os Magnatas do Tráfico Negreiro (Séculos XVI e XVII)*. São Paulo, 1981.
——. *Os Cristãos-Novos e o Comércio no Atlântico Meridional (Com enfoque nas Capitanias do Sul, 1530–1680)*. São Paulo, 1978.
Sangree, Walter H. "The Social Functions of Beer Drinking in Bantu Tiriki," in D. J. Pittman and C. S. Snyder, eds. *Society, Culture, and Drinking Patterns*. New York, 1962, pp. 6–21.
Santos, Corcino M. dos. *O Rio de Janeiro e a Conjuntura Atlântica*. Rio de Janeiro, 1993.
——. *Relações Comerciais do Rio de Janeiro com Lisboa (1763–1808)*. Rio de Janeiro, 1980.
——. "Relações de Angola com o Rio de Janeiro (1736–1808)," *Estudos Históricos*. No. 12, 1973, pp. 7–68.
Santos, João M. dos. "Angola na Governação dos Filipes: Uma Perspectiva de História Económica e Social," *Revista de História Económica e Social*. No. 3, 1979, pp. 53–76.
Santos, José de Almeida. *Luanda d'Outros Tempos*. Luanda, 1970.
Santos, Luis Gonçalves dos. *Memórias para Servir à História do Reino do Brasil*. Rio de Janeiro, 1943. 2 Vols.
Saul, Mahir. "Beer, Sorghum and Women: Production for the Market in Rural Upper Volta," *Africa* (London). Vol. 51, 1981, pp. 746–764.
Saunders, A. C. de C. M. *A Social History of Black Slaves and Freedmen in Portugal, 1441–1555*. Cambridge, 1982.
Sautter, Gilles. *De l'Atlantique au Fleuve Congo: une géographie de sous-peuplement*. Paris, 1966. 2 Vols.
Scardaville, Michael C. "Alcohol Abuse and Tavern Reform in Late Colonial Mexico City," *Hispanic American Historical Review*. Vol. 60, 1980, pp. 643–671.

Schneider, Susan. *O Marquês de Pombal e o Vinho do Porto: Dependência e Subdesenvolvimento em Portugal no Século XVIII*. Lisbon, 1980.

Schilz, Thomas F. "Brandy and Beaver Pelts: Assiniboine-European Trading Patterns, 1695–1805," *Saskatchewan History*. Vol. 37, 1984, pp. 95–102.

Schivelbusch, Wolfgang. *Tastes of Paradise: A Social History of Spices, Stimulants, and Intoxicants*. New York, 1992 (trans. by David Jacobson).

Schwartz, Stuart B. "Plantations and Peripheries, c. 1580–c. 1750," in Leslie Bethell, ed. *Colonial Brazil*. Cambridge, 1987, pp. 66–144.

Searing, James F. *West African Slavery and Atlantic Commerce: The Senegal River Valley, 1700–1860*. Cambridge, 1994.

Serrano, Carlos M. H. *Os Senhores da Terra e os Homens do Mar: Antropologia de um reino africano*. São Paulo, 1983.

Serrão, Joaquim V. ed. *O Vinho na História Portuguesa, Séculos XIII–XIX*. Porto, 1983.

Sheriff, Abdul. *Slaves, Spices and Ivory in Zanzibar: Integration of an East African Commercial Empire into the World Economy, 1770–1873*. London, 1987.

Silva, Joaquim Lino da, "O *Zea mays* e os milhos africanos na costa oriental da Africa: Discussão em torno de documentos Antigos," *Garcia de Orta, Série Geográfica*. Vol. 14, 1993, pp. 15–40.

Silva, Maria Júlia de Oliveira e. *Fidalgos-Mercadores no Século XVIII: Duarte Sodré Pereira*. Lisbon, 1992.

Simonetti, Giuseppe. "P. Giacinto Brugiotti da Vetralla e la sua Missione al Congo (1651–1657)," *Bolletino della Società Geografica Italiana*. Vol. 8, 1907, pp. 305–322 and 369–381.

Simonsen, Roberto C. *História Económica do Brasil (1500–1820)*. São Paulo, 1978.

Skidmore-Hess, Cathy. "Soldiers and Smallpox: The 1626 Portuguese Campaign against Njinga of Matamba in Angola," in Robert H. Harms, Joseph C. Miller, David S. Newbury, and Michele D. Wagner, eds., *Paths Towards the Past: African Historical Essays in Honor of Jan Vansina*. Atlanta, 1994, pp. 395–413.

Stanley, G. F. "The Indians and the Brandy Trade during the Ancien Régime," *Revue d'Histoire de l'Amérique Française*. Vol. 6, 1953, pp. 489–505.

Taunay, Affonso Escragnolle de. *Subsidios para a História do Tráfico Africano no Brasil*. São Paulo, 1941.

Taylor, William B. *Drinking, Homicide, and Rebellion in Colonial Mexican Villages*. Stanford, 1979.

Teil, Joseph du. "La prohibition de l'alcool de traite en Afrique," *Revue Indigène*. Vol. 4, 1909, pp. 1–12.

Thomas, Robert P. and Bean, Richard N. "The Fishers of Men: The Profits of the Slave Trade," *Journal of Economic History*. Vol. 34, 1974, pp. 885–914.

Thompson, Peter. *Rum Punch and Revolution: Taverngoing and Public Life in Eighteenth-Century Philadelphia*. Philadelphia, 1999.

———. "'The Friendly Glass': Drink and Gentility in Colonial Philadelphia," *Pennsylvania Magazine of History and Biography*. Vol. 133, 1989, pp. 549–573.

Thornton, John K. *Africa and Africans in the Making of the Atlantic World, 1400–1800*. Cambridge, 1998 (2nd edition).

———. "Legitimacy and Political Power: Queen Njinga, 1624–63," *Journal of African History*. Vol. 32, 1991, pp. 25–40.

———. "The Art of War in Angola, 1575–1680," *Comparative Studies in Society and History*. Vol. 30, 1988, pp. 360–378.

———. "The Correspondence of the Kongo Kings, 1614–35: Problems of Internal Written Evidence on a Central African Kingdom," *Paideuma*. Vol. 33, 1987, pp. 407–421.

———. *The Kingdom of Kongo: Civil War and Transition, 1641–1718*. Madison, 1983.

———. "The Kingdom of Kongo, ca. 1390–1678: The Development of an African Social Formation," *Cahiers d'études africaines*. Vol. 23, 1982, pp. 325–342.

——. "Early Kongo-Portuguese Relations: A New Interpretation," *History in Africa.* Vol. 8, 1981, pp. 183–204.

——. "The Slave Trade in Eighteenth Century Angola: Effects on Demographic Structures," *Canadian Journal of African Studies.* Vol. 14, 1980, pp. 417–427.

——. "A Resurrection for the Jaga," *Cahiers d'études africaines.* Vol. 18, 1978, pp. 223–228.

Umunna, Ifekandu. "The Drinking Culture of a Nigerian Community: Onitsha," *Quarterly Journal of Studies on Alcohol,* Vol. 28, 1967, pp. 529–537.

Vachon, André. "L'Eau-de-vie dans la société indienne," *Report of the Canadian Historical Association* (Ottawa), 1960, pp. 22–32.

Vansina, Jan. "The Foundation of the Kingdom of Kasanje," *Journal of African History.* Vol. IV, 1963, pp. 355–374.

——. *Oral Tradition: A Study in Historical Methodology.* Chicago, 1965, (trans. from the original 1960 French edition by H. M. Wright).

——. "More on the Invasions of Kongo and Angola by the Jaga and the Lunda," *Journal of African History.* Vol. VII, 1966, pp. 421–429.

——. *Kingdoms of the Savanna: A History of Central African States Until European Occupation.* Madison, 1966,

——. "Anthropologists and the Third Dimension," *Africa.* Vol. XXXIX, 1969, pp 62–68.

——. *The Tio Kingdom of the Middle Congo, 1880–1892.* London, 1973.

——. *The Children of Woot: A History of the Kuba Peoples.* Madison, 1978.

——. "Finding Food and the History of Precolonial Africa: A Plea," *African Economic History.* Vol. 7, 1979, pp. 9–20.

——. "Memory and Oral Tradition," in Miller, *The African Past Speaks,* pp. 262–279.

——. "Equatorial Africa and Angola: Migrations and the Emergence of the First States," in D. T. Niane, ed. *General History of Africa—IV: Africa from the Twelfth to the Sixteenth Century.* Paris, 1984, pp. 551–577.

——. "Histoire du manioc en Afrique centrale avant 1850," *Paideuma.* Vol. 43, 1997, pp. 255–279.

Vellut, Jean-Luc. "Notes sur le Lunda et la frontière luso africaine (1700 1900)," *Études d'histoire africaine.* Vol. 3, 1972, pp. 61–166.

——. "Le royaume de Cassange et les réseaux luso-africains (ca. 1750–1810)," *Cahiers d'études africaines.* Vol. 15, 1975, pp. 117–136.

——, "Diversification de l'économie de cuillette: miel et cire dans les sociétés de la forêt claire d'Afrique centrale (c. 1750–1950)," *African Economic History.* Vol. 7, 1979, pp. 93–112.

Venâncio, José Carlos. *A Economia de Luanda e Hinterland no Século XVIII: Um Estudo de Sociologia Histórica.* Lisbon, 1996.

Verger, Pierre. "Rôle joué par le tabac de Bahia dans la traite des esclaves au Golfe de Bénin," *Cahiers d'études africaines.* Vol. 4, 1964, pp. 349–369.

——. *Trade Relations Between the Bight of Benin and Bahia from the 17th to the 19th Century.* Ibadan, 1976.

Vieira, Alberto. *Os Escravos no Arquipélago da Madeira: Séculos XV a XVII.* Funchal, 1991.

Vilar, Enriqueta Vila. "La Sublevacion de Portugal y la Trata de Negros," *Ibero-Amerikanisches Archiv.* Vol. 2, 1976, pp. 171–192.

——. *Hispanoamerica Y El Comercio de Esclavos.* Sevilla, 1977.

Vogt, John, *Portuguese Rule on the Gold Coast 1469–1682.* Athens, 1979.

Warner, Rebecca H., and Rosett, Henry. "The Effects of Drinking on Offspring: An Historical Survey of American and British Literature," *Journal of Studies on Alcohol.* Vol. 36, 1975, pp. 1395–1420.

Web, Sidney., and Webb, Beatrice. *The History of Liquor Licensing, Principally from 1700 to 1800.* Hamden, Conn., 1963 reprint.

Wheeler, Douglas L., and Pélissier, René. *Angola.* New York, 1971.

White, Bruce M. "A Skilled Game of Exchange: Ojibway Fur Trade Protocal," *Minnesota History*. Vol 50, 1987, pp. 232–236.

——. "'Give Us a Little Milk': The Social and Cultural Significance of Gift Giving on the Lake Superior Fur Trade," *Minnesota History*. Vol 48, 1982, pp. 66–71.

Williams, Eric. *Capitalism and Slavery*. Chapel Hill, 1944.

Willis, Justin. "*Enkurma sikitoi*: drink, commoditization and power in Maasai society," *International Journal of African Historical Studies*. Vol. 32, 1999, pp. 339–358.

——. *Potent Brews: A Social History of Alcohol in East Africa, 1850–1999*. Athens, OH, 2002.

Winkler, Allan M. "Drinking on the American Frontier," *Quarterly Journal of Studies on Alcohol*. Vol. 29, 1968, pp. 413–445.

Wrightson, Keith. "Alehouses, Order and Reformation in Rural England, 1590–1660," in Eileen Yeo and Stephen Yeo, eds. *Popular Culture and Class Conflict, 1590–1914: Explorations in the History of Labour and Leisure*. Brighton, 1981, pp. 2–11.

Wyndham, H. A. "The Problem of West African Liquor Traffic," *Journal of the Royal Institute of International Affairs*. Vol. 9, 1930, pp. 801–818.

Yoder, John C. *The Kanyok of Zaire: An Institutional and Ideological History to 1895*. Cambridge, 1992.

Yoder, Paton. "Tavern Regulation in Virginia: Rationale and Reality," *Virginia Magazine of History and Biography*. Vol. 87, 1979, pp. 259–278.

IV. *Unpublished Secondary Sources*

Agiri, Babatunde A. "Kola in Western Nigeria, 1850–1950: A History of the Cultivation of Colanitida in Egba-Owode, Ijebu-Remo, Iwo and Oto Areas," Ph.D. dissertation, University of Wisconsin, 1972.

Bardwell, Ross L. "The Governors of Portugal South Atlantic Empire in the Seventeenth Century: Social Background, Qualifications, Selection, Reward," Ph.D. dissertation, University of California at Santa Barbara, 1974.

Bauss, Rudolph W. "Rio de Janeiro: The Rise of Late Colonial Brazil's Dominant Emporium, 1777–1808," Ph.D. dissertation, Tulane University, 1977.

Cruz e Silva, Rosa M. M. da. "Njinga Mbandi e o Poder," Paper presented at the Canadian Association of African Studies Annual Meeting, Montreal, 13–16 May, 1992.

Elbl, Ivana. "The Portuguese Trade with West Africa, 1440–1521," Ph.D. dissertation, University of Toronto, 1986.

El Sheikh, Mahmoud A. R. "State, Cloves, and Planters: A Reappraisal of British Imperialism in Zanzibar, 1890–1938," Ph.D. dissertation, University of California at Los Angeles, 1986.

Ferreira, Roquinaldo A. "Dos Sertões ao Atlântico: Trafico Ilegal de Escravos e Comercio Licito em Angola, 1830–1860," M. A. thesis, Universidade Federal do Rio de Janeiro, 1996.

Geller, Jeremy R. "Predynastic Beer Production at Hierakonpolis, Upper Egypt: Archaeological Evidence and Anthropological Implications," Ph.D. dissertation, Washington University, 1992.

Heywood, Linda M. "Production, Trade and Power: The Political Economy of Central Angola, 1850–1930," Ph.D. dissertation, Columbia University, 1984.

Hoover, J. Jeffrey. "The Seduction of Ruwej: Reconstructing Ruund History (The Nuclear Lunda: Zaire, Angola, Zambia)," Ph.D. dissertation, Yale University, 1978.

Karasch, Mary C. "The Brazilian Slavers and the Illegal Slave Trade, 1836–1851," M. A. thesis, University of Wisconsin, 1967.

Lugar, Catherine. "The Merchant Community of Salvador, Bahia, 1780–1830," Ph.D. dissertation, State University of New York (Stony Brook), 1980.

McDougall, Elizabeth A. "The Ijil Salt Industry: Its Role in the Pre-Colonial Economy of the Western Sudan," Ph.D. dissertation, University of Birmingham, 1980.

Miller, Joseph C. "Quantities and Currencies: Bargaining for Slaves on the Fringes of the World Capitalist Economy." Paper presented at the Congresso Internacional sobre a Escravidão, São Paulo, June 7–11, 1988.

Pantoja, Selma A. "O Encontro nas Terras de Além-Mar: Os Espaços Urbanos do Rio de Janeiro, Luanda, e Ilha de Moçambique na era da Ilustração," Ph.D. dissertation, Universidade de São Paulo, 1994.

Pardo, Anne W. "A Comparative Study of the Portuguese Colonies of Angola and Brazil and their Interdependence from 1648–1825," Ph.D. dissertation, Boston University, 1977.

Pirio, Gregory R. "Commerce, Industry and Empire: The Making of Modern Portuguese Colonialism in Angola and Mozambique," Ph.D. dissertation, University of California at Los Angeles, 1982.

Power, Joan C. "The History of Keana's Salt Industry c. 1780–1900: The Mechanics of Gender in a Precolonial Economy," M. A. thesis, Dalhousie University, 1985.

Rayner, Mary I. "Wine and Slaves: The Failure of an Export Economy and the Ending of Slavery in the Cape Colony, 1806–1835," Ph.D. dissertation, Duke University, 1986.

Skidmore-Hess, Cathy. "Bones and Baptism: Symbols and Ideology in the Career of Nzinga," Paper presented at the Canadian Association of African Studies Annual Meeting, Montreal, 13–16 May, 1992.

Wheeler, Douglas L. "The Portuguese in Angola 1836–1891: A Study in Expansion and Administration," Ph.D. dissertation, Boston University, 1963.

INDEX

THE ATLANTIC WORLD

ISSN 1570–0542

1. Postma, J. & V. Enthoven (eds.). *Riches from Atlantic Commerce.* Dutch Transatlantic Trade and Shipping, 1585-1817. 2003.
   ISBN 90 04 12562 0
2. Curto, J.C. *Enslaving Spirits.* The Portuguese-Brazilian Alcohol Trade at Luanda and its Hinterland, c. 1550-1830. 2004.
   ISBN 90 04 13175 2